ALANA FAIRCHILD

CRYSTAL GODDESSES
888

LIVING THE SACRED FEMININE

BLUE ANGEL®
PUBLISHING

CRYSTAL GODDESSES 888
Living the Sacred Feminine

This printing 2020
Copyright © 2015 Alana Fairchild

Published by Blue Angel Publishing®
80 Glen Tower Drive, Glen Waverley
Victoria, Australia 3150
Email: info@blueangelonline.com
Website: www.blueangelonline.com

Edited by Leela Williams

Artwork Copyright © 2015 Jane Marin

Blue Angel is a registered trademark of Blue Angel Gallery Pty. Ltd.

ISBN: 978-1-922161-25-3

DEDICATION

Dedicated to the courageous hearts who
honour her wisdom and live her love.

ACKNOWLEDGEMENTS

With special thanks to the many teachers and guides, from Heaven
and Earth, who have supported me on this path of feminine
wisdom. I always say the Divine Mother helps the helpers, and she
has given me so much grace in the form of a wonderful publisher,
caring editor, clever (and funny!) manager, amazing admin angel,
talented graphic designer, not to mention the organisational
goddesses devoted to the path of love that assist me in bringing the
Divine Mother's work to the world through workshops and tours.
Gratitude and thanks from the depths of my heart.

CONTENTS

INTRODUCTION

WHY AM I ATTRACTED TO THIS BOOK?

The many facets and faces of the Goddess are an expression of the Divine Feminine. This does not mean they are only relevant to women. Men may also be interested in the path of the Divine Feminine and such men are growing in number. These men are not interested in limited definitions of masculinity that deny feeling, tenderness and passionate relationships. Instead, they want to incorporate those qualities into their experience of being a modern man. Such men will be attracted to working with this book too.

The Divine Feminine is awakening now. This is a spiritual rebalancing of the Divine Masculine and feminine presence. The masculine needs the feminine for grounding and the feminine needs the masculine for lightness of spirit. The rebalancing of feminine and masculine principles into a more harmonious relationship is moving the human race forward. It is expanding the current level of consciousness in the human heart.

The awakening of the Divine Feminine is part of a new teaching for the entire human race. This program is running on a soul level with the lesson to love and honour creation as a valid and beautiful expression of divinity. This teaching is needed to heal the unconscious separation of spirit and matter that we have experienced since the inception of patriarchy (the slowly dying system of social organisation based on the subjugation, not only of women, but of men too). Men and women have been cast into limiting roles that deny feminine consciousness and therefore obstruct genuine nourishment and aliveness of the human soul. Patriarchy and its tendency to honour intellect and reason above all else has played an important role in developing human consciousness, but the need for that way of being (or thinking, to put it more accurately) has long been surpassed by the greater need for an expanded consciousness that honours feeling and connection so that life may continue to flourish on this planet.

There are particular souls at the forefront of this shift in consciousness that are helping light the way for others. You have been drawn to this book because you are one of those souls. Much of the material in this book will make sense to you straight away and may even mirror what you already know. It might also challenge or confront you. Choose to be in your heart and sit with the information presented here, to find a way in which it can strengthen your healing presence in the world.

It is important to realise this new consciousness is not a return to old ways, prior to patriarchal systems and the rise of intellectualism. Nor is it about rejecting or being ashamed of what has been. Our current level of consciousness cannot support us for much longer. This is not something to feel guilty or fearful about. It is the natural ending of one phase, in favour of a more enlightened and aware stage of human evolution. We would not keep repeating kindergarten if we were ready for first grade, and so it is with spiritual evolution. As a species, we are spiritually growing up. The consciousness of the Divine Feminine is the next step in the waking up and growing process.

Each of us has the ability to help birth this new consciousness on Earth by honouring the Divine Feminine energy in our personal lives and on our spiritual journeys. How and what we choose to give birth to, how we choose to nourish and 'be a parent' to our creations and how willing we are to release it into the world, is how we access, develop and express our feminine consciousness, whether we are male or female.

At the core of Divine Feminine consciousness is power. It is the power to know and choose what we value. When the feminine knows what is of genuine value, the masculine in us (again, whether we are male or female in body) can choose to honour her by setting priorities and boundaries that support those values. To be able to really locate our values, we have to be able to tap into our genuine feelings. It is nearly impossible to discern what has real value, is truly important and authentically moves us, if we cannot feel. If you have ever tried to work something out with your mind, you will know it can argue rather convincingly for one truth and then just as compellingly for its opposing truth. The mind can justify virtually anything. This is something I learned in law school! At the time, I found my own ability to rationalise and argue for opposing truths rather disturbing. However, it taught me to trust in what I felt to be true rather than in what I could intellectually convince myself of at any given time. That was a step on to the path of the Divine Feminine.

When you are moved by the truths of your heart, irrespective of logic or reasoning, then you are living the Divine Feminine principle of heart-centred living. Of course, logic and intellect have their place and usefulness and great gains have been made within humanity through the development of those qualities. However, it is not wise to render a master out of that which is meant to be a servant. Reasoning is useful, yes, but not when it comes to determining the core values on which we base our life choices, decisions and actions.

The foundation of our lives needs to come from passionate love and genuine feeling, if we are to have the energy we need to really live, as opposed to just existing and going through the motions. Without that genuine heart-centred passion, life becomes a chore as we try to force ourselves to do what we think we should, rather than what we feel impelled to do from a heart-inspired place. To live the spiritual life – which is challenging at times, to say the least – requires tremendous energy. Love is the most powerful fuel there is. It will keep us motivated, disciplined, humorous and inspired long after the intellectual reasoning and 'shoulds' have dried up.

Those that work with Divine Feminine energy are brave, rebellious and loving. The nature of the Divine Feminine is to heal and transform consciousness. The Divine Feminine is the mother of life and nurtures all creation, but alongside an inherent respect for all of life there is also a rebellious streak that is constantly seeking to evolve. Perhaps because of this, those that walk the path of the Divine Feminine tend to go against the mainstream. This can manifest in subtle ways such as how someone thinks or more obviously in their choice of lifestyle or work. Devotees of the feminine path cannot stand the mainstream idea of what life is supposed to be. They find systems, structures, demands and lack of imagination soul destroying. As well as denying creativity, mainstream practice places constraints on our freedom to grow and become all that we can possibly be! In their hearts, those that are opened to the Divine Feminine, love life and want to be free. More than that, they want this freedom for all beings.

If you see this in yourself, you are recognising your devotion to the feminine divine. It is not about denying the value of the Divine Masculine. This shift of consciousness is about restoring the Divine Feminine to her rightful place, allowing for both leadership and living from the heart. The Divine Masculine light can then protect, strengthen, honour and serve the heart-centred way rather than being in the world in ways that no longer support human spiritual evolution.

It takes a lot of courage to walk this path because it actively denies what is generally still accepted as the right way to live in mainstream consciousness. The old systems of dominance and intellectualism are on their way out, but it is a slow death and many are ignorant of the beautiful, alternative realities available to us and are therefore fearful of any change. Those who have the wisdom, insight and courage to embrace this change are pioneers in consciousness who need to hold onto love, patience, strength and determination to help encourage others across the bridge of faith and trust, into an awareness of the Divine Feminine that is urging humanity forward on the spiritual path.

People can cross the bridge of trust into new life more easily as they switch off from being mentally conditioned by the mass media and begin to feel and think for themselves – rather than reacting based on unchallenged opinions, largely created by external forces interested in manipulating the masses for their own personal gain. Mass media promotes fear and feelings of insecurity. There is so much idiocy and toxic conditioning in mass media that it can be a relief to step out of it. Yet letting go of our intake of mass media (print, film, TV, other forms of media) and consuming with far greater discretion and discernment it is not without its sacrifices. Standing up and thinking for yourself can feel isolating – at least for a while, until you gravitate towards other conscious humans who recognise the vibration of awakening within you and can relate to you at that level.

Also, on this path there will be times when you feel like you might be going crazy. This is because you are becoming sane in an insane world. You will not feel like you fit into typical cultural situations, nor are you supposed to. You were born to stand out. You were born to show a different way is not only possible, but preferable. You might even recognise this internally, but that doesn't mean your path will be free of challenge. You will have the most powerful beings in the Universe as your helpers. This is rather reassuring, but big souls take on big tasks and at times you will feel like this path asks a lot of you. Personally, not taking this path is such a miserable alternative that I don't typically mind what is asked of me. Of course, sometimes it is really difficult and being able to stay true to ourselves during such challenges is part of the task to help humanity move forward.

You were given the divine intelligence, courage and wisdom to be able to do this and thrive. You have so much loving assistance from goddesses, who form the many arms of the Divine Mother, and the crystalline kingdom (or queendom!) to support you. The Holy Mother wants what you want in your heart too. We are all in this together. We are on the same team, working for the divine success and fulfilment of the human race, even if some seem like they are being dragged into it kicking and screaming. If you have ever tried to have an authentic conversation with someone when they want to remain numb and glued to the TV or latest techno-gadget, you know what I mean.

As surprising as it may seem, the Divine Masculine actually wants the Divine Feminine to be honoured. It gives him a chance to become the divine man he always wanted to become: a protective, passionate, sacred warrior fighting for the noblest of causes – love. He wants to shine his luminous, uplifting light into the feminine heart, thus evoking joy. Men and the masculine energy more generally, have the need within them to become all of the beautiful, strong, passionate and protective beings that they can be. If you are a man or woman who feels respect for all that masculine energy can be, and compassion for the wounding that patriarchy has brought on men (as well as women) in forcing them to play a role rather than be authentic and whole, then you will understand the very important role masculine energy plays in the awakening of the Divine Feminine. Masculine and feminine energies are distinct, but not separate from each other. For one to grow and heal, the other must responsively evolve. They must both be allowed to grow more whole and loving within themselves and towards each other so as they can function as a harmonious, passionate, and supportive marriage. This divine partnership will allow life to unfold on this planet as human beings and human culture become so much more wise, compassionate, empowering and free.

However, first things first. We have to step out of unconsciousness and onto the sacred feminine path. As the feminine heals, so too does the masculine, and eventually genuine oneness and harmony can be experienced as relief, peace, and clear purpose unveiled in our hearts. The all-important first step onto the Divine Feminine path is taken through bringing the body to consciousness. Coming to consciousness means bearing pain and learning (as odd as it may sound) to bear bliss, ecstasy and passion, too. In essence, the first step is to become present to all of life without shutting down, turning away, running away, hiding or resisting. This might sound simple, and certainly there are many simple ways to trigger that consciousness, but will hardly be easy. We need courage. We need to remember why we are doing the work. We need perspective and we need trust.

Consciousness in the body is naturally stimulated through physical activity *during which we remain present*. Dancing or yoga are examples. However, if our mind is not with our sensations in our body, but is dissociated through drugs or over-thinking, then consciousness can elude us. Yoga or dance practice can be a case of 'going through the motions' rather than catalysing consciousness. Of course, it is better than not doing anything. If you are going to put in the effort of practice, being aware and willing to bring your mind to your task will help you so much. You are worth that. Without such awareness, a whole life can be spent just going through the motions. With awareness, even making breakfast in the morning can be a meditation in awakening consciousness.

This is less about what is done (though those things *are* important, especially when they support our overall wellbeing) and more about how present we are in our actions. Eventually this cultivates a sense of 'being' even in our 'doing'. Through awareness, consciousness can come, bringing insight, feeling, intuition, wisdom and presence.

Another practice that tends to stimulate consciousness in the body is journaling. This is not just undertaken as analysis, but as a deeper process of getting in touch with your feelings and sensations. It might also involve working with the intuitive intelligence of dreams and visions, which you can easily do through drawing or writing about dream sequences or imagery.

If journaling is not enough or quite right for you, you can also incorporate dance, art, creating altars or any other form of creative self-expression. Spending time in nature, stepping out of your daily routine and getting to the beach, for example, might be enough to help you drop out of your head and into your heart. Music can do this for a lot of people. It can move us beyond our mind and into our bodies. Also working with the healing processes in this book (and throughout the entire *Crystal Spirituality Series*) will support you in that reconnection. The healing processes are also available as downloadable audio recordings, proving that technology and all things, can be used with awareness to serve the body and the feminine path, rather than to disconnect us from ourselves.

Getting in touch with the body is the basic premise for access to the Divine Feminine path. Often, it can be the biggest stumbling block because of what happens when we begin that process. You only have to think back to when you started your spiritual path, and recollect how much emotion and pain you encountered when you began your personal healing work. Whatever backlog we have stored in our bodies has to come out. When we begin, it can seem like there is a hell of a lot there. Early on my personal healing path this lifetime, I wondered if the grief and anger would ever end. After decades of practice, I now feel (more often than not) as though I am living in the present moment rather than conditioned by unresolved past pain. Awareness and healing are part of an ongoing process. The sooner you start, the better. I moved through that unresolved pain by bringing my body to consciousness and honouring what came out emotionally. I still use that approach as a way to live and move through emotional 'stuff' that arises from time to time, especially if I am going through deep personal transformation. It is a dedication to knowing truth and getting to a place within my body that is increasingly less reactive (due to unresolved past pain being triggered) and increasingly more responsive (which can only happen when we are in the present moment) to life.

The more sensitive we are, the more we will be able to access and clear stored pain in our bodies. Sometimes it will be our own stuff, especially if we are really going deep into our journey this lifetime and making spiritual progress towards the absolute remembrance of ourselves as pure divine beings. Often, there will be a lot of old stuff, such as shame, guilt, anger and fear, that needs to be released in order for us to be able to feel and witness the truth of our being. It can be hard to do that when it is obscured with layers of stuff from this or other lifetimes. The body knows how to release that stuff, but we need to do our part, by becoming present, taking the feminine journey and allowing the body to do what it knows how to do – heal itself.

At times you may also sense the body is clearing an ancestral legacy of unconscious, unresolved pain which was unintentionally yet inevitably handed down through the generations. That continues until someone is strong enough to bear conscious witness to it, process it and let it go. Sensitivity and strength are required to do this work. Sometimes it seems like a tremendous challenge, but it is actually empowering as the clearer we are able to become through personal healing, the more space there is within us to receive divine grace and experience the absolute magic that such grace brings to our life. You could say the rewards far outweigh the effort, though I will be the first to admit there are times when this won't seem comforting. There is great effort required to bear the release of pain, to confront our suffering, and still have enough trust in this process that we don't shut down from it prematurely, but allow it to work its way through us and be released.

This can be all the more challenging in the early stages as the personal healing can be intense and we are yet to discover how wonderful the reward that follows actually is. We may have dreamed about what living a magical sort of life might be like. I certainly did. But I didn't really know what it was like and how it would work until I began to experience it first-hand. I also had no clue about how painful the path of healing would be, and continues to be at times, in order to stay in tune with the grace of the Divine Mother. The grace is worth it, but ironically perhaps, the path of grace doesn't always feel so graceful – especially if we are going through such deep healing that we feel as though a part of us is dying. Even if we know at some level that dying is a way to allow for new life, it doesn't necessarily make it any less painful at the time.

It takes a lot of inner work to be ready to even begin this path of bringing the body to consciousness and Divine Feminine awakening. Humanity as a whole is only just starting to emerge out of the unconsciousness patriarchal system based on competition, win-lose, dominance, apparent personal success at the expense of another and getting ahead no matter what. There is so much unresolved pain underneath those sorts of behaviours. Part of our heart and being gets cut off when we even attempt to live like that. When we begin to bring our body to consciousness all that pain needs to be released. No matter how convincing a deceptive appearance might be to the mind, the body knows a lie from what is real. The mind needs to learn to stop trying to shut down the responses of the body and instead become strong enough to open up to them, to bear witness and to bring compassion, even when those responses are not necessarily understood.

When I was working at a particular phase of self-healing, I connected with horses. I was amazed at their energy and how immediately responsive they were to the emotional energy of myself or others around them. You couldn't fake anything emotionally with a horse. If you were fearful, no matter how brave you pretended to be, they would be skittish or ignore your attempts at authority and go their own way. If you attempted to be tough, but were actually a soft-touch underneath, they would know. This happened to me on a horse whispering course. The horse just came and buried its head on my shoulder. I was so moved by the tenderness and trust of that action, that I failed miserably at remaining genuinely tough and disinterested enough to successfully master the art of horse-training, where you establish yourself as the 'alpha animal'. Instead I just opted to appreciate their immediacy, honesty and lack of pretension. You always knew where you stood with them – preferably not within kicking distance of their hind legs.

As I learned more about horses, I realised why so many therapists worked with horses and addicts. In a culture like ours, at this stage in evolution, addiction becomes something of a way of life for us, where unconscious habits are enacted daily in an effort to soothe unresolved pain. The pain within is the intelligent part. It is the part of us that is saying, "This is nuts! I am dying inside! I cannot live like this!" The part of us that is freaked out by the truthfulness inside, opts for addiction instead. Perhaps the addiction-oriented part of us is worried that people will think we are weird or a failure if we confess our true feelings. Maybe we believe that we can't survive without whatever it is (a job, a relationship, an ideal etc.) we are holding onto for support, even though it is wearing us down and destroying us in the process. Through addiction we try to numb things out in order to cope with the internal conflict between needing to let go and not being sure we are ready or capable enough to grow and move on.

However, when we let go of our pain and release suffering from childhood or other lifetimes, your body will speak clearly and honestly from a completely accurate, intuitive place. It is like a horse. Free of the intellectual mind, it just cannot lie. It has its own kind of intelligence. We have been taught to disconnect from our bodies and our truths, sometimes simply through the socialisation process (e.g. sitting at a school or office desk for hours on end). To some extent this cannot be avoided, but in other ways it is an unnecessary extreme where we are virtually medicated by social dictates in order not to feel, so we will continue to half live the half existence we are taught is normal.

It breaks my heart to see it. Mostly because I know it is not essential as so many believe it to be. As our bodies awaken to the truth – that the idea life has to be a particular way is a learned belief and not true – our hearts do break. Perhaps for wasted effort, unnecessary suffering, or in relief that the nightmare can be laid to rest and a new way of living explored. This is honourable heartbreak that allows us to let go of what has been and take action to live differently and shine the light for others to realise that they can choose to do the same.

I have had people admit to being jealous of what they perceive my life to be, and how I lived it. What surprised me most is that these were often people very close to me who should have realised how hard I work to be able to experience some freedom in my life. Greater freedom has always entailed greater responsibility. If freedom seems to be the absence of responsibility, then somewhere along the line, that freedom has probably turned into escapism and that is not freedom at all, for the inevitable encounter with whatever it is that you are running from will have to come eventually.

The grace I have been given in my life is available to anyone who is willing to do the inner work necessary to be able to receive it. It is not the punishing, self-denying effort I once imagined work to be. I became absolutely depressed when I contemplated a career in law as it was not a good fit for me, and the thought of it loomed large and dark as a never-ending work schedule with no time to actually live! This is a different kind of work, with its own challenges. Although others might scoff at how easy it seems, they quake in their boots when it comes time to actually do it!

This is the work of trusting yourself and the Divine. It is the inner-healing work that leads to outer change, of being willing to let go and face our fears, and of growing stronger in the process. We are all taking that journey to the extent to which we are capable.

On the Divine Feminine path, it takes a strong masculine spirit (in women and men) to be able to go far. Such strength of spirit is arrived at through our own self-work in this and/or other lifetimes, which has empowered us to face our inner pain and to work consciously with the truths of our body. For some of us, many of us, that will entail feeling the feelings of the earth at times, of the entire human race, of the animals. With the amount of suffering that exists, this can sometimes feel rather overwhelming, especially for a sensitive. We must learn to have compassion and kindness for ourselves and not purposefully throw ourselves into emotional oceans of suffering so that we feel we are drowning in it. I did this unconsciously for much of my childhood and young adulthood. It took genuine rage for me to say 'no' to that way of being. It didn't mean that I stopped loving, or that I stopped being moved very deeply by my emotions and by compassion. Rather it meant that I learned how to serve more people by cutting off those that wanted to vampire from me, and be more supportive to those taking responsibility for their own healing. I had to learn to say 'no' in order to more boldly say 'yes' to life and my life's work.

The strong masculine spirit in each of us is refined through experience after experience of having to stand up for what we know is true, even when that means going against popular opinion or challenging our own views on what it is to love or to be free. When it seems there is still endless work to be done, this is the part of us that says, "That is enough, this body needs love and compassion too, today is a day for me to rest." It is the part of us that is unafraid of being broken down by emotion – ours or the feelings of the Earth Mother – because it understands the value of rebuilding, especially after great destruction or loss. The masculine spirit also helps us walk in natural balance so that our process is tempered and unfolding to the degree that will challenge rather than annihilate us. It helps us know when to say yes to life's challenges and when we actually do need to take pause and rally ourselves before leaping forward. It is the strength in us that can say, even at our most vulnerable times, "I love you. Let me hold you now. Just be with me and curl up on the lounge with a good book, or gaze at this beautiful view, and rest for a while."

Or when a different response is needed: "You are strong enough to get through this. You are going to be just fine and this pain will pass soon."

Once you are on the path of the Divine Feminine, inner work is an on-going process. It is not constant and seems to come in waves. It has ups where we are more externally oriented in the world, and dips where we are more internally oriented to work on whatever needs healing and attention within us. In the dips, it can feel like we are living in another world. The outer world can lose its pull when we are diving deep within ourselves. I have lived like that for a few moments or a few hours and for much longer periods. Once I was in that world for more than seven years. It was a long, long time to be in such a space and it took a lot of courage to go in and to stay there until the work was sufficiently integrated. It also required the strength and wisdom to know how and when to come out and back into the physical world. Coming back was actually just as painful and challenging and I understand why babies have a good cry and scream when they come into the world! At first, being in a space of deep, inner healing can feel like being in a womb as our primary focus is on our growth. It can be hard to go into it and leave the world behind, and just as hard to come out as it means leaving the sanctuary of our solitude.

On the feminine path, we learn how to make the transition between inner and outer orientation more easily and swiftly. For advanced souls it is often part of our spiritual growth to go through at least one prolonged period of self-healing and focus on the inner world. Eventually we will learn to live in the inner world and engage in the outer world. As we get used to travelling from the inner to the outer world and back again, distinctions do soften somewhat. For example, we can channel mid-conversation or be cooking dinner in Sydney while channelling soul light and healing to someone over in the United Kingdom. An advanced soul could be sitting on a beach, enjoying the sense of community playfully going on around us, whilst having a moment of deep internal reflection with spontaneous awareness of some block or issue that is resolving itself in that moment. The feminine awareness is not linear and time/space limited. It is expansive and multifaceted. It is one of her powers, one of many that are bestowed upon us as we tread this path.

Many of the readers of this book will already be on the feminine path as healers. Your spiritual growth means you are being divinely trained on the inner planes as teachers, healers and guides whether you formally work that way or not. You are so needed to lead humanity into the new way. This leadership may express itself through your vocation in the metaphysical field, but it could just as valuably express itself in how you raise your children, in your attitude in the workplace, within your relationships or through your art, music, writing or other creative pursuits. Most profoundly, it will reveal itself in how you choose to be true to your own feminine knowledge and the values of your heart in a world that is just beginning to learn the necessity of such wisdom for us to thrive as a species and as a planet.

I give thanks to your soul, for the courage to incarnate as a woman in this lifetime, or as a man who has the wisdom and sense to recognise and honour the feminine principle. May you taste the delights of feminine power and potency, and have the strength to experience what it is to be a wise woman or man of wisdom. Share your knowledge with others to cultivate a new human consciousness of loving support and wisdom on this planet, so that the Divine Feminine and the Divine Masculine may eventually thrive together in loving harmony on a higher turn of the evolutionary spiral of consciousness.

HOW DO I KNOW IF I AM ON THE DIVINE FEMININE PATH?

When the Divine Feminine chooses to work with you – and it is always her choice – you will know it.

For me, it began with a crisis of sorts. I was happily engaged in my love affair with the divinely masculine worlds of spirit and light, when all of a sudden, it just closed up and I felt like I was being plunged headfirst, into the earth. I felt like a big turnip. It might sound strange, but I genuinely felt as though my crown chakra, once at one with the energies of light, sky and heaven, had been tipped upside down and plugged directly into the earth. It felt really odd and I didn't enjoy it much. The way I had sourced my power up until that time – directly from the light – was no longer available to me. I felt lost, disoriented and confused. I certainly felt 'in the dark' which was not where I naturally preferred to dwell.

It took me a long, long time to get used to those worlds and to begin to experience their beauty and wisdom. This came through dream work at first, then yoga and dance, and eventually music and singing as well. These were all gifts that could come only through having a body. I could dream of the joy of singing, and often did, but it could not manifest in the physical world as direct experience until I gave up my love affair with the light and learned to love the earth equally.

I will talk much more on this process in *Crystal Stars 11.11* because those of you who are more accustomed to the light than the earth will find it helpful. For now, it is enough to say that this was an initiation from the divine path of the masculine light, into the divine-feminine path of wisdom which comes through the body, the heart, and is earned through consciously integrating life experience.

I remained in the dark, inner worlds mentioned earlier for seven years. It wasn't as though I chose that length of time consciously, it just took me a while to learn what I needed to. During that time I couldn't work with spirit in the same way that I had previously. It was a crisis in my work and I felt many of my clients falling away. During that time, my ability to teach receded and the inspiration to run classes or workshops dried up completely. I just had no urge for it. When my spiritual abilities returned they were stronger than ever, but at the time I didn't know if that would be the case. I didn't really understand much of what was happening, except that I was going into the void, and would have to bear it for some kind of learning experience. Beyond that, I knew nothing.

In my time in the darkness of the Divine Mother's womb I learned many things, including the need for balance. As someone with a tendency towards extreme behaviour, this took me a while and I have no doubt I am still learning it at a deeper level. As I was so internally oriented during those years, my dreams were vivid and sometimes very disturbing. Through those dreams, I was healing at a deep, deep level and releasing emotions I could not consciously access in my waking state.

This was an invitation for me to connect with the mysterious, enigmatic and healing worlds of the Divine Feminine, with her intuitive and strange symbolic language, her sense of humour and healing genius, all of which came to life through my dreams. In time I began to trust in my dreams and eventually, in my bodily intuitions as well. I discovered that this body was an animal with her own intelligence, like a horse. She was so unerringly accurate, the only time confusion arose was when I didn't listen to her or didn't like what she was telling me, and tried to find a way to change things, rather than accept and move through it.

This all gave me an entirely different understanding of what human beings need to become enlightened. It wasn't just masculine spirit, but a loving, healed relationship with feminine creativity as manifested in all of nature, including our own bodies. This balance enables us to experience the fullness of life. Incarnation is not some blip or mistake on the ladder of evolutionary progress. It is an important part of the enlightenment process. It is a way to bring the light of the spirit to life, through genuine, deep, passionate and serving love.

Those of you with a passion for animals, the oceans and trees will know how strong that love needs to be for real healing, guardianship and appreciation of those divine creations to endure. Those of you already on the path of the Divine Feminine, will know that love and appreciation for animals and nature is a powerful, motivating force. As a person who walks a shamanic path – which for me is a path that integrates the conscious and unconscious with the spiritual realms of light and dark, to bring healing and awakening – the healing power of animals is very real. I work with animals as totems through dreams and when they physically come into my life, they help me too.

Animals help us remember that there is so much more to life than our intellectual minds. I remember hearing spiritual teacher, Andrew Harvey, talk about his special relationship to the cat who was his spirit animal and soul healer for many years. When he talked of the death of his cat, everyone in the room was moved to tears, himself included. He then mentioned a previous workshop where, after hearing the same story, a young woman politely asked, "But why do we really need the animals?" He responded, "Young lady, I cannot answer you right because I feel like I want to kill you!" How she responded to such a pronouncement I do not know and could not ask because I was simultaneously so disturbed and amused by his response that I couldn't think straight. For people that understand the love and aliveness animals bring to human existence, the question asked by that young woman is a sign of a damaged soul who cannot feel the connection to the natural world that sustains a remembrance of the natural, feminine wildness within us.

Some years ago I taught workshops in a country town in New South Wales. Enthusiastic for some exercise, I decided to go for a run in the bush around the property I was staying at. Unintentionally, I ran until I couldn't see the house and realised I had gotten myself lost! After a moment of acute embarrassment at my city-girl uselessness in such a situation, and another of freaking out at being genuinely lost in the bush with no means of seeking human assistance, I called out to Mother Earth for help. A group of kangaroos appeared moments later. They stared at me and I stared at them. Eventually I said, "I need to get back to the house, but I don't know which direction to head." Like something out of a cosmic episode of *Skippy* they bound off in a particular direction. I sighed, "Oh well, I have done weirder things in my life," and ran after them. They led me straight back to the house. I was rather less ambitious in my running from that point onwards and in even greater awe of Mother Nature – and her kangaroos.

A few years back I happened upon a supplier of animal fur at a local beach market. She sourced her furs from pest species that are culled (in Australia that is typically rabbit). I had always automatically rejected fur from a moral standpoint, but there was something in me that gravitated to her market stall. I was uncertain of what it was and was disturbed by it. Despite the inner conflict, something in me stirred at a deep level. As I touched that fur and put it on my body, I felt so very close the earth, to Mother Nature, to the spirit of the animal that provided the fur and to my own body. It was surprising, beautiful and disturbing to my moral viewpoint. However, I could not deny that it grounded me in a powerful way that I had not previously experienced.

Sometimes it can be harder for me to tolerate animal suffering than human suffering. This is a quirk in my nature that I know many others share. I did not want to be a hypocrite as walking my talk has always been so important to me. It is the authenticity of my journey that makes what I have to say most helpful for others. I needed to be in integrity with myself. Even with all that, I could not deny the oneness I experienced through the connection with the fur. I knew there was something else going on. More than the fur, this experience was about accepting another part of myself. A short time later I was unexpectedly initiated as a shaman on the inner planes, in the middle of teaching a workshop. Through that initiation, I was given the ability to work with earth energy to heal the human soul and promote spiritual growth in a more powerful, new and deeper way.

The entire experience – being drawn to the market stall, confronting my own judgment of the part of me that wore the fur and felt healed and plugged into nature through doing so, and being stunned as that same part of me became a healer in a deeper and more powerful way – was an initiation onto the path of the Divine Feminine. It was a surprising transformation that was not revealed immediately, but eventually I understood what was happening and the wisdom in it, even though my mind struggled with the process.

Typically, my encounters with the Divine Feminine are unexpected. This is often because she is bringing something to life that I am not yet in contact with, am ignorant of or do not fully understand. Every genuine encounter on her path can feel surprising, even disturbing, and always calls for growth beyond what we feel comfortable with or certain of at the time. Sometimes this path will lead us in ways that are not only unexpected, but are not even particularly desired. If we feel moved by love, from within, without expectation or attachment, and then no matter what our mind tells us, the invisible, but palpable will of the Divine Feminine will be at work in our lives. If we are to serve her and become whole, we must follow her in the trust that her wisdom will become evident in time.

In that process, I had to acknowledge and honour my dark side and my light side both privately and in the public eye. I would rather be real and whole, as darkness and light, and underneath all of that be coming from my heart, rather than appearing to be superficial and one-dimensional. As the Divine Feminine demands wholeness, the latter would not be helpful for those genuinely seeking to walk this path. It just so happened that in my dark side there was a shamanic healer who wanted to work with earth energies in partnership with the energy healer who worked with the Divine Masculine energies I was more comfortable with in my light side. Together they were far more potent and effective than on their own, but I had to have a lot of love in my heart and a greater ability to accept all of myself, in order for that partnership to occur. And of course, I didn't know until towards the end of the process – that took me years to work through – that it would be such a beautiful marriage. I could only trust and do my inner work.

Of course, there are those that criticise the darkness in themselves and others, and I understand that. Loving is hard work at times. The mind will sometimes rebel and I get it – I really do. I appreciate those who defend the animal communities. The charities I sponsor are primarily focussed on animal welfare because that is what moves my heart, so I do understand the sacred rage behind the passion to defend the undefended. That is also a face of the Divine Feminine, but we do need to be careful not to contribute to the culture of fear and hate that diminishes rather than cultivates compassion. I have stumbled across online images of people performing horrible acts of animal cruelty and I weep when I see them. I pray fervently to the Divine Mother because it is the only thing I can do in those moments to bear the suffering. I pray for her to liberate the animal and the lost soul of the person who could bring themselves to do what they are doing, because truly, they need love more than they need judgment or hate.

The feminine path is not about being all nice and soft. You only have to look at the goddess in some of her fiercer forms to realise that she has her dark face and a rage that is entirely appropriate, but how we express it is so important. Rage can be used as a tool of love and transformation, rather than a degenerative device of hate and fear. Those of us on the path of love may be side-tracked into fear and hate, and be tempted into taking pot-shots at each other from some moral high ground. While it is good to be discerning, undermining other healers on the path is not necessarily going to contribute to our cause!

A dear friend of mine, who is vegetarian, was viciously accused of being a murderer by a woman who criticised her for not being completely vegan. This woman posted "murderer" all over my friend's Facebook page. Now my friend is a gentle and powerful lightworker and is an authentic and loving teacher for many thousands of people on the feminine path. Through her work, she is doing so much more for the world that is constructive and based in love, than those who are coming from fear and hate. No matter how justified, passionate or noble intentions might be, we can have discernment and leave others to walk their own path. Help each other when we can, step back and let the Divine do its magic when we cannot, but trying to tear another down out of jealousy, judgment, fear or hate doesn't help the light – except by forcing us to grow stronger in our compassion to outgrow it. The weapon of choice of the Divine Feminine is always love.

Understand that we are all darkness and light, and choose wisely which parts of your inner self you will feed. Yes, underneath all of that, there is just one big, throbbing bliss-bomb of a spiritual being, but we are here to learn and grow by engaging with the material world. That is the path of the Divine Feminine. In her creation there are light and dark aspects – of which we are a part whilst we are incarnate in this world. We get to choose how to respond to that. Will it be with love or with fear?

Love doesn't mean that we cannot be strong, or even fight for what we want and what we feel is true. Love is powerful. It fights differently to fear. Part of the feminine wisdom is that the end never justifies the means. Hating someone to end hate will not work. We have to grow beyond it. We have to work intelligently with what we have at our disposal to align ourselves with love. This is our real power. Part of how I do this, is to work on the consciousness within humanity that causes the problems in the first place. I do this first within myself and it then translates out into the work that I share with others. Others may not work at such a grass-roots level and may be more political or activism based, and that's wonderful. We all have to reach out to help each other according to the grace and gifts we have been given.

Ninety-nine percent of what I receive back from the world is love and I am profoundly grateful for the acceptance, appreciation and thanks that I receive for the work that I do. However, there is that small percentage that prefers to attack rather than support me. I accept this as a part of life. What saddens me in those moments is that the ego has triumphed over the heart because every human being has free will to choose love or fear in any given moment. No matter whether that person thinks they are justified in their comments, to act with fear (which is what fuels aggression) is not a triumph of love.

We gain power when we work with the goddesses. We will be challenged about how we use that power. Is it to further fear or to further love? Self-righteousness can blur the lines between the two. We can always choose. Sometimes we need to be careful with our choices. With greater power, there are greater karmic ramifications for our actions. There have been times when a comment I felt was perfectly acceptable, has been met with a reaction that was all out of proportion to what I expected. What to me seemed like a tiny drop, for another was perceived as a huge wave!

We are responsible only for our own reactions, not the reactions of others. However, we can certainly use the responses of the world around us to help us monitor how we are working with the growing power we have been offered through our healing work with the goddess. How will we use that power? What will we do with it? Can we be sensitive to its effect upon others and therefore utilise it with ever more compassion? It is always our own choice and responsibility. This is why these teachings are only given on the more advanced stages of the soul path, when we have enough maturity (hopefully!) to be fully accountable. Higher levels of teaching are denied until we are responsible enough to pass the initial 'tests' of how we work with our power. You may think you are a beginner in all of this, but you would not be connecting with me and this work if you were not beyond the basics and moving into a deeper consciousness that allows for your soul to fulfil its mission of spiritual leadership upon Earth at this time. You are reading this book so you are ready for this journey, or more than likely, are already on it. This book will bring you the pieces of the puzzle of which you are in need.

When you are on a mission of spiritual leadership (whether obviously or more undercover) you will understand that you are here to heal not only yourself, but to make a positive healing contribution to the world as well. You'll be passionate about various causes and that is as it should be. The world needs that passion to fuel conscious action. You will also understand that it is through healing ourselves that the world around us becomes ripe for transformation. So we each begin to work with what has been given to us – a body, consciousness, individuality, life experiences, challenges and opportunities. From this, great growth and healing can happen. When we are plugged into feminine consciousness we understand there is no separation. When we become healthy, we bring that energy to others and they are empowered to choose health too, if they so wish.

On the feminine path we learn to trust in the natural tendency towards wholeness and growth, and our job is to tend to our inner gardens – to weed, to fertilise (with the bones of what we are letting go) and to trust the right amount of sunshine and water will come to us from the light of spirit, the heat of our passions and the emotional flow of our feelings.

WORKING WITH GODDESSES

This and the other books in this *Crystal Spirituality Series*, including *Crystal Angels 444* and *Crystal Masters 333*, were written to assist your surrender into the loving guidance that emanates from highly advanced spiritual guides. In this case, into the faces of the Divine Feminine that want to help you succeed on your life path. You are attracted to this information now which means this process has already begun for you.

The goddesses themselves have a rich history that has manifested in various cultures, with different characteristics and tendencies. Underneath their multifarious appearance is the one great beating heart. In the same way that a woman can be gentle one moment, passionate the next, then tender, funny, playful or sad, so too the great goddess shows herself in infinite ways. No matter which face she is showing, it is all the one divine being underneath, the nature of whom is cosmic, unconditional love. Just as an adoring mother responds to her child, she nurtures our soul in its spiritual growth.

When we begin to work consciously with goddess energy, our life changes. Goddesses are big, bold and vivacious energies. Even the more introverted goddesses are large personalities and we have to be careful to allow them to heal and flow through us, rather than identifying as being them. This can happen if our ego is feeling particularly weakened or challenged at any given time in our life and wants to grab a hold of something it perceives will block any threats to its existence.

Imagining oneself as a goddess is a way of blocking out the darker and less palatable aspects of our physical mortality for a moment or two. However, it is extremely unhealthy because we are not goddesses and are not meant to be. We are divine humans. We are meant to honour our spiritual nature and to love and accept the human body we are blessed with as well.

To play at being a goddess, without honouring our human limitations or learning to allow her energy to flow through us, is a recipe for disaster. It is like the story of Icarus, with his wings fashioned from feathers and wax. In his thrill of flight, he flew too close to the sun, the wax on the wings melted and that was that. Human beings, even divine ones, are not meant to fly too close to the light of the great sun. We are meant to live on Earth and work with the light of the heavens. We are here for a reason, and while there are days when one can understand why such a fantasy might appeal, it is not to try to escape the earth and run away to the heavens. Getting carried away and trying to live as though we are a goddess or above matters of the earth, just creates unholy brats and makes everyone's lives miserable. Eventually, such people are plunged back into the ocean of earthly, emotional lessons.

Realising that goddesses are not just mythical or fictional characters, but real, living beings that hold great power can cure us of any desire for fanciful flight such as posturing as if we are actually Isis, for example. I had an experience recently at a workshop where a lovely young woman came up to me and confessed that a healer had told her she *was* Isis in a past life. I have no doubt others have been told similar stories involving Isis, other goddesses or various historical figures – Cleopatra comes to mind. Sometimes the pain of this present lifetime can be so great that the ego is lured by the idea of a truly fantastical past life. The fantasy can feel so good to the ego that is difficult to resist. Nonetheless, this particular woman was confused rather than empowered by the information she had received. It brought her relief to hear that her healer may have believed in what she was saying at the time and held good intentions, but that I saw things differently. I explained that she might carry the spirit of Isis in her heart, even whilst the goddess Isis was energetically still very much alive and doing her part in the greater spiritual work for the betterment of humanity. I suggested that this woman was meant to be herself, not Isis. She could love the goddess and even relate to her story and mission (and you may too) but she was still meant to be her own unique divine spark which is just as sacred as the goddess. In fact it *is* an expression of the goddess, just as Isis is. This information calmed her confusion and helped her feel good about herself again. Surrendering in unconditional love is the safest and most sensible way to work with the energy of the goddesses for the greater good.

More so than with the beautiful angelic beings and Ascended Masters, I have found that the goddesses work in a way that tends to throw you off your game. This is not in a destructive or negative sense, but they will choose how to work with you, what you are best suited to (which may or may not be what you think) and move you forward on your most genuine path. Sometimes that means making peace with parts of yourself you would rather avoid. Most of my initiation into shamanic work with both the natural and spiritual worlds (rather than just the spiritual worlds, which was a gift I was born with) has come through meeting and learning to accept and hold compassion for the darkness in me, in the human heart and in the world of nature more generally. I know I am a being of light, but in the interplay of that light with consciousness in the world of forms, both light and darkness will manifest through me. It has not been an easy journey to take, but the fruits of that journey have been vast and enabled me to serve the light of my own soul far more effectively, and this has helped more people in the process. The darkness can be made to serve the light and perhaps it is even more accurate to say that the darkness can serve love in how we choose to respond to it. It is better work with darkness as intelligently as we can, rather than fearing or trying to avoid it as it thus becomes even more unconscious and less under the guiding counsel of our hearts.

I try to be as conscious of the darkness as I can and to work with the gift of light, but it would be foolish and irresponsible to deny there is a dark side to my nature. I have to be aware of it and hold compassion for it. To take that particular journey has been the only way I have been able to learn how to grow larger in compassion than in the fear of darkness and fear itself. You cannot become intelligent in your responses to something if you don't even acknowledge it exists. This doesn't mean I indulge in the darkness of evil in the world, in my own consciousness or in others. I hold compassion and actively seek out awareness of that surprisingly sneaky tendency to want to destroy life rather than honour it. It can surprise us with its subtlety and is not always as obviously repellent as one might expect. Sometimes that quality can be extremely seductive and it is only when we come through an experience that we realise it has been serving death rather than life. Perfectionism is one such example. Sometimes we only learn the difference between what is serving death and what is serving life through the experience of both. The mind cannot guide us on this. Only the heart can discern what serves life and what undermines it as it may come under the guise of logic, safety, rationality or righteousness. Goddesses don't judge, but they will rally for love with great passion, whilst accepting all experiences can be made to serve love, and ultimately will.

When the Great Goddess stomps through your life, things will never be the same again. And believe me, she can stomp! Often in practical shoes and with little regard for whatever you might think is sacrosanct, spiritual and beyond reproach. That has certainly been her calling card in my life. She has systematically stripped everything from me that I wanted to hold on to or thought I needed and was bound by. It sounds nasty – it certainly wasn't pretty much of the time – but I believe it is because one of her many gifts to me is freedom.

In working with this material I suggest that you add the simple act of calling your higher self and the guidance that loves you unconditionally to your daily practice. You will be grateful for the loving support and kindness. You can do this simply by saying, at least once a day, "I call on the guidance that loves me unconditionally, please help me today." If you are having a shocker of a day, do it often! This will help you deal with the challenges and receive the opportunities that the Divine Feminine is going to bring to you on her path of awakening. She will bring you whatever your soul needs to thrive. This may make little sense to the ego, but when we are in prayer and trust we know it will work out beautifully. We do need to be prepared to go with our life experiences, accepting them for what they are, even if we don't always understand the higher reason for it. This is called ... living!

MANIFESTING – WHAT IS IT?

Several years ago, I ran a project with a few powerful and spiritually aligned women. We gathered for a meeting to discuss what we wanted to create. One of the women started with a bold statement about how we needed to be very detailed, down to the last degree, to visualise every aspect of it and go from there. I felt my heart sink. It was the exact opposite of how I worked!

I realised we were at odds with each other and I hadn't even opened my mouth yet. I had some serious doubts about the project and sure enough the wheels fell off soon after. It was challenging at the time. She was one of those people who seemed to believe it was her role to point out where I was going wrong and how I should do things differently. This wasn't particularly helpful to our cause, but it did show us, right from the beginning, that we were not going to be a good energetic match in the long term.

From that experience, I learned more about the apparently non-typical way in which I manifest. In fact, as far as I am concerned, even to say that I manifest is putting it back to front. My experience is one of opening to consciousness and then following my life path, no matter where it leads me and what it asks of me. Of course, there are some tantrums along the way. Obedience is not my natural tendency, even to the divine genius, though I whole-heartedly accept it is far more brilliant than I. In opening up, I am shown the next step in the divine plan. At certain times, I will see and know enough of what is happening to realise what is being manifested through me. At other times, I consciously participate in each step, but overall am surrendered to not knowing the bigger picture. Even when I know some parts of the bigger picture, it can often be many years before I realise how the creative process has been at work around and through me. So, I am the divine being manifested. I am being acted upon in conscious alignment and surrender. That's the bigger truth.

The healing processes in this book are to help us on that path. We get out of the way and divinity happens with all its glory.

Now of course there are the smaller level manifestations, the things that I feel are created through my intention and the response of the Universe to what I want or need in that moment. This is the more everyday level of manifestation – the parking spaces, bargain shopping deals, best time to go grocery shopping, houses to live in, car repairs and basic lifestyle needs. Sometimes that type of manifestation happens 'accidentally'. By that, I mean without conscious realisation, because there really are no accidents and the Divine is in constant alignment with the brilliant plan of evolution.

At other times we need to do some micro manifestation in the moment – the parking spot is a good example. So we ask for help – from our parking angels, for example. Or we need to find a lost pet so we call on the angels of lost things and ask for their help. Both of these angelic groups are amazing and can help you too. All you need do is ask them for help. Literally. Just say, "Parking angels, please help me find a great parking space now," or "Angels of lost things, please help me find my lost pet, thank you!"

With the goddesses we are going to manifest for our physical as well as our spiritual lives. There is no distinction in their realm, so the Divine Feminine will assist us in manifesting everything from a great dinner where magic flows and the ingredients just come together deliciously, to the right loving relationship to help us on the next step of our spiritual growth.

Now you can take the approach of the detailed visualisation. It does work. I have manifested cars, places to live, outfits for performance, technology and all sorts of things through that method. I have asked for perfect timing so that deliveries arrive in the short window when I am at home to receive them and books that were impossible to find have turned up in second-hand bookstores, ready for me to purchase. I even manifested a beautiful silk kaftan through this visualisation method.

Those of you that have seen me in person, will know my 'work uniform' is sometimes a vibrantly coloured kaftan dress from an Australian designer. Her clothes are beautiful but rather expensive, and I love to nab a bargain in a sale when possible (thanks to the bargain shopping angels). In a recent collection of hers, she featured oriental designs. One kaftan with beautiful colours and dragon motifs caught my eye, and I could see myself wearing it when talking about Kuan Yin. However, it was rather expensive and not yet available. For a brief moment other garments made with the same fabric were available in store, but that particular kaftan was available in very limited numbers and proved hard to come by. Apparently the small amount that were available sold out as soon as they came into the store and the design wasn't available in the online boutique.

Some months later this designer announced an online sale on Facebook. These sales can be more terrifying than the old-school department store sales my grandmother told me about. Once when she was trying on a new shoe, an over-eager shopper grabbed the shoe my grandmother had worn into the store, out of the sale bin. "That's my shoe!" protested my grandmother. "No," the other woman cried, "I got it, it's mine!" My shocked grandmother, despite her polite, non-confrontational nature, demanded that the woman return the shoe to her and eventually she did. Perhaps that woman should have called on the bargain shopping angels to help her find what was meant for her, which clearly was not my grandmother's shoes!

Anyway, I somehow managed to get through the maelstrom of typical server crashes and problems that occur when so many people attempt to purchase at the same time when this designer has an online sale. I browsed through the sale items. My beloved 'Kuan Yin' kaftan wasn't there, but I did want to purchase a kaftan at such a great discount (I do have a bargainista streak!) and found one that appealed to me. It was different to the one that I loved, but I liked the look of it and the discount.

Later that day I was purchasing groceries in a shopping centre where the designer had a store. It occurred to me that I could go and see if they had the kaftan I had purchased in store so I could see what it looked like 'in person' so to speak. Rather a back-to-front approach, I'll grant you, but that's what I did. It was in store and I didn't like it quite as much as the colours weren't as vibrant as they appeared online, but it was still lovely and I knew I would enjoy wearing it. I enquired again about the kaftan I liked, only to be informed that they were sold out and were no longer available. I mentally shrugged and figured I would find a second-hand one somehow, because I believed it would come to me eventually.

A few days later my purchase from the online sale arrived. As I unwrapped it, I couldn't believe my eyes. There sitting before me was the 'Kuan Yin' kaftan that had never been made available for sale online and was sold out. It had been sent to me courtesy of a 'mistake' made by whoever had packed my order. I knew I had manifested it without intending to do. I did wear it to speak about Kuan Yin at the *Mind Body Spirit Festival* in Sydney and I enjoyed that experience and wearing my vibrant dress, very much.

However, there has been plenty of times when I was not been pleased with the results of this method. A highly-prized legal position that made me absolutely miserable comes to mind. I certainly manifested what I wanted, sometimes rather passionately. As I was coming from my mind, and the limited viewpoint of what I could actually see, know and desire at the time, the results were not always what I hoped for in substance, even though I got what I had specifically asked for. After using this mind-driven manifesting technique to successfully climb a couple of mountains, only to discover they were not the right mountains for me, I decided to quit that method and began to move more from my heart and soul. I figured the Divine knew what I needed in order to grow, even when I didn't consciously know myself. As a bonus, the Divine would also know the best way to bring what I needed to me. So I shifted from manifesting in great detail to manifesting in greater trust. I became precise about how I wanted to feel and the overall plan, but very open to how it would all come together. I wanted to serve, fulfil my soul destiny, live my truths with courage and honesty in an inspirational way, and to create, write, teach, dance, sing, heal, channel, perform, inspire and also to connect with the highest and greatest level of divinity possible for me. I trusted the Divine would lead me on a continually unfolding pathway towards whatever that life-package was going to look like. And, that is exactly what has happened.

I still like to manifest a 'kaftan' from time to time, but my main focus is on the bigger picture. If I am focusing on something I want in my life – such as somewhere to live – I give the essentials, but not the form. In this example, I might ask for a home that will be good for me to heal in, that moves my heart, that is close to nature and that will suit me. I then trust in what comes to me. If I need to tweak the essentials, for example if I realise I need somewhere that has more space or light, then I do that, but I trust more than I direct. There is a far greater intelligence than my own limited consciousness guiding my path and I love and trust in that.

When we work at this level, we are always manifesting and creating, but it is happening on a bigger level than our immediate conscious mind and body can sense so there may be times when we lose faith in the process. There have been periods of time, more than ten years actually, when I was busy working towards what I am doing today. I wanted to be doing what I am doing right at this moment about nine and a half years ago! I didn't realise how much needed to be in place to enable me to step forward and be what I wanted to be. These changes happened within me, but also in the lives of the very important people who help me do what I do in the world.

That trend of forward thinking continues in me! I have projects I would like manifested now, but I am not exactly sure what they will be. I mean, I know the spirit of them, but I am waiting to become more aware of their heart and to receive enough of their form energetically so that I can say, "Right, I get what it is now – on we go!" It is then that the process really kicks into gear, taking shape, attracting the right people and opportunities to move forward. I hope that it won't take another ten years of work to bring them to be. My feeling is that it might be another year or two, but really, one cannot know what one cannot know. In this sort of manifestation, we have to live it into being. We aren't in control of the process from an intellectual level, we just have to go with it and trust.

It is important to realise the divine being in us is always creating and is sometimes working at a divine soul level that our minds can't comprehend. Even when we can't see it, manifestation is happening, but on a far greater scale and we have to accept the Divine knows what it is doing, and the timing to do it in. So, we need trust and then we see results.

HOW THE GODDESSES OPERATE IN THE WORLD

Goddesses are endlessly resourceful. They will manifest through people, as situations and through messages that repeat again and again until you realise what is coming through. About ten years ago, a client told me she had set the CD stacker in her car to randomly select songs, but one tune was being played more randomly than most. It was often repeated three or more times and once, was actually selected at random seven times in a row! The song seemed to relate directly to a life experience my client was having. "Do you think there is a message for me in the lyrics?" she asked. I suggested, that, "Yes, there quite likely is."

Goddesses are real forces and can appear in many guises. In their teachings it is said they will sometimes shapeshift into animal form, taking on the guise of a dog, or a cat and the like. Gaia is certainly known to pass on messages and guidance through her animal friends. The goddesses will also speak to us through books and teachings. If there is something I have written in this book that feels like it really speaks to you, in that it vibrates at a level of truth that seems so perfectly appropriate for what you are experiencing, you can be sure that the Divine Feminine is reaching out to you through those particular words. It doesn't matter if those words can be read by someone else, and even resonate for someone else too. If they are clicking for you, then she had them written by me, for you. And that's that.

The goddesses serve the Divine Feminine plan of love. They move through life events and circumstances, weaving situations into creation so that humanity can evolve as a group and as individuals, through their spiritual learning. They may work through the forces of natural events, or through energetically supporting humanity in learning a lesson – with a loving caress or a short, sharp slap, depending on what will best serve love. Life is the divine classroom through which human beings are instructed in spiritual growth, and the goddesses weave the threads of life, of which we are a part, into a rich tapestry of sacred, loving creation.

WHY AND HOW CAN I WORK WITH THEM?

You will choose to work with goddesses if you are called to – because at that point, you are going to want to do so. You can work with them in whatever way you feel intuitively drawn to, provided you always state, aloud, that your work is to come from unconditional love.

Goddesses vibrate at different levels of reality, depending on what we can access. For example, if we were to work with Circe, the goddess of drugs and medicinal plants, we could use her energy to poison or to heal depending on whether we are coming from a place of compassion and love or otherwise. It is the same for the goddesses, but the experience will differ based on the consciousness of the person doing the work.

It is important to remember that goddesses are empowering energies. They make us energetically more powerful, but be mindful that working with higher beings does not mitigate universal law. So, if someone is working with goddess energy from a lower level of consciousness by going about casting spells that violate free will or sending curses, their actions and intentions will return to them amplified as karma. I sincerely doubt that anyone drawn to my work would be resonating at that particular level of consciousness, but it is helpful to learn about how consciousness operates in our universe. If we are working with goddesses to liberate the human soul, we will gain so much love, support and assistance on our path. But how we work is always our choice to make.

For a brief time, I studied with a spiritual teacher who spoke about having some restraint in our use of power. She said someone had annoyed her and she was momentarily tempted to 'throw them into the fire' of her anger – of course, she didn't do it. I wasn't sure whether to be appreciative that she didn't do it, or disturbed that the thought had even crossed her mind.

Then sometime later, I had a dark moment of my own, where I felt very, very angry with someone, and it flashed through my heart that I wanted that person to suffer. Considering that I have dedicated my life to the compassionate liberation of the soul, this was quite a sobering experience for me. It was an encounter with the shadow Hera, the goddess who just had enough of being treated poorly by her misbehaving husband and was not adverse to unleashing absolute wrath upon those that disrespected her. Fortunately, it didn't consume me and I was able to witness it as a passing darkness, recognise it for what it was and have compassion for the part of my being that was in the wounding and reacting to it. I responded to it by acknowledging and affirming that I understood and accepted the feeling, but it wasn't who I was, and it didn't go any further than that. I was able to come back to my more natural, compassionate state for myself and for the other person involved, and that was the end of that.

The point is, that when you have power, from time to time you will be tested on how you would use it. Personally, I am grateful for this. I know it can be all too easy to get caught up in excuses and give ourselves permission to do something we would truly regret later on, if we were not kept in check by these little (but significant) tests along the way. In keeping the work pure and clean, by constantly calling on unconditional love to be the guiding force in any spiritual work we do, and by holding the intention that our work be for the greatest good, we are covered, so to speak.

It is also good to note that some goddesses will be channelled through you and you may even come to temporarily embody some in healing service, which is quite an experience. It places a certain demand on the physical body, but can be so powerful in liberating people out of their 'stuff' quickly and effectively. In some cultures, such as in India, this is more typically accepted. Recently, one of my clients shared that her father would often become Kali, a dark goddess whom we will meet later on, and channel all sorts of things during his trances. In *Crystal Masters 333* and in this book, we will discuss discernment in relation to receiving messages from those claiming to channel other beings. Even if someone is genuinely channelling another being, their own 'stuff' can often distort or colour the original message in a way that might not be so helpful. Discernment allows us to take what is useful and leave the rest behind, with compassion. When it comes to channelling goddess energies, it is best to respond in the same way.

Know that goddesses will never belong to you or to anyone else, even if someone claims to channel their energy or embody their presence and regardless of how genuine and powerful that embodiment may temporarily be. Goddesses don't belong to anyone! They are goddesses! So they will flow through us, but like divine power, we can never orchestrate or own their energy. We can learn to align with their frequency, endeavour to be as clear and pure a channel as possible and deal with the stuff that comes up for us. Working with goddesses will force us to grow, in order to keep up with the high frequency – perhaps even more than the people on the receiving end of that energy.

When you realise you are beginning to serve a particular goddess, it can be incredibly blissful. They can be so sneaky and sometimes it has been years before I realised a certain being has been working with me, deeply, for a long time and, for whatever reason, has chosen a particular moment to bring her presence and identity to my conscious awareness. Knowing she also works with others teaches us not to be possessive of her, to love her freely and to know that she loves us utterly, without restraint. The more freedom there is and the lighter the bond is held, the deeper the devotion and the passion will become. It can be quite an education on how to love and be loved.

Although various goddesses have their religious and spiritual traditions through which they have come into human awareness, they are not limited by them. Nor are we limited in who we can or cannot work with based on our own backgrounds. I know that there will be people who are uncomfortable with this, and I apologise if that is a reader of this work. I ask that you trust in your own path of love and work with the expression of the Divine that feels truthful for you.

There will also be many people who feel absolutely comfortable with the idea of one divine source being reached via many religious and spiritual pathways. I feel very fortunate in how I was raised in regards to this. I had a fascination for many different religious traditions, even as a child. I was sometimes attracted to, sometimes repelled by, but always fascinated and curious by different iconography. I always knew, at some level, there was only love behind it all.

WHY THESE PARTICULAR GODDESSES?

There are so many goddesses from a variety of traditions. In this book, I chose to share the ones who have chosen to work with me over the years. As I have been empowered and initiated into their paths, I felt I could be constructive in sharing their wisdom and grace with you.

Although there are many healing goddess energies available to us, I believe that these goddesses are particularly relevant and helpful at this particular point in human evolutionary history. As my work is for practical spirituality in the now, this was a major plus point.

As with all my work, it is intuitively constructed, so I trust in the greater plan behind the choices.

WHAT IS 888?

Numbers hold both vibrations and messages. I absolutely knew that this book would hold the eight vibration in high frequency, hence the multiple eights. I would have had 88888888 if I could, but I think it might have been a bit visually confusing for the cover!

The eight vibration speaks of mastery, power, authority, strength and leadership. These might seem to be masculine qualities, and in a sense they are, but it is through feminine wisdom that these qualities become refined to the point that they serve love rather than dominate through fear. The Divine Feminine is the empowering, guiding, leading force of consciousness on our planet at this time. She is calling to those of us with enough sense to realise this, to step into our power and to not be afraid of our empowerment. Through the eight vibration, she is asking us to realise that we have taken enough responsibility for ourselves and what we are putting out into the world and that we are now to be trusted with her power, because we will use it for the greater good. Even if we do take a moment to manifest a parking space – with the understanding that in the world of the Divine Mother, everyone gets a perfect parking space – there is no essential reality of triumph of one over the other or of reality being win-lose. There is only the choice of whether to empower that reality or not. I choose not!

I have such a passion for sacred numbers, and the Universe has been going berserk with communication via numbers since I began writing this series – even more than usual! It has been funny, beautiful and really so very strong. So I have written an additional book on it, as an offering to help you work even more deeply with number vibrations for healing, without having to be a numerologist. It is called *Messages in the Numbers* and is published by Blue Angel.For now however, it is enough to know that this entire book brings you healing through the eight vibration, just as *Crystal Masters 333* brings you healing through the master number thirty-three vibration and *Crystal Angels 444* brings you healing through the master vibration of forty-four.

HOW TO WORK WITH THE CRYSTALS

With the exception of mica (which needs very careful cleaning with a delicate dust cloth so it doesn't flake off in your hands) and citrine (which doesn't actually need cleansing), you can cleanse your crystals regularly especially if you or another person have been touching them. If they are just working their magic in your room, for example, they don't need cleansing quite as often. You'll learn to feel when they are 'full' and need some clearing before they can begin to work again. That could be a period of weeks or months.

If you are feeling confident, you can even clear and program a quartz crystal to cleanse all the crystals in your collection with each full moon. To do this, simply hold the quartz in your left hand and call upon the Crystal Angel of Clear Quartz, and the beings who love you unconditionally, including your higher self or soul. You would then thank the crystal for its service and ask that it be cleared of all negative energy and previous programs. You then place your right hand above it and instruct it to cleanse each crystal in your home (for example) with pure white light until they are clear of any negative energy at each full moon, until instructed to stop doing so.

Another powerful cleansing method is visualisation. Imagine a vibrant violet light, flecked with white, sparkling and crackling above the crown of your head. Allow it to flow down over your forehead and into your mouth before blowing it out over your crystal. Hold the intention for this beautiful violet energy to cleanse all negativity. Do this for at least seven breaths, until it feels clean. With practice you will become more focused and be able to clear a crystal with one short, sharp breath. Another system is to play beautiful music, such as a CD with the OM chant or other mantras (I have created an album called *Sacred Voice*, a DVD called *Mantra Dance*, and yet another album called *Voice of the Soul* that contain mantras you may like to use for this purpose) as well as burning incense to clear the space and your crystals all at once.

Always cleanse your crystals before and after using them in healing, particularly if they have touched your body. If the crystal doesn't get handled then cleansing every few months, or every few days or weeks if there is a lot of emotional energy or stress in your home, will be fine. When a crystal is clean it feels vibrant and clear, but when it is dirty it will feel like sunlight trying to get through a dirty window. This heaviness is accumulated because your crystal has been working hard to clear and harmonise energy.

You cannot over cleanse a crystal nor can you clear its good energy. Cleansing just removes any extraneous energy. It is safe and will not harm you or the stone. Water or sunlight can affect some crystals and cause fading or dissolving. Halite, a type of salt, is one example. It is beautiful and pink halite is particularly stunning, but will melt and dissolve easily! If in doubt, stick to using breath, light or smoke and smudging to cleanse your crystals. You can smudge using a feather or your breath to gently direct the smoke from your favourite incense (more traditionally frankincense or myrrh) 'through' the crystal with the intention of cleansing it.

Many people wonder where the negative energy goes. It doesn't actually go anywhere. Instead, when we use the breath technique, it gets transmuted, from one form into another. This is one of the healing properties of violet light and St Germain whom we met in *Crystal Masters 333*. If you feel unsure about the breath technique, then simply hold the crystal in one hand, raise the other one and say out loud (if possible, or silently in your mind if you prefer): "I call upon the beings of unconditional love who can assist with cleansing my crystal and transmuting negativity energy into unconditional love. Through my own free will. So be it!" Leave it at that or go about burning your incense and/or playing your music.

Crystals worn in contact with the body should be cleansed more frequently than those left in your environment. There are no hard and fast rules so simply trust your intuition. Sometimes it is like they speak to you psychically and ask to be cleansed. A bit like when you see those dirty cars on the road, and someone has cheekily traced "wash me" through the accumulated dirt on the back windscreen!

WHAT IS A CRYSTAL ANGEL?

Every crystal has its own angel. It is sometimes called a nature spirit, oversoul or deva. The word deva translates from Sanskrit into English as 'Shining One'. These crystal angels are the spirit, consciousness, wisdom and vibration of the entire crystal 'species'. These are the beings we call upon in our healing processes.

If you were holding a piece of amazonite, for example, which might have a lovely blue-green hue, you are working with the energy of that individual crystal, plus the entire higher consciousness of all amazonite everywhere in the Universe. It does not matter if the stone is still in the ground or even on a distant planet, every piece of amazonite ranging from the bluest green to the greenest blue is energetically linked to every other piece of amazonite through the consciousness of the Crystal Angel of Amazonite.

We tap into this divine, holographic unity through intention! Your particular piece will have its own unique energy, depending on its unique colour, shape and size. Yet it is aligned via the angel to all amazonite energies. This is why even a small piece of crystal can be very powerful.

The crystal angel will help you tap into the greater power, healing properties and energetic potency of that particular crystal type, as well as to the special personality of the individual piece you are working with. Once you are able to connect to the crystal angels, you do not actually need to have the physical stone with you. This may surprise you, but I have worked with this technique for years. If someone is struggling and a crystal intuitively comes to mind, I simply call upon the angel of that crystal and ask for its consciousness to channel into the body and soul of my client through unconditional love. It works every time. In addition, I do not need to rummage around in my crystal cupboard to see if I have the exact stone that holds the vibration they need in that moment.

Working with crystals is fun and beautiful. We can make the experience more tangible as we learn to sense their unique energy. It is good to know that there is more than one way to tap into the healing intelligence of crystals, especially if we feel attracted to a certain crystal that is not physically available. All we have to do is close our eyes for a moment and silently or audibly say: "Through unconditional love, I call upon the Crystal Angel of Malachite (or whatever crystal it is that you need) and I ask you to bring your healing power into my body, mind and soul now, with compassionate grace. Through my own free will. So be it." Breathe in and out slowly, with your awareness in your heart and an intention to receive. All done!

HOW DO I WORK WITH THE MANDALAS?

In this book, as in the first and second in this series, *Crystal Angels 444* and *Crystal Masters 333*, we work with mandalas as possible replacements for the physical stones. They may be used in the healing process in the same way as regular stones: in your healing room, under your pillow at night for healing, to look at, or to perhaps meditate upon. Let your heart guide you.

HOW DO I READ THE HEALING PROCESSES *AND* DO THEM?

Healing processes go deep and you can either read them as you go or record them beforehand, perhaps on your mobile phone or computer, and then play them back. If you do this, speak slowly and clearly. You need a slower pace when meditating because you are entering a deeper, more spiritual space.

I have included one healing process for each chapter. I find the healing of body, mind and soul comes together easily in one process in each chapter, as it did in *Crystal Masters 333*, although in the first in the series, *Crystal Angels 444*, three different processes were included. Blue Angel has released these processes as downloadable sound files (on CDBaby, Amazon, iTunes etc) and is also working on publishing an app with the healing processes on them as an inexpensive and practical way for you to connect with my voice and energy, as well as to complete your healing process with less effort – always a good plan! You can find out more on my website, www.alanafairchild.com.

Finally, it is a good idea to mention to your doctor or therapist that you are doing energy work, especially if you are on a mental health program or medication. If your healthcare provider believes in energy work, he or she needs to know how to support your journey. If you discover your healthcare provider does not support your decision, you might consider changing your provider. One of my Reiki teachers used to emphasise to all students that energy changes consciousness so make sure you are in consultation with an open-minded healthcare provider as you do this work. You deserve such care.

1.

TARA (MOTHER OF THE WORLD)
TIBETAN QUARTZ (PURITY)

MANIFESTING THROUGH COMPASSION

She hears the cries of the world. They are sounds resounding within her own heart. Even before we recognise our own sadness, fear and anger, she is aware of it and is responding with love. A constant stream of compassion emanates from her and those who suffer are called into the soothing love of her grace.

TARA (MOTHER OF THE WORLD)

In the Tibetan Buddhist tradition, Tara is known as the saviour goddess. She is pictured in many colours, but most commonly in green and white, which represent her different aspects. She is fierce, loving, wise and protective.

On a recent teaching tour, I had a personal encounter with the Goddess Tara in a more intimate and powerful way than I had previously experienced. Many people compare her to Kuan Yin and some even believe she is the same being. I felt the emanation of Tara was similar to Kuan Yin, but I didn't sense they were one and the same. Ultimately, all goddesses come from the one source, yet their emanations can be very individualistic. Much like human beings! So I wanted to know Tara more individually, to really feel her essential divinity in its uniqueness.

Like most divine encounters, I was led into it by an intelligent sequence of events, intuitions and synchronicities. I had no idea what was happening at a deeper level until after the encounter. I was teaching in rural Australia. The tour was organised by a client I had worked with for over ten years. Devoted to the path of love and very respectful of the work I do, she tirelessly poured her energy into organising a wonderful tour through which I had the opportunity to meet many new people and share the experience of divine love. The tour gained quite a bit of attention as we shared our adventures on Facebook. The responses were of excitement and enthusiasm, but there was negativity from one person in particular.

Divine protection is present even when we don't know that we need it – this is just one of the things that astounds me! In such instances, after I realise what has happened, I am left so humbled by the grace that has been afforded to me so that I can get on with my work. When that divine protection seems to be absent, it is because I am learning something valuable in the process of an experience and I can handle it on my own. When that learning has taken place, the protection is there once again and I am held in a compassionate realm of grace.

During this tour, the organiser mentioned a woman I had met a year prior. Although I have a memory like an elephant and usually remember people and their energy fields with tremendous recall, whenever my client mentioned this other woman, I drew a complete mental blank. I was unable to place who she was and my client would have to explain, until I said, "Oh yes! I remember. How is she going?" I would then recall talking with the woman a year or so earlier and even some of the things I said to her. I remembered her with some affection, as she struck me as direct and fun. However, I seemed to instantly forget all about her so that the next time she was mentioned, I would again draw a mental blank. My client would explain who she was, I would remember for a short time, then completely forget all over again. This happened a couple of times and it was so odd that my client and I both noticed it, but I didn't think about it much beyond that.

A few days later, I was doing my early morning yoga and meditation ritual. My practice is never the same from one day to the next. Different feelings, different mental states and different physical sensations arise. On this particular day, I was taken into an unusually deep and blissful state. Tears poured down my face as I was practicing yoga and in meditation, I simply cried. There was so much love, so much tenderness and so much bliss. I had no words for it, I was just in it. I felt very fragile afterwards, but also incredibly blessed.

Feeling as though I was utterly glowing, I emerged from that delicate state and began to prepare breakfast. My client told me the woman whom I kept forgetting had not forgotten me. She had written some nasty, attacking comments about both of us on Facebook just that morning, whilst I was deep in bliss. I recognised the love that I held for that woman and the thought of her sending hate my way saddened me greatly. I understood that her own story was going on behind her comments, but nonetheless I didn't appreciate her actions towards us. I replied on Facebook and acknowledged her right to her opinion, but asked that she not post negative or attacking comments on my Facebook page.

That evening I dreamed my client told me the woman had retreated off Facebook. Sure enough there was no reply to my remark, but sadly, I thought she was likely to be back in a few days after she had licked her wounds (I had been loving, but firm with her) with another attack that attempted to justify her behaviour. This tends to be the way those in ego attack behave. They need to feel justified and would often keep going with incredible energy and determination until they felt so. I had not given in to her behaviour or accepted her remarks. She would be back to try and gain justification from me – to have me feel put down in order that she may feel propped up.

About three days later, I arose for my early morning practice and felt overcome with a deep compulsion to connect with Tara. I created a playlist of music for my practice that included the long Tara chant from my *Sacred Voice* album and began my practice.

As I moved through yoga and meditation, I again felt overcome with emotion. I heard a voice announce, "She cries the tears of the world" and tears streamed down my face as I felt my heart breaking open with her tenderness and love. Eventually I was drawn into deep meditation. I suddenly saw Tara, her eyes so close to mine that it shocked me. Then she was dancing over me. Her foot had an open eye in it, staring at me. I sensed she could see everything. Then unexpectedly, I was one with her and she was holding a small kitten. I suddenly realised it wasn't a kitten this vast being was holding, it was the entire Earth. She held the Earth in her loving hands. I fell into deep bliss and awe, and was transported to a place of shivering energy that pulsated through my body and beyond. I felt myself expand into deep, compassionate peace. There was so much purity in her love. After the attacking hatred that had been directed at me, I was so grateful to feel the purity of love again.

Sure enough, I came out of that profound experience to find that the woman had posted more negativity on Facebook. I realised that her comments on Facebook were accompanied by some unwanted psychic energy that was also directed at me. She was too consumed by her own projections to be able to relate to me with any awareness, so I let her go, trusting that she would get the help she needed from a source that she could accept, when she was ready for it to happen. I blocked her on Facebook and energetically. It was relatively easy to do this because the grace that Tara had given me had centred me in my heart so that I could deal with the confrontation from a place of love and peace.

At the times the attacks were happening, in the profound compassion of the Universal Mother, I was lifted into a state of divine love so that I wouldn't be harmed. The attack seemed so small, sad and petty, even though I could feel the power of the hate this woman was acting out, in her own wounded way, and I felt saddened because I genuinely loved her and wished her well. I had no conscious awareness of the attacks when they were happening, I was simply moved by the Divine into so much compassionate grace that I was protected from them.

I believe this protection was given to me because on so many levels the work I was doing on that tour was hard going and was given in genuine, loving service. The protection allowed the tour to reach people, to be successful and not become derailed by ill will. If I had been drawn into the hate the woman was projecting, my own vibration would have dropped and my ability to support others would have decreased. The grace of the Mother helped me avoid that undesirable outcome.

Even the effect of the tour's publicity on this woman was part of the grace of Tara, but what she chose to do with what emerged was up to her individual free will. She could face her pain and seek to heal it, thereby opening up to receive even further grace from the Divine Mother to support her in her work and professional development, or she could project it out and blame others for her pain. This time she chose the latter, but perhaps in future she will choose otherwise and become free to share her own considerable healing gifts with the world. That is her choice. The Mother of the World loves all equally. She gives what is needed and will help all who ask her. When she calls, and we respond, her gifts are extraordinarily beautiful.

What Tara can provide us with – if we allow it – is the grace to heal. Healing takes work. It isn't a magic moment with no effort involved on our part, though you might be surprised at how many people think that way and will hand all their power over to a healer – or even a goddess – in the hope of circumventing the difficult part of their healing process. The grace required for healing is a type of magic, but it doesn't end our responsibility. It is more like getting a super-charged spiritual vitamin shot, with the energy we need to be able to gain insights, trigger shifts of consciousness and integrate what we have learned so that we can implement new behaviours that are more aligned with our developing consciousness.

In my experience, Tara's grace is capable of empowering and supporting us to heal even the most stubbornly resistant wounds within. Through Tara, issues that may have been immoveable for decades, suddenly begin to destabilise so that healing becomes a real possibility. As this starts to occur, it can feel like an extraordinary, miraculous and unfathomable lightening of our load. When you have lived with a wound for a long time, you can come to believe it is a part of you and nothing can be done about it. You might not even be able to imagine life without it, especially where the wound is a deep and pervasive presence within you and therefore in your life. Yet, Tara is so much vaster than any of our struggles. Her grace changes what is possible for us.

The humiliation wound tends to run deep, mostly in the unconscious and is extremely resistant to healing. I believe this was the wound at play in the example of attacking behaviour outlined above. I have encountered it so many times and in so many different types of people, that I have come to believe it is something of an emotional and psychological epidemic in modern culture. The humiliation wound lies beneath toxic and unresolved experiences of rejection.

Rejection may be actual or perceived, perhaps through various unpleasant experiences interpreted as being rebuffed or discarded. An example of the feeling of rejection that may give rise to a humiliation wound is where someone sensed they didn't fit in with others as a child at school or were treated with ridicule or bullying. The rejection may have been felt as a result of a parent leaving due to divorce or a parent not being present due to illness, addiction or death. To a child, these experiences can feel like abandonment, which is tantamount to rejection, and may leave them with a profound sense of 'what is wrong with me?' This feeling operates deep in the psyche of that child. Of course, there might have been an actual rejection too. Being classified as a 'mistake' or unwanted pregnancy, or the more subtle, but just as scarring rejection of someone's uniqueness or other qualities that were beyond the capacity of their caretakers to love, honour and accept, are examples of actual rejection. We may have been rejected culturally because we didn't fit in or come from the same background as those around us. Rejection can also be gender based, if someone was born a girl when a boy was wanted, or vice versa.

The rejection wound tends to occur when we are vulnerable and do not feel strong enough within ourselves to allow another's actions or comments to simply 'bounce off' our healthy self-esteem, so it can cut very deep. This can happen in childhood when we are relatively defenceless, or in someone who has experienced quite a happy and nurturing childhood, but encounters a low point where their self-esteem takes a bit of a beating due to circumstances beyond their control. Perhaps someone's self-worth was worn down by a relationship that started out reasonably healthy, but ended up toxic and destructive, with unexpressed feelings and constant little rejections that bred resentment and confusion.

Rejection can also be transmitted down the family line, from ancestor to ancestor, through a family system that is not yet able to confront the wound and resolve it. It might have originated in a generation that lived as migrants and always felt somewhat ostracised from the community around them, or from a line of witches, healers or psychics in one's family history (known or unknown) or even mental illness (again, known or unknown) which resulted in an ancestor being considered a social outcast. Until someone in the family (which is probably going to be you!) is wise and aware enough to do healing on the matter for themselves, by digging deep and realising that the energy of a wounding doesn't just 'go away' because someone dies. It has to be worked through and resolved or the painful legacy will continue.

No matter how we arrived at our increased state of vulnerability, the humiliation consequent to the experience of rejection becomes an insidious poison inside of us. The belief in our fundamental unworthiness and wrongness of self, shows up in various behaviours. Again, we might be able to catch the behaviours before we can really get to the wound underneath, confront it with love and begin to let it go. We might rationally know that a parent leaving due to divorce was not particularly about us, and yet, as a child we might have felt deeply disturbed, abandoned, rejected or betrayed. A child who is unable to express those complex feelings or was not given permission to express something as taboo as anger or grief, is likely to have internalised and pushed down their emotions as an unconscious belief that they drove a parent away (after all, the belief that the world revolves around them is part of a child's way of relating to the world – for better or worse).

Behaviours that signify the presence of humiliation might include negative self-talk, choosing partners that don't treat them well, or treating their body with disrespect, criticism and unhealthy tendencies, even when they consciously aim to look after themselves, eat well and be self-loving. In people with a more severe humiliation wound, there can be a deeply painful splitting off of the self. In such cases, a sense of absolute hatred for the self that was so cruelly cast aside and not loved as it needed to be, is hidden so deep within that the person themselves will hardly recognise it consciously. That self-hate can come out in destructive behaviours that burst forth at different times. Examples are drunk driving, getting into fight, hurting the people they love or trying to push them away.

The humiliation wound is one of the most hidden, usually with defensive behaviour that suggests anything but humiliation or rejection. The arrogance of judgment, superiority, over-confidence and the belief that you can always be in control often mask the wound. Hidden underneath is a fear of being invisible, worthless or nothing much, and feeling powerless to do anything about it. As if overcompensating, the humiliated self can present a face of beauty, charm, seductiveness and allure, so that no one can believe there is a problem at all – apart from an excess of self-confidence! However, it only takes a glance from the eye of the heart to realise that underneath the seductive qualities and charisma – that make for compelling and magnetic personalities – is an unreachable quality. No matter how warm and open they appear, if you happen to threaten their defences in any way (even unintentionally), you will quite likely be on the receiving end of an extremely powerful pent-up rage designed to protect the person from feeling the excruciating pain of the original rejection and humiliation.

The more brightly and beautifully these people seem to burn, the stronger and more potent the humiliation wound operating within will be. They will attract and charm many around them, seducing others with a similar unconscious wound, and with a strict (though likely unconscious) set of rules to remain in control at all times, so that they will avoid the genuine intimacy and vulnerability that could set them up for re-wounding.

I have met a few healers with this wound. They can appear to be so open, giving, generous and supportive, but when you scratch even a tiny bit beneath the surface, you find it is all glitter and no gold. If you were to try to get within an inch of them in genuine friendship, they would turn on you viciously, making sure you never want to get near them again. Or they may try to humiliate you in some way to reinforce their feelings of control and power, so that they cannot be hurt by you. They will not be vulnerable to you, even if you had no intention of anything other than genuine friendship.

No matter how close you may want to get to these people, even if you are in bed with them as a lover, you will never really be able to touch them, because their inner self has become so small and tucked away, hiding within themselves with so many defences, layers and scars, that they are not available to be touched. The result is that you can pour as much love as you can muster into the friendship or relationship, but it will be like pouring water onto scorched, barren earth – it will be unable to penetrate the hard, dry surface.

On the surface, these people can appear to be very successful and often have legions of devotees. Their seductive ways can be very appealing and will make people feel special, chosen and lucky to be in their company, until the power games and manipulations start – a masterful skill developed as a way to survive and avoid further rejection – and then you will start to feel hardness and pain in your interactions with these people.

If you are sensitive and have done some work on this in yourself, you will learn to spot these people and not fall prey to the illusions they so masterfully weave. You will instead hold yourself with compassionate awareness. Many years of inner work are often required before you learn to see what is really going on. You have to recognise and heal the wound in yourself before you can hope to avoid getting entangled in it with another. The fact that others don't see what is really going on might puzzle you at first, but eventually you will realise that they don't see it because they have the same unresolved wound in themselves.

Typical of the humiliation wound is a tendency to either idealise or degrade the self or others. We are either the best in the world, or the worst. That other person is an angel, or the anti-Christ! Or if we are not the most beautiful, it means we are ugly and not worth anything other than self-loathing and hatred. It is an extremely painful state to be in.

It is particularly painful in relationships because if the wound is active, we tend to attract partners that idealise and degrade us too. It can be very confusing! One minute we are the bee's knees and the most beautiful creature ever, and the next we either need to get rid of that bit of fat there, are not worth noticing at all or we didn't do the washing up properly and overall are such a disappointment. This triggers the shame and uncertainty that wears down our self-esteem and ensures we will be in too much pain to summon up the energy to leave and too much angst to summon up the energy to get closer to or try to heal the pain of the other person in the relationship. This pattern of behaviour is fairly typical for a person acting out the humiliation wound because they want you around, but not too close! It is a perfect recipe to avoid further rejection.

Rejection – real or perceived – can dig deep into our sense of self and create a stubborn but relatively unconscious belief that we are not okay, but are unworthy, particularly of what we want the most. It is that combination of stubborn fixity and unconsciousness that makes it so challenging to heal. We can't heal what we do not acknowledge. We can usually only acknowledge this wound by beginning to notice its effects in our lives. We see the symptoms before we can hope to directly see and heal the wound.

When that wounding is present, any time we see someone else receiving love, affection, acknowledgment or admiration, or anything that we ourselves would like to have, it is like rubbing salt into an open wound. It is genuinely painful for us. We might attempt to mask the pain with judgment and hide our jealousy with criticism of the other.

I had an experience of this when I went for a psychic reading recently. I am usually extremely careful about who I go to for any kind of healing support or psychic assistance. Whilst I will see healers whenever I feel it is beneficial, I only see a psychic once every two or three years when I am in a deeply transformational process and feel I could use the benefit of another's insight. A woman was recommended by someone I knew as being "the only other psychic I have been to who is anywhere near your level" and I had heard of her in other contexts as being very good. As I was at a time in my life when I had a lot of question marks, I decided to risk it and off I trotted to receive further clarity about the two big steps I was working towards at the time – the ending of the relationship I was in and the subsequent relocation to a new residence.

As a psychic she was actually pretty good. Her manner was very different to mine. Personality wise we were like chalk and cheese, so that was to be expected. What I instantly liked about her was that she was very honest and upfront. You couldn't help but feel that she would tell you what she sensed without any hesitation. This is what I most enjoyed about her – except that she was also very critical and made some unsavoury remarks about a particular person who was instrumental in my career. I had not brought this person up as I had no particular issue with him. I actually liked and was grateful for his presence in my life. She brought him up herself and was forthcoming with her poor opinion. That she would speak of someone else in this way was a bit disturbing to me, but I figured that was her way and didn't take it on, nor let it affect my opinion of him. It was just her stuff.

Towards the end of the reading she suddenly said, "I am sorry for making those remarks. I feel like such a bitch but when you walked in and I realised these things about you, I felt like you were living my life, the life I wanted."

As it turned out, she had approached this man previously, as well as some other key figures in my professional life, for assistance and they had decided not to go ahead with her. She felt rejected and was expressing that with her criticism of others.

I told her that her work was well-known and she obviously wanted to help people, but our energies were very different and the people that I worked with might not be the best fit for her to work with, and vice versa. What she did with that information I do not know. After the session she said that she wanted to help me and continued to make contact with me, which left me feeling increasingly uncomfortable, despite the fact that I knew she meant well. Eventually I chose to discreetly break off any further contact with her. As for the person who recommended her as a healer like me, well this woman was so like *her* it was astounding. Go figure!

At least this psychic had the guts to admit that she was jealous. I wasn't particularly comfortable in the session with her for a number of reasons, but I did respect her honesty. She understood that her jealousy was her inner self saying, "I want that too! Why can't I be loved also?"

We can stay with the feelings that come from the rejection wound and acknowledge that we are actually worthy of love, but first we have to stop rejecting ourselves by acting out the old wound. We need to pay attention to our feelings, to own and take responsibility for them rather than blaming others. Judgment or blame isn't just a rejection of another. It is the rejection of ourselves and of our feelings of pain that is prompting the judgment.

Of course, it is hard to realise this if the pain is buried so deep that it is hard to consciously access. That is why we need ways to bring the body and its stored memories and feelings to consciousness. We do this through the methods outlined in the introduction and the healing processes at the end of each chapter throughout this book. Bringing the body to consciousness through healing work releases old emotional 'stuff' and thereby frees us to have a different life experience, rather than constantly re-experiencing old wounds because we haven't been willing or ready to confront the feelings and move on. It can take time to be ready and willing to do this. However, it is better and more conducive to getting to that place if we acknowledge what is really happening here. That means accepting that if we are judging, then there is pain within us. Judgments are about the one passing judgment, more so than the person being judged. Taking this approach will resolve the situation most quickly. It doesn't mean that the other person doesn't have their work to do too. Don't we all? But in taking responsibility, you can heal. You can't do another person's work for them. You can judge all you want, but you will just be spinning your wheels and going nowhere. You won't be helping them get anywhere either, regardless of how 'well-meaning' your comments might be.

Once you start to sense the quality of this wound, you will see it a lot in our culture: in the media and television (especially in reality TV with its fascination for degrading, shaming, exposing or ridiculing others), in fashion and film industries, in the typical office, in the psychological and emotional violence of many corporate operations and management (treating bodies like chattel to be pushed into an office chair for eight hours a day), in gyms and many yoga schools (where worship of the perfect physique or posture can become more important than respect and compassion for the body and a genuine desire for balanced wellbeing), even in spiritual communities (where power can be seen as flowing from the teacher and not from the greater heart of the Divine that beats in every living heart). Anywhere that you feel you are not good enough (even if the outward message appears to be saying otherwise) and anywhere that you feel you are being controlled through emotional manipulation or subjected to excessively controlling rules that limit your basic, personal freedoms to express an opinion or to move your body freely, you will be witnessing this wound at work.

It has come to be my belief that most members of modern society are nursing this wound to some extent. As we have been socially conditioned to believe that we must earn love and acceptance, there is a profound social wounding around rejection and consequent humiliation.

If you are passionate about freedom, and want to be 'allowed' to just be yourself and live your life as you see fit without a need for approval from others, then you are one of the brave whom are destined to break free of this wound. You are a liberator. You are here to heal the wound within you and to show others the way.

As the wound heals within ourselves – through grace, doing our inner work, trusting we can be helped and a willingness to run the risk of being vulnerable again – rejection no longer instantly translates into humiliation.

Once we have repaired our self-esteem, rejection is just rejection. It is just a part of life. You will realise and accept that not everybody will love you and that's okay. It is not about you, it is just their choice and it is fine. It is quite likely that you won't love everybody either! You might hold goodwill for all beings and still want to avoid some people as if they were the plague, because being around their energy is unpleasant for you. Such is life. It is neither good, nor bad – it just is. Surrender judgment and in its place, you will discover a purity of heart.

TIBETAN QUARTZ (PURITY)

Tibetan quartz, sometimes called Tibetan black quartz, is a powerful healing crystal. It may appear as mostly clear with minimal black inclusions and may also have a lot of black material within it – usually carbon – and also appear as almost grey.

I first experienced Tibetan quartz with a client of mine. We were looking at a selection of pieces a mutual friend had in her crystal store in Mackay, North Queensland. We sat at the counter gazing at the pieces before us. My client had chosen the smallest, most unobtrusive piece. Being a humble person, she was able to find the beauty in that which others might pass over. I gently picked up her small crystal to examine it more closely. I nearly dropped it instantly! As soon as I held it, the crystal burst forth with an enormous, "OM!"

I looked wide-eyed at my client, "Did you hear that?" Half laughing, half in shock at how the smallest, apparently most unimpressive crystal had the loudest and most powerful vibration, I asked, "That loud OM? Did you hear that?" She burst into a fit of giggles, as did I. Then we realised we had unintentionally gone through the store owner's personal collection rather than what was for sale. Naughty lightworkers! The owner came into the room, saw what we had done, scolded us good naturedly and promptly asked us to put the pieces back into her collection. I was a bit sad not to be taking some of those pieces home with me, but I knew I would not forget the sound of that OM!

All Tibetan quartz holds the manifestation and healing vibration of OM, though obviously – at least in my experience – some pieces emanate it more powerfully than others. Louder isn't necessarily better, more powerful isn't necessarily better. Finding the right piece for you is what matters most. Sometimes we do better with gentler energy and sometimes with stronger energy. We must trust in what we feel at any given time. Intuitively we know what we need and will draw it to us.

When we are able to surrender into the OM, it can clear our energy field and our home, and bring great peace. Combining the OM with quartz (which also happens to hold the exceptionally spiritual and pure vibrations of the land of Tibet) creates an incredibly pure, exquisite healing energy.

Not so long ago, my best friend and I were having a little getaway at the beautiful Crystal Castle in Mullumbimby, Australia. After so much hard work, we were ready to play. Laughing our heads off – as we are prone to do – and generally disturbing the quietness of the place, we wandered about and soaked up the atmosphere.

In the midst of our raucous cackles, we suddenly heard a resounding OM as *The Great Bell Chant* (End of All Suffering), began. This is a stunningly beautiful prayer and piece of music, spoken by Vietnamese Buddhist monk and spiritual teacher Thich Nhat Hanh, and chanted by another monk, Brother Phap Niem, the latter of whom has a voice so drenched in compassion, light and serenity that it sends chills through my entire body. This recording is played daily at the Crystal Castle, pumped out through large speakers so that it fills the grounds with sacred sound.

Our playful antics calmed down and everything around us felt as though it became still.

As I heard the voice of the monk chanting, my body shivered with bliss and my friend's hand spontaneously went to rest on her heart. "Oh," we both said and fell into silence as the purity of the chant bathed us in compassion and purity.

After the chant finished, some seven or so minutes later, we felt changed and cleansed. The sacred vibration had cleared something within us, allowing us to let go of all the hard work we had been doing and come into the present moment. This was part of a powerful, healing weekend getaway that I will talk about further in the chapter on Saraswati and ammonite. This is how Tibetan quartz works. The powerful vibration clears, purifies and powerfully recalibrates our individual energy fields and the energy fields around us. Just as Tara lifted me into bliss, Tibetan quartz and its OM vibration, lifts us into the truth of compassion, light and love. It won't always be as dramatic as these examples, but it is an extremely powerful stone and it will work cumulatively over time.

Tibetan quartz is particularly useful for healers and people who tend to pick up negativity easily because they are sensitive or energetically open. A Vedic astrologer explained it to me, "You are a clean soul, like a beautiful piece of pure white paper, and dark energies will want to write on it!" It was a very vivid way to describe the situation. You will know if this is you because you will be quite noticeably affected by the moods of people around you and the environment that you are in. This is a double-edged sword. If you are in a shopping centre or location where there has been a trauma or tragedy of some kind, you will feel it and need to clear yourself afterwards to feel like yourself again.

Fortunately the plus side of this openness and sensitivity is that any time spent in nature or places of genuine spiritual communion will restore you quite powerfully and often quite quickly. As my friend and I were driving towards Mullumbimby and the Crystal Castle we had a moment when we wondered if we were getting anywhere near the place. We had never been there before and as both of our phones had long run out of charge, we had to rely on our internal GPS, which is often quite skewed when we are together. We seem to generate a slightly chaotic field of energy when we are together – loving, creative and healing, but also a bit wild!

As we drove in the direction we figured we were meant to be heading, I actually felt the energy of the Crystal Castle in my crown chakra. I could feel the peace of the place. I was struck by two thoughts. Firstly, it was more powerful than I thought it would be, given that I could feel it before we could physically see the place. Secondly, we probably weren't far away. A moment or two later, we saw a street sign for it and drove up the winding driveway.

It was a similar sensation to what happens for me when driving down the south coast of New South Wales towards Wollongong. On the way I pass by a large Buddhist temple, the Nan Tien Temple. You can actually feel the energetic field of peace around the temple. I always know when I am near it because I feel my heart opening as calming light enters my body and I relax. Some moments later it will come into view. The first time I experienced this, I didn't know why it was happening and it was only when I saw the temple that I understood. I was awed at how powerful that vibration was and how physically it could be felt. If you know anything about the traffic and heavy industry that one encounters driving down to Wollongong, then you will realise the energetic field of peace around the temple, able to cut through such dense pollution (on many levels), is powerful indeed.

Tibetan quartz provides a similar field of purification and peacefulness around us and our home. It is something like a monk or a monastery in a crystal. If you have a space where there is sickness – of mind or body – or where nightmares or arguments take place, there may well be a problem in the energetic field of the Earth in that spot, as well as within its inhabitants. Tibetan quartz placed in the corners of that room will be very helpful.

If you or a loved one are recovering from any course of drugs, radiation, chemotherapy, or toxicity on a physical, emotional or mental level (such as from being in an abusive relationship of any sort), Tibetan quartz will help to purify all levels of your being and restore you to the realisation of your fundamental purity.

If you feel you have become dark, depressed, worn down, hostile or bitter and hateful because of various life experiences, remember this is not who you are. You are a pure being of light and love. You just need to shift identification from the reactions to the essence. Tibetan quartz helps shift the reactions so you can more easily experience your essential purity, without denying the human experiences that are helping you to grow.

Please, remember that the OM vibration will still be there in the stone, affecting the environment around you, even if you cannot physically hear.

If you have Tibetan quartz in an area where you sleep or unwind and you find that you cannot rest while it is there, it means your sensitivity is developing. You may simply need to move the stone to another part of your home so there is less stimulation in your sleeping area. Others will find the stone very calming. It really is a case of sensing and trusting what feels right for you.

MANIFESTING THROUGH COMPASSION

Manifesting through compassion is an advanced practice accessible to those who are able to trust in divine love. This can be quite challenging when what is happening seems to be other than what we have wished for! As the expression goes, "It is easier to trust in feast, than in famine." In the chapter on Gaia and her wild grace we will explore the gift of both feast and famine further, but for now, all we need is the understanding that compassion exists within all that takes place, and we are being loved into fruition through that compassion.

To manifest through compassion we are asked to let go of much of what we have been taught is essential in order to create. Action still plays a vital role in our manifestation process and in the chapter on Durga we will learn more about the difference between consciously inspired action and thrashing out this way and that, using our will to try and force things to happen.

Rather than doing and outer activity, manifestation through compassion draws upon being, our inner attitude and our ability to surrender into the divine plan to generate a magnetic attraction for all that we need to thrive. This doesn't mean that action and doing are denied. It just means that our focus shifts and our internal process becomes the primary means through which we manifest. Any action flows naturally from that inner state of being and, subsequently, less is often required than we might expect.

At the basis of manifestation through compassion is the understanding and total acceptance that the Universe is fundamentally benevolent and supports our desire for spiritual liberation. Even when we are presented with challenge, it comes with protection, support and compassion. The challenge is meant to help us grow. It is a blessing. It may be disguised or hard to see at first, but it is a blessing nonetheless.

Your ability to surrender into compassion is determined by your acceptance of the Universe as a supportive, creative, loving and intelligent being. We will struggle to accept compassion as a powerful creative force if we cannot accept there is a greater, fundamentally loving intelligence that calls to us from within our hearts and always guides us back to love. Can you sense how essential it is to heal the humiliation wound in order for us to be able to manifest from compassion? That wound would have us trusting and believing in rejection, unworthiness and shame rather than in love!

If we can grow and learn to trust in the fundamentally loving nature of the Universe, then the creative power of compassion begins to thrive within our hearts and can be expressed in our lives. We can manifest for ourselves in apparently miraculous ways, but the most beautiful part of this process is that we are manifesting not only 'things' but also a way of being that is grounded in trust and loving surrender. This benefits not only us, but all sentient beings. We are bringing 'good' energy, as healing consciousness, through our being and out into the world.

As we grow spiritually, we become increasingly aware of how the Universe mirrors us. We move through various situations in our lives. Some appear to be positive and constructive, and others seem challenging or destructive. How we respond to 'opportunity' and 'challenge' determines what is manifested through these experiences. Does heartbreak allow us to love more or does it close us down in fear? Perhaps we fear at first, but after a while become determined not to let pain block our ability to love and choose to be even more open to love through the stretching of our heart. One who can bear great loss can open to greater love.

Through this growth we sense that how we respond is how the Universe responds to us. That is the mirror effect. When we are giving and we are open, life responds in kind. When we are discerning and able to cast something aside that is no longer for us – be it a situation, relationship or object – the Universe responds by bringing more of what is right for us. When we respond in fear, the Universe cannot so easily reach us with its loving light. When we are open in love and trust, it can reach us more easily. It is not an issue of being loved less or more by the Divine. It is an issue of it being somewhat harder to hug someone when their arms are closed over their chest!

When it comes to manifesting through compassion we are open, detached and loving, and so we can experience the reflection of the Universe as having greater compassion towards ourselves. We become softer, more forgiving, kinder to ourselves and others and we let go of judgment, which is one of the most liberating and healing shifts we can have. We don't lose our discernment, we simply become capable of letting ourselves and others find their own way. We might become quite passionate about offering prayer and kind thoughts to those who are really suffering and acting out in cruelty, hate and violence.

Although it can be hard not to recoil from such people or situations when we encounter them, staying in the heart and praying for healing is more constructive. If we judge, we can compassionately forgive ourselves for not recognising our own pain and move into prayer, rather than judging ourselves for judging and continuing the cycle! If I encounter something truly cruel, I often have no words for it. I just feel. So, I pray from that place of feeling. I just call out in my heart to the Divine Mother with my feelings. It is my prayer for healing myself for not being able to accept a person's actions, and for the being who is in so much pain that they are, perhaps, unconsciously acting it out.

What we manifest through compassion is greater peace and an acceptance of the trials and tribulations that are a natural part of the life journey. It can be surprising just how much of our suffering comes from how we judge a situation or a person, rather than the actual experience in question. As judgment and our resistance to what is placed before us lessens, it changes how we see things. We stop interpreting obstacles in life to mean that we aren't worthy, or that we are bad people. We just see life presenting something to us that isn't what we thought we wanted and question how to respond to it. As we take this journey something significant happens within us. We open up and become more agreeable to our journey as it plays itself out as it will. We are softer and more malleable to our divine essence when it expresses itself, even though our minds may sometimes wonder what on earth is going on. When things do not go as expected, we don't label them failures, we just see it as life offering us growth. If we so choose, we can take that and run with it with a peaceful heart. We can accept our pain, work through it and let it go in time, when we are ready. We are in compassion and we are able to receive more because of this softening of our hearts.

Manifestation then becomes an act of grace rather than will. We allow life to happen through us and our own life begins to resemble the divine destiny that we are all moving closer to each day – even on those days when things seem a little haywire.

When we manifest through compassion we allow divine love to flow through us and be the fuel that lights our fire or the hand that moulds clay into form. It is then a matter of creation happening through us. Even though at one level we might feel as though we aren't doing anything, on another level we are working very hard on ourselves and our own inner world, to clear out and come to a place of innate purity so that divine love can flow through us into the world. We come closer to the Divine when we are not holding ourselves back from its flow. When we become a source of compassion, the Universe is able to return that compassion to us and we are lifted into love in the process.

What we create through this process is more peace, more love, less fear, greater flow and a closer and more intimate relationship with the divine essence which is the truth hiding in every desire we have – whether we think we want to manifest a kaftan, a greater enlightenment, something in between, or all of the above!

Being able to go into the compassionate well of our own hearts means we can more easily let go of hate, fear and the additional suffering they tend to draw into our lives if they are not felt and released naturally and easily. We can then become closer to the gentle face of the Divine.

All from this one, simple (though not always easy) practice of cultivating compassion.

HEALING PROCESS

If you feel yourself getting entangled in hate, fear, judgment, gossip, political machinations in the work place or power games in your relationships, and you feel degraded or drained by it, then this healing practice will be helpful for you. It will help you work on shifting the humiliation wound as well as healing your heart and opening you up to the great power of compassion that can develop within the purity of your heart.

If you are working on a deeper level on your spiritual path, there will be times when you will be shown great darkness and suffering in the world, in your own experience and in your various encounters with humans and other beings. At times, you may be shown great darkness in yourself. You will need to learn how to bear the knowledge and experience of the darker face of creation within you or around you with compassion. Compassion will prevent you from closing down in shock or becoming overwhelmed, disheartened or burdened by what you have come to see or know. Remember that within the encounter of darkness, lies the opportunity for love to be served and for healing to occur. We choose how to respond. The Divine Mother can make any darkness serve love through healing. Compassion allows that to happen.

It is sometimes hard not to become angry or frightened when unconscious wounding is acted out by various people and organisations on this planet – even by ourselves at times. We might need the sacred rage of Sekhmet to fight against it, and we will meet her later on in this book, but we may also need the cooling grace of Tara's compassion to soothe our inflamed hearts so that we don't burn ourselves out. You won't be able to do your work as an activist if you are exhausted!

We are all growing and evolving into love as one human race. This practice will be helpful at those times when impatience or frustration gets the better of you and you unintentionally find yourself moving out of compassionate peace and into judgment. We can act and be powerful from a place of compassion, but in judgment, can quickly lose our effectiveness and lower our vibration. We can end up getting drawn into energy-draining attacks and weaken rather than support each other on our healing journey of love.

Give yourself the gift of restorative compassion through this healing process at any time you feel yourself caught up in judgment rather than discernment and need to return to the purity of your own heart.

The Process

If possible choose a space where you can be relatively undisturbed. If you have a Tara chant, or other soft healing music that takes you into your heart, you may like to play that softly in the background.

Using either a piece of Tibetan quartz, and/or the healing Tara mandala in this book, create an altar for yourself to gaze at during your practice. You may like to light a candle or burn some incense. Make your altar as ornate or as simple as you wish.

Hold your hands open, palms facing upwards to the heavens and say out loud, "I call upon the Mother Tara, she of unconditional grace and unconditional love, who cries the tears of the world. Save us! Mother, take us into compassion!"

Close your eyes and breathe at least eight breaths in and out, as you imagine or perceive the light of Tara descending from above and pooling as light in your upturned hands. Notice whether that light has a feeling or colour associated with it.

When you are ready, turn your hands over and send the light you have received into your altar. Do this by holding your palms above your altar and imagining compassion drip from your hands like holy water, so naturally, so easily and with little effort.

Then turn your palms downwards towards the Earth, and say the following out loud, "I call upon the Crystal Angel of Tibetan Black Quartz. I call upon purity, upon the power of OM, upon your purification of the suffering of the world. May the suffering of the world end, upon the compassionate breath of the Divine Mother, as she utters the sound of love. May all beings be happy and free. So be it."

Imagine or perceive white light with black spirals of cleansing energy rise up out of the earth and gather at the palms of your hands. Let this power naturally be pulled to you for at least eight slow breaths, in and out.

When you are ready, gently face your palms to your altar and imagine or perceive the energy you have gathered pouring into your altar.

Then sit or lie comfortably so that you can gaze at your altar. If you can, imagine your altar in your mind's eye. You may wish to close your eyes, or to sit with your eyes softly focused (not staring hard) at your altar.

Say the following, "The Mother of the World and her healing crystals, generate peace and love so that all of creation, even in the darkest moments and places, can feel the light and love of her compassionate grace, as suffering is released and hearts open into her loving balm of compassion. All beings shall be happy and free. By the Mother's grace, so it shall be."

Gently sit, gazing at the altar and feel the truth of your words resonate through the altar. You may sense, feel or perceive energy moving. You may feel emotional and the practice may be strong or very subtle for you. Whatever happens, have compassion and simply be. You might feel negative energy leaving your body or rushing through you. Trust that Tara will guide you and protect you through this process.

Sit with this for at least eight slow breaths in and out and when you are ready, place your hands in prayer position and repeat the following mantra that calls in the grace of Tara. Say it out loud at least eight times. A sound guide to pronounce the mantra is below.

OM TARE TUTARE TURE SOHAM

OM (rhymes with Tom) TARE (Tar-Ray) Tu (Two) TARE (Tar-Ray) TURE (Two-Ray) SOHAM (SO-HUM).

When you have finished, close your eyes and place your hands in prayer and let the healing energy settle for a moment.

Say, "May this healing energy go where it is most needed."

If you have a particular issue that needs healing then add, "And I ask for healing on this issue of ... so that I may serve the light to the best of my ability, thank you."

When you are done, simply place your hands in prayer position at your brow and bow your head lightly to your fingertips. Then open your eyes and gently clear your altar.

This healing brings the energy of compassion into you, naturally bringing healing to the world and triggering healing of your own issues as your being purifies.

Be gentle with yourself after this process as it can be quite emotional at times. Feel free to complete this process at any time you are disturbed by something you see or hear within you or in the world around you. So much healing is needed now and this is a simple and effective way to help tip the scales towards compassion more quickly.

May you be blessed in your efforts and richly and justly rewarded.

2.

LAKSHMI (SELF-WORTH)
DENDRITIC AGATE (PLENTY)

MANIFESTING THROUGH LIMITLESSNESS

From deep within she shines as a golden light, warming your heart with divine love. She urges you to remember what you are. For in remembering that you are divine, you become receptive to her plentiful gifts. True abundance in all ways – prosperity, wellness, fullness of life, enlightenment of the soul. She is the bearer of plenty, and to those centred in the heart, her generosity is without end.

LAKSHMI (SELF-WORTH)

Lakshmi is the divine goddess of prosperity and spiritual enlightenment from the ancient spiritual traditions of India. She is sensual, feminine and beautiful. She is said to bless those that love her with attractiveness, wealth, charisma, spiritual talents and enlightenment. A rather appealing combination of blessings!

The story of Lakshmi's creation helps us understand the path we go through on a human level to access her presence in our lives. There are two things I love about stories from ancient India. Firstly, they can be likened to divine soap opera, as they are so complex, with many twists and turns and varying characters that are constantly reincarnating as someone else. You can never, ever get bored or predict what will happen next! Secondly, they are absolutely epic in scale. When I started exploring the spiritual stories of India, I was amazed at the sheer scope of their perspective. It seemed like there was no limit to what the stories could teach us about. They were not overly focused on human drama, although how to deal with being human is certain a feature. The stories also speak about divine energy, its multifaceted nature and offer instruction about the evolution of the Earth and the formation of the Universe. The stories can be rather complex, so I am giving you my version of Lakshmi's tale in the hope it will distil the helpful elements for my purpose here and not offend anyone with its relative simplicity.

The birth of Lakshmi starts with many great and powerful beings, including those that serve the light and those that served the dark, gossiping about a divine nectar. Word got around that this divine nectar could provide instant karmic healing which would bring the end of struggle and provide great divine power. As if that wasn't enough, it would also deliver immortality. This was rather too much to resist and so every being – angelic and demonic – wanted to get a hold of it!

However, the divine nectar was lodged deep in the recesses of creation and could only be liberated by churning the ocean of consciousness. That was no small feat, but if accomplished, the force of that churning would dislodge and propel the nectar up and out of its hiding place, where it could be accessed. Quite likely by those with the fastest reflexes to grab for it! The demons hoped they would get to it first and the angels hoped that the powers that served the light would get to it first.

Eventually the squabbles about who would get their hands on the nectar and what they would do with it subsided and the forces of light and dark decided they would have to stop all their posturing and work together to complete the huge task of churning the ocean of consciousness so greatly that the nectar could be forced out of its hiding place. Otherwise, it would just stay hidden forever.

Eventually a snake offered himself as the 'churning stick' and the various beings of light and dark grabbed his tail and began to churn together. They lunged and heaved, churning consciousness this way and that. Slowly but surely, their toiling to and fro built up enough energy that the ocean of consciousness began to move and swirl in a spiral, with ever-greater momentum.

As this momentum moved towards its peak, a golden form of light rose up from the depths and emerged out of the swirling vortex of consciousness. The most beautiful feminine form ever beheld stepped out of that golden light. It was the divine nectar, in the form of a drop-dead gorgeous woman! The churning stopped as all the beings who had squabbled over the nectar stared at this stunning creature. Jaws dropped for a moment of awestruck silence, and then they each declared they were going to have her as their own!

Before a war ensued, she calmly announced that she was Lakshmi and would choose for herself where she wished to be, thank you very much, putting each one of those great beings firmly in their place. She casually sauntered over to Vishnu, who holds the Christ consciousness of 'God is Love' in his heart and said, "I choose to be with you" and that was that. The others were humbled by her choice to be devoted to love and chose to serve her with devotion instead of being selfish.

Now that is quite a story. It is also very relevant to what we go through as human beings learning to open up to Lakshmi and her golden grace. We cannot get to her through the half measure of only recognising the light within us or in creation. We have to come to recognise that darkness exists, and that when consciously accepted, we can work with it to serve our own spiritual growth.

In India, where this story originates, the presence of light and dark alongside each other is obvious and generally accepted. India is learning and growing as a nation, just as any other, but spiritually they are rather well ahead of the bell curve when compared to modern Western nations. Speak to someone from India, even with only a little religious education, and they will be quite open about demons, angels and the unfolding plan of the Universe. In the West, we have to journey quite deeply into spirituality, way beyond the basics offered to us, before we get to the grit of such matters.

I experienced India for the first time in this body when I travelled there as a teenager. I had just completed high school and was excited to be taking my first trip overseas. I stepped off the plane and waited to meet my friend and her relatives who were on the other side of the glass wall at security in the airport. India was an immediate shock to my senses on many levels. I had never travelled to a place like that before. I couldn't get used to the smell. My sense of smell has always been acute and the scents were so strong it was like being cloaked under a blanket that never completely lifted off me the entire time I was there. The number of people and the completely different notion of personal space was also a bit of a shock. I can still feel someone's presence and think they are standing right behind me, only to turn around and find they are farther away than I thought. But in India! Well, there seemed to be a completely different notion of personal space – not really one at all. A local woman, a complete stranger, chose to rest her head on my shoulder while she snoozed on a packed train. She didn't bother asking, she just did it. I was completely uncomfortable with the constant begging and the noise. There were military men with machine guns parading about and riots had taken over Mumbai.

Aside from the culture shock, there was colour and a timelessness about the place that I was instantly drawn to, as well as a deep spiritual heritage and the food – my goodness it was so good. I also found an incredible hospitality and friendliness in many people. There was an aliveness and energy in India that was completely raw, without pretence of any kind and I was fascinated, repelled, transported and mesmerised by it. All in all, India was a place that changed my young view of the world and opened me up to paradox. At the time, I didn't consciously realise I was having a divine experience. Bleakness and beauty, light and dark, majesty and mayhem were all jumbled up together, without shame, without hiding, without denial. It was all just there, as part of existence, naked and willing to be beheld.

That is the Divine. It is the paradox of light and dark, the enormity of all that is – for what else is there but divinity? Even in darkness. Is there anywhere that the Divine is not? Of course not! We honour our hearts and act with integrity. If we are descendants of angels, loving the light and wanting to serve love, then that is what we do. However, we don't pretend that we are divine to the exclusion of the rest of creation. We just play our part in the unfolding of the big, spiritual drama of life and don't try to understand the Divine, because – as Lakshmi and India teach us – the Divine is not to be understood, not logically anyway. The heart can get to wisdom that the mind cannot fathom. Lakshmi blesses us with so much of what life has to offer, from spiritual enlightenment to great material wealth and wellbeing. We can only receive her when we accept that darkness plays a role in the divine drama of life, just as much as the light.

Anyone who has managed to gain wisdom through a traumatic experience will know that sometimes the dark can be a powerful teacher. With her golden consciousness, Lakshmi offers us transcendence from the struggle between the light and dark within us and in the world around us, and allows us to simply walk the path of love. Her wisdom and blessings are obtained by allowing the friction of the struggles we go through in life to give birth to the divine being who chooses to live in the heart, in much the same way that the churning of angels and demons liberated her golden essence from its quiet dwelling in the undisturbed ocean of consciousness. It was the friction, the war between light and dark, and the desire for spiritual success that culminated in her arising. We can't turn away from the darkness to find her golden love, we have to work with it.

When we call upon Lakshmi, which we will do in the healing process below, we are essentially saying that we are ready to surrender our identification with our struggles. We are no longer those struggles. We recognise them as a method through which our consciousness is developed so that the golden light of the Divine can manifest through us, as us. Whilst we accept that the challenging conflicts between light and dark within us and in the world around us, serve our growth, we can also be ready to open up to the higher purpose of conflict – the birthing of divine consciousness. When we are ready to serve love above all else – even above our judgments of darkness or our desire for no more suffering – we move into acceptance and total surrender to the unfathomable divine plan of creation. Most of the time it won't make any sense, but our hearts don't need logic, they just need wisdom, love, passionate purpose and conviction. Only then will Lakshmi finally have access to us, for she chooses to live in the heart that dwells in love. When we have an open channel to her, we live life from a divine perspective. We are more open and accepting, have less need of forcing the Divine to fit into our belief systems and are more capable of bearing the mystery and unknowingness of the Divine because that is what we will find. Then her abundance of material and spiritual gifts are given to us so freely.

There is no limit to her offering, because in love, all is. Some may believe that wealth and spiritual enlightenment are mutually exclusive and that one must give up the world to find the spirit. As we learn to see beyond the material coverings that veil the divine light, and to see and feel the light, the separation of the two paths may be helpful. However, there will be a time when the path of love will ask us to bring the spiritual and material together as one living divine creation. Lakshmi teaches us, in the completeness and limitlessness of her gifts, that ultimately everything can serve the path of love. It is how we respond to things, people or situations that matters, not our opinion of them. Do we discern the truth and act accordingly, without judgment but with a firm sense of the choice that resonates with our hearts? Lakshmi is of love, but she is no fool! She chooses to serve that which will increase what is meaningful to her – love. She did not choose some flighty god with a superiority complex, who claimed he could just take her for himself. She chose the one who was open, receptive and respectful of her right and power to choose her own destiny, and powerful and loving in his own right. She chose the Lord of Love as her consort, her beloved, as the one she would support with her power, wisdom and light. She did not hesitate to choose who would feel best to her, who would serve her and therefore be a worthy being to serve in return. She models a marvellous demonstration of unerring good taste, discernment, self-worth and self-respect!

It is so much easier to be open to life once we have shifted any old wounds about indignity or shame and have thereby opened up to a fundamental realisation of our innate worth. When we give ourselves permission to cultivate self-respect and self-worth, we naturally behave differently. We stop believing that we have to defend ourselves against our life experiences and instead believe that life wants to nurture us into being. Lakshmi helps uproot and clear old issues of shaming, especially around our bodies and sexuality.

Probably my favourite Lakshmi story is about a young woman who was devoted to her and did ceremonies to invoke Lakshmi until she felt she was one with her mysteries and teachings. Word got around about this woman's spiritual potency and how advanced she was. Eventually people spoke so highly of her that some gods became curious about her and wanted to see if all the praise was true. So the three Hindu faces of the Divine Masculine, Shiva, Vishnu and Brahma, decided to get together and test her spiritual prowess (proving that even when they are divine, men can still behave – at least sometimes – like boys!).

The male gods dressed themselves as beggars and went knocking on the young woman's door. Honouring the Indian cultural tenet that any guest is to be treated as though he or she were God, she graciously allowed them to enter her home and offered them food and shelter for the night. When she went to prepare them dinner, they decided they would test her by insulting her and told her they wanted her to feed them whilst she was topless. In any culture that would be considered a questionable request, but in India at that time, it was probably the most offensive comment that could be made.

Rather than shrink back in fear, or feel ashamed or ridiculed, she carefully asked them if this is what they really wanted. "Yes," they affirmed, "this is what we want!"

She nodded and went over to her water dish where she enacted her daily ceremonies in devotion to Lakshmi. She cupped some sacred water in her hand and before the three misbehaving gods had a chance to work out what she was up to, she sprinkled the water on them transforming them into babies. She then fed each one in turn from her breast.

There are so many interpretations of this story and its healing messages, but the one I took from it was that through devotion this woman transformed the situation without aggression and managed to remain in a position of respect, empowerment and, one must say, humorous resourcefulness. She did not allow the situation to be internalised as degrading to her. When we are sensitive we can feel degraded by another's disrespect of us. Lakshmi helps us learn to stay centred in our self-esteem and to realise that other's attitudes are about them – not us, and are in no way a reflection of our innate value.

I had an experience of this once, rather unexpectedly. I was walking in a nearby shopping mall, having collected some groceries, when a man turned and leered at me with so much lust. As I gazed at him doing so I noticed something interesting. I didn't feel anything. In the past, I suspect I would have felt shamed, dirty or perhaps the need to hide myself away from his disrespectful gaze. What I felt, however, was exactly the same about myself as I had before I encountered him. I felt just fine about myself. I noticed his behaviour and what he was trying to do, which was (most likely unconsciously) project on to me and offload from himself his own shame and issues to do with sexual desire and women, but I wasn't having any of it! I didn't even feel anger at the time. I didn't need to, I actually just felt compassion for him. It wasn't contrived, it just happened and I was grateful for it.

All of this happened in a few seconds, but it was enough to empower me for many future interactions. In the past I had often felt degraded by men who treated me as a sexual object, disrespectfully, lustfully and without an interest in who I am or caring if I was at all interested in them. I believe it was a similar phenomenon to that of women who have been sexually abused in more obvious ways and struggle with a compelling feeling of guilt and misplaced responsibility, as though somehow she had 'asked for it', even though her will was violated. If I was being desired by a man who treated me respectfully, it was a lovely experience. If I was desired by a man who had some real issues about women and sexuality to work through, I would often register his shame as though it was my own, as though it was about my body – which of course, it was not! Through my work to heal my self-esteem over the years, I discovered an unexpected and most welcome side effect. I no longer unconsciously took on that unresolved shame of men. I could leave it with them. That was their story. It had nothing to do with me or my body.

In the check-in queue at the airport recently, after a powerful spiritual talk, I was feeling very peaceful and vibrant. I was dressed and behaving in the same way I usually do, but I was filled with Shakti, divine energy, and people typically respond to that, even if it is unconscious. When I am in such states, people will often just come over and want to talk to me, or people stare at me. It can be a bit disconcerting, but then I tend to people watch too, so I can't complain! If you are a healer, you may find that you have similar experiences with people being drawn to you, perhaps sexually, but also in other ways, after you have done a day of healing. They want to connect with you, because they sense, often unconsciously, the energy in you and they are responding to it.

In the queue at the airport, I could feel someone trying to hook into me energetically as they were drawn to the energy they sensed in me. I turned around instinctively and saw an older and rather disturbed looking man staring right at me. He tried to send something energetic into me, but I wasn't interested and simply turned away. I could feel his thoughts though. They were dark, they were about him recognising the purity in me and wanting to sully and destroy it. In my heart, I received his message and I quietly sent one in return to his soul. I said to him, "You don't want to destroy my purity. You want to remember that you are beautiful and not the darkness that is trying to destroy you. You cannot destroy purity. You just need to stop fearing it. It is in you. You are not this darkness you imagine yourself to be."

I didn't feel disturbed or shamed by this man. Again I just felt compassion, but it was the gift of Lakshmi that allowed that response in me. The gift of her grace of self-worth brought the realisation that I have the power to choose how I feel about myself and no one else has any power to alter that.

This subtle way of standing in our own presence and responding to the wounding of others is invisible, but powerful. It is real healing work. It can be exceptionally helpful for those of us on the healing path who do at least some, if not all, of our spiritual work undercover, to realise how important it is to increasing the wellbeing of humanity.

There are so many truly powerful healers that are not in the public eye at all and even those that do have a high public profile will often do a lot of work out of public view, often far more than what is visible to most people. We become more empowered to be of service when we know that what we do is effective and helpful, whether it is consciously recognised by others or not. We are always karmically rewarded with grace – in a variety of ways – when we offer healing, whether it is recognised in a public way or not.

Sometimes a soul can actually help others more effectively when they are out of the public eye. At other times a soul will work effectively with a public profile. It all depends on what the soul needs for growth and how it can best serve. Lakshmi helps us realise this and not make judgments about our own value and worth based on the recognition that we may or may not receive from others. This is very liberating! It helps us to discern for ourselves the value of what we do. If you are in the public eye and you cop criticism from those that like to pass judgment upon you, then Lakshmi helps you stay centred in your light and continue with your work, allowing others to have their choice about how they live and act in the world, from fear or from love, just as you do.

I had been an admirer of Lakshmi, from a distance really, for quite some time. Kali – whom we will meet later in this book – was always my first love as a goddess. I didn't consciously choose for that to be the case, she was just the energy that I was unconsciously drawn to beyond many others for quite some time. Kali is such a big energy, provocative, taboo, terrifying to many and certainly powerful. I wasn't sure if other goddesses would be quite so demanding of personal healing as she was. Eventually, as I began to work with Kuan Yin, and then Isis, Saraswati and of course, Lakshmi, and all of the goddesses we meet in this book, I realised that although they may not seem as intimidating as Kali, working with any face of the Divine Feminine is going to demand a lot from us in terms of personal healing. The deeper we want to go into a goddesses' wisdom and presence, the more that will be asked of us. Lakshmi is no exception to that.

As I deepened my personal connection to Lakshmi, I realised how much work I still had to do around receiving her grace. This came up when I was preparing to run a dance workshop dedicated to Lakshmi with my dearest friend. We discussed the basic outline, but the actual event was weeks and weeks away, so we decided to let it percolate. And percolate it did. As I mentioned in the introduction, even the intention to work with these Divine Feminine energies is enough to set the healing process in motion, and as we get into unresolved wounds it often feels more painful before it feels better.

During the weeks that followed our original decision to run a Lakshmi class, I worked with her mantra. I use mantra a lot in my sound healing work, but I also understand that there is a whole other level of power that is activated in a mantra when we don't just say it. When we have the consciousness to be able to become one with a mantra, to embody within our being what it is that it calls forth, we can become a living version of that mantra. Now that's something! The Lakshmi mantra was one power I wasn't sure I had access to with the same potency I had with Kali, Durga, or Saraswati, for example. My intention was to awaken the latent power of Lakshmi within me, enough that I could have something of deep worth to offer to the beautiful group who would undoubtedly gather for the goddess night.

Over the weeks leading up to the class, I was unexpectedly cast into old issues I had not thought about in years. It was as if every unresolved aspect of me that would block Lakshmi's grace arose, apparently unbidden. Of course, my intention to connect with Lakshmi had set this healing process in motion; I just had no idea how much I had set afoot in setting that intention! All my blocks to her grace were laid out before me as I battled with issues of self-worth, self-esteem and feeling like I was not good enough. It was so unexpected and yucky feeling (to use a non-technical term) that I didn't immediately make the connection between my emotional healing crisis and the divine energy I sought to become more intimate with. When I eventually did, I was able to work with it more effectively and enthusiastically, but for several days, I had no clue what was going on except that I was in a real mess (to use another non-technical term).

As I worked through the issues and feelings that arose, I came to realise that Lakshmi would hold herself back from us out of grace. If we asked for her blessing and all it would give rise to was painful resistance, because our desire for her blessings of beauty and wealth, for example, came from wanting to compensate for not feeling good enough, then her blessing would actually resolve the 'not good enough' wound before anything else could come to us. So if all we were comfortable accepting was the feeling that we weren't good enough or weren't deserving, then there wasn't much she could do but bring that stuff up to be healed so that she could deliver the next level of her grace – which might be rather more enjoyable! All of my issues were triggered because she was reaching for me as I had asked her to. She was offering me her blessings and I was responding with, "Oh no! I couldn't possibly accept!" It was unconscious, well less so by that point, but that is why I didn't feel as familiar with her potency as I did with other faces of the Divine Feminine. I just hadn't healed the issues that would block me feeling her presence. Once healed, she could become just as alive in me as any other divine being.

I felt comfortable with being powerful, so Kali was just fine for me. I felt at ease with self-expression and using my voice, so Saraswati was comfortable for me too. I was still asked to grow in connection with them, and there were some confronting challenges in that for me too, of course. But I was very aware of what was happening. With Lakshmi, much of what was within me that deadened her effect in my life was deeply unconscious. She has been working through me, shifting those layers and gently bringing them to consciousness so that I can heal and move closer to her, ever since. Sometimes she seems to enlist the aid of another divine being to assist our work together, but she is always there, answering that prayer for the sort of intimacy and connection to her most powerful offering of her wisdom that I can make.

On the goddess night, my dear friend and I led the group through our rituals and healing processes. I sang the Lakshmi mantras with my friend playing the crystal singing bowls. I shared my Lakshmi stories, which I have shared with you above, and taught the Lakshmi mantra (a version of which I will teach you below). We then danced and chanted the Lakshmi mantra as a group. As usual, when the group did this it felt like the air was pregnant with sound. In this case, it felt like a field of thick golden light had filled the space, and it was as if we were dancing and singing within it. Then my friend took over and the dance journey fired up. It got so rowdy and out of control in a playful way, that when my friend leaned over and whispered, "Club Lakshmi!" We both laughed.

At the end of the night, to ground the wild frenzy of dancing and potent energy work, we went around the circle, opening up feedback and questions. One woman in particular, one of the most enthusiastic and appreciative women I have ever met – she is a fizzing bliss bomb of complimentary loveliness – absolutely lavished me with compliments. Anything she could think of, she complimented me on. My hair, my voice, my earrings – "My god, so gorgeous, where did you get them?" – my outfit, my dancing, the music, my teachings, that I looked like Lakshmi, so golden, and on it went. What I felt was that Lakshmi was radiating out of her as a golden field of light. I could feel her in the beauty of this woman's words and I could feel myself absolutely accepting, with happiness and gratitude (rather than embarrassment or denial) all that she was sending my way. It was truly delightful. I had taken another step on the path of love to Lakshmi in just simply receiving without apology or demur.

For men and women who have been denied the dignity of respect and worth, who have been shamed in any way, who have suffered from being chronically misjudged or misunderstood, there can be a subtle chipping away effect, wearing away our sense of worth and self-regard bit by bit. We often don't realise it consciously as we just get on with life until, perhaps, we catch ourselves putting ourselves down and wondering why we keep doing that, or we don't even bother reaching for something or someone we really want because we don't imagine our desire will amount to anything. Perhaps we have become so used to people not really getting us or seeing us that we give up even wanting to be seen. Especially for souls with such a beautiful light that can genuinely help heal the world simply through its presence, this is a sad state of affairs, and Lakshmi would like to help us change it!

People were usually shocked when they found out I was studying law. I assumed it was because they imagined my readiness to laugh, new age spiritual orientation and wild corkscrew curls, signified a lack in intelligence. I never took it personally or as an insult. What did get me down was that I was apparently so hard to fathom. The very honest psychic I mentioned in the previous chapter actually told me people greatly underestimated me because I was sweet and friendly, and did not realise just how much iron will and strength I had within me. This has been true at times. I can count on one hand the people I know who accurately see me and know what I am capable of. Although, that may be changing as my work becomes more visible, but I can relate to past experiences of it. Sometimes people look at you without really seeing you. I have the sense you might understand exactly what I am saying here. Anyway, I wasn't exactly happy about that state of affairs, but was not one of those types who found it natural to go about informing the world at large of their fabulousness. I figured those who bothered to really pay attention and see what lies within would turn up along the way and that they would be discerning – a quality I always appreciated and respected – along with having substance and maturity, and a healthy dose of irreverence and humour – but I digress!

So not so long ago, I became closer friends with a woman I had known socially for over a year. At our first dinner together, she revealed another side of herself. I couldn't believe how insightful, intelligent, bright and capable this woman was. I always liked her and found her to be lovely, but she had cloaked this whole other side of her from me. She was a trained psychiatrist. Now that takes years upon years of study and, I believe, is an accomplishment to be proud of. I quizzed her passionately. Why hide this about yourself? You are so amazing! Let people know! She responded that I was probably a better psychiatrist than she and she didn't want to make people uncomfortable. I just sighed as I recognised my own tendency to keep to myself and even get a bit shy when people are awed by what I do for a living. Genuine interest, I can handle, but stark admiration can make me very shy indeed. When she said she was stunned by how psychologically aware I was, I realised I hadn't really talked or shared much of myself with her either. We were each a revelation to the other. What a lovely surprise and learning experience that was. The hand of Lakshmi was at work there, gently urging us to no longer hide our respective qualities but to let them be seen more freely.

A few days ago I was at a rowdy, wild drumming circle with a group of people, some of whom I knew, but most of whom I did not. Feeling so much playfulness and energy buzzing the group, it felt natural for me to grab a microphone and add some rowdy, wild chanting into the mix. I felt the energy flow and whipped it up into a frenzy of divine energy as drummers drummed and dancers danced. After the moment had passed, I did what I tend to do which is step 'off centre stage'. Once the moment for performance or offering is over, I can become quite introverted again. One of the drummers told me how much he loved it, that he let my voice move him and the energy became so wild and free and it was very exciting. Then a woman, a dancer, bounded over to me, "You are amazing! Thank you, thank you!" She bowed and kissed my feet, and she said, "Don't hide yourself, your sounds, they pull the negativity out of people, what a gift you are!"

After being so open – when I sing or perform or teach, I don't hold anything back, it's all just there, given according to how much the group can receive – it felt good to be affirmed in such a loving way. I thanked them both for their loving words and actions.

I might never be the type to sit at a dinner party and wax lyrical about what a talented healer I am (as obnoxious as that behaviour may sound, this sort of people often have very good businesses because they aren't afraid of promoting themselves!) but I do hope I am learning to share myself more openly with others, not out of immature self-importance, but out of mature self-respect. That is just one of the many blessings of Lakshmi, and a way to open ourselves to many more of her gifts.

She says that she weaves the golden path, and we need only follow one thread. Take one step at a time and when it is time for the next step, she shall guide us along the way.

I would also like to mention here that Lakshmi is said to bring luck or good fortune. I know people who say that they don't believe in luck, that we create our own reality and that is that. I don't believe these two things are incompatible. Luck or good fortune is a frequency that allows us to be in the right place at the right time and to consciously receive the gift of turning opportunities into benefits. We might call it synchronicity. Some people are more easily able to do this than others. As the frequency of luck is with them in greater abundance, they are just more comfortable with it, open to life and expecting goodness without attaching to how or through who or when it appears. Lakshmi operates on that same joyful, playful and open frequency. As we work with her, we are more able to plug in to her way of being in the world and our ability to 'be lucky' increases too.

The biggest Lakshmi blessing I can offer you, from which all others will flow, is this: "May you come to realise your true worth, beloved."

DENDRITIC AGATE (PLENTY)

This is such a visually beautiful crystal. It usually features white, blue and black, or black and brown tones. It doesn't usually contain banded patterns like most other agates. Instead it has markings that are fernlike and are sometimes so intricate that they resemble a hand-painted image rather than a naturally formed pattern.

The first time I saw dendritic agate I had no idea what sort of stone it was, but I fell in love with it instantly. I couldn't believe it wasn't hand painted and when I realised it was natural I was just in awe. I stood staring at it for quite a while. I think the store assistant thought there was something quite wrong with me. Fortunately by that point I had done enough work on my self-worth not to worry about that, and instead I kept on staring, mesmerised by the beauty I saw in the stone.

Dendritic agate is often used in jewellery, which is how I first came across it. It can be found in tumbled stones as well. Although it is treasured as a stone of wealth, wellbeing and good fortune, it is inexpensive. I think this says something important. It is a stone of plenty that brings great wealth, yet it is not unobtainable. Dendritic agate is not about wealth for a privileged few. It is about abundance as a way of living and making abundance more accessible. It makes dreams and that which we yearn for seem possible rather than some distant fantasy.

Like the earth itself, there is an innate intelligence in this stone. It has an ability to create systems that support and balance each other and the plant like patterning on dendritic agate hints at this. This stone carries the wisdom of ecosystem and connection. The patterning looks as if it is growing on the stone, living and thriving before one's eyes.

To open up to wellbeing and prosperity in order to manifest dreams and desires, we need to feel connected to other people, places and energy sources. If we are sensitive and have learned to withdraw in order to deal with aggression, density or other lower vibration realities, then we can find our way to wealth in all its forms a lot more challenging. After all, money is attached to people, love comes through connection, and enlightenment is based on an acceptance and loving regard for all things. To take those steps, we need to learn how to connect. This also means learning how to manage our energy and the impact that others have on us. This is something Lakshmi supports us in doing. Dendritic agate teaches us how to make connections, how to open up and how to allow life to happen through us. It can also help us learn how to become creative and resourceful (like nature!) in dealing with energies that deplete rather than nourish us. We can use that which needs to be released or allowed to wither and die (whether that be a quality within us or a relationship that is not healthy) as fertiliser to bring to life the seeds that would help us live and thrive too.

The combination of dendritic agate and Lakshmi, who teaches us to look for the goldenness that can even come through the battle of light and dark within or around us, can help us to transform our relationship to the world, to humanity, to money and to wealth in all its forms. We can function in the world and be true to ourselves without being scared of the energies of others. Even if we consciously choose not to invite particular energy into our lives, we can still accept its existence as a part of life more generally, and decide how and to what extent, we will interact with it from a place of integrity.

As we mentioned above, Lakshmi holds the energy of self-worth. Part of this is the power to choose where one wishes to align oneself. In her case it was with the Lord of Love. Good choice! When we bring that energy of choice into connection with others, we can feel more empowered, discerning and allow ourselves to set boundaries. There may well be times when a person is so wounded and toxic in their behaviour that any boundary you set will be insufficient and it would probably be wisest to cut contact with them cleanly and completely. However, there will be other times when we can heal the relationship by healing how we choose to relate within it. With its innate intelligence to support adaptability, growth, abundance and plenty, dendritic agate supports us in naturally detecting how and when to let go and how and when to tweak our attitudes and responses in relationship. We therefore have the best of both situations! We can choose to be in the world and in relationships, and benefit from what this can offer us. This also means we can be of benefit to the world and of benefit in our relationships, because we aren't hiding, but engaging consciously.

With dendritic agate, the power of choosing to engage is turned into a manifesting tool that can become very powerful. We can attract what we need through fast-moving electrical impulses that travel along invisible lines of connection between us and what is needed. The energy can flow quickly and what is needed finds its way to us more seamlessly because there are countless channels open through which we can receive. The more we are engaged and open, the more the Divine Feminine can share herself with us through the people and opportunities that will serve the path of love. This is not about settling for bad behaviour in your relationships in the name of remaining open. In her lessons on self-worth Lakshmi teaches us that is a 'no go'. What it means is that we can, through the frequency of our hearts, attract more and more valuable allies to our cause so that we can all benefit.

If you are lucky enough to witness even just a moment of this electrical attraction that leads to manifestation in action, you will probably be utterly awestruck by how fast and effective it really is. It's like playing super-fast Ping-Pong: we emit frequencies and the rest of the Universe responds in instant manifestation! Dendritic agate is known as a slow-working crystal, which is completely appropriate for this process. It helps us to slow down and remain receptive, rather than getting over-excited by the manifestation process. It helps our nerve fibres to strengthen so that even as we expose ourselves to more and more of the world, and to divine energies and frequencies such as Lakshmi, our bodies can integrate our experiences and cope with our challenges without collapsing into stress or fear, but by gently and naturally continuing to open up to receive more and more love, in the spirit of true abundance and plenty.

MANIFESTING THROUGH LIMITLESSNESS

I often say I have manifested things in my life despite my best efforts. Despite my thoughts, my expectations and even with my relatively open-minded nature, the divine perspective always consists of a broader horizon, and as such, knows best in terms of what is needed and will bring fulfilment.

Our basic preconceptions about spirituality and money, and whether or not they can go together with integrity generally suggest that we may need to let go of self-imposed limitations in thought, attitude and belief to allow Lakshmi to weave her golden magic through our lives. Dendritic agate gently, but firmly and consistently, encourages us to be as the Divine, that is, to be as nature, constantly opening and evolving without creative limits. We have to be willing to bear the unknown and to remain open to possibilities. It we want to live in a familiar, known world, this is going to cause us some heartache until we realise that security doesn't come from anything other than our own fundamental realisation that the Universe loves us and is urging us to grow.

As mentioned in the introduction and throughout each chapter, there are many ways to manifest. Sometimes struggle and trying to force something actually ends up pushing it further away. We project the belief that we have to get something, when we could actually begin to settle into the notion that energetically we already have what we are seeking within us. We just have to tap into that energy and grow it enough to naturally attract like-minded people or higher-vibration situations into our lives. When we act 'as if' rather than 'if only' we energetically shift from 'wanting' to 'claiming.'

When I began working with Lakshmi I was already well on my path. I was surprised by how much stuff came up about self-worth when I began to create the dance workshop mentioned earlier. When I am going to teach, I always find that anything I need to master in order to embody the teaching will arise in advance of the workshop. I had done a lot of work on self-esteem and self-worth many years previously, so I was shocked at how much more deeply I needed to look at my attitudes towards what I felt I deserved and my beliefs about spending money. I found an odd little quirk in my behaviour. I seemed to be more at ease about spending in small amounts than in one larger purchase, even if I ended up spending the same or even less in the one larger sum.

When I realised I was doing this, I began to question why as I wanted to see if I could release the beliefs that were surrounding this pattern. What had I unconsciously made spending larger amounts of money mean? I realised that, somewhere, I was still holding on to a really old belief that I couldn't have what I wanted, so I was compensating by getting more of what I didn't really want. It was a funny sort of unconscious bargaining with myself. It didn't have much of a bearing on financial reality, because I was channelling a similar amount of money into many things, instead of one thing. When I gave myself permission to have the one thing I really wanted, and to enjoy it, I no longer needed quite so many second choices!

The more I worked on this, the more the situation improved. I subsequently felt happier and began to take better care of myself more naturally and easily in other areas of my life. I enjoyed a balance between wholesome discipline, the enjoyment of my simple but blessed quality of life, my choices and even my possessions so much more. Because I felt happier and more nurtured, I was also able to part with what I didn't really love (or did love, but didn't really feel that I needed anymore) with greater ease and happiness. I recently cleared out over ninety percent of my book and crystal collection, partially in a private sale, partially in donations, and was stunned by how comfortable I was in doing so. It had taken over twenty years to handpick that collection and the contents of it were precious to me. A part of why I was comfortable with the process was because it was the right thing, at the right time as suggested by my higher guidance which I trust implicitly. It was also that I felt ready and willing to do so within myself.

Surprisingly, the process was incredibly freeing and I felt genuine pleasure at some of my beautiful crystals and books finding loving new homes, and that the hundreds of books I donated to the local library would give them a truly amazing spirituality and healing collection that could help many people. I realised the crystals I needed in my life had changed and the ones that I had once held on to for my own growth now wanted to serve others. I wanted to honour their wishes, out of a tremendous appreciation for all they had helped me with on my path, so I let them go. Sometimes they asked to go to a particular person, so I simply wrapped them up as a surprise gift and sent them along with their book order. I trusted they knew where they needed to be.

This was part of my personal work to release the limitations I had unconsciously placed upon myself. Now limitations are not bad per se. Sometimes they are very helpful. Limits on how we spend our time and with whom, on our desire to 'push', on how much we indulge or discipline ourselves, or on how much we deny ourselves before asking for help can all be rather helpful.

The limitlessness of Lakshmi's healing, and the power of dendritic agate is not about being a superwoman or superman devoid of human limitation. It is about shifting the way we think and behave so that the Divine can do what it does – which is offer genius solutions to situations that our more limited thinking might deem unsolvable or unavoidable. It is about getting out of our own way, learning to feel comfortable with not knowing how something is going to work out and still trusting that it will. This is the ultimate attitude of trusting optimism that leads to our surrender into the genius of divine creation.

HEALING PROCESS

You will know you need this healing process if you feel stuck in how you expect things should be. If things are not matching up to your expectations no matter how hard you try or how hard you pray, this is for you. This is usually a sign that either timing is an issue (in which case surrendering into Lakshmi will help you relax and flow) or that the Divine has a better idea in store for you, in which case surrendering your attitudes and allowing dendritic agate to work its magic will help you receive that better opportunity instead.

The Process

Create some privacy for yourself by turning off your mobile or taking the landline phone off the hook. Turn off your computer and if you wish play some nice peaceful music that makes you feel good. You may like to burn some incense or light a candle, whatever feels soothing, indulgent and comforting to you.

Take a dendritic agate crystal, if you have it, and/or the mandala for Lakshmi and dendritic agate.

Find a place to sit and relax, and make sure you have enough layers of clothing on so that your body is a comfortable temperature.

Allow yourself to gaze at the crystal and/or the mandala. Say the following passage out loud. You don't have to speak loudly, however, it is about putting the vibration of the sound into space. Really feel the words as you speak them. Take your time and speak from the heart, "I call on Lakshmi who is unconditional love. I call forth your healing golden light and surrender into the bliss of your love. I call upon the Crystal Angel of Dendritic Agate, and the healing power of Mother Earth expressed through this crystal. I call upon my own divine soul and healing journey now, so that transformation may be deep, merciful and pure. So be it!"

Close your eyes and place one hand on your heart and the other on your belly. Breathe gently in and out. Imagine that with each breath in, you are allowing your awareness of the day-to-day world to fall away and with each exhale you are dropping into your heart.

When you feel your awareness is comfortably within your own being, perceive or imagine that there is a sparkling, golden light fizzing brightly above your body. This is the energy of Lakshmi. Imagine it shining down on you as golden rays of light, perhaps sense it as a lovely, warm-feeling energy.

Beneath you there is a sense of pleasant, cool-feeling energy. This is the energy of dendritic agate. Imagine it bringing a calm, light feeling of pleasant coolness into your body, rising up from the cool, vast earth.

Take your time to relax with these energies, both the coolness and the warmth, and let yourself feel as though you are floating, held and restful in these vibrations.

When you are ready, place your awareness in your belly, underneath your resting hand and say the following, "Of my own free will, I now choose to release any cords of connection from relationships, situations, memories or objects that are holding me back from opening up to the next level of divine abundance and healing solutions available to me. I release any shame, conscious or unconscious, any issues of self-esteem or self-worth, from this or any lifetime, that are getting in the way of me receiving the blessings of prosperity and healing from the Divine Mother, now. Through the grace of Lakshmi, so be it."

Imagine the golden light that is fizzing above you, move in through the top of your head, down through your head, into your throat, down into your chest and heart, and then along your arms and into your hands.

Hold one hand at your heart and one hand at your belly as the light fizzes, and gently but firmly flicks away any cords of connection that are not healthy for you. Whether you are conscious of this happening or not, it is enough that you are doing this practice and it will happen.

When the fizzing feels like it has stopped, or at least eight breaths later, allow your awareness to move deeper into your heart. Imagine or perceive any situation or difficulty you would like to have solved or a situation that you would like to manifest for yourself or the world. See, sense or feel it in your heart. Imagine you can open up the back of your heart chakra and breathe the situation or prayer out through the back of your heart into the cool dendritic agate energy beneath you. Imagine the earth sucking it down into the crystalline layer of dendritic agate.

Relax and be in the cool, pleasant feeling of relaxation and peace.

Slowly become aware that the dendritic agate has absorbed your issue for healing, your intention for creation or both. The energy is now moving swiftly through the crystalline layer, growing and swirling out towards the solution. The right people, opportunities, healing and grace are now being drawn to you through the intelligence of the Earth's magnetic field. Just relax as though you are floating and imagine that the energetic intelligence of the crystal is floating up from beneath you, gently in through the back of your heart and flowing through your entire being until you are filled with crystalline light and it pours out beyond your skin to create a field of light within and around you. You are in harmony with the solution and the manifestation now.

Just relax and breathe slowly for eight breaths.

When you are ready to finish this healing process, imagine that the golden light of Lakshmi is ignited as two shining, golden energy bursts in your heart and your belly.

Gently sit up and say the following mantra, or ancient prayer to Lakshmi, at least eight times to close the practice. Imagine the sound of the mantra going all the way into your body, strengthening that golden light in your heart, belly and anywhere else it needs to go.

This prayer means, "I call upon the abundance of the supreme feminine principle of divine prosperity, beauty, healing and enlightenment and I surrender into her healing wisdom and grace." A sounding-out or pronunciation guide is included below.

OM SHRIM MAHA LAKSHMI YEI SWAHA

OM (rhymes with Tom) SHRIM (sounds like shreem) MAHA (sounds like Ma-Huh)

LAKSHMI (sounds like Luck-Smee) Yei (sounds like yay) SWAHA (sounds like Swa-huh).

Imagine the sound moving through you as you speak it slowly and aloud. Take your time. As you practice it, you will learn to say it easily.

Once you feel you have said this mantra enough to close your practice, just sit up and gaze at your mandala and/or crystal and say, "May I experience the abundance, prosperity and enlightenment that can best serve the divine plan. I give permission for blocks to this to be removed with her loving grace so that I may blossom and live a truly abundant life in harmony with the divine plan. So be it."

When you are ready, place your hands in prayer at your heart and bow your head.

You have then completed the healing process.

After a few days or in stronger cases, a few weeks, you will find that the necessary clearing has happened through dreams, life circumstances and situations. Don't be surprised if issues about self-worth, money, receiving or giving, setting boundaries, believing in your own beauty, or any other related issues arise during this time. Just notice them, give thanks for the healing process that is forcing those issues to be shed. If it gets too much to simply observe, then repeat the above healing process up to three more times, no more than once a week. Take your time and work with the mandala in between. You can place it near your bedside to assist you in integrating this work whilst you sleep. You are worth the effort that it takes to see this right through to completion.

3.

SEKHMET (SACRED RAGE)
FIRE AGATE (INNER FIRE)

MANIFESTING THROUGH PASSION

A wild goddess roars as she strides powerfully across the burning desert. With the body of a woman and the head of a lioness, she emanates beauty and power. She destroys that which is in her divine way with the burning fire of her presence. Only truth can withstand the intensity of her rage against all that is unjust, all that deters love and obstructs life. She is the righteous destruction of that which must end, in service to life.

SEKHMET (SACRED RAGE)

As a little girl I was obsessed with my mother's book collection, which included oversized books with full colour maps of the world. The gypsy in me was already dreaming of discovering new lands and I would gaze at different places on the map, wondering what they were like and what it would be like to visit them. Her collection also featured a large, full colour book on the history of humanity, with a section on Ancient Egypt. The colourful pictures ignited my imagination. Sitting with my head buried in that book, I felt as though I was transported beyond the four walls of the cool, dark lounge room and back through time.

Mesmerised, I would gaze at the pictures of the strangely beautiful goddesses of Ancient Egypt. Without words or concepts to explain what I was feeling, I was overcome. Something about them captured my heart. It was like meeting a long lost friend, after having a sort of amnesia that made you forget how you ever knew them. The connection was so palpable and there was no doubt it was real. I knew them, without knowing how I knew them. It was a connection that I felt even more strongly when I finally travelled to Egypt in my early twenties.

Sekhmet in particular, along with Isis and Bast, felt like sisters of my soul. Sekhmet, with her womanly body and lioness head, seemed to emanate strength and power. I felt safe with her. Her name comes from the Egyptian word 'sekhem' which translates as power and literally means 'she who is powerful.' One of her particular titles which appeals to me greatly, is 'the one before whom evil trembles'.

Sekhmet is a solar goddess who holds the power of the sun. She is also the deliverer of divine justice, the power through which karma is enacted. She functions as the protector of Ma'at (the goddess of justice and divine law in Ancient Egypt) and her titles also include, 'She who loves Ma'at and detests evil'. She doesn't analyse and decide karma; she just acts with immediacy and unwavering purpose, at one with divine truth.

Perhaps because of this, Sekhmet is known as a goddess of destruction. She had a popular and powerful cult following in Egypt and her destructive bloodlust was said to be pacified only when she became unintentionally intoxicated. This is a great metaphor that helps us understand Sekhmet's wisdom teachings. From out of the intense fire that annihilates all that no longer serves us, we will, at some point, need to surrender into bliss and playful abandon. All that intensity must be balanced with joy, or it can become destructive beyond that which is helpful. This is why Bastet (associated with sensuality and joyful play) is the balancing divine sister energy to Sekhmet.

Sekhmet is a goddess of war, victory and as unlikely as it might seem at first, of healing medicine. She was known as the Lady of Life and was the patron goddess of physicians and the priests who performed healing. Sekhmet provides protection for those who do healing work through her destructive side and her constructive side – they are both one and the same for her, as she is like a living sun, creating and destroying life in accordance with divine will. Sometimes she is called Nesert or flame and referred to as the midday sun in the desert, such is her power. She is the brightest and most powerful light.

As healers, we need the power of the light in service to life and we need help in dealing with the powerful darkness that is often drawn to such light. We need the destructive part of her, for it is part of her protective field of energy and consciousness.

I was wearing a Sekhmet pendant when out and about one day, and an Egyptian man came and asked me, "Are you a healer?" Somewhat surprised, I responded in the affirmative and asked how he knew. He responded, "Well I see you are wearing Sekhmet. She is for healers!" It seemed like the most obvious thing in the world to him. He understood Sekhmet and the power of sacred rage that serves love.

When we are in a healing profession, on a path of divine personal healing or both, we need to heal our relationship to our emotions. Anger often gets a bad rap as a destructive emotion and our typical role models for anger are negatively stereotyped. Perhaps we see anger as violent or aggressive actions used to punish or shame. It is very a powerful emotion and when it arises we often don't know what to do with it energetically. However, we can always choose how to express the powerful sensations of anger.

I have worked with clients over the years, particularly when I was a psychotherapist, who were very frightened of their anger. When they were young, they had been shamed by their parents into believing their anger was very bad indeed. One client in particular was concerned that her anger might destroy me. This client's higher self was trying to bring her mother's fear and rejection of her anger to consciousness in our work together. The mother had her own reasons for denying her daughter's anger. Perhaps the mother had never learned to accept, claim and own the anger in herself and didn't have the awareness not to pass her patterning on to her daughter. I had a couple of brief encounters with the client's mother during the course of the treatment and found her to be passive-aggressive and critical. This helped me understand the issues my client was dealing with. From what I could sense, the mother feared and rejected anything that could emotionally and psychologically separate her daughter from her. The daughter had unconsciously internalised her mother's emotional reactions to her anger and believed them to be some sort of truth. She believed her anger was bad and to be avoided at all costs.

She had to bring this realisation into conscious awareness, in order to put her reaction to her anger into a more accurate perspective. Until she consciously claimed her anger, she would keep acting it out in very painful and self-destructive ways, because emotions hidden within don't go away. They do end up being acted out unconsciously or, eventually, concreted into illness. This client would get very angry with herself and harm herself through dangerous, self-destructive activities. Eventually the therapeutic relationship took over and she was able to experience some of her anger in the context of our relationship. On the rare occasion that she allowed herself to become angry at me, it led to therapeutic breakthrough when she realised I was still there for her, with regard, in the aftermath of her heated expression. No one had been destroyed and life could go on.

It took some time, but she began to release the fear and rejection of her anger. She recognised her trouble expressing anger stemmed from her mother's issues and was not founded on the true value of her own anger at all. In doing so, she was able to reclaim the energy and power her anger was trying to give birth to. It was pushing her to let go of the suffocating psychological hold she had allowed her mother to exercise over her and to redefine their relationship by setting boundaries on her mother's behaviour and choosing how she wished to live her life for herself. This would be healing and helpful for both of them. She was unable to set the needed boundaries so she could free herself to make her own decisions while she was locked in to her childhood pattern of avoiding her anger. She had to go through the pain of acknowledging the judgment of her anger in order to release it and claim its benefit.

Learning to heal our relationship with our anger is rarely an easy task. It is probably the most feared, misdirected, misused and misunderstood emotion in modern Western culture. If you are more gentle-hearted, it can be a difficult and uncomfortable feeling to endure. I usually don't enjoy feeling anger when it does arise, but I do find it helpful because it will be alerting me to something. Anger – as with any emotion – expresses something to us from our intuition or deeper feelings that could be extremely useful to our wellbeing. Anger might tell me I need to take better care of myself, to get some rest or to set some stronger boundaries with certain people. It may also be a message that I need to step away from a particular person who is draining my energy, that I need to get out of my head and into my heart, or perhaps that I need to have an afternoon off and treat myself in to some fun.

There are lots of useful messages underneath the feeling of anger, but I have to connect with it before I can sense what lies beneath. If I was to get swept up in unconsciously dumping my rage at another, blaming or attacking them for all the things I have judged they are doing wrong, then I would lose the opportunity to find the nugget of guidance underneath my anger. I would also poison my relationship with that person in the process.

Anger is a powerful and potentially destructive emotion if not handled with wisdom. Most of us were not taught to respond to our anger with wisdom, so it can be terrifying even to imagine feeling really angry. We simply don't know what to do with it, especially if we don't want to hurt other people by lashing out with it. Fortunately, Sekhmet can help us with this. Her presence helps us to learn how to consciously respond to our anger and we will tap into this lesson during our healing process below.

I still remember one fight I had with my younger brother. He criticised me for something that I didn't believe was justified. It wasn't that we had a difference of opinion that angered me, but that he had appointed himself as the judge of me. To say this made me really, really cranky would be an understatement. After hanging up the phone on that conversation, I had so much anger pumping through me that all I could do was fidget. So, I just went with that. I walked around the lounge room in circles (it wasn't a huge apartment!) and ranted, out loud, to the Divine. I called on the angels of healing and anyone else that could listen to me in unconditional love, and said, "Hey, I need to talk this through, can you please listen and block any negative energy from coming in or going out ... thanks!" I didn't want my words to become an unintentional psychic attack towards my brother but I did need to get all my feelings out and come to some sense about what was making me so mad.

I spent quite some time walking and talking out that anger. I talked as if I had the best sounding board in the world listening to me. I probably did! I just worked through it, talking it out, until I felt some insight fall into place. I realised that a good portion of what I was feeling was my own sense of injustice, but also, a hefty amount of anger actually belonged to my brother who felt helplessly manipulated at being cast into a role of taking care of my mother's needs and was very angry about it. He couldn't process that consciously and he needed to vent. I happened to be the one he directed his rage towards, which was part of why the encounter felt so unjust to me – because it wasn't authentic, it was dumping. However, I had compassion. I grew up in the same family dynamic as him and so I had first-hand experience and understood that although it was often loving, there were some challenging aspects to handle as well. All that rage, boiling up inside of me, just passed. It evaporated and I was free, clearer about what was going on and able to let it go. I have always found journaling or 'talking it out' to the angels in my lounge room to be helpful ways to process emotion. Of course, if someone were to stumble upon me having a passionate conversation with 'mid-air' I would surely seem quite mad!

Then there is the other side of anger, when someone is unable to contain their anger and doesn't internalise it towards themselves but projects it out at you. It can feel like psychic attack, emotional abuse, or may even manifest in physical abuse. We might feel our own fear towards their anger, or even their own fear of their anger as they realise that indeed, they are out of control.

I knew a man who was like this. He would keep his anger repressed for as long as possible. I am not sure why. Perhaps he didn't want to be an angry person or he was scared of behaving in a way that wasn't in control and calm, which was his more typical way of being. He suffered with recurring depression for many years until he learned to express his anger. He didn't learn to do that very consciously, but it did alleviate his depression! Eventually he would just erupt like a volcano. He would act out physically, sometimes yelling, banging doors, punching a wall, throwing a laundry basket down the yard. Whilst it was a good method of overcoming depression, there needed to be some development in how he expressed his anger if he was going to mature emotionally. His behaviour shut down communication in his intimate relationship and prevented him from being able to really deal with what was happening for him.

Unfortunately for his relationship, he felt it was acceptable behaviour. While he admitted it was not ideal, he did not see it as worth doing anything about. His unwillingness to put effort into dealing with his emotional energy in a more constructive way drove a divide between him and his partner, who couldn't relate to him emotionally. This was largely because he didn't really want to relate emotionally – to himself or to her. His partner felt very sad about this and ironically perhaps, angry too. However, she chose to respect his right to choose how he wanted to live. He had every right to dictate how much energy he would put into personal growth. She decided she also had the right to choose how she wanted to live. The truth was that they couldn't live well together or relate emotionally in a way that satisfied his partner, and they ended the relationship despite a great deal of emotional attachment, love and affection between them both.

Our anger can end up destroying us from the inside with disease if we internalise it and destroy the love, trust and openness in our relationships if we direct it outwards. We are right to consider it a powerful force and to tread carefully. However, if we are so frightened of it that we will not look into it, anger can end up unconsciously destroying our bodies and relationships anyway. As we know, avoiding something doesn't make it go away. We have to deal with it directly.

With anger this means learning to hold awareness in the fire of rage – not resisting it, but not allowing it to consume us to the point of unconscious acting out either. It can take years of inner work to be able to bear witness to powerful emotions, allow them to run their course, and *then* choose how we will respond. Sometimes no response is required. Sometimes an important decision and action will need to be put in motion. Until we can be with the feeling, and breathe and connect with the truth lying beneath it, we won't know if an action is required or not. The truth might be that a relationship needs to end, that someone is not honouring us or that we need to calmly, clearly and assertively set a boundary, but the problem is not with the emotion itself. The problem comes when we try to act from our anger or to act out our anger.

Expressing ourselves when we are in the heat of anger, or trying to solve something at that moment, is unlikely to bring the most successful outcome. The phrase 'blind rage' gives us a hint! After the anger passes we can see things more clearly, but when it is firing within us, we might lack perspective. Of course, we could be angry in a moment of fierce clarity. That is possible. Action after the heat of passion has cooled is still likely to be the wiser course to take. We are more likely to approach the situation at hand more constructively once the anger has worked through us and we are able to respond with a cool, calm head. We don't invalidate the anger, we listen to it and respond as needs be.

I sometimes deal with my anger by discharging it with physical movement. I might dance or do some exercise. I have clients that sing very loudly in their car with the windows wound up as it is the only way they feel they have the privacy the need to release the emotion. More often, I actually just stand still and breathe, whilst it rips through me like a wild fire. I feel as though I am a living flame in those moments … Nesert, like Sekhmet.

As intense as the flame of anger is, it tends to pass reasonably quickly and then comes the opportunity to ask myself, "Does anything need to be done with this?" Sometimes there is not. It could be that I am just tired or overheated, and someone or something has irritated me in my already volatile state and I get cranky. I need to let my anger rise and fall, so I can realise I need a break, to bring myself into a more centred state again. However, sometimes another person does something and I am really mad about it. Is that person capable of a conversation about the issue? When I have calmed down, I might put feelers out, and tentatively broach the subject to see if we can have a conscious conversation about it. If the person is just interested in blame or being defensive, then I won't usually bother going any further with it. If the person wants to actually talk about it, then we might come to know each other better, and each of us can learn something and grow. Of course I have had moments where I have just laid it all out there bluntly but I prefer not to do this, as you cannot 'unsay' what has been said. Most often, once I realise where someone is coming from, I end up feeling compassion (even if it takes a while) and just move on and let it go.

When we are learning to stand in the truth of our feelings, including anger, it is helpful not to put impossible standards on ourselves. There have been times where I have been so frustrated, overwhelmed and exasperated with someone's behaviour, that I have just let it rip, so to speak. For me that means speaking – sometimes with a loud voice and a lot of emotion – the truth of what I am feeling. Now, generally speaking, I would prefer to be calm but in those moments I really wasn't capable of that. The two situations I can recall (and I am sure there were plenty of others over the course of the last thirty nine years!) both involved relationships where there were long-term patterns of emotional manipulation that I did not appreciate at all. One was with a close family member, the other with a romantic partner. In both situations, when I did just explode – even though I was mortified at my behaviour the moment afterwards – the people in question were so shocked that they paid attention, immediately apologised for their behaviour and both stopped doing what was so painful to me. This was so shocking to me. Firstly, because neither of them were particularly apologetic types. Secondly, because even though I felt I had lost control over myself, the communication was effective. I expect this was because I was speaking my truth from the heart, even if it was more wildly done than usual.

As I reflected upon my behaviour with my mentor some days afterwards, she made a comment that stayed with me. She remarked that perhaps what had happened was what was needed. It certainly didn't destroy the relationships in question, it just made them more respectful. I wanted to share this with you because in our attempts to be conscious with this potentially destructive emotion, we can be too hard on ourselves and overly critical when we don't feel we handled it with enough consciousness. It's good to want to work on ourselves, and become more aware and conscious in how we are in our relationships. But we are also allowed to be human. It isn't helpful to aim for perfection – it is wiser to commit to making progress.

This does not mean behaving abusively in a relationship is permissible. Abusive behaviour is an emotional, psychological and spiritual sickness that needs to be acknowledged and tended to for the wellbeing of the relationship as well as the soul of the individual. It does mean there might be times when things get emotionally messy. Not only is this to be expected, but sometimes it is actually constructive and helpful. It can be a step into honesty and vulnerability, and from that, if the other person can handle it, intimacy can develop.

How do you know if the other person can handle it? If someone is emotionally, spiritually and/or psychologically sick, then they will be unable to honour and receive vulnerability with compassion. Instead they may respond to your vulnerability by attempting to manipulate or control you, through shaming, criticism, judgment or any other sort of mental or emotional games and power plays. You might not be sure if this abuse is happening or not. It can be very hard to discern when we are actually *in* that pattern and it isn't until later when we look back that we realise the extent of the dysfunctional and abusive behaviour and how much we have outgrown it, thankfully.

However, you will know enough to sense if something isn't right. If after sharing something openly, you don't feel closer to that person, but rather you feel bad about yourself – weak, shamed, dirty, icky or unsafe – then you can be pretty sure something is happening in your relationship that isn't particularly healthy. These feelings are your inner self letting you know that something is askew in the relationship or within you, and you'll need to investigate that further to empower yourself and be healthier emotionally. If you sense these sort of responses happening for you in any of your relationships, then you'll need your anger! It will help you to say, "No, this is not acceptable." It will also give you the energy and motivation you need to do some work on why you are in such a pattern in the first place and help you feel feisty enough to ask for (and act on) divine assistance to help you outgrow painful patterns. You are worthy of this!

Potential for healing exists when we are accepting of and increasingly conscious with our anger by using it as a fire that can lead us to honesty and insight, rather than a stick of dynamite with which to blast other people. As we get to that place, a pathway opens up for us. Anger will not only be relevant to our personal, emotional journey in relationships, it will become relevant on our spiritual journey. Accepting our emotions, and being willing to deal with them maturely, allows energy to flow in the body. Our energetic digestion is enhanced and we can process, metabolise and release energy more effectively. Emotional states can flow, things that may once have taken years to process, can energetically metabolise more swiftly and thereby, perhaps, we might naturally work through an issue in a matter of days or weeks, instead of years.

When our energy field can flow, we tend to have more energy on all levels, including physically. We are fitter and healthier all round. This state is brought about by learning to love ourselves more unconditionally and therefore provides more unconditional acceptance for ourselves and our various emotional states. As our emotional pain from the past is gently cleared and we become increasingly oriented on the present moment, we are in effect clearing out our bodies so that there is empty space through which light can erupt from within our cells. Spiritual presence will develop quite naturally in spaciousness. Our job is to work towards providing that spaciousness, which in itself is like inviting the Divine to reside within your body.

As we work to own our anger, and all of our emotions, we become more attractive to the spiritual light and more inviting of its presence. It might sound strange that working through our anger can bring more light, but it does. The Divine is in all things, the Goddess lives in all of life and in all our life experiences and she wants to be honoured completely.

I had an experience of this recently in a conscious dance gathering. I had made a shamanic offering of an earth blessing with voice, crystal bowls and my shamanic drum. I felt a lot of love within me and very connected to my body and soul, and with the entire group, which I always do when I offer healing in a group context.

The group was then led through the five elements with various music to support the quality of each element. As we moved into fire, a song came on, a heavy metal song called *Killing in the Name* by a group called Rage Against the Machine (which I have always thought was a rather brilliant name). The song is powerful. However, it was very unexpected in a conscious dance class – and a laugh of glee erupted from me when it first came on. Then I dropped back into my body and I felt waves of oneness in the group as all those bodies moved with the music. I could feel the anger in each one of us. I could literally feel the anger and rage at how people were treated and anger at what was going on politically in the world, pulsing in all of our cells. As we danced, yelled, and really let loose, something unexpected happened within me. I felt the presence of the Goddess. I was one with her and she was one with me and with all of us in that space. We were the cells in her body as she danced. The rage, not what I once thought it to be, was revealed as a golden wave of light. There was ecstasy in it simply because it was divine, it was alive, and it was sheer, utter joy and bliss. I don't mean that I stepped out of the rage and anger and suddenly became all lovey-dovey. That rage was still exactly what it was – but I was able to experience it as a divine phenomenon not only in my mind and awareness, but in my visceral being. It was a powerful experience of aliveness and of absolute living love. I knew I had been dancing the Divine.

When I shared my experience of that oneness and ecstasy with the group afterwards, some knew what I meant but one girl had a strong reaction to my experience. She seemed to think that I had missed the point of feeling anger for what was happening in the world. That was not the case. I could still feel that anger but had received a gift of grace in feeling the truth that was veiled in sacred rage – that of ecstatic love.

It is my absolute belief that within every experience and beneath all of existence, is love. I don't mean this is in any fluffy way, but in a very real way. Whatever shows up in our lives is simply an invitation from the Universe for us to know this. Even if that is anger. When we aren't holding back, holding in or believing we are not worthy or capable of what is required of us for healing, we are in a vibration of increasing love. Like can attract like rather easily. The Universe will offer us many invitations to know the truth of life, of the Divine. As we accept these invitations, we will go through plenty of emotional healing work and as a result the light within us can grow stronger.

As we become brave enough to honour our emotions, including our anger, we are initiated deeper into the sacred terrain of Sekhmet. She guides us into the truth our bodies hold within their cells, and we will eventually find that we are tapping into a deep cellular rage. This can be so potent, it makes our once impressive anger seem like the small flame of a candle compared to the light of the sun! I have been in that state – where it is so powerful that I can barely contain it. We need the impressive container of Sekhmet with her fierceness, power and wisdom to support us as we begin to work consciously with this big energy. It is not comfortable or pleasant to access, until we come to grace with it, as I experienced during the conscious dance gathering. However, even in its discomfort, it is truthful, liberating and can open us up to our life path and purpose with tremendous energy, passion and clarity. But, at least initially, it often involves bearing great pain.

Rage exists deep within each of us for a reason. It is too much to just casually access, as though we could be humming quite happily to ourselves and then remark politely to our neighbour, "Oh my, I want to tear my hair out at the state of the oceans!" before heading off to buy some milk. When you tap into this rage, or more accurately, when it begins to reveal itself to you, you will realise you are encountering a wild face of the Divine. It isn't casual. It isn't gentle. It is truth, but it is truth that roots you to the spot and leaves you breathless. When I have encountered this energy, I have had to collapse onto the floor, push my palms and feet into the earth to try and ground myself, and breathe in and out as though I was about to give birth! I couldn't think straight, the amount of energy pulsing through my body was so strong. If I had been able to stand up and move,

I would have pulled at my hair and run wild down the street screaming in horror and anguish! As it was, big strange sounds erupted from my body and I was just in the rage and pain of the Earth, of the Divine Mother, of God, of the Universe and every being! It is no small thing. No wonder I could only bear it for a few brief moments before it shut off again and with relief, I was released into myself once more.

However, those brief moments were enough for me to immediately understand the teachings from the Sufi tradition (we will look at these when we meet the mystic sages Rumi and Shams in *Crystal Saints & Sages 777*) that tell us love is a mad woman, tearing off her clothes and running wild on a mountain. I could see her pulling at her hair and screaming. Yes! I completely understood! I learned so much about the fierce compassion of the Divine in that moment, more than I could have in years of study. I understood that every moment we are not coming from our own heart nor honouring our own soul, is the equivalent of sauntering up to the sacred goddess and sticking pins in her eyes! Of course she is going to scream. Of course she is going to have to let out all that feeling through floods, droughts, volcanic eruptions, etc. We thwart and disrespect her when we thwart our own spiritual growth and disrespect any part of ourselves. We must stop this now. Perhaps this is not easily done, but in that moment, oh yes, it was crystal clear.

I once had a student with whom I shared a considerable amount of my energy and time. She had taken all I had offered as a guide, teacher and mentor, apparently with respect and devotion. Then came a situation where she felt challenged by the pain that was arising within her and by my response to that pain, which was to ask her to confront it. She wanted me to soothe it away and I wanted her to stay with it. However, her ego's need for protection from the pain was too great. She chose instead to lash out and attack me in anger, as though I wasn't doing my job properly because she was in pain. Over a decade of love, nurturing, guidance and teaching was tossed aside, just like that. She took something that was precious, the trust that I thought we had cultivated towards each other in our spiritual relationship, and destroyed it with her rage.

Instead of honouring my presence in her life as a blessing for which she could have gratitude, she had come to feel entitled to me and therefore that I should behave in the way she believed I should. I despaired. Her beautiful soul, with so much potential, was stunted and locked in the grip of her ego. I was devastated.

Then a fierce rage came over me and I was jolted out of despair and into passion. I loved the human soul! It was the most important thing! Its survival was the reason I had committed to take the earthly journey, to play my small role in the grander scheme of human spiritual evolution, in the first place. It was far too precious to be allowed to be gobbled up by ego. If my former student chose her ego over her soul, I certainly didn't have to do so.

Rather than try to continue on with her, I did what I felt was divinely correct and cut her loose. Somewhere along the course of our relationship she had started using my presence in her life to boost her ego rather than support her soul and that had to stop. I withdrew completely from any further involvement with her. I knew the Divine loved her unconditionally and she would attract the right teaching situation for her soul growth. I didn't feel that was through me anymore.

Then I remembered the Bible teaching from Jesus' Sermon on the Mount that we must have wisdom about what we share and with whom. The teaching is that we are not to give what is holy to the dogs, nor cast our pearls before swine, lest they trample them under their feet, and turn and tear them to pieces. I thought of a comment that my Vedic astrologer, Rajan Sharma, once told me. He told me to be assertive and not to allow the jealousies or negativity of others to manipulate me, just because I have a softness, an ocean of love, within me. Both of these teachings were about sacred rage. Not the raging self-protection of an ego needing to be right, but the sacred rage that honours our spiritual growth above those ego needs.

I took a look at my client list through eyes made clearer by that sacred rage and began to make some further changes. If a relationship was not feeding the soul of the person anymore, as it had become too dependent or I simply felt divine guidance urging me to push them from the nest, so to speak, I began a gentle but firm process of terminating that connection from a place of love. This was easy for some and very difficult for others. I loved them too much to play any role, even an unwitting one, in leading them away from their soul.

Through the cleansing of that rage, these actions took place swiftly. What happened as a result of that spaciousness was that I had so much more energy. I couldn't believe how draining those relationships had become. They were feeding off me and I naturally had so much energy that I didn't realise it until they were disconnected and I felt all that I had been giving to them flooding back to me. It was startling.

All the energy that returned to me through this process was fairly quickly redirected into an ambitious publishing schedule and these books are part of what was born through that energy. Instead of the work reaching a select number of students, those who have the courage, commitment and responsibility to pick up this book, work through it (it isn't easy going at times, I am sure) and value the teachings enough to really take them in, will be the ones that I reach. I always benefit from spiritual teaching to the extent that I am willing to do the work necessary. I figure this way, those that are mature enough will benefit from what I can offer, and I won't be wasting my time or energy, or unintentionally denying those that really do want what I am offering. It just happened that way. The rage helped me shift out of what I was doing into a more intelligent and efficient way of operating and it is my sincerest wish that whoever can genuinely benefit from these words will receive it.

As we encounter rage, there will be destructive aspects to it. If we do our emotional work and learn to honour the rage that we feel, rather than dump it or direct it at another, it can become a useful source of energy for change. It isn't trying to destroy us, although any unresolved fear of our anger will certainly have to be worked through before we feel safe enough to approach the honest experience of rage within us. It won't feel pretty at the time. We will need to be centred in our hearts and held in loving containment by higher beings that can deal with that sort of energy – like Sekhmet. Then we can become constructive in the experience of rage.

In goddess traditions from all over the world there is always a fierce face of the Divine Feminine. She is the one who refuses to put up with human beings using their free will in ways that do not serve life. She speaks through the body and she will yell, scream and cry at injustice and suffering, particularly at those that have the power to do something about it and do not do anything. She is the internal cracking whip that compels us to act, flow, surrender, offer a contribution, share our resources and be honest, kind, furious and determined not take it anymore!

The more conscious we are in our bodies, the more connected with are from the heart to Mother Earth and divine love, and the more we may find rage within. It may seem counter-intuitive that the more love we have, the more anger we have. But, this is sacred rage we are speaking of and if we have great love and a desire to be of great service in this world, we need fuel for our divine fire. Raging against what destroys rather than nurtures life is the fire that truly passionate world servers use in order to have the strength to stay on the path and not just throw their hands in the air in defeat, believing it's all too much to deal with, so why bother. The sacred rage within is transformed into the energy and the drive to serve love that empowers them to keep going.

Our rage might be about being chained to a desk, like an animal in a cage, expected to perform so unnaturally in artificial lighting for eight hours a day, while our body is increasingly shut down and stultified. It might be rage at the blatantly stupid decision of a politician to dump toxic material onto a beautiful reef or remove protection from rainforest areas. That short-sighted, greed-driven decision might make you incandescent with rage – I am pretty sure it is not just me! You could rage because you feel like you always have to be kind, polite and spiritual when you really just want to stand out from the crowd and scream at the top of your lungs about something or other, and soon!

Rage is fierce, and when it is channelled and contained through the presence of Sekhmet, sacred and holy. You'll know the difference between sacred rage and plain old ego-driven rage, because the ego driven emotion will be all about you being right, make you feel justified in behaving in some quite appalling ways (believing the end justifies the means) and it won't change anything. Ego driven rage is about keeping things the way you want them to be. Sacred rage is about shifting the status quo, letting go of control and allowing the force of healing change to flow through you. You will feel the power of it, but it won't make your ego feel powerful! If anything, you will feel exceptionally humbled by it because you will recognise the hand of the Divine working through you and you will just do your best to stay in your heart while staying true to the compelling urge to take action and do whatever it is you are guided to do. Sacred rage is the healed energy of empowerment that we can tap into as we heal our old, toxic relationship to anger and rage from the past, opening up to become an empowered vehicle for divine justice – remember, Sekhmet loves Ma'at and detests evil! Sacred rage serves truth and denounces untruths.

It is essential for healers to have access to their sacred rage because, amongst other things, it prevents us from falling asleep! One cannot become complacent, comfortable, inert or bored when the fire of the Goddess burns in the belly and sends a torrent of healing energy to the heart and head! One has to do something with all that energy. We have to shine, glow and share in order to know truth, speak kindness and love! We have to be alive and in doing so, our divine essence can take root in the world and grow. This is the whole point of us being here in a body in the first place.

May you feel the loving fire of the Holy Mother within you, be ever more deeply moved with passion and clarity into your life path and purpose, and absolutely, from the depths of your heart, roar with love.

FIRE AGATE (PRESENCE)

I was captivated when I first saw fire agate. It was a bit like I imagine the first human being to see fire might have felt. There was some kind of magic in it, and I couldn't wait to hold it and feel its energy (I expect this was a more pleasant experience than the first person to try and do that with actual fire). It held the coolness of agate and the stimulating heat of fire.

The colours are not particularly vivid in fire agate, it tends to have a more earthy appearance but is very beautiful. It features tones of red and brown, and sometimes quite subtle grey and white. When it is polished, it can look like a living fire is whirling underneath the sheen, within the crystal. The bands of colour bring a sense of movement like that of living fire. It truly is a stunning stone. It is relatively inexpensive, though not always easily found.

Fire agate brings energy to the lower chakras, which is incredibly helpful for those on the spiritual path who may tend to dwell in the upper centres and are learning to bring our heavenly natures down to Earth. If you have loads of ideas, a passion for many different causes or areas of interest that you would like to study, or many different visions for how you might like to create your life, but they aren't translating into the physical world in a palpable way, then you can benefit from fire agate.

If you work in an office or any job where you use your mind a lot and would like to bring more energy into your body, so that you can sleep better, have more energy for exercise and doing chores or running errands without feeling worn out so that all you can do is slump in front of the TV at the end of the day, then fire agate can help you too. I imagine rather a lot of readers dashing out to purchase a piece to put on their spouses' desk at work! You might want to place a second piece in the lounge room (near the TV!).

If you have suffered from overexposure to violence, from visual aggression on television, psychic aggression from those suffering around you, the emotional violence of a toxic relationship or otherwise, then fire agate will be beneficial for you. It helps us deal with the effects of physical, emotional or psychological violence by gently but powerfully rebuilding your sense of inner strength and guiding you to remember that you not only survived, but are here reading about how to grow and flourish. You are more than a survivor; you are a thriver.

If you had, or still have, a tendency towards depression (which can be a symptom of chronic overexposure to violence and repressing the responsive rage), chronic fatigue, blocked creativity or energy flow, a sense of helplessness or hopelessness, or have many ideas but not enough energy to bring them to fruition, then fire agate may help to reignite the energy within that will push through the blockages. Emotion may come up. That is good! It is a sign that things are moving and you are going to be able to break free from stagnant patterning that probably hasn't been helping you create what you want anyway.If you already have a lot of inner heat and passion, fire agate can actually help you rebalance your inner fire and direct it towards the heart. The coolness of agate can naturally help you find your sense of purpose and clarity amongst the fire of your passion and emotions. Like Sekhmet, fire agate cuts through inessentials. It will help you find your focus so that you can act on what is useful and necessary in the now, rather than getting caught up in past happenings or stuck in visions of the future to the extent that you lose your footing and your ability to take constructive action in the present moment to ensure those visions are brought to life.

Fire agate helps to ground our presence, awareness and focus in the body. From presence we are able to feel greater clarity and make more helpful decisions about what needs to be attended to first. If you are one of those achievement-oriented people who perhaps make lots of lists, feels overwhelmed and then suffers from procrastination because you have given yourself too much to do, then fire agate can help you ground, come back to the now and get on with what needs to be accomplished so that your lists can actually get shorter rather than cluttered with never-ending, ever-increasing demands. Fire agate will actually support you in getting cranky enough to say 'no' to the pushy, driving part of you that puts inappropriate demands on yourself and in turn will help you to cut back on excess 'doing' so that you can focus your energy on what is meaningful to you. Instead of feeling busier and busier, running around in circles, getting less and less done you will do less while increasing your actual productivity.

If you have a tendency to feel lightheaded or spaced out, fire agate will encourage you to come back into your body and learn to feel how nice it can be to simply be present. If you have a lot of mental stress – from work, financial concerns, relationship dramas or family emergencies – then fire agate helps you draw up energy from the earth, through your lower chakras, to support you. If we don't do this we can unconsciously use up our personal energy reserves from the heart. If we are a giving sort of person, we can be in the habit of doing this without realising it. If it is happening, then we will end up feeling weak, drained and even as though we are coming down with a cough, respiratory issue, infection or virus. Boosting the immune system through adequate rest, relaxation, good nutrition and supplements will really help, but we also need to find a different way to source our energy and fire agate can help us access the vast reserves of energy that are available to us from the loving earth that supports such an abundance of life, so gracefully.

We might also have a tendency to go into our heads during a crisis, to try and work everything out. This can lead to headaches, mental exhaustion, feeling strung out, insomnia or mental anguish, particularly if the stress relates to a long-term condition such as an enduring illness or long-term relationship or financial issue. Again we need to learn how to come back into our bodies. Exercise can help us do this, especially if it involves bringing focus into the body as in yoga balance poses rather than mindless movement which can just add to our stress if we push too hard.

Connecting to our sensual, sexual and creative energy can also help rebalance us when we are too intensely in our thoughts. Fire agate helps to boost our sexual energy and our ability to be with that energy in a loving, accepting and grateful way that will draw us back into the present moment.

Fire agate has the dual effect of stimulating and grounding us. It can inspire you and at the same time encourage you to feel relaxed, comfortable and secure, so it is perfect for those of us that tend to worry rather than trust and feel good about our unfolding life path.

Fire agate is also known for its protective properties, again linking it to the power of Sekhmet. It creates a field of energy around the wearer or the person working with this stone and deals with negativity sent by others – whether it is done unintentionally or purposefully. It operates rather differently to the way other stones work. Some absorb negative energy, others simply deflect it, but fire agate blocks the attack and returns it to the sender with the spiritual awareness of what the sender is doing. Other stones may also help the receiver of an attack to let it go. Fire agate serves the sender through karmic teaching, which they can choose to learn from as they wish. Remember Sekhmet, who resonates with the frequency of fire agate, serves Ma'at (divine law, truth and justice) and detests evil (ignorance, and unwillingness to grow and serve the soul). Sometimes the only way for a person to learn is to become aware of what they are doing. We don't decide this for ourselves nor do we make the arrogant assumption that we can teach others their own truth. We can only ever live from our heart and express our light – the Divine takes care of all the rest. We can trust in that.

Fire agate is a powerful stone, but it is also gentle enough to use with children. However, note whether they become too stimulated or active with this stone, and if so switch to something softer such as carnelian which will bring grounding and protection in a gentler way. Alternatively, only let the child 'play' with fire agate in the mornings, once or twice a week instead of all day, every day. The same goes for sensitive adults who may find the stone strong enough to use from time to time, rather than every day.

MANIFESTING THROUGH PASSION

Could there be anything more exciting than manifesting through passion? It certainly sounds marvellous and it is, but it does come with a challenge.

For those of us that are cooler by nature – perhaps more analytical with a tendency to step back and reflect before acting – learning to tap into passion can be a helpful step towards wholeness and it can bring vivacity, life and the excitement of change and growth into our lives.

Those of us who are already quite flamboyant or excitable personalities, sometimes have to learn how to ground and temper our passion with the coolness of strategy, schedule and daily discipline. Perhaps this doesn't sound so exciting, but it does offer us the wonderful benefit of actually translating our passion into reality, rather than letting it fizzle out, or even worse, burn us out with emotional exhaustion and compassion fatigue – even though we truly want to make a difference in the world.

When it is balanced, passion is a powerful fuel for our life's work. Sometimes people imagine that if you love what you do, all the work goes out of it. It ceases to become work and is only joyful. That's not really true. Well, it's maybe a little bit true, but not completely.

When you are living and serving from the heart, there is going to be bliss and ecstasy, without a doubt. But there will also be deep, heart-wrenching, heart-breaking growth, so that we can keep growing stronger and more surrendered in divine power, and therefore more effective at what we do. That's why we need passion. Why would you bother doing the work and going through the excruciating agony even if it does bring ecstasy with it, if you weren't so completely in love with what you are doing?

Those that live with passion might strike envy in the hearts of many, but it does take work. True passion will have you bearing the moments when you have to work and you don't want to, when you want to be free and escape and you have to bear the commitment of love, discipline, boredom, frustration, uncertainty or fear. Passion keeps you going when you'd just rather not. Passion can inspire and empower you to take leaps that you wouldn't otherwise think were possible, because you know that you have the breath of the Universe lifting you via invisible wings, because you are living your divine destiny.

If you don't know what your destiny is, don't worry. It knows you and is reaching for you, unfurling itself in grace through you, every day. You might not have a clear glimpse of it yet, but it sees you. It is your divinity. It is happening. If you don't yet know your great, grand, singular life passion, don't worry about that either. We might think it's a thing or a job, but sometimes it is something far greater than that.

A friend of mine – actually, the lovely woman I spoke about in the last chapter who is trained as a psychiatrist and is so very unassuming about how amazing she is – told me recently that she is looking for her passion. I liked her honesty. It got me to thinking about what my passion actually is. As I sat here writing this book, I thought of all the things I do – writing, teaching, singing, creating, composing, studying different types of metaphysical and spiritual teachings, going through heartbreak, dealing with disappointments, learning to identify and meet my needs and wants, playing in nature, walking on the beach, talking with God, dancing with the Goddess, channelling, healing, lying in the sun, travelling, doing yoga in airports, dreaming, manifesting, dealing with the cat throwing up fur balls in the morning, choosing what to have for breakfast and having gratitude that those last two things don't happen too close together. All of these things from the apparently most mundane to the apparently most precious and rare, are all about honouring life. To me this means accepting that the purpose of life – from my little perspective and for the purpose of my unique, passionate life path – is the enlightenment of the human soul. That is my passion. It is the great burning love affair from which all other passions emanate and that all other passions serve. The divine awakening of the human soul is the reason people tell me they love me when they meet me when I am working. Often the words just burst out of their mouths and I can honestly respond by saying I love them too. Because I do. I love the soul. Your soul. I want it to burst aflame with divine love and for you to know it is holy.

However, there are times when passion is hard to access. I am sure you have had those moments. You are in the thick of a challenging growth spurt, everything seems topsy-turvy and you really can imagine dropping all the balls you have been struggling to keep in the air and sneaking off for a vacation on a tropical island where there is no phone coverage and no demands upon you (apart from what bikini to wear and which part of the beach to lie on). When my best friend or I are having 'one of those days' we often remind each other how lucky we are to have the passion for our work that we do. It is a treasure, even though there is heartache in continuously trying to bring this passion to greater and greater manifestation. Nonetheless, we are grateful for it and deep in my heart I wish that each being who wants to discover their passion may be beautifully and perfectly led into it.

HEALING PROCESS

The healing process below is strengthening for those that are open to receiving more divine support, energetic fuel for passion and the restorative, supportive, cool, balancing earth energy of agate, to further their discovery and manifestation of their passionate purpose.

You'll need a space that feels private and comfortable for your body. Remember to turn off electrical devices that aren't necessary for your healing ritual. You may wish to play rousing music that you love in the background, so long as it doesn't disturb your focus. Having a cushion or blanket handy is also recommended for later in the healing process.

You can have a small candle burning. You will also need your fire agate crystal and/or the crystal mandala. If you have an image of Sekhmet that you love, or a statue or necklace, feel free to bring that into your sacred space and place it on your altar too.

Your altar can be a table that is cleared for this ritual and is afterwards restored to a resting place for feet and coffee cups! If you have a dedicated space or small table for your healing work, then do use that, but you can still work with this healing process even if you do not have such a space set aside.

The Process

Light your candle and place your crystal and/or mandala and any other sacred object/s for your ritual healing nearby.

If possible, start by standing with your two feet at hip width and your legs strong and steady on the ground with your feet feeling connected to the earth beneath you. Don't lock your knees, keep them strong and straight, but naturally so, as forcing the joints to lock will block the energy flow. If you cannot stand up or it just doesn't feel right to do so, sit in a way where you can really let your awareness drop into the lower half of your body so that you can feel connected to the earth element beneath you.

When you are ready, say the following aloud, "I call on the Crystal Angel of Fire Agate and ask for your protection, grounding into presence, passionate fire and restorative, cool containment."

Close your eyes or gaze at your crystal or mandala, and be aware of the energy of the earth reaching up to you. There is cool, soft agate, strong and restoring, circling around you from left to right, swirling gently and holding you safe.

Then there is the heat of the molten core of the Earth, the power of fire rising up in a swirling, living energy of red, orange and white, and bringing life-force all the way up from the soles of your feet to your belly and then up to your heart. It circles around you from right to left.

Allow yourself to see, sense or feel the cool grey of the agate mixed with the red, orange and white tones of the fire energy. Allow the fire to go where it is needed and the coolness to go where it is needed, in perfect balance within and all around your body in your greater energy field. You may sense this consciously or you may choose to just surrender and allow it to happen naturally.

You may now like to sit down, if you have not done so already, and close your eyes and relax into this process for at least eight slow breaths, in and out.

When you are ready, say the following out loud, "I call upon Sekhmet, ancient one of power and light, who loves unconditionally. I call upon your radiance, She Who Loves Ma'at and detests evil! She before whom evil trembles! Bring me your healing, ancient mother, bring me your strength, your truth and your passion, through unconditional love, so be it!"

Become aware of a burning sun that appears above you with a red lioness face within it. This is Sekhmet. She may gaze steadily or roar. Just notice her with reverence and respect. She will appear to you however she chooses.

Allow her light to shine and be with that light in whatever way feels best for you. It may be that you step into her light, that it shines into your heart or any part of your body that has been subject to disease that arises from blocked anger or suppressed rage. It may be that her light turns into fire and burns away cords of connection to toxic relationships or situations from the past. Just be with what is happening, whether it is fully conscious for you or not.

Relax into this process for at least eight breaths.

When you are ready, say from the heart, slowly and with feeling, "I now choose of my own free will and through the Divine Mother Sekhmet's power, to purge and release any attachment, entity, memory, attitude, belief or thought form, as well as its past, present or future effects, that are holding me back from the recognition and full expression of my highest divine passion in this lifetime. I choose to release any shame, degradation, suffering and injustice that I have experienced or witnessed. I choose to claim my passionate purpose and devote myself in service to the unfolding of my divinity upon this Earth, above all else. All that is in my life serves this as I serve life. I give my permission, from the heart and in the protection of unconditional love, to Sekhmet who loves me unconditionally, to bring me the blessings and healing that I need so that this may be so. Through the light of Ra, the passion of Sekhmet and the unconditional love of the Universe, this is now so."

Breathe in and out for at least eight breaths as you allow these words to resonate and be consumed in the fire of Sekhmet. You may experience feelings or sensations as this takes place. Just be with whatever happens for you and know that it is as it should be.

When you are ready, repeat the following words aloud. Say them with breath and intention to allow that energy to build within you. When you have said the phrase, finish with a noisy breath out and stick out your tongue! Then repeat the process again and again for at least eight times, until you feel that it is enough for you. With this exercise you are building the energy of Ra (the solar energy, the Sun) who contains Sekhmet, and Sekhmet herself who burns with the passionate light of Ra, in your energy field. It is the balance of power and containment that will help you burn through any obstacles on the way to finding and/or furthering your divine passion. Sticking out your tongue allows for a release of energy as the divine energy emanates within and causes a detoxification process to begin.

The phrase is **SEKHMET RA** (sounds like SECK-MET-RAH).

When you have finished saying your phrase, you can sit, stand or lie down, whichever feels right for you and say the following, "I give my body permission in this sacred space to release the anger, rage and emotional reactions that have encouraged the suppression of those feelings, from my body, mind and energy field. I do this now in the grace field of divinity. Help me access the true fire of my nature, tempered with cooling grace, so that I may serve fearlessly in the world and live my truth in all of my relationships. For the greater good, so be it."

When you are ready, be brave and allow your body to move or rest. You might feel a cool field of energy sucking the toxicity out of you. You might feel quite unwell whilst this is happening, but you will feel much more well again afterwards, so stay with it if possible. You might feel like crying or yelling. You might like to scream into a pillow or blanket if you are worried about disturbing your neighbours or family. You might feel like jumping up and down or thumping the floor (again a cushion or blanket might be handy here). You might feel frozen solid. As big or as small as your response might be, just be with it without judgment.

When you are ready, simply come back to your breath and rest for a moment.

Finish your ritual by placing your hands in prayer at your heart and say aloud, "I am cleansed. I am blessed. My sacred rage is completely acceptable to me. It shows my truths and I accept these truths without fear. I am supported by the Divine and by life, in taking action based on my truth that serves life and love. By the power of Sekhmet, this is so."

Bring your hands up to your forehead in prayer position and bow your head lightly to your fingertips. When you are ready, simply clear your space and gently, in your own time, return to your daily life.

After this healing process, which is quite powerful, you might have anger or other issues arise for no particular reason, or quite strong dreams. Try not to judge yourself for this and take time to have a salt bath or ocean swim, as you gracefully and gratefully let your body cleanse itself. You will feel so much better for it in a few weeks or even within days. You might like to journal your anger or simply dance or move your body as you wait for the rise and fall of emotions to take place. Please notice if you feel more clarity about changes needed in your relationships or life situation and give yourself permission to take action, gently but firmly, as needed. If you feel drawn to repeat this exercise again it might be best to wait for a few weeks to give yourself time to adjust to the healing effects.

4.

SARASWATI (SOUND)
AMMONITE (SPIRAL)

MANIFESTING THROUGH WORD

Spirals of light radiate from her in all directions. She issues the word and worlds are formed according to her intent. Energy rises and expands, transforming into new realities, again and again. With her every sound, worlds end and are reborn. Her power is absolute.

SARASWATI (SOUND)

I have felt a particular soul affinity with Saraswati, the ancient Vedic goddess of sound, healing and wisdom, for a long, long time. I have noticed that my closest friends also have a soul affinity with her. Perhaps this is a matter of like attracting like. Whether male or female, my nearest and dearest soul pals tend to be musicians or dancers, interested in spiritual knowledge, usually writers and profoundly moved by sound through music, mantra or word. Thinking of four of my closest friends (two male and two female), I am intrigued at how we have all this in common and yet we are all so different.

Sound healing, the terrain of Saraswati, is certainly becoming more and more popular as a surging forth of awakened sound healers and crystal healers occurs. Crystal healing works with vibration through sound as well. It is not easily audible to the physical ear, although the sound of crystals can be heard clairaudiently by some or felt intuitively by others. If you have ever experienced sound through a thumping great bass speaker, you know that sound can be heard *and* felt, both emotionally and physically. When I work with my crystal bowls for music and sound healing, people certainly feel them very strongly, as well as hear them.

If you are a healer, someone who loves music, dance, books and learning, or are interested in the power of your words and how to use them to manifest, then you are connecting with Saraswati. If you feel drawn to sing, to learn music, to study or to tap into your own wisdom, then she is calling to you also.

One of my favourite spiritual mentors, a wonderful English woman who is absolutely hilarious, naughty and utterly unique, once told me that as soon as someone said to her, "Oh you can't do that," about anything she wanted to create, her instant response was to say (at least inwardly), "Watch me! I'll do it!" We both laughed at this, recognising the rebellious streak we have in common. She is a true Saraswati woman. She writes, teaches, manifests and tunes in to her intuition to help people in business, in spiritual growth and in all areas of life really. She marches to her own beat and chooses to live according to her own values, one of which is to help people find their truths. Saraswati is connected to the throat chakra in energetic healing and making choices based on our own values – whether another really understands them or agrees with us is irrelevant. Her work honours the power and grace that Saraswati emanates.

There are numerous stories of Saraswati in the ancient Indian teaching stories or Vedas. One story that appealed to me is about her and her husband Brahma. Saraswati and Brahma are offered a gift by some devoted priests who wish to create a sacred ceremony for them. This special event is to happen at the exact moment of a very rare and powerful planetary alignment.

Brahma is delighted! It will be wonderful to be so honoured! He tells his wife of the details and the importance of the exact timing and she agrees to receive the gift of the ceremony. She says that she will be there and gives her permission for the preparations to go ahead. Enormous effort goes into those preparations as the great ceremony draws near.

On the day of the ceremony, Saraswati is preparing herself in her temple, whilst the priests, attendees, helpers and organisers swarm about to have everything just right, and in perfect time with the auspicious planetary alignment. At the site where the ceremony will occur, Brahma sits upon his throne, ready, waiting and a bit nervous as the clock is ticking. The essential timing is a narrow window of opportunity that cannot be missed or repeated, and his beautiful wife is yet to appear. Nervously he instructs an attendant to run with a message to his wife so that she remembers to be on time.

The attendant runs to the temple room and even more nervously knocks on the great doors, and calls out, "Dear beloved Saraswati, please forgive me for bothering you, but Brahma says to remind you that it is almost time to start!" Saraswati languidly calls back, "Yes, yes, I know, I have said I will be there."

Brahma receives the message and is satisfied for another minute or so, but as the final minutes pass by there is still no sight of Saraswati. Many people have gathered to witness the event and with the empty throne beside him, Brahma becomes very nervous. He sends more attendants and receives the same return message from Saraswati. Still her throne remains empty and the planetary alignment is about to begin! She is nowhere to be seen.

In the final moments, all the people are gathered, all the priests are ready, even the gods (of which there are many in the ancient Indian tradition) have all gathered to witness this momentous event. Everyone is there. Everyone! Except Saraswati!

Brahma checks on the time again. Only a moment left! He calls one of his attendants and says, "Quick! The alignment is about to happen at any moment and my wife is STILL not here! Run and find me a replacement wife who can sit at the throne beside me, so that this great ceremony and all the good fortune it will bring, can take place! Hurry!"

The flustered attendant rushes through the crowds and sees a young woman. He grabs her hand and says, "Will you come and help Brahma? He needs you!" The young woman is shocked to be called upon but agrees and she is thrust into Saraswati's throne, just as the priests are about to begin.

As the priest draws breath to begin the ceremony, right at the moment of the alignment, Saraswati appears with absolutely precise and perfect timing. She moves to take her throne beside her husband and sees it is occupied by another.

I imagine the expression, 'you could have heard a pin drop' would apply here.

Brahma looks at her, horrified. The crowd is mortified at the embarrassing situation and the young girl is terrified. Only the other gods seem amused and snicker away in their front row seats.

Saraswati rises up in full anger and demands to know why her throne is being used by another. Brahma huffs and puffs and tries to blame her for arriving at the last minute but Saraswati will not have any of it. The gods pipe up and tell her to stop fussing and she turns to them with a series of reprimanding statements that teach each of them not to disrespect her in a traumatic, though seemingly far-fetched way. The gods scoff at what she has said, declaring it impossible. Of course, many lifetimes later it does occur and they sing a different song in the end, but for now, they don't believe her words.

The girl however comes to be blessed by Saraswati. Her pure heart and good nature in trying to serve is honoured by the goddess. She bestows a sacred honour upon the girl in return for her devotion. The girl becomes a patron goddess for those who seek spiritual enlightenment but don't have all the training of priests and monks, to be assisted on their divine path. The girl is named Gayatri and has a special mantra or prayer named after her so that all beings may claim enlightenment, if they so choose.

Saraswati departs leaving the room in chaos. All of her angry words, uttered to teach the gods more wisdom, eventually manifest just as she had spoken them. If Brahma been able to hold complete and utter trust in the word of his powerful, divine wife everything would have turned out rather differently. As it was, he was chastised and told that he would never again have a ceremony dedicated to him, and he is not worshipped with ceremonies in the way other gods are in India. Poor Brahma! But Saraswati was not to be doubted. It seems the old saying is true – hell hath no fury like a woman scorned.

This story teaches us something of the power and grace of Saraswati. Her teaching is that we are to hold absolute trust in divine timing, even if things seem to be 'of the eleventh hour' and getting very close to deadline. Divine timing happens at the right time. That's that. It doesn't happen earlier, and it doesn't happen later. If you are anything like me, with a tendency to want to jump on in and sort everything out as swiftly as possible, and perhaps find it difficult to sit back in chaos and let each part of the process have its own time to rise and fall, then this is a particularly important lesson.

If you have a visionary ability and tend to see the writing on the wall for people, places, situations or relationships – as I also tend to do – restraint, patience and the ability to allow all to unfold in its own time is another of Saraswati's teachings. If we try to rush and force things to happen before time, it can get messy! I have had many experiences of this and I realised, over time, that I was creating issues where there need not be any. Being raised as a take-charge, can-do kind of woman, it took a long time for me to learn when patience was needed as opposed to action. I had to develop trust in divine timing. As guidance has said to me many times, "What is the point in rushing for a bus, if it's not going to be there when you arrive?"

When we push rather than trust, karmic lessons can be brought to bear to teach us things that we possibly wouldn't have needed if we were just able to hold absolute trust that when we ask something of the Divine, the response will come in the perfect way and in the perfect time. If you have been guilty of pushing and shoving rather than graciously allowing, and I count myself in that category, don't worry too much. It might not make your life easier, but the Divine has a way of turning anything into a lesson that can ultimately be helpful. In the case of Gayatri, the young woman who did her best in the situation at hand, great blessings were evoked and those blessings are still serving millions of people who chant the Gayatri mantra for enlightenment every day, helping to heal and awaken the world.

To receive the blessing of Saraswati, trust is paramount. It is easier to trust when we remember the power of sound, which Saraswati made very clear through this story. The utterances that she made were not believed possible by the gods who received her words. They were arrogant and scoffed at her. Yet events conspired so that the apparently impossible was made possible and did occur. Great learning and wisdom happened through those experiences. There were plenty of challenges in the situations that arose too, all through which learning could take place. In this story, Saraswati teaches us that what is said with clear intention will be. It might take us on unexpected journeys, it might cause chaos, upheaval and even great personal challenges on the way to the fulfilment of the manifestation, but it will happen. She is not a force outside of us. She lives within us. As human beings we have the power of sound within us, too. We might scoff like those gods before their learning, and believe that something is impossible, but nothing is impossible. The flow of time makes things possible. We have to trust in that, learn patience and have respect for the creative power of the word.

This is one reason why we need to grow an awareness of our words. The teaching, 'what we speak about we bring about,' is based on the understanding that all creation begins with sound. In the Rig Veda, a sacred text predating Christianity by more than a thousand years, and also in the Bible, this teaching is summed up fairly succinctly with the statement, "In the beginning, was the word."

Sound is more palpable and powerful than light in moving through water. Think of the depths of the oceans and how whales communicate with incredible precision in that vast space with limited light. It is through sound. We live and breathe within what appears to be a physical world but it is actually an astral field. The world appears to be made of air, water, earth and fire (and is, on one level) but if we were to see it at a higher level, all those elements of air, water, earth and fire – the building blocks of manifest creation – actually exist within a type of cosmic ocean. What we conceive of as reality, including the physical world and our thoughts, feelings, sensations, emotions and beliefs, takes form within a glue-like substance, like jelly or plasma, called the astral plane. In a way, we are all sea creatures swimming in a greater spiritual ocean. Beyond that ocean is the divine realm. It is the light from which even the astral field is derived. To heal or manifest in the world, we have to deal with the astral field. That is our environment and any progress we make spiritually or otherwise, happens according to the state of that spiritual oceanic environment through which we live and breathe.

I worked with light as a healer for many years before I worked more fully with sound. I always knew the words I chose were part of that healing process, but once I really began to work with sound with intention, using my words, but also mantra and singing, the power of the work leapt up to an entirely new level. I was shocked! I was also happy. And careful. I knew thoughts have the power to create reality, but words are like thoughts on steroids. Words are extremely powerful.

As I worked with sound in mantra – sacred words in prayer form to manifest certain realities – my own energy grew more powerful. I was the same soul I had always been, but the sounds were clearing, healing and rearranging the astral field within and all around me so that more of the soul light that I was could pour through into oneness with my body. As a result my spiritual potency increased. I was in my true nature as much as I ever was. As I grow, that is how I feel. I am the same, always the same, even whilst the form, the feelings, the body and the energy field that expresses what I always am, have been and will be, change rather dramatically. I just become more of what I am and what I have always known myself to be.

Working with mantra and sacred sound was changing my life, from the inside out. The more sensitive we are, the more we will immediately feel the effect of sound. Light can be very, very helpful and I find it is best to work with both light and sound. Sound often moves us at a physical and emotional level in a different way to light. Hearing a piece of music can transform your mood and make you want to dance. Now imagine adding intentional spiritual energy to that sound, with love for healing. It is quite a potent combination! As we become aware of this potency, we can become more aware of what we listen to and discern for ourselves what feels good.

Saraswati teaches us that even the most unlikely events can and will occur through clear intention and sound. There is a teaching from the beautiful, spiritual master Yogananda, whom we met in *Crystal Masters 333*, that karmic law states that every human wish must find fulfilment. This is such a potent teaching. It means that everything we wish for will ultimately come to be. It makes us realise perhaps, that we really should be careful what we wish for! This actually happens, right down to our smallest wishes and desires.

Recently I was invited to spend New Year's Day at my sister-in-law's house for a feast with family. I was going to bring something for dessert. I thought of a particular cake shop near to my previous address. They had delicious desserts and not being one to bake unless it is strictly necessary, I knew I could find something in one of their stores. I had only moved house a few weeks before and when I searched for the store locations on the internet, I could see there wasn't one anywhere close by. I tried to work out how I could get to one of their stores but found it all a bit too hard because they were all so far away. Eventually, I figured I could just find a cake shop locally and all would be fine.

A week or so earlier, I had tea with a new friend at a quirky bookstore/cafe on Bondi Beach in Sydney's Eastern Suburbs. We had a lovely conversation about all sorts of things, mostly spiritual experiences, and it was wonderful to meet someone who was so pure of heart, open and kind. She told me about her experience with a Vedic astrologer and said, "I would love for you to see him, I'll send you his details." I had always been so curious about Vedic astrology and within a day I decided to go ahead and book a session with him. As a trained Western astrologer, I was interested in comparing it to the ancient Indian method. The appointment was set for the morning of New Year's Eve.

As I took the long drive to his home for the session, I was curious about what he would say. It was actually extremely helpful and clarifying, with the expansive, natural spiritual focus that typifies India's wisdom traditions. A short way into my trip home after the session, I decided to stop off at a shopping centre where I felt I would be able to buy dessert for the following day and get some lunch. I did both of these things and was feeling happy and uplifted from my session and was contemplating all the astrologer had said.

I jumped back in the car for the long journey home to the northern beaches, switched on my GPS and drove out of the car park. Suddenly, I couldn't understand a simple instruction from the GPS. Was I supposed to turn left or right out of the shopping centre car park? I later realised the GPS was directing me to the left, but I got confused and thought I was supposed to drive straight ahead. As the GPS re-routed my journey I wondered why on earth I had got the directions so confused.

I glanced up and there on the left was a cake shop in the franchise I had intended to purchase dessert from! It was tucked away in a small group of shops just around the corner from the shopping centre I had been in. I had no idea one of those stores was so nearby, but there it was. I didn't stop because I was happy with what I had purchased at the other store, but I was stunned because here was the result of the manifestation I had earlier set in motion. Finding one of those stores, at the right time, randomly and unexpectedly in the right place fulfilled my original intention.

Things like this happen for me often, but they make me giggle nonetheless. Sometimes manifesting feels like playing a game with life. You put out an intention and wait to see how it will quirkily form and come back to you.

The more refined your astral field, the quicker manifestation can happen. The denser the astral field within and around someone, the slower and more laborious this process can be. The density of the astral plane is determined by the quality of the vibrations within our body and in the thoughts, feelings, emotions, belief systems and bodies of those around us. The thicker and heavier a belief, for example, the denser the astral field will be. If it is cluttered and full, there are obstacles and obfuscations. Manifesting with a dense astral field might be likened to swimming in an ocean when there is a mud slick, oil spill, thick seaweed, debris or perhaps even the wreckage of an old ship blocking the way.

The more fear-based our beliefs, the denser the vibration they create. Our soul may be filled with love, but if our bodies are clogged up with unprocessed childhood trauma or have been soaking up fear-based negativity from the world around without the relief of cleansing release, then our astral field will be too heavy and dense for the love of our soul to shine through and make a change. It can be frustrating to know that you are a divine and pure spirit when you are experiencing life as a trudging great effort to combat negativity and not feel defeated.

As unpleasant as it can feel, there is nothing wrong with this situation. I have been through it many times – the love that I felt was within me wasn't yet reflected in my life experience. It is just a part of our growth. We have to remember that the life we live today is not the whole story. It is just one stage of the process. Your soul is a shining divine light and it wants to manifest its presence in your life so that it is gradually infused with the soul's own qualities of joy, ecstasy and bliss. This is not a state of never feeling sadness again, which is not helpful, but a way of completely changing our orientation to life that frees us from our fear of living. However, we do have to do the work to facilitate this process. In this, Saraswati helps us with her healing power of sound.

Most of us have to deal with the energy of fear in our bodies that is very old. Survival fear that originates with our ancestors leads us to take rather than receive, to compete rather than encourage, and other outmoded behaviours that don't resonate with the soul vibration of love. Fear is slow moving, sticky energy. It tends to attract dirt, dust, and clutter. So, while what we want can begin to come towards us, in response to our intention, there is much more for it to get through in order to actually reach us. Sometimes what we want might be so huge, that we need to clear some space in our astral field by doing some heavy lifting in our inner work to clear out 'old wreckages' (For example, the residue of trauma from relationship breakups or family secrets.) If we don't do the inner work, it might take many lifetimes for what we are manifesting to reach us. If we don't see the world responding to our intentions, we might deduce that manifestation doesn't work or that we can't do it, when actually we just need to refine our vibration, make space and become more receptive to the creation that we have set in motion.

If you are a visionary person and what you are manifesting is nothing short of a completely different life to what you have experienced thus far – perhaps taking you from poor health and poverty into vibrant wellbeing and prosperity or from an office job that makes you want to pick up your computer and throw it at the wall in frustration to a vocation that fulfils your soul and breaks your heart with its beauty and sublime peace – then that is wonderful! It also means that you are going to need to do a lot of work on your astral field, within yourself, in your personal healing work, in the vibration around you, and in how and to whom you relate.

If you are resonating at a heavier density than what you want to manifest, because the energy around you in mainstream culture and the beliefs with which you were born are based more in fear than love, then you will need some healing before your dream can manifest in the physical world. If you wish to manifest something that resonates at a level of love, bliss, peace and trust, then I applaud you. I have taken this leap many times and will undoubtedly continue to do so. It is a process, not a one-off manifesting event. As we continue to manifest and evolve our consciousness, we become capable of living with more love and greater light. On each turn of the spiral, our inner world changes and so does the world around us.

I speak not only of changing ourselves but the world around us. Whilst I am not suggesting you try to change others (we each need to take responsibility for our own journey), it is highly likely that as you do the work of self-healing, your relationships are going to change. You might find some soul mates will be on the path with you deeply and for a long time. Others might not be able to tolerate the higher vibration of your frequency, and may even actively (though unconsciously) try to undermine your healing work to keep you at a vibration with which they feel more comfortable. This may be because they don't want to lose you but are unwilling to do the work on themselves to grow along with you. However, that is never going to work well in the long term and will breed resentment. Eventually you will have to be free to live your truth, even if that means some sad parting of ways. You will of course have space to attract more people of like-vibration into your life. It can be a sad part of the path, and also a joyful one.

When you do this work on yourself, the types of relationships you can enjoy expand dramatically. The experience of love deepens and becomes increasingly unconditional, pure and very vast. If your relationships lean towards mutuality, in that you are loving the world more and being more genuinely and deeply loved by people you encounter, then manifestation will happen in a more powerful way. When more than one person gathers to create something, magic can happen. When the extra arms, legs, eyes and heart are united in love, synergy happens.

Synergy is when the combined field of two or more things is greater than the sum of its parts. It happens in cooking and it can happen in group endeavours! The individual qualities of each part are enhanced by each other, creating something greater together. When the higher frequencies of love begin to replace fear and trauma in our astral field, we begin to attract – quite naturally – more helpful and synergistic relationships. Synchronicity and joy then become part of our natural way of manifesting, adding some variation to the hard slog that is more dominant in our approach to creation when we are operating in lower vibrational, heavier, denser astral fields. The Divine is always at work, always remarkable, always bringing you closer to your intentions, but when we are in love rather than fear, the process is more visible, immediate, electrical, wild and joyful. Will there still be work to be done? Of course! But there will not *only* be hard work to be done! There will be an experience of effortlessness and flow as well.

I experienced this with one of my most beautiful, long-term and devoted students. We write to each other and usually conduct our sessions through email. We are like old soul friends, writing letters backwards and forwards, and as a result a sublime relationship with the Divine and each other has unfolded within each of us.

I serve her with great love and she loves me deeply in return. No matter what I offer her in a reading – be it something that thrills her, repels and challenges her, touches her with gentle sensitivity, or confronts, disturbs and sends her reeling for weeks – she takes responsibility for her responses, deals with them and returns to me, ready to receive, again and again. She receives my spirit and accepts whatever it delivers. She loves me in a way that is more unconditional than typical. Her response allows me to be the Divine without restraint in her sessions. As a result of this, a very special spiritual relationship has developed between us, which has supported her in some tremendous steps on her path, and has done exactly the same for me.

I have known myself as Divine more through the work I have done with her because she is so open, willing and capable of receiving that from me. As I sit and write to her, I am often swept away by waves of energy so strong that I close my eyes as they roll up to heaven. Whilst in this ecstatic state, my fingers just type, somehow stringing sentences together and delivering messages whilst the energy flows. She feels this energy as if she is in the room with me when she receives the sessions. Some sessions are gentle, some are so strong as to be repelling for a time. Together, through the sacred relationship, we are lifted into increasing divinity and both our lives have gone through some powerful transformations. I suspect they will continue to do so through what I can only describe as the amount of God allowed to happen in our connection to each other.

I usually write the session in one sitting of an hour (or upon occasion two or three hours), but in one instance I wrote to her over a couple of days and one evening. The session typically unfolded as a spontaneous channelling where I just experienced it as it was happening and had no sense of what it would become. The sessions are always an adventure for both of us, you see.

As the session came through, so did the feeling that something important was taking place on the spiritual plane, and it would come through, directly pouring into the astral field of my mind, emotion and body. As I wrote, a spiritual name came through for my dear student. A spiritual name is a gift that is given to help us on our path. It contains – with the wisdom of Saraswati and her healing power of sound – a seed which will manifest into form when the beloved receives and uses the name. It is like a personal mantra. The name may or may not change over the course of a lifetime. Then again, we may not receive a spiritual name in this lifetime. If it is needed, you can be sure it will come to you at the right time – again, divine timing is Saraswati's terrain.

I was not in the habit of giving spiritual names, and this was the first name I had consciously given another whilst in this body, so it was special for both of us. The energy that came through for this name was incredible. I felt as though a portion of the sky had opened up and was reading the words as I wrote them with increasingly startled eyes as I realised what was taking place. The love that poured through me, which I feel again now as I write this, was so potent. I felt as though I was experiencing a divine birth. It was incredible. I knew the experience would shift this beloved's energy and open up a pathway for her to fulfil her destiny, part of which is to be a bringer of the love and wisdom of Saraswati through writing. She is a very talented writer already, and has an extraordinary ability to express herself verbally too. She has Saraswati's talent for words.

The session had already taken quite some time and I was due to go out for an evening of spontaneous music with my two close friends. I stepped back from the session flooded with love and practically floated out the door, determined to complete the session the following day before emailing it to my dear student.

That evening, the energy for the session continued. My friends and I have a particular way of jamming together. One feels something and starts, another joins in, then the other and we let the energy between the three of us become what it wants to be. We each have the ability not to force anything, but to come into deep oneness with each other to channel sound, mantra and music. It is always a blissful, special experience that leaves us sitting about in silence, grinning at each other like love-struck fools afterwards. Sometimes people come along and listen to our jams and just to be transported along with us.

During this particular evening, a cascading rush of piano melody, crystal singing bowls and the beautiful, haunting drums came with the spontaneous chanting of the Saraswati mantra and the new spiritual name of my beloved student, part of which included Saraswati's name. As the music and the love poured through, I was so grateful that something had prompted me to record it. The next day I finished writing the session and emailed it, with instructions on how to complete the naming process with a ritual, and an MP3 recording of the music from the evening before to accompany the ritual and give sound to the feeling that came through in the session. It was a beautiful turning point in our divine relationship and so very special.

Afterwards, I realised this had all happened on this beloved's 'naming day' from her religious upbringing and I couldn't help but feel Saraswati's signature in the perfect timing. Her signature is particularly obvious in the moments that happen, without us asking, without us expecting, with such perfection that we cannot help but realise the divine presence, with all its benevolent love and nurturing, is urging us deeper into manifesting our divine destiny.

We can use healing sound to help us refine our astral field so that the world within us and around us shifts, thus becoming more capable of manifesting the visions of our heart, but we have to be willing to do the work that comes with that. That means dealing with the emotions – anger, fear, loss, sadness – that will arise as we let go of what once was and open up to what can be. This might involve letting go of childhood programming or an identity or a status we once held on to. It could mean giving up things we once believed were important or anything else preventing us from being ready and becoming clear enough to receive more of our own light into this world where we really need and want it to be.

Grief can occur when what is being released is no longer helpful, needed or even really loved. Grief will be more powerful if what is being released is still loved, but is to be sacrificed on the altar of growth. What we sacrifice on the path of love is never a waste, never a mistake, but this doesn't mean it is an easy process. It can be very painful and we might have to call on all the reserves of truth and faith we have within us to bear the process of letting go.

If your manifestation involves not only you but many others – for example, if you want to create a spiritual vocation in which hundreds of thousands of people will be blessed and touched by your work (and why not think such bold, loving thoughts?) – you can expect to need to work on your astral field over and over again. Your energy field will need to grow clear, strong and powerful enough for the messages you are bringing through to be stable, direct and clear enough to be able to reach the astral fields of those hundreds of thousands of people. Imagine the depths of the ocean, especially if it is cluttered or polluted. Only the brightest sunlight can cut through the muck and penetrate it to bring light. If you want to reach others with your message, you will need your light to be strongly present in the astral field and able to shine through the darkness that may haunt some people, to bring light to their minds, hearts and bodies to help them on their path. Only when the light shines brightly enough can it cut through the mental confusion and doubt, the emotional fear and the superficiality of appearances on the physical level to bring a sense of peace, trust and love into the hearts of those you want to assist.

For your light to be strong enough to do this, work on yourself as the 'guinea pig' in the 'spiritual science lab' of life. This is how the work we do on ourselves can genuinely assist others. Those who can receive what you are offering will probably have already done some work on themselves too. Perhaps quite a lot. Of course, there are parts of the ocean that cannot receive the sunlight as it is just too dense for the light to filter through to, and that is part of life. There will be people with astral fields like this, who just cannot open up to the light as yet. We have to accept this and work with those who are able to work with us. We don't try to change nature as that would be foolishness, instead we learn to work with her ways.

In Saraswati's story, her words took lifetimes to manifest. This helps us to understand that our soul goals for growth can span over many lifetimes. This lifetime is complete in and of itself, yet it is also part of a bigger pattern. Remembering this can help us have more compassion for the things that we can't seem to master and to realise that we don't have to be everything, we just need to be ourselves. We are in an experience of greater soul manifestation. If you are the sort of person who dreams big, it doesn't mean your dreams can't happen this lifetime. The very fact that those dreams have come out of your heart suggests that perhaps you have already spent lifetimes working towards being ready for the manifestation in this lifetime. However, part of Saraswati's wisdom is in her patience. Her intention never waivers. She never doubts. She just waits, knowing the perfect time will come.

This means that everything happening in this lifetime serves your own heart-centred manifestation even if it is challenging at times. So, we can remember that what we speak about will manifest; it is only a question of to what extent and when. Even if the effect is not instant, remember that your words have power. Through this understanding, we can begin to be wiser, more careful, more intentional and more loving in what we speak of and how. Remember also that everything we speak of is directed out into the world and towards ourselves as well. Our words can be curses or blessings and when we lose track of what we are saying, there is always a chance to come back to our hearts and ask for forgiveness, mercy and compassion. Everything we say is a broadcast out to a very attentive, responsive and powerful universe. The Universe is a creative field and whilst we don't control it, we do have a part in co-creating along with it because we are a living part of its creative intelligence. Our words become threads in a living tapestry that is the life we are co-creating with the divine power of sound, care of Saraswati.

If you want to work on your astral field with sound, the healing process at the end of this and other chapters of this book will support you.

AMMONITE (SPIRALS)

Ammonite is the fossilized shell of an extinct species of molluscs. These ancient creatures once inhabited the world's oceans and their remnants are now found in marine rocks. The connection between water and the creative process is honoured in many traditions. Water is a powerful conductor of sound, which Saraswati teaches us is the potent, creative force. Water contains the energy needed to support creation, like the fluid in the womb of the mother. The combination of strength and fluid grace of water reminds us of the strength of intention and the surrender we need in all conscious manifestation.

The spiral formation in ammonite is at the basis of creation. It is the form that is replicated through our DNA, our chakras, and throughout nature. It is even seen in the spiral formation in which our Milky Way galaxy turns.

Ammonite helps to create a smooth-flowing energy pattern that is aligned with natural life-force. If you have a tendency to rush head first into situations and only later realise it wasn't such a good idea or that you have unintentionally caused a bit of ruckus, then ammonite is a great stone to have near you as it will ground you into the body and hence into the power of your inner connection with the natural spiralling energy of life. If you are meant to be an agent of divine chaos (and no doubt, some of us are just built this way – at least for now) then the divine impulse of love will become the guiding force of your actions so you will create upheaval as needed and remain in harmony with universal flow. If this is not your role, ammonite will help you avoid ruffling feathers unnecessarily.

If you have a tendency not to finish things you start, have lots of frustrating stops and starts in your creative process, or feel you have too much unfinished business in your life, then ammonite can help you clear the excess, focus on your priorities and find your way through to peace. If you have a lot of chaos within you or around you because you are going through major growth spurts, spiritually speaking (or even physically speaking – for teens, for example), ammonite can help you ground and find a calm centre within the storms of change.

Given you are reading this book, it is assumed you are a relatively deep thinker already and so this next point is unlikely to be an issue for you. However, it might be beneficial to know that ammonite also helps us get beneath the surface of a situation and find the real issue within. If someone has a tendency towards superficiality and skimming the surface, an unwillingness or inability to see connections between events and consciousness or is unable to learn from one's history and therefore repeats it, then ammonite is helpful.

The ability to look beneath the surface can apply to those of us on the healing path who are stuck seeing an issue in one particular way. In working with ammonite, we may sometimes find absolutely nothing but 'hot air' underneath an issue and realise all the drama is no more than habitual reactions firing off. In seeing this we can simply shift our perspective and choose not to empower the drama any further. Most often, we gratefully find an issue will just run out of steam or fall away of its own accord when we cease adding fuel to the fire. At other times, ammonite will help us understand our issue in a different light so we can get somewhere new in the healing process. Perhaps rather than thinking that a relationship issue is about not being good enough or the other person being selfish, we might just realise that our struggles in the relationship are because our fundamental needs aren't being met and the relationship just isn't healthy for us – or the other person.

Its grounding quality, makes ammonite helpful when you are working with big soul transformations. By their nature these can be rather chaotic and cause a lot of change and upheaval in your physical life as the soul seeks to express itself with less restraint and greater freedom. I recently had such an experience on a road-trip with my best friend who had moved from Sydney to Noosa. I was on the tail end of a North Queensland tour and we decided to teach a healing dance workshop that we used to do together when she was based in Sydney. Then, we thought we would hot-foot it to Byron Bay to explore, shop, laugh and play for a couple of days for a much-needed break.

In the months leading up to our mini-break, we were both unexpectedly and absolutely swamped with work. The time to organise the holiday and the workshop was becoming less and less and then, I had a dream. I dreamed that we both decided not to do the workshop and to just go on holiday instead! Considering we are both practically workaholics, this was a most surprising dream. However, a few weeks after the dream that is exactly what we decided to do. We may be borderline workaholics, but we still know how to relax and have fun! After a year apart, there was much excited, preholiday squealing going on before we met up. We missed each other a lot.

I had the lovely but not necessarily common experience of all my travel arrangements falling into place effortlessly. I travel a fair bit for work so I know this isn't always going to be the case and I was grateful. My flights were all on time and my luggage was the first off the plane. I knew I had an hour to wait for my pre-booked coach to take me up to the Sunshine Coast, but I headed down to the collection area, just so I knew where it was. I easily found the collection point and just as I did so an earlier scheduled coach from the same company that I had pre-booked with pulled up. I went straight up to the driver and asked if it was possible for me to take this coach instead of waiting another hour and he graciously granted my request. I texted my friend and it was more convenient for her if I was an hour earlier too. I felt as though the Universe was just giving me green light after green light for this little holiday.

It was so delightful to see my friend again. We talked, walked, talked some more, managed to stop talking enough to eat and then talked again. Time flew by and soon the hour was upon us to hire a car and drive down to Byron Bay. For those of you not familiar with Byron Bay, it is a spiritual, alternative, new age hot spot for Australia. On the easterly most point of the East Coast, it has a thriving energy. Around it are sacred Aboriginal initiation grounds and lakes. I was told that for the indigenous population the intense energy of the area makes it a place to pass through rather than to live in permanently. My music producer, whom I have worked with for over ten years, has told me that most couples who go to Byron do not stay together because the energy there is so strong it causes whatever is 'broken' in a relationship to come to the surface where it would have to be dealt with. All in all, having never been to Byron Bay before, I was very curious to experience it for myself.

My friend was all set to leave her family behind for two whole days, something I don't think has ever happened before! Eventually we were in the car, beginning our girl's weekend away for real. At that moment, something happened. Before I tell you, let me just say that we are both intelligent women that have managed to travel around the world, at times on our own, and are well able to find our way around!

However, from the moment we stepped into our soul-time together for those two days, there was a sense of chaos. It wasn't negative or disruptive, but it was unsettling (and somehow also hilarious). We managed to drive in the wrong direction. Twice. As in taking a turn, and then moments later, taking that exact same wrong turn again. We managed to take the wrong turn offs and all sorts of debacles. Somehow we did manage to get where we wanted to go and in pretty good time but with an overriding feeling of disorientation. Intuitively, I kept sensing spirals of energy being whipped up around us as though we were being lifted into a silent cyclone and spun about until it was hard to say which was up or down. It was as if our inner compasses were going haywire.

The next morning, before breakfast, my friend and I enjoyed our time and space to do our spiritual practice. We both loved Saraswati and spontaneously decided she would be the musical theme of our morning practice. I pulled out a Saraswati playlist I had used in a class and we set about our morning practice in our lovely, open, white and bright room at a small, boutique lodge in Byron Bay. In companionable ease, listening to the music and the breath, my friend stretched, danced and then rested, while I did yoga and meditation. During our practice, I had the overwhelming sense that our souls were in some sort of creative cahoots with each other. I recognised a lot of power flying about that room. I couldn't say what it was in logical terms, but I knew in my heart that we were healing and empowering each other as well as opening to the Divine Mother Saraswati and her ways of creative manifestation. I felt there was some underlying meaning to our spontaneous choice of Saraswati themed music for our morning.

We went off for breakfast and began our exploration of Byron Bay and the beautiful surrounding towns. We talked, meandered, moved unconsciously in spirals in our conversation and our movement. Through this whole, mostly playful, process we talked deeply and honestly and put something into action for ourselves at a deeper level. The changes that have been happening for both of us since that weekend are powerful and tangible. So much so, that even as we are thinking of planning our next trip, we keep wondering if we are we quite ready for it! Have we integrated all the change from this last weekend away? What would happen next?

The spirals of chaos I felt, accompanied us back to Noosa as we meandered all over the place again with more hilarious antics. These were actually the creative spiralling of our soul energy in creation, an experience of Saraswati herself.

On the way home, amidst our spirals of disorientation we managed to get where we needed to be and stopped off at Mooloolaba for dinner. As we wandered about the beachfront we saw a huge new age store that was having a half-price sale on all its goods, including many crystals. My heart skipped a beat, I said thanks to the Bargain Angels, and in we went. I gravitated straight towards a large statue, sitting on her own, and of course, it was Saraswati. I called my friend over and pointed her out. "I think she is for you," I said. I could see my friend fall in love with her on the spot! Some hours later, after dinner, we went back and claimed the statue and she now sits in my dear friend's home, as the patron saint of the wonderful healing work that she does in the world through dance, wisdom and music, which are of course Saraswati's particular gifts.

Those spirals, which ammonite helps us tap into, are the manifestation of the creative energy of Saraswati that sets creation in motion so powerfully that at times it may feel like it overwhelms our sensibilities. These are the same spirals in ammonite, though with the crystal they are grounded and anchored and thus, can be softer and easier to integrate. This is good to remember if you are having one of those days where you feel that perhaps you are going backwards, or things are falling apart. Those are the times when the spirals of creation are spinning so that sometimes we appear to be further from a goal than ever before but are simply at the beginning point of an ascending turn of the spiral, about to move closer to the goal than ever before. Ammonite reminds us that every turn of the spiral, every twist, no matter whether it seems to move us closer or further away, leads us to the centre.

MANIFESTING THROUGH WORD

There is an expression in New Age circles that what you speak about, you bring about. Sort of like you are what you speak (as well, perhaps, as what you eat). I remember my first spiritual teacher calling me 'clairvoyant' long before I had ever consciously considered that to be the case. I was at the very beginning of my spiritual studies in this lifetime and coming back to my heart after a rather dramatic divergence off into the world of academia to study law – not from passion, but because I was listening to the voices of social conditioning rather than my own inner voice at the time.

To hear this teacher, who I admired so greatly, refer to me as already awakened to some extent gave me a great amount of confidence and trust in the subtle forces within that were guiding me onto a very different path. Through her description of me, I gave myself permission to see myself as such. It wasn't long afterwards that the natural inner sight I had taken for granted when I was younger became more real for me as a young adult. I developed much more trust in myself and my perceptive abilities and my steps forward on my path became more swift, determined and sure-footed. Sure I had my stumbles, but I trusted my sense of where I was headed more often than not.

I learned that the words we choose to use about ourselves are actually rather powerful in creating our self-image. When that self-image comes from an open and loving heart it can be leaned upon to support our growth. To acknowledge my natural abilities and have hope that one day I could be as strong and powerful as I perceived my teacher to be, required me to have a positive and hopeful self-image. That self-image was supported by how I thought about myself and how I talked about myself to others. I found that the more I gave myself permission to accept and trust in the sense of self I was tapping into, the stronger I was when I encountered someone who wanted to try to undermine, control or straight out tell me who I was, as if they knew my heart better than I did.

Eventually, even through moments of self-doubt, my sense of self became strong enough that it didn't waiver, even when some years down the track, my own beloved teacher judged and criticised me for issues she only admitted were her own quite some time later. That was an extremely painful and challenging situation, though it proved to be one of most helpful pushes I have ever received to really trust myself above what anyone else may say, no matter how much authority I may have invested in them. Although it hurt at the time, I was extremely grateful for the grace that she demonstrated later on by apologising and being upfront about her behaviour. I respected that greatly.

Learning about the power of word from her, and from the teachers that followed, helped me develop and grow a sense of self that was strong enough to take the battering that comes with spiritual growth. You don't want to assume that you know everything – even yourself – so completely that you shut off to greater learning and wisdom, but at the same time, you don't cast aside your inner authority and unintentionally give others power over you. You can be open, you can even be willing to be uncertain or 'not know' a lot of the time and still be able to trust that if something just doesn't seem quite right that you will trust that inner warning.

HEALING PROCESS

If you are going through challenges, be they relationship issues with another, or with your own self, where you feel as though people are trying to tell you who you are, or what you are, and you need to find your own sense of self, your own truth, your own words and expression, then this healing will be helpful for you. You might simply be going through a test to see if you can claim the truth of who you are and express it. When a friend of mine told her mother that she was a healer, her mother responded somewhat caustically, "What, like Jesus?" Rather than being shut down by this, my friend coolly replied, "Yes, something like that." She claimed her reality and her knowledge of her abilities calmly and honestly. She didn't allow herself to be shut down, judged or shamed, nor did she try and make herself better than another. She just expressed and shared herself honestly in the world. As we give ourselves permission to do this, our path opens up to us.

If you are wanting to manifest something that is genuinely aligned with your soul path or if you are able to take an even more advanced attitude and are willing to allow your own soul to manifest itself through you, no matter what the ups and downs of the journey might be, then this healing will help you too.

The Process

Find a place where you can be still and undisturbed, with some privacy if possible. Either have a pen and paper or your journal with you. Healing music or silence is extremely important in this particular healing process. Choose what feels right for you. Take the mandala and/or your crystal and be seated, with your journal or pen and paper within easy reach.

Take a moment to come into your heart by placing your hands in prayer at your chest and closing your eyes. Breathe in and out for at least eight slow, conscious breaths and as you do so, imagine that your awareness can leave the day-to-day world behind as you open up into sacred space.

Say aloud if possible, "I call upon my higher self and the higher self of my higher self. I call upon Saraswati who loves me unconditionally. I call upon the Crystal Angel of Ammonite and the ancient spiral wisdom. I call upon the unconditional love, mercy and protection of the Divine Mother to assist me in soul-aligned manifestation now. So be it."

Take your time and write a list of what you want to manifest. You can create anything you want! Don't come from fear or lack, though. You will enjoy the manifestation process far more if you focus on what would feel loving, fun, authentic and beautiful to your own heart. We are designed so that our needs are taken care of as we blossom into our truths. We don't have to try to be other than what we are in order to have divine success in life. We just need to be ourselves. So be true to you. What would make your heart sing?

You may already be clear about what you would like to create or you may be open to be shown what the Divine has in store for you as you grow and heal. If you are uncertain of your list, then simply write "My soul manifests completely through me, as me, in unconditional love now." You can add this to your list if you wish. It is good to take your time with your list and keep it simple. It can be the most powerful when written as a statement of what is true rather than of what you want – For example, "Soul love is in my life and fills my heart now" or "Gratitude fills my heart for blessings of abundance and prosperity now."

Take your time with your list. When you are ready place it where you can easily read it.

Gaze at the crystal or mandala and gently place your right finger at the outermost point of the spiral. Go through the list of what you intend to manifest and one-by-one read each item out loud. At the end of each statement, gently trace the outer edge of the spiral all the way into the centre and pause for a moment breathing in and exhaling fully when your finger reaches the centre of the spiral. Then remove your finger and start again until you have completed your list. Remember you can do this process at any time and more isn't necessarily better. You can have one statement or twenty or more. It is up to you to choose what feels best for you at this time.

When you have finished your list say, "Through the blessings of the Divine Mother, and the perfect timing of divine grace, this will be so."

Put your hands in prayer and say the following mantra to anchor your practice at least eight times. The pronunciation guide is below.

OM EIM SARASWATIYEI NAMAHA

OM (rhymes with TOM) EIM (sounds like I'M) Saraswati (SAR-AZ-VAR-TEE) Yei (YAY) NAMAHA (rhymes with Yamaha).

When you are ready, simply bow your head to your hands in prayer for a moment and feel connected with your heart in gratitude for all the wonderful and empowering gifts that are coming to you to further your ability to serve love in the world.

Then simply clear your place and you are done with this ritual. Notice your words and thoughts in the coming days and weeks. If you catch yourself thinking negatively, just send love from your heart to your mind and reassure your mind that it is okay, as everything is already in the flow of change and creation. Be kind to yourself.

5.

ISHTAR (DEFIANCE)
ASTROPHYLLITE (REBIRTH)

MANIFESTING THROUGH DIGNITY

From the heavens she descended to Earth. The cosmos, her cloak, the star of Venus, her body, and the light of love burning in her eyes. Able to triumph even over death, she is subsumed completely into the power of love. For those that receive her, their light shines brighter and what is wounded comes to light so that healing may occur. For those that dare open their heart to her, the light of her loving gaze restores a divine remembrance of their true nature.

ISHTAR (DEFIANCE)

The ancient goddess Ishtar was known throughout various civilisations several thousand years before the time of Christ. In the Sumerian culture she was known as Inanna. The Phoenicians referred to her as Astarte. In ancient Babylon she was Ishtar.

In all of her guises, Ishtar is feisty, defiant and demanding. She wants to be adored, to love and be loved. When doors are closed to her through some rule or other and regardless of whether that rule has ever been thwarted or broken before, her response is to declare that if those doors are not opened to her, she will bust through them and kick them open if needs be, to have her way. This attitude allowed her to have life experiences that were denied to others. They were challenging but transforming. She does not shy away from the challenges inherent in her adventures but she also demands that she succeed. She is a bold and fearless goddess.

Ishtar was said to be the star we know as Venus, the brightest star in our sky, apart from the Sun. As Venus, she is always in progression, shifting her position as the morning star to become the evening star, in a continuing dance with the Earth before disappearing behind the Sun and rising as the morning star once more.

In ageless wisdom, Venus is recognised as a highly evolved planet that assists Earth like a sisterly, spiritual guide along her evolutionary path to higher consciousness. Ishtar contains this higher consciousness and light and is known as a goddess of love, fertility and sexuality, and also of war. Throughout the ages she has been loved, worshipped and feared, and her energy was believed to bring beauty but often great chaos and upheaval as well.

Venus holds a higher consciousness. Higher consciousness contains a higher voltage of divine electricity. The effects of an intense higher consciousness for those on the receiving end, depend on the finesse with which the consciousness is delivered and the state of the vessel that is receiving. Any issues and any talents, abilities or gifts, in the mind, body or soul of the receiving vehicle – be it a person or a place or a planet – will be amplified by the intensity of the higher consciousness. If there is just enough difference in the voltage of the giver and the receiver, then the shift can be helpful, uplifting, loving and illuminating. The receiver will feel better, more well, energised and happier. If there is a lot of disparity between the giver and the receiver, then the result can be less pleasant, even though that higher consciousness is essentially love. Like being burned by the sun, when exposure is too great for the receiving vessel the results may be painful. Instead of feeling uplifted, the receiver might experience upheaval, acting out, fear, terror, chaos or war. Instead of being drawn to the energy, they might feel repelled and want to get away from it. This is especially the case if the receiver has a lot of fear inside them that starts to arise in response to the presence of love and they are not able to stand it. Love is a powerful force. As strange as it may seem, sometimes more love is not necessarily more helpful. What is helpful is enough love for growth and healing. Enough is best.

This goes some way to explain the mixed responses that Ishtar and indeed most of the goddesses have evoked from humanity over the past thousands of years. As we heal ourselves, we are able to receive higher consciousness and experience it as nurturing. Sometimes it will evoke pain, yes. As we grow, we experience more of life and become able to bear it. To bear great suffering, be it our own or the suffering of the world as part of our greater being, and to bear the passionate yearning for the Divine that fills our heart with devotion, requires tremendous emotional, mental and physical strength. That comes with time and a willingness to meet with life as the ultimate spiritual personal trainer and build our divine strength through experience. This becomes possible if we believe that life always knows what will help us reach the next level, what will allow us to be served and to serve, and how to deliver that to us through our experiences. With the healing of self-acceptance and inner dignity that Ishtar brings to us, we become ready, willing and capable of receiving all the divine radiance that she wishes to shine into our hearts through the unfolding of our life journey. We don't personalise 'negative' events in our lives, we see them as opportunities through which we are being offered the chance to become all that we can be. By the hand of a great and loving intelligence.

In the teaching stories of Ishtar, she is dedicated to the expansion of consciousness, which she knows to be love. She descends to the underworld, the world of death, and is able to emerge from that experience back into life again, just as Venus descends in the west as the evening star, is not visible for a time and eventually rises in the east as the morning star. For Ishtar this is not a near-death experience, it is a death experience, but one that leads to life.

Even though she is the Queen of Heaven and Earth, Ishtar was told that she could not have dominion over death. That power belongs to the Queen of the Underworld, her sister, Erishkegal. Ishtar refuses to accept that death would have power over her because she knows herself to be love – the ultimate consciousness. So despite every being and every law urging against it, she strides off to the gates of the underworld and pounds on the doors, demanding they be opened to her. She has the energy of command so that nothing is withheld from her. She demands not as a child, for she is most willing to bear the suffering that comes with her requests and take responsibility for her growth through that suffering. She demands as a lover of life who defiantly pokes her tongue out at rules and tradition, and asserts that she will know and experience all that is, for she is worthy of all of life and she will have it! Not only that. She is love and therefore nothing will tame her spirit or be the 'end' of her.

This attitude is rather unusual and the terrifying gates of death that lead to the underworld are not accustomed to having goddesses threatening to kick them down. The gates open and Ishtar steps into what proves to be an adventure more challenging than even she anticipated.

Life can be like this at times. We want to manifest something. We want our life and the way we live, to be bigger than the fears that dominate mass consciousness. We don't want to be limited by the fear of not having enough, fear for our survival or fear in any form. We may try to shrug it off and live a different way, rebelling from our hearts against all that would say to us, "You cannot live with the freedom and playfulness and abundance that you want, you just can't!" In our hearts we declare, "But I will! I cannot give in to fear! I don't know how it can work out, but it has to!" When we not only think this, but start to believe it and act on it in a way that thwarts mainstream consciousness and the mass belief of what is possible, then Ishtar is alive and kicking in us.

I went through something similar when I decided I didn't want to pursue law as a career because I felt like, for me, it would end up being like a living death. I remember standing in a shopping centre, gazing at some lovely, new furniture. I was at the point where I wanted to move out from the nest of my family home and live the independent existence I enjoyed when travelling. I wanted to live my own life, but to do this I would need things. Like a bed. And a lounge. I looked at the price tags of the items I loved and sighed. I couldn't imagine ever being able to purchase something so expensive.

For a moment this thought lodged in my mind: "If I want these things, I will have to stick with law as a career so I can earn a good income." Very quickly, the Ishtar-like rebellion kicked in. "No! I want wealth, but I want it on my own terms. I want it from the heart. I will not sell my soul to acquire it! It will come to me! But in a different way!" In that moment, much to the consternation of my family, I decided I would step away from law and put it behind me.

My loving grandmother was trying to keep up with all the changes taking place in her granddaughter who was on the cusp of young adulthood. When I told her I was not going to take up law as a career and was going to do spiritual work instead, she didn't quite know what to make of it, "Are you sure you don't want to be a barrister, Alana? You'll have champagne tastes on a beer budget!" I would sigh and reassure her, that certainly I would be okay and felt no regret about casting law aside, even after spending the better part of five years completing my university degree. It was true. I had no regrets about that decision and have not once imagined my life could have continued down that path with any degree of happiness. Whenever my grandmother noticed me with my head deep in some book on witchcraft or chakras or hear me talking about spirit guides, she would say, "That's fine Alana, but do you still love Jesus?" My response was yes, I most certainly did. Eventually, she saw that I was becoming happier and healthier despite the struggles my choice brought up for me and she came to some peace with my decisions.

I had an Ishtar-like determination to live life on my own terms, rather boldly too I might add, considering I couldn't see anyone around me living that way at the time. All I could see was hard work that mostly drained the life-force out of you and made you miserable and anxious, in order to earn enough money to survive. I dared to demand something different for myself but there was a price to be paid for that boldness.

So … Ishtar exercises her bold power of choice and descends into the underworld and has some unexpected prices to pay. At each of the seven gates something of great value to her is taken away. These things are most important to her – she can't imagine living without them as she believes they are part of who she is. She gives up her crown, her royalty, her powers of dominion, her physical vitality and strength, her arrogance and pride, even her spirit, until eventually there is nothing left. She is weakened, stripped bare of her powers and identity, until she is completely naked, far from her loved ones and the world she has known – alone in the depths of hell. She is then taken to meet her dark sister, Erishkegal, the Queen and Mistress of Death who rules the underworld. Erishkegal hangs Ishtar, who is in the throes of death, on a meat hook. There she hangs dead, for three days and nights.

My decision to defy the traditional way of life I was raised to believe in and claim my divine right to choose how I wanted to live, including my financial wellbeing, was in alignment with my heart. It was also a choice that couldn't manifest without a lot of transformation on my part.

Those of you who have gone through any kind of transformational process will already know it is something akin to going through a death. The process involves the death of who we once thought we were so that we can become a different, more whole, version of ourselves. That might involve a lot of pain, especially if the process of transformation involves parting with an identity or belief system we have used to support ourselves in some way. If we found we could love ourselves, so long as we never did anything we considered truly unacceptable, or we believed we were worthy because we had intelligence, or that we had worth because we were a lawyer, doctor, a good person who never got angry or a mother, and so forth, then you can pretty much assume that in transformational processes, those beliefs are going to be challenged.

It's hard to bear the loss of things we love. It might be a person we thought we couldn't live without or even the person we thought we were that has to be released so that we can become more of who we really are. This might mean accepting we are a less one-dimensional being and far more complex with darkness and light. That might be hard for us, or for those that expect us to keep behaving as we always have done, to accept.

Sometimes, it is not only internal change that occurs in the transformational process, but external change too. We might be forced to move or feel we have no choice but to end a relationship or stop seeing family members who are toxic to our health. In those choices, we have loss. There is also a chance for new starts, but there is loss nonetheless. To process loss, we need to grieve. Even if we are happy at one level to give up what we are releasing, it cannot be let go of without being mourned. That means pain, sadness, anger, grief and that is part of the healing process. It is not fun, but being stuck in the past and unable to move forward would ultimately be even less fun.

In terms of the financial part of my journey, I had essentially said to the Divine, "I want wealth through love, no other way." I was certainly not going to accept it through fear or by going against my heart and declared, "I just won't stand for that." It was rather a big prayer, when you think about it, but I didn't think about it much at the time. I just couldn't imagine being happy any other way. Like Ishtar, I just pounded on the doors that were closed to me and said, "I don't care if everyone else is doing something in a certain way. I want to get to what I want! So remove any obstacles right now and let me in!"

And, the Divine answered my prayer. And, it did not involve me falling madly in love with a billionaire and being swept off into a decadent lifestyle beyond my wildest fantasies. No, rather the powers that be felt my path would be better served through a different mode of transformation. I entered into a truly difficult and challenging time of self-healing so that I could actually exist financially in the world, according to what I had decreed. Do you think I had any idea what I was actually setting myself up for at the time? Certainly not! But would I have done it anyway? Absolutely. What other choice is there, really? Either live by fear or face it. Both are hard but at least the pain in the latter approach actually ends at some point and offers a different reality at the end of the process. I am, however, the first to admit this is easier to accept now I am somewhat further along in the process, than it was at the beginning when I felt like my life was going to hell in a hand basket. At the time it actually felt like my world had collapsed in on me and I had no idea how or if I was going to be able to continue on.

Life experience after life experience challenged me financially. Now don't misunderstand me, I received blessings too. Through it all I was somehow able to sustain myself, if at times just barely. Nonetheless, I was always okay. I could hardly bring myself to rest easy based on those blessings, due to the intensity of the fear being unleashed within me so that it could be cleared. I might have been okay in that moment, but what about the next day? And the one after that? Suddenly I wasn't dreaming of big, white lounge chairs with a hefty price tag. I was having nightmares of something far worse than financial limitation, I feared for my basic survival. What was most real to me, most confronting, most attention grabbing, was my belief in the struggle. I was actually facing my own internalised anxiety about money, control and survival. It was a powerful beast to confront. I thought I could simply decide not to live a life based on fear for my own survival and anxiety about money, both of which spawned issues of control and power. I had no clue how deep the genuine, at times deeply challenging, self-healing work would be in order for me to even approach the way that I wanted to live in the world. Before I could receive anything of the sort, I had to go through the process of getting out of my own way. Until I began to let go of what I had known, I didn't realise just how much I was in my own way! There were various entrenched beliefs and behaviours to break free of. I was willing to do the work when it came up, but I had no idea exactly what would be asked of me.

There were times when that journey was very, very difficult. At one point, I was living in the most expensive property I had ever lived in, had more debt than I had ever had, with a partner whom I knew was not particularly responsible financially and wouldn't be able to support me should I need it. For an income, I was relying completely on spiritual readings. One day, I realised I literally had twenty cents in my bank account and there was no clear indication of when I would earn any further income or how much it might be. A part of me knew that if the Universe was supporting me, it didn't matter whether I had twenty cents or no cents. If I needed something, it would come and I would be safe. At that level I also knew that I was manifesting my worst fears and testing myself to trust. I knew that if I could trust in the Universe then, when so many potential financial disasters hung on the brink of every moment, I would have attained a level of trust that was very powerful indeed. However, the power of the belief that control is required for one to be safe was still very strong in me at that time. So, despite my inner knowing, at another level, I was absolutely clutched by terror and fear.

That terror and fear took me into a phase of emotional struggle that lasted approximately eighteen months and manifested in daily panic attacks and a terror so overwhelming that I did readings for myself daily to try and calm my mind. The calmness would last for the duration of the reading but the terror would return in full force soon after. It was a living emotional and psychological nightmare. The only time I felt peace in my heart during that entire period was when I was doing readings for people, when I would then enter into a conscious connection with guidance and become focused on the other person. I believe it was the light that came through those readings, rather than the income, that helped me have enough trust (on some level) to face the fear over and over again until I could move all the way through it.

During that time, in fact throughout my entire life, I somehow managed to get by financially. If I need it, money comes. I have been supported by the Universe so that I can do my work. I was at that time too, although I was so blinded by fear I could hardly recognise it. When I needed money to go to a healer, it was there for me. When I needed to buy food or pay rent, I always managed to do so. In time, I became free from debt, got rid of my credit cards and felt more financially stable, if not quite yet at the point I originally envisioned when I made my declaration. However, I was out of the depths of suffering and was learning to trust and relax more. The more I did that, the easier the Universe could respond to me with what I needed. I hadn't quite managed to convince the Universe that what I needed was a lovely home in the Maldives where I could relax for three months of every year, adored by a loving, sexy and wealthy husband (for example), but I was getting by and I felt grateful for that. I was also so very grateful to have eventually been able to receive peace in my heart, so that the terror could give way to a more accurate perspective and the realisation that even if I had no clue how, and no immediate power to force a resolution, things could and would work out for me in whatever way they were supposed to and I didn't really need to worry about it.

As I continued through the process, I had to let go of lots of things I had been raised to believe were essential for feeling safe, strong and powerful. Like control. And also the belief that I always had to feel safe, strong and powerful in order to actually be safe, strong and powerful! At that time I had no experience of the new way, but I had a desire for it. I didn't know how I would need to grow and change to partake of the manifestation I wanted. I didn't fully realise that the manifestation could only happen to the extent that I grew to be able to receive it. Even though I was raised to believe that trusting the Universe to provide for me with absolute surrender was immature and silly (at best) or sheer lunacy (at worst), at some level I did understand that this was exactly what was being asked of me and it was okay to go with that. I could have what I asked for, but as to how it came to me, I just had to trust.

The idea of a descent into a dangerous and dark world through which we can heal and therefore grow exists in shamanic traditions and other transformational healing paths such as Jungian psychotherapy. The necessity for experiences that strip away our identities and attachments to the outer world, as well as the instruction gleaned in experiences of loss, grief and the death of the old in order to take on the new, is universally recognised. It is the same journey, with a different perspective, that Christ took through his descent into the dark night of the soul in the Garden of Gethsemane, his consequent crucifixion and his resurrection. This is the same journey Ishtar takes in her wisdom stories.

The descent and its associated death is the fertiliser for new life. It can be good to remember this when we feel things falling apart or slipping away at different times in our lives. Even if we haven't made some bold declaration, life still happens and sometimes we are just called to live bigger. That means some things – even if we have loved them and still do – will be too small for that bigger existence and will have to go. This is in service to our growth. We can sometimes get stuck focussing on what is ending and that is part of the grieving process. However, to hold even the faintest recognition at a deeper level that this ending is part of a greater beginning can provide us with enough hope to bear the experience of grief, loss, terror, pain or growing through the shadow of death as we are led into new life.

An underworld experience, or descent, might be triggered by a deep and overwhelming grief due to death, divorce, a tragedy or even the death of an identity (perhaps through children leaving the nest or a redundancy at work) that leads to disorientation, uncertainty and a deep questioning about who we are and what our purpose might be. Our underworld journey might happen through depression, a crisis of consciousness between our emerging spiritual path and conflict with our previous 'roles' of mother, good daughter, devoted wife, or an illness in our bodies or in the body or mind of a loved one where we feel helpless to assist.

For advanced souls, the journey into the underworld sometimes has no apparent outer trigger at all. The internal process is just as strong and real as if there was an external 'cause' but the advanced soul has the additional test of whether they will accept their call to descend simply by honouring their feelings, even though nothing seems to be wrong in their lives to warrant going into a transformational process.

In such cases, the soul is inwardly growing and this will at some point involve entering into darkness as a way towards wholeness. It can be even more challenging to be in this sort of situation. I have heard many times from clients that they would find it easier to accept the darkness they were experiencing if there seemed to be some sort of reason for it. However, there is a reason, it is just divine rather than physically visible. The growth that is being acquired through the experience is reason enough. The trust that is required by the person going through such an experience builds more divine power in their soul. If they are here to do healing work, for example, the soul needs power to be effective in that work. The dark night is likely to be part of their spiritual training. It can be a tough task not to doubt your sanity or invalidate your experience when there is no logical way to justify the darkness. Yet, the advanced soul will go through the experience and honour their inner truths no matter whether they seem logical or not. Ishtar is all about life and truth and doesn't give a hoot for logical explanations or justification. She can help us accept the truth of our experience without needing to explain it and without being able to rationalise it.

No matter what the apparent reason for the descent is, when it happens, you will feel it. Resisting it will eventually become impossible. If we don't go willingly when it is our time to descend, we will be forced to do so through illness, depression, injury or other forces outside of our conscious control. Sometimes, if we don't realise what is happening is supposed to be a descent, and do not work consciously with the feelings and experiences that come up for us, we can end up feeling almost zombie-like. Life doesn't hold the same appeal. We might fall into addiction to try and avoid the underground pull of inner orientation and inner healing, or criticise ourselves and wonder why we can't have more energy, be more focused, or more energised. We might have less energy for exercise, less interest in sex or go in the other direction and try to resist the process through acting out with excessive exercise, sex, shopping, drinking or socialising until those things become so destructive we have to stop, or some other crisis is evoked and we are forced to turn within.

It is said that when Ishtar descended to the underworld all sexual relations in the outer world halted. This speaks of the reorientation of our natural energies when moving into a deep healing crisis. If the descent is into something very challenging, we may need the energy we would normally use for socialising, play, exercise, sex, study or work to be redirected into energetically financing our healing process. This is temporary, but it can be difficult for those in our lives who may feel we have suddenly dropped off the radar or are no longer putting energy into a relationship. It is not uncommon when going through our own underworld experience to find that life ceases to function as per usual in the outer world. We can only do our best to explain this to our loved ones, so they might understand, even in part, what is happening. We can also pray that all involved will be guided through the process.

As hard as it can be, we have to trust in this process. There are no half measures in a descent. If we try to come out before we have been dead for three days, symbolically speaking, our new life won't have had time to form and the full healing will not have taken place. The full richness of the process needs time to occur. We need to let ourselves hang on the metaphorical meat hook for as long as needs be.

In modern culture, we are generally taught to try and pull ourselves out of downward spiralling consciousness as if it was a bad mood to be avoided. Buck up! Smile! Be grateful for all you have! This attitude is helpful at times, but when you need a descent in order to grow, platitudes are not going to do anything for you. It is like trying to stop the onslaught of a tsunami with an umbrella. You are just going to have to go with it and see where it takes you.

The downward spiral into the underworld is not a bad mood. It can bring us an incredible energy, a series of insights and a deeper connection to our genuine selves that allows us to realise we are ready to release what we no longer need, in order to be open to the new life bursting forth from within. Just like a seed that can only begin its journey of growth from the darkness, sometimes we need darkness too. It is sort of like being pruned of excess so that we may flourish when it is time for the spring again. Any temporary redirection of our energy within by working with dreams, visions, insights and meditations will help us when we re-emerge (which we will naturally do!). Just as we were pulled down, we will be pushed up when the time is right. At the time of re-emergence, we will be lighter, clearer, more purposeful and able to bring even more of ourselves to the relationships we are continuing on with and the new ones that we will attract into our lives.

The shaman and the healer both understand, at a high-level of intelligent evolution, that death can feed life. Of course, it can destroy it too. By shutting off from growth or resisting our life experiences and where they are leading us to, the death energy can become repressive and destructive towards the new life seeking to emerge from within us. When we can accept the death of that which we have defined ourselves to be and we can shed our need to understand, in favour of a willingness to be, to live and to respond to life honestly, and from the heart and soul as much as we can, then Ishtar's fighting spirit rises within us. Her defiant intention to passionately unite herself with all of life becomes alive in us. It is more powerful than fear and more arousing than the need to control.

There is no part of Ishtar's being that says to life, "Well, yes I want what you have to offer me but only if I don't need to change or be uncomfortable, confronted or challenged." Instead, she boldly rushes forth declaring to life, "I will have you! All of you! Bring it on!"

She is never humiliated by what is asked of her. If a lover spurns her or someone behaves in a disappointing manner, with anything less than the adoration and devotion she knows she deserves, she does not hesitate to express her opinion on the matter. A gentle and restrained goddess she is not!

Her relentless pouring forth of light comes from a place of not holding anything back. She doesn't hold shame nor guilt within her, so she is able to be herself unconditionally. She shows up to all her life experiences with openness, honesty and doesn't flinch in the face of what those who suffer from shame and guilt might find to be a humiliating source of indignity. For her, it is just part of opening to the totality of life. If she has to get naked and hang on a hook in her quest for complete and utter empowerment through love, then so be it. She doesn't interpret life events as a personal attack or judgment of her value. She just engages with them as learning experiences. If we have a tendency to feel ashamed, embarrassed, humiliated or less worthy due to a set of circumstances or another person's behaviour, the bold self-love and dignity of Ishtar can help us learn be in our own corner and not allow situations beyond our control or other people's consciousness drag us down or undermine our self-esteem and self-belief.

Ishtar also teaches us the lesson of absolute trust in love. It is love and compassion that ultimately frees Ishtar to rise up from the underworld restored. Her dark sister, Erishkegal, Queen of the Underworld is actually in agony when Ishtar is hanging dead on the meat hook. The story goes that Erishkegal is trying to give birth at the time. She is trying to bring life through but, to do this, she needs what Ishtar is – love. They both need each other. When the Erishkegal in us is in agony, we feel her pain. It was her trying to give birth to me when I was in terror and horror every day for a year. The pain I felt was my dark-self trying to give birth to new life, trying to tap into the parts of me I hadn't yet accessed, the parts that were unconditionally trusting of life, so that I could surrender into the greater plan the Universe holds for me. Only one thing can save Eriskegal from her agony and it is the same thing that saves Ishtar by bringing her back to life. That is love.

The story goes that two small, furry creatures from the world above, armed with instructions from a wise man about how to rescue Ishtar, venture down into the underworld on a mission to bring their precious queen back to life. Word had got out, you see, that the goddess was stripped bare and lay dead in the underworld, which was not where she belonged. She was love. She belonged to life, not death. What is interesting about this little, fur-faced duo is that the next stage of the story, its resolution, depends upon them even though they don't really have a lot of power. What they do have is the ability to carry out their instructions faithfully, which they do. They march right up to Erishkegal as she lies about her dark throne moaning and writhing in agony. They were instructed by the wise man, to simply repeat everything she says or does. Presumably not in the manner of an annoying childhood game where someone drives you to distraction by repeating everything you say with an irritating gleam in their eye, but in the style of a compassionate counsellor who listens to what you say and reflects it back to you so you feel heard and understood (this is referred to as mirroring). If you have ever been in the latter situation you will know how completely healing it can be in and of itself. Certainly, it works for

Erishkegal. These furry, little creatures respond to her completely and remain present through what she is going through. Erishkegal feels something in that presence. They alleviate her loneliness and she can bear her birthing process. She offers them a reward for their kindness and assistance in her hour of need and they claim Ishtar as their prize, which is granted.

It is love that brings this teaching story to fruition. Whenever we are going through the rigors of transformation it helps to remember why! There are times on my path when what is asked of me is demanding beyond all expectation. I have coped with things I did not believe I could, except that I actually went through it and because I didn't have much warning, I just got on with it. Sometimes, I even did it with a modicum of grace and poise – sometimes not so much.

In my personal growth, I have accepted many deaths of myself. It is what has allowed me to continually create and move forward on my path – sometimes with quite significant leaps. When I am confronted with something that seems a bit too much or I wonder if I will be able to endure what is being asked of me, I remember why I am in that position. I remember how much I love the Divine and the yearning for unrestrained divinity that fills my heart. I remember how I felt when someone's soul called out to me and I could respond effectively. I remember how heartbroken I was when someone struggled to find me and the work that could help them, and how I have raged at obstacles that lie between myself and a genuine seeker on the path. I remember how much I genuinely love the souls I help through taking this journey, and how deeply and unconditionally I want to share that love. I also remember the wisdom of those little, furry faces. I do my best to have compassion for my struggles and pain, and to acknowledge myself. If I cannot then I seek help from someone who can help me bear witness to what is happening so that with presence, awareness, honesty and acknowledgement, I can find it easier to move through it. That was, and is, what brings me forward through the many deaths of the transformational process and back into the world, over and over again.

Those of us on the path as healers need love to pull us through whatever is asked of us. Sometimes we have to descend for our own growth, but also for our ability to reach others. At this time in evolutionary history, the darkness is quite rich and ripe, the birthing pains of transformation are very strong, and people can get lost, confused, disoriented and even fearful. As healers, we need to have compassion and empathy for the human plight. That compassion is often attained through our own struggles. We really know what it is like for someone who is struggling because we have taken the journey ourselves. Through that hard-won wisdom, we can relate to others and they can relate to us. This is something special about Ishtar. She has been through the suffering and knows what it is to love and be loved. She teaches us how to use our experiences to better serve life and to heal our own hearts and the world.

ASTROPHYLLITE (REBIRTH)

I love Ishtar deeply. When it came time to feel for the crystal that would work with her energy –that is filled with contradictions of grace, love, war, birthing, death and the heavens – I was uncertain. I asked the divine ones to help me know which stone to work with.

Some ten minutes before I started to write this chapter, I shuffled some papers on my desk and a flat, shiny, black stone with silvery feathering fell out and hit the floor. I picked it up and placed it next to the laptop. At one point, while I was sitting with the intuitive feeling of the themes for this chapter, I picked it up and unconsciously held it against my forehead for a few moments. Then I drew my hand away and gazed at the stone, suddenly conscious of what I had been doing. Astrophyllite! Of course! It was a perfect complement to Ishtar's consciousness. Just like life and Ishtar, it has the unusual property of including a complete range of vibrations from the quite low and dense to the rarefied and refined. It can therefore be used by anyone, and will bring light into all of the chakras to create balance and alignment wherever it is needed. Its illumination brings light to what we need to see and know.

Astrophyllite means 'sheet of stars' and with its dark black, shiny surface and silvery inclusions that shimmer in the light, it reminds me of gazing at a rich black night sky with comet tails and shooting stars bursting forth in all directions. When I gaze at astrophyllite, it is like a universe is contained within the stone. I feel as though a multitude of doorways would open wide, portals to other planes of consciousness would become available and I could astral travel to worlds beyond this one, if I could energetically drop right into it. All of this could happen through deep and open connection to this stone that contains worlds within it and access to worlds beyond it.

It is a relatively rare crystal but can be found in tumbled stones at reasonable prices. The leaf or feather-shaped inclusions can be silver or bronze in tone.

Astrophyllite supports our journeys or descents into the underworld, into crisis for healing and transformation, because it holds the wisdom of release, death and rebirth. It holds the deep truth that an ending is a beginning, like the serpent biting its own tail. When a door is closing it is not because we are denied. It is because we are being asked to take a different pathway, a different way through. There is something more aligned, more appropriate that is taking place and we are to take that pathway instead.

The attitude of never giving up, of simply looking for the other way through, is the equivalent of Ishtar busting down doors that were closed to her. She didn't declare that it must happen how she wanted it to happen, she declared that she would not be denied. Astrophyllite helps us remember that we have universes within us, that we are boundless, limitless spiritual beings and that we can be open to all of life. It helps us let go of attachment to how we think things should come to us and to let go of attachment to a closed door, and to instantly shift and look for where the door is opening for us. Just like Ishtar, we expect life and universal love to support our growth and offer us all that is. It therefore becomes easier to let go of things that are dying away and to open up to that which is thriving with life and calling us to it.

Astrophyllite is a birthing stone and part of its healing properties include the balancing of hormones which is physically, psychologically and spiritually helpful for all stages of birth. Hormonal balance helps us surrender some of the stress that we attribute to change, to feel more aligned with the grace of transformation, to accept the inevitable letting go that is asked of us, and rather than feeling the emptiness of loss, letting it become a vehicle through which we can allow so much more to come to our opening being.

Astrophyllite supports out-of-body experiences as well as physical healing. With deep transformation and the resulting change, one of the necessities for peace of mind, is that we learn to shift perspective. We can sometimes feel stuck in how we have come to see a person, place or relationship and interact out of habit rather than responsiveness. It can begin to feel as though the situation or relationship in question is a parody of itself, rather than a living, spontaneous expression of life. This can bring us emotional or psychological security of the known entity, but at the same time we have to be careful that it doesn't crush the living spirit of freedom, authenticity and spontaneity in a relationship or other life situation, lest we end up feeling like we are acting in our life and relationships rather more like reality TV than reality.

Astrophyllite helps us shift out of our expectations to open up to other perspectives. If you have ever learned something new about someone you have known for years and found that you looked at them differently, that your connection became more vivid and interesting, infused with new life and fresh perspective, then you have experienced the gift that astrophyllite can help us access. It helps us open up our perceptive faculties to become more sensitive, aware and more responsive to life as a result of this.

Astrophyllite helps us to live in acceptance of the now whilst remaining conscious that what we choose to do and be now is always an invitation for future experience to manifest. It helps us connect with our ability to vision a future while staying in the miraculous present moment, where we take the practical steps to birth that vision. As this stone helps us know ourselves by letting go of what no longer serves, it also helps us find our life path and purpose. Our divine path and purpose become increasingly obvious, the more we know who we are because our purpose and path are essentially to become all of who we are. Our divine path is an expression of our essence. It is not something outside of us to find, it is something within us seeking to be born in all its magnificence. Astrophyllite helps us realise that within us there is a universe of possibility. It helps us allow that possibility to manifest.

This is a visionary stone that helps us connect with our innate psychic abilities and refine them so that we are not victims of what we see, but rather, have an ability to see more and more from the heart. This allows us to see with curiosity, rather than judgment, what a soul is creating in a particular life situation and for what learning purpose that situation is being evoked. The light that it evokes from within is like a searchlight inside of us so we can see the next step to take. We might get a big searchlight that gives us far reaching vision or we may be moving through so much that all we need to see is the next step and then the next step and so forth. We simply work with what is given to us and step forward in that light, in trust.

MANIFESTING THROUGH DIGNITY

One of the Hopi teachings from the Native American tradition for the New Age shift of consciousness is that we need to learn not to take things personally. There is so much shifting that we are going to get caught up in the movement of it and at times we will realise it is much larger than one individual. Although we have free will as to how we respond to this process, at another level we came here to Earth to take this journey – all of it.

When something appears to 'go wrong' because our ego thinks it should be otherwise, it doesn't have to mean anything more than life is just happening. There is always a bigger perspective to be had and the bigger the perspective the more our fundamental divine dignity is intact. There is no shame at that level, nothing to feel humiliated by or anything you have failed in. There is just the divine spiritual light having the experience of being made manifest. To the soul, it is a wild, exciting and interesting journey.

I have seen my own soul essence, and the souls of others, during various points in our respective life journey. Far from shining more sombrely during particularly devastating challenges and the breaking down of the ego, usually it boldly shines with more awe-inspiring radiance than ever before! I find this somewhat humbling from the ego perspective and it does offer us hope. When you are brave enough to be present through the dying away of certain things in life and conscious enough to witness the birth that is happening as part of that process, you might recognise for yourself that your soul is on fire with divine radiance. Whilst I have been in the throes of my own personality breaking apart and the suffering that can entail, I have had the bizarre experience of realising that my soul is lighting up like the sun in the room with me. I usually have a little quip with my soul saying, "This body and mind sees that you are loving this but this body and mind need compassion too!" At which point there is a sense of love rather than only light in the room.

There is a fundamental purity in the spiritual being that dwells within our bodies. Our soul essence is never tainted or diminished, but only grows brighter through experience over the course of thousands and thousands of lifetimes. When we are able to accept this part of ourselves and come to identify with it more, instead of mistaking ourselves for actually being our bodies (rather than just loving them), a profound shift in manifestation occurs. We start to realise our innate, divine, royal nature and unshakeable dignity. We become far more wild and life-loving as a result. We don't have to hide ourselves from possible shame or humiliation because we don't empower it as true in the way that we once may have done. We are able to let loose and express ourselves. If you have ever watched a performer or an athlete completely lose themselves in what they were doing and felt something stir in you – a yearning that you couldn't quite identify – then you were tapping into this need for inner dignity that allows you the freedom to completely and fearlessly let go and live.

To manifest through the dignity of Ishtar is to allow your lust for life and your desire to taste all that there is to emerge and you will become bigger, more emboldened and stronger for it. It requires a belief in yourself and a trust in life that you shall be led into experiences that are right for you at the time they are right for you. The right experiences, in right timing mean that you are not overly broken or squashed by life, but jolted or gently nudged just enough so that you will recover by growing.

If you have ever suffered from perfectionism, thinking anything less than the best will bring shame to yourself or others, then you will enjoy reclaiming your dignity as you realise it is not conditional in any way, it just is. No matter what your experiences, no matter what others may make of your experiences, you have an untainted, fundamental dignity within you. When you accept and honour this, you will have so much daring that your life will open up to adventures that can manifest things you may have wished for but never truly dreamed were possible.

HEALING PROCESS

This is a good all-round healing process for any time you are feeling shamed or down-trodden by a setback or challenging life experience, are beating yourself up for not being 'further along' on your path or in life, or after you have spent time in an toxic relationship or friendship that leaves you not feeling good about yourself (perhaps consider whether or not you want to continue with such relationships as part of your healing dedication in this ritual). It is also a good chakra cleanser any time you are readying yourself to take another step on your path and you want the power of Ishtar so you can really go for it without holding back.

The Process

You will need seven tea lights or other candles. If you wish, you can choose candles for the colour of each chakra: red, orange, yellow, green or pink, light blue, dark blue and purple or white. You will need a lighter or matches and your mandala and/or crystal.

Turn off electrical equipment and communication devices like phones and email if possible, so that you can focus on being in the moment with your healing. Close any windows that could blow out the candles or cause a wafting curtain, for example, to catch fire. Make sure that you are in a fireproof area and that the candle is not somewhere a child or family pet could easily reach.

Lay out your candles in a row of seven. If you are using coloured candles, start with red and move all the way through to white or purple. Don't light any yet, but have your matches or lighter in easy reach.

Lay out your mandala and/or crystal near your body and sit comfortably.

Start by saying the following with your hands at your heart, but with the palms open and turned upwards to receive.

"I call upon my divine essence, my higher self, my soul, and upon the ancient divine one, Ishtar who loves me unconditionally. Ishtara. Astarte. Inanna. Divine Mother. Golden One. Venus. She who is wild with the love of life and fears no evil. She, of endless names. Ishtar, who loves me unconditionally, be with me beloved, bless me with your radiance and glory. I call upon the Crystal Angel of Astrophyllite, stone of the earth and the stars and all that lies between. I call upon the healing, clearing and protection of divine love, light and power now. For the greatest good and through mercy and wisdom, so be it."

When you are ready, hold your crystal in your hand at a level where you can comfortably gaze at it. If you are only using the mandala, rest your open hands with the palms lightly on the picture, leaving enough room in the centre to gaze at the image of the crystal.

Gaze at the crystal/mandala and allow your eyesight to become a bit soft, blurry or diffuse. Don't try to focus, just let your eyes relax a bit or let them close if you like. When you are ready, settle back, relax and imagine or perceive you are stepping into sacred space.

All around you is endless blackness with feathery bursts of light. There is bronze, silver, pale green and white in a spectacular array. It is like you are floating in a beautiful universe, with stars dying in a burst of flames before being reborn again. This wild cosmic dance is happening in all directions around you. Just be with it and see if you can feel the energy of it – free, raw, beautiful and powerful.

Relax and breathe in and out, at least eight times.

When you are ready, become aware of a set of stairs descending beneath you. They seem to emerge out of the darkness and deep within that darkness there is an incredibly bright shining star. This is Ishtar, Venus, Goddess of Ancient Times. You may sense within the star the figure of a goddess or simply sense light, colour or even the sound of her voice. Let yourself be with what happens for you and trust.

She speaks to you, "I have called you through time and space to reclaim the brilliance of the light within you. I am your heavenly sister and we share the same divine heritage. Step forward now and shed your doubts and shame. Be one with my radiance, my dear divine one. I will help you now."

Imagine that you are stepping, perhaps even running or dancing, out of your clothes, out of your identities, becoming a star of light. Descend with her, down the stairs and into a place of great darkness. You are unafraid. She is with you and together you shine brilliantly.

In the depths of the darkest place you can reach together, allow yourself to truly let go of and leave behind all that you no longer need. Say the following, "I cast aside with love and without regret, all that I no longer need. In service to love I let go fearlessly and with great trust in what I am becoming and the eternal being of light that I am. My heavenly sister, Ishtar is my witness, and I receive her healing grace deep in my soul. So be it."

Relax and breathe in and out, at least eight times.

As you light your first candle say, "My base chakra is cleared of survival fears, tribal wounding and I dwell in trust. My needs are met and my soul family gathers around me, attracted into my life now. So be it."

Look at the lit candle and visualise or intend that your base chakra is a clearly glowing, vibrant red at the base of your spine. Then imagine or perceive that you and Ishtar are ascending one level from the depths of darkness, back towards pure light.

Light your second candle and say, "My sacral chakra is cleared of emotional blockages and old guilt of sexual control and psychic cords that are not of unconditional love, now. I choose to be present to my own shadow, the parts of me that I find hard to accept, with compassion. I choose to flow with my natural emotional, creative and sexual energies, in loving acceptance of myself. So be it."

Look at your second lit candle and visualise or intend that the sacrum or hips and belly are shining with clear, vibrant orange. Then imagine or perceive that you and Ishtar are ascending another step or level up from the depths of darkness towards the light.

Light your third candle and say, "My solar plexus chakra is cleared of shame, conscious and unconscious, from this or any lifetime. I take the learning and let go of the karmic memory of any shame or shaming, humiliation, degradation or diminishment, so that I may serve love, now. I embrace my dignity, my inner sovereignty and empowerment.

So be it."

Gaze at your lit candle and visualise or intend that at the abdomen, your solar plexus chakra, is clearly glowing with a vibrant yellow colour. Then imagine or perceive that you and Ishtar are ascending another level from the depths of darkness, back towards pure light.

Light your fourth candle and say, "My heart chakra is cleared of any impediment to love. Old wounds, betrayals, un-forgiveness, struggle or heartbreak is released now with gratitude for how strong my heart has become, so open to love despite my past hurts and suffering. I trust my heart and I honour its need to love and be loved. So be it."

Look at your lit candle and visualise or intend that at the centre of your chest, your heart chakra, is clearly glowing with vibrant green, soft pink or both. Then imagine or perceive that you and Ishtar are ascending one more level from the depths of darkness, back towards pure light.

Light your fifth candle and say, "My voice is freed from fear, silencing and shame. My throat chakra is cleared of any vows, decrees and curses upon myself or others that I have ever made, consciously or unconsciously, now. My truth shines through me without holding back. So be it."

Look at your lit candle and visualise or intend that at the base of your throat where your throat chakra spins and shines is glowing with a clear vibrant sky blue colour. Then imagine or perceive that you and Ishtar are ascending another level from the depths of darkness, back towards pure light.

Light your sixth candle and say, "My third eye chakra is open and sees clearly. What I see I do not fear. I see truth. I see love. I see reality. I trust in what I see and I trust in where it leads me, for I see also that I am held lovingly and completely within divine protection always. So be it."

Look at your lit candle and visualise or intend that at the centre of your eyebrows, your third eye chakra is clear and glowing with vibrant, dark indigo-blue. Then imagine or perceive that you and Ishtar are ascending one more level from the depths of darkness, back towards pure light.

Light your seventh candle and say, "My crown chakra is free from any implant, traumatic imprint from abuse, or obstruction between myself and the Divine. I trust in my own divine connection. I live my own divine nature. I am loved, protected and illumined by divine light always. So be it."

Look at your lit candle and visualise or intend that at the crown of your head, your crown chakra is a clear, glowing, vibrant purple or shining bright white in colour and opening as if it has a thousand petals, to the brightest, purest sunlight.

Then imagine or perceive that you and Ishtar are ascending the final level from the depths of darkness, stepping into pure light. Say, "I am unafraid and I am reborn, with my heavenly sister Ishtar at my side."

You and Ishtar step through the pure light and back into manifest reality. Come back into your body, with your awareness at your feet, feeling the air on your skin and the temperature of your room, the sensation of warm blood in your veins, your heart beating in your chest and the in and out flow or your breath. Stay there for at least eight breaths and in your own time, put your hands at your heart in prayer position and bow your head to finish.

Gaze at your lit candles and know that you are different to how you began this process. Take your time to extinguish the candles gently, or if they are not a fire hazard and you are remaining nearby, leave the candles burning for a while and allow the energy of what you have accessed from deep within, to rise up.

Notice your intuitions, behaviours and any differences in you or in how others react to you over the coming weeks as signs your inner work is beginning to unfold.

6.

HECATE (CROSSROADS)
MICA (SYNTHESIS)

MANIFESTING THROUGH CHOICE

She stands where all paths meet, at the centre of the crossroads. From her all directions and possibilities flow. She is eternal and wise. She sees all and knows all. Cloaked in robes of black, her will is not used to impose a decision upon us, but to evoke a choice from us. What will you choose? Her power and grace are activated through the making of a choice. Only then can life unfold in all its mystery.

HECATE (CROSSROADS)

Hecate (Hek-Ah-Tay) is the Greek name for the goddess of crossroads, gateways and choices as well as crafts involving herbs, medicines and poisons. She was worshipped in numerous cities and cultures including Ancient Greece and Rome.

It was taught that she resided in the underworld, the same place where Ishtar (whom we met in the previous chapter) made her descent. However, Hecate didn't just descend there, it is her terrain.

Hecate's symbols are keys, torches and dogs. Keys represent her ability to provide us with what is needed to pass through new thresholds by unlocking doors to the opportunities and worlds that become available to us when we exercise our power of choice. Often the first choice we need to make is choosing to acknowledge that we have the power of choice. We always do. When we believe there is no choice within a situation it is because we have limited our thinking in some way. If we ever feel we have no choice, then we aren't seeing something clearly.

I have heard, "but I don't have a choice" so often in my years working with people. It might be the feeling that we don't have a choice to be happy in our lives because of how another person in our life behaves. We don't have a choice about how they behave, that is true. But we do have a choice about how we respond to that behaviour. Sometimes simply choosing not to engage in the negative behaviour of another is enough. Sometimes that can shift a relationship dynamic and move it in a healthier direction. Sometimes the relationship dynamic is too intractable, not pliable enough to respond to energies of change and therefore can only continue in one particular pattern or break under the stress (rather than adapt to the stress) of choices that evoke the energy of change.

I was once in a relationship for several years that wasn't a particularly happy one, even though I loved my partner very deeply and he loved me deeply also. We had a choice about what happened in that relationship. We had lots of choices. They all led to us eventually parting. Before I eventually chose to find another place to live and move on from that relationship, I chose to stay put. I did this because even though I was unhappy with the connection between us on a number of levels, I also wanted to be with him. Even after many, many attempts to change the relationship dynamic failed, I hung in there, hoping for growth. That was my choice. The results of that choice were that my happiness in the relationship declined over the years. I was happy and fulfilled in my work, in my friendships that meant so much to me and in many other areas of my life, but not, sadly enough, in my primary relationship. His choices contributed to the increasing unhappiness in the relationship, but my choice to stay was just as important. I never felt I had to stay or I had to leave, until right at the end of the relationship. Although my love for him was as strong as always, in the end I felt my love for my own being had to be stronger. If I was to choose growth over self-destruction, then I had to leave. The growing unhappiness in the relationship was draining my strength and undermining my self-confidence. I had reached a point where I met Hecate at the crossroads, jangling her keys. I felt as though one of those keys would liberate me from what seemed to be turning into a prison of unhappiness, but it wasn't an easy choice for me. I would have to walk away from the man I deeply loved. I felt devastated and shocked by the nature of the choice before me. I moved slowly and painfully through an emotional process of disbelief into the eventual acceptance that I would have to sacrifice the relationship. At that moment, I accepted a key from Hecate. Soon after, her spiritual key became the actual key to the new home I found for myself (with plenty of spiritual assistance which I will mention later on in this book).

I had met Hecate at a crossroads I never wanted to encounter, but recognised it, eventually accepted it, and used my power of choice to step out of the relationship I was in and choose the possibility of a new life for myself. As I took that step, extraordinary things began to happen for me. As I chose myself, the Universe chose me too and I was assisted in learning to love myself in a deeper way and able to heal past patterns and behaviours that I had not been able to shift up until that point. I began to know happiness in a deeper way than ever before, even while I was grieving the loss of the man I had loved.

Torches, another of Hecate's spiritual tools and symbols, represent her ability to shine light in the darkness, or bring knowledge to what is otherwise unknown, so that progress may be made. Often when we are stuck in a situation and can't see a way out of it or what a possible choice could be, we are approaching the crossroads where the decision making power lies, but are just not quite close enough to catch the light of Hecate's torch.

In truth, the power of choice is always within us, but sometimes it's hard for us to accept or see it because we don't really want to enter into what is being asked of us. The prospect of making a choice that will take us onto an unfamiliar path might be too frightening or even so exciting and wonderful that we don't believe it could possibly work out. So we hesitate, look the other way, believe in our stories about not having a choice and postpone the inevitable decision making moment. Sometimes we actually need these actions to help us slow down and bide our time, while we gather the strength and readiness to make an important decision in our lives.

The relationship I described above was never going to end in marriage as we had each hoped at different points. Despite wanting it to be otherwise, there were some severe limitations in the relationship that became even more difficult to manage as I grew on my path. The reason that I ended up leaving was not a new reason; the dynamics that caused the unhappiness between us had existed throughout our entire connection. They just grew progressively more obvious until the light of Hecate's torch was so bright and the choice that lay before me so clear that I was unable to put it aside for just one more day or month or year. It had become too obvious and I had no way of pretending otherwise.

By that time I had gathered enough strength to be able to make the choice I needed to make. My partner had reached a similar place of awareness within himself by then too. Although he acknowledged that he wanted me to stay, he could also acknowledge that the relationship wasn't working. Nonetheless, when I made my choice to walk out the door it was so painful and distressing that I realised why I had needed to be so patient with myself. I wouldn't have been ready to do it any sooner. Hecate had been flashing her torch in my direction for some time, but I really had to be utterly certain that I couldn't stand the pain of the relationship anymore because the pain of leaving was almost more than I could bear. I knew it was an essential step on my path, but my goodness! If there had been even the slightest hope that I could remain and not be negatively impacted by the relationship, I would have stayed. I needed absolute certainty before I could summon up the strength to go, even though it prolonged the pain and delayed my final choice to acknowledge what wasn't working and to move on with my life.

Hecate's totem animal is the dog. In mythology dogs, such as the three-headed Cerberus, guard the underworld to prevent the living from entering and the dead from leaving. Anubis, the dog or jackal-headed god from Ancient Egypt, had a similar role as God of the Underworld. Dogs have often symbolised guardians of the thresholds much like modern-day watchdogs or household guard dogs. However, Cerberus was not just a watchdog. It is said his heightened canine sense of smell was able to detect the purity of a human soul with one sniff. The impact of his flawless vision was thrice multiplied by virtue of his three heads that represent knowledge and vision of the past, the present and the future. Cerberus also had an appetite for live meat. In short, not much could get by this three-headed hound of hell!

Thresholds, especially when they involve great leaps of consciousness from one way of life to the next, are not easy to get through. They involve great personal growth in preparation for the leap. It can take years of preparation and we usually have no idea we are being trained in readiness for a future life event. Our consciousness will be honed during that preparation period. We might be tested on similar issues over and over again, whilst we wonder if we are ever going to get the point of it all so we can be free from this repeating karmic pattern. At a greater level our soul is learning to handle a particular sort of energetic pattern.

Imagine the soul is a shaman or medicine man from a tribal community working with plants and nature to keep his tribe spiritually and physically healthy. The shaman discovers a plant that can help him open his consciousness to worlds of powerful energy he can use for the wellbeing of his tribe. However, he knows that others have tried to use this plant and become very sick and some have even died. It has poisons in it that prevent those who are not yet ready from using the plant. Those who were too immature to handle the power the plant grants with responsibility would rush in and try to access its gifts for instant fixes or gratification. Those not prepared to pass the threshold into a greater consciousness, and lack preparation and wisdom, were led to their demise. Only those who are mature, wise and patient will be granted access to the power of the plant and the greater consciousness it can bestow. So little by little the shaman begins ingesting the plant, allowing the healing power of his own body to learn how to work with the poison. He applies the wisdom of nature – patience, trust in his body's natural healing power and the ability to balance the energies of life and death – to slowly develop an immunity within himself to the negative effects of the plant. He develops a relationship with the plant. He comes to understand it, to become one with it in his own body and it becomes his ally. Eventually he is able to work with the energy of the plant for healing purposes, without sickness or death. He is granted access past the threshold of the ordinary world and into the greater world that the plant opens up in his consciousness.

The 'plants' the soul is learning to work with in its quest for greater consciousness are life experiences. On the way to greater love, for example, we will often break our hearts open and go through more extensive grief than we have ever had to bear, or face more fear than we thought we could possibly handle. The way we process our responses to life events (such as the ending of a relationship) can be likened to learning how to metabolise the 'poisons' of a plant. They could destroy us by permanently shutting down our hearts. However, if we respond with intelligence, patience, trust and awareness they could actually make us stronger and empower our hearts to fearlessly open to love and willingly surrender to its genius with absolute trust. We can then become empowered to serve our 'tribe' more effectively from a place of genuinely expanded consciousness.

This process of growth requires that we pass through thresholds of consciousness. If you are capable of a lot of growth, you will face these thresholds on a regular basis. Sometimes it will seem as though each is more daunting than the last! At other times, passing through thresholds will become more graceful as we master something of the process required: trust, surrender and flowing into what is with absolute acceptance.

If we are not going to undertake quite so much growth in a lifetime, and there are many legitimate reasons for a soul to opt for a slower path, then we will find our journey involves less of these initiatory thresholds and is likely to proceed at a gentler pace. The path of accelerated growth can have quite a bit of turbulence at times. Whether we experience life as gentle, bumpy or both there are two great thresholds every human will encounter – birth and death. Those on a conscious evolutionary path of personal healing and spiritual growth will encounter many more symbolic birth and death thresholds throughout a lifetime.

The three-headed dog that stands by Hecate's side and guards the thresholds between life and death symbolises the genuine challenge facing anyone who seeks to take the leap into a new world. The gift of new life is often hard won. Even when it is offered with gentle grace from the Divine, we generally have to let go of something to reach for it. This can ask a lot of us. However, there are ways for us to get through this process with less struggle. In the stories of Ancient Greece, only two heroes were able to get the better of Cerberus and cross from death into the world of life. These myths teach us the two ways we can get past the three-headed dog, or in other words, what is necessary for us to cross our thresholds in life.

Hercules, the original superman with incredible strength, is the first to successfully get past the hound of hell. He puts Cerberus in a choke hold and knocks him out! This doesn't actually mean we should go around thumping our way through life, clubbing anything in our way into submission! Hercules' action doesn't kill Cerberus but it does leave the dog unconscious long enough for him to complete his task. We can draw wisdom from this myth. There will be times when making a choice at a certain crossroads in our lives and passing to the next threshold, will mean taking a step that might seem impossible to us at some level. There may be such strong resistance to taking the action we need that we could fail to even try. By the time we decide to take the step, we are probably going to need so much strength of will that we will refuse to listen to any resistance within us that would prevent us from moving ahead anyway. It is the equivalent of putting a choke hold on it and knocking it out with our sheer determination to cross the threshold into new life, even though it's only temporary.

I had an experience of this with the ending of the relationship I spoke of above. On the day I was leaving, I was so heartbroken; I could barely keep myself together. The thought of the sheer physical effort involved in moving house was so great, when I was already so emotionally distraught, that it felt absolutely overwhelming to me. I pushed on through it bit by bit but there was one moment where my resistance to move on was so strong that even when we were two thirds through the move and unpacking at the new place, I had a moment that completely winded me. It had the strong, almost irresistible urge to tell the men to start packing the truck back up, turn around and go back!

I couldn't believe I was feeling that way, but there it was. I had to use all the power of my will to snap myself out of it and force myself to keep going. I made a bargain with myself to aid that process. I would just complete the move and see how I felt in a few days. I knew at some level that if I could just get through moving day I would begin to settle down and be able to process my grief, begin my new life and I would be alright. But the Hercules within me had quite a fight with my inner Cerberus who was not going to let me transition out of my dying relationship and into my new life without a fight!

Finally the move was completed. I unpacked the house over the next couple of days and began to settle into my new surroundings. I felt the beautiful healing energy of the place and began to heal my heart. I felt more happiness, even amongst the painful waves of grief, as I was able to just relax and be myself without the pain of the relationship hanging over my head anymore. I took my time to grieve and begin my healing process. I had knocked out my resistance for long enough to allow myself to cross the threshold into my new life. I still had emotional work to do to make the transition in heart and mind as well as in body, but I had given myself the opportunity to do so. I needed the strength of Hercules to do it!

The other myth that teaches us how to overcome that feisty, terrifying Cerberus is that of Orpheus who uses what my mother would have called, "music to soothe the savage beast." When I was a little girl, I would sit at the piano in the lounge room and play Beethoven. It quite likely looked and sounded surprising for a young girl to be playing such emotionally mature and powerful, dark and mournful music. But I loved his work. It enabled me to pour a world of dark childhood emotions out through my fingertips. Although I naturally have quite a sunny nature, I am very familiar with the worlds of darker emotion and feelings. Sometimes I felt as though I had thunderstorms within me, even though the weather outside might have been sunny and bright. I needed to express those storms, and as a child music was a helpful way for me to do so. It still is! So I would sit in the cool dark lounge room and let my little fingers beat out notes of mournful, haunting music.

We had an Afghan dog at the time. He was a stray that my brothers and I eventually nagged my mother into keeping. He was wild, with long legs, soft grey fur, a mischievous streak and natural speed. He would escape the house, jump over fences and attempt to outrun speeding cars as he dashed across the main road we lived on. Once he got free, he would saunter off to the local park to fall in love with visiting horses out for some exercise and follow them around with lovesick devotion. Possibly because they were the only thing faster and larger than him in the local dog park! He had also stolen a lamb roast left to cool on stranger's windowsill. I expect they never solved the mystery of what happened to their Sunday lunch that day. He would generally get himself into all sorts of mischief. Even when he was relatively still, he was trouble. He would chew the spines off the library books my mother borrowed (he seemed to like the smell and taste of the glue in the binding) until she was banned from any further borrowing. She was absolutely mortified! Deprived of library books, he would gnaw at the skirting boards in the house as he lay on his back in bliss, legs askew, leaving teeth marks in the otherwise beautifully polished wood. He was proud, beautiful and a right royal pain in the behind. Thankfully he didn't have three heads like Cerberus. He wreaked enough havoc with just one! Still I absolutely adored him. His crazy antics and constant naughtiness only abated when I played the piano. In he would wander and lie flat on the ground, as if lulled into a trance. My mother would quietly pass by the lounge room door, notice the idyllic picture and comment that my music was soothing the savage beast.

In the Greek myth, Orpheus descends to the underworld and risks death to try to bring his deceased beloved, Eurydice, back to life. He uses music, playing his beautiful lyre to lull the Cerberus to sleep so that he may pass.

Music was Orpheus' divine gift. It might be your divine gift too. Your divine gift may also be your spiritual connection to the angels, your ability to pray with conviction from your heart, your skilful healing work with crystals, your devotion to a particular goddess, the love you have in your heart for your work, your children or your passion for dance or art. It might be your love of nature or your genuine appreciation for life and the desire to really live rather than exist and to inspire others to do the same. It might be many things. Whatever it is, you can rely upon it and use it to inspire you beyond any resistance you might encounter and help you make your transition despite any obstacles in your way.

Orpheus uses his gift to overcome the obstacle of crossing from one world into the next. What is beautiful about this myth is that it gives us another way. We might need the strength and will of Hercules as well, but we may find the gentler path filled with softness and soul can be an effective ally in overcoming even the most apparently fearsome obstacles.

Part of my reason for leaving the relationship was my genuine love for the Divine that I wanted to continue to serve. To do that I knew I had to take another step on my path, I had to continue to grow. I knew I couldn't do take the step if I remained in the relationship, no matter how much I wanted to do so or how much I wished the relationship was flexible enough to grow with me. I wanted to grow into what I could sense I was becoming. It was my divine gift, to become all of myself. It was the voice of love that called me towards that self. No matter how rough all the other parts of the break-up process seemed to be, that gentle, constant urging of love to let go, to trust, and to move with authenticity towards what I sensed was calling me forward was always there. It was soothing and incredibly powerful. It was devotion to love that was the invisible power holding me through the death of the relationship and allowing me to move through it.

Sometimes you'll need both of these approaches to pass Cerberus, strength of will and your divine gift – of devotion, of insight, of passion, of surrender, of trust. Sometimes you will be blessed to discover the third way of passing Cerberus, where he actually just stands back lets you pass without challenge. This is what happens when your pathway seems to open up magically before you and great change happens surprisingly easily. In the Greek myths, this is what happens for Persephone (also known as Kore and Proserpina), whom we will meet later on in this book. The gateways between the worlds open up for her at the turning of the seasons. This tells us that there will be a time when it is right for us to cross over either between life and death, death and birth, or from one threshold to another, to start a new part of our journey. At that time, we have gone through the training, the preparation and we are just ready. So it happens. This is the gift of divine timing and Hecate knows it and honours it.

Hecate was called upon to protect households from restless spirits and ghosts. She was also worshipped at doorways and crossroads to protect travellers from harm. She presides over city limits and walls, and in modern terms, this would include the boundaries of what is known and unknown. She is a liminal or medial goddess in that she provides connection and communication between worlds, be it Heaven and Earth or the known present and the unknown future that calls us to it.

She was credited with the power to create or hold back storms and was revered by sailors for this. This applies just as much for those of us doing emotional healing work. As it relates to the element of water, Hecate can assist us in securing safe passage through storms of emotional turmoil.

Originally Hecate was pictured as a singular goddess, but over time she came to be portrayed in triple form. In modern day pagan traditions that are based on the wisdom and love of the natural world, she is often regarded as the crone aspect of the triple goddess (which includes maiden or virgin, mother and crone). Crone wisdom is that of unconditional love. However, Hecate is rarely considered soft and gentle as one might expect from a goddess of unconditional love. Crone wisdom is compassionate. It is insightful and honest. It has no personal ego agenda. It is clean, pure, unattached and the only interest Crone wisdom has is in your growth.

One of my favourite Jungian writers, the truly wonderful Marion Woodman, explained how she experienced the wisdom of the crone through her male therapist. The crone is not about being a woman, per se, it is about holding a certain type of real, truthful, unconditional wisdom. To illustrate her point she shared something from her own life. Her dog, her dear companion, had only just died. Already her story takes us into the realm of Hecate.

She went to her scheduled therapy session that day and spent the better part of an hour talking about everything other than the passing of her beloved dog. At the end of her session, her therapist made a remark that prompted Marion to mention that her dog had just died. Her therapist was overcome! He made the sad observation that she had spent the entire session talking about rubbish when her soul animal had died! What a waste! It wasn't a gentle comment. It was however a truthful one that took her into her heart and into the truth. The wisdom of the crone broke through the defences that led Marion to avoid dealing with her pain of loss. This shows how us much can be accomplished in a few seconds of truthful and compassionate exchange.

Crone wisdom is powerful. It is not limited to those of a certain age or gender. It is ageless, but does require a depth of maturity that often only comes with age for it to come to fruition. However, it can exist in those who are young but have a maturity that is surprising for their age. These are the people who are more comfortable with people older than themselves, even as young children, and have perhaps always felt older than their years. They are often called old souls. If you are reading this book you are likely to be an old soul yourself.

There is sometimes jealousy over such wisdom amongst spiritual seekers. The crone has a certain power and when it is consciously held it is lovingly inclusive but some will sense that power, their inability to control it and want to cut it down. This is more likely to be the case if such people believe they are the ones who hold the power or own the people or territory involved, as if genuine power or spiritual students could somehow be claimed as their own personal property. The desire for power, control and to play at being god rather than going through the surrender required to genuinely experience divinity is a shadow side of spiritual growth.

This happened with a student of one of my colleagues. He became so entranced with his psychic abilities as they awakened that he ended up using them as though they were for his benefit alone. The power of the crone – detachment and compassion – were not as developed as his psychic ability to see, read and unfortunately manipulate people. The expression of his power became karmically unclean. What I mean is that his actions were not neutral because they were tainted by personal attachment and motivation, not simply to divine service as is the actions of a crone.

He used his impressive abilities to manipulate other people for self-serving ends. Often these were women who believed that his compelling insight into their nature came from a genuine heart connection with them and mistook his insight for intimacy. They did not see it as a calculated use of his intuitive abilities to seduce them. This false interest in them was more about him enjoying his power of insight rather than any genuine interest in them as a person. Coupled with his good looks, fit body and charming personality, it made for an irresistible combination for a number of women.

His teacher was a student of mine and when she sought me out for guidance on how to deal with the issue, I felt disappointed, surprised and angry. The man in question had received shaktipat or energy transmissions from me on several occasions and I knew these had been instrumental to opening up his spiritual powers in this lifetime. I worried that I had bestowed too much upon him but knew that I gave freely from love. I had to trust that this was part of his own learning and that it was the Divine rather than I that allowed for spiritual reawakening and more than all that, the Divine knew what it was doing! However, I felt strong about offering clear guidance and teachings to try and abate the further creation of negative karma. I spoke with my student and stressed the importance of teaching him about the ethics (or lack thereof) of what he was doing and if that was insufficient, to explain that karmically this was going to come back and bite him in the backside later on and it wouldn't be pleasant! I told her to emphasise that he would be forced to take responsibility for his actions at some point. He could not just continue with the free ride he thought he was on without slamming into a wall at some point.

When one of the women he had slept with became pregnant with his child, he did take on some responsibility as a father, even though he had no particular interest in the relationship. Perhaps this was the beginning of karmic rebalancing for his behaviour. My involvement in this man's spiritual growth was limited and so I don't know what has developed in his situation as yet. I do know that the karmic rebalancing will happen eventually according to divine wisdom. Maybe it is only through the experience of karmic rebalancing that this talented young man will be able to take the next steps on his path and perhaps even develop the spiritual power of detachment and compassion so that he can put his considerable talents to work for more worthy pursuits.

Crone energy is only accessed after many – often painful – deaths of our sense of self and control in the world. This is why crones are free from even the hidden arrogance that many healers unconsciously carry that may have us lapsing into the belief that we know what another should do in their lives and when and how they should do it. Crones have experienced too much of the divine mystery to fall into the trap of believing that they know anything of divine will, other than it is usually utterly unfathomable, works with an undeniable genius of loving grace and that they are best to surrender to it unquestioningly.

Crones know that they are never anything greater than custodians of the divine power that passes through them. They are able to recognise that power and they have responsibility for how powerful they become through the presence of the divine power flowing through them, but they do not claim it as theirs. They recognise they are neither the originators nor the directors of divine power, but simply a conduit through which it passes. They recognise their role as a pure vessel through which divine power can manifest and they do their work to that end. They do so by scorching their own attachments to outcomes again and again, and learning to surrender more deeply into the service of the greater truth.

This is rather different to the ego-thrilling game of playing with power and using our gifts to boost our ego or make ourselves feel special. Whilst that is a typical part of the path to spiritual maturity, it is nowhere near the level of consciousness of the crone. The crone is what is left when that sort of ego has been cleared out of. It isn't much fun to go through that cleansing (to put it mildly, it is a type of agony) but the power that can flow into our emptier-self is genuine divine presence and very helpful for the healing and empowerment of humanity.

Within the crone there is a spaciousness which is not in conflict or competition with others, but simply has a loving respect for all beings. This might not sound like much, but the genuine expression of this is rare and precious. If you meet a crone, you will know it. You will feel completely free from judgment or condescension in their presence. You'll feel that you are seen and received, neither over nor underestimated and loved unconditionally. You'll be held accountable for all the magnificence of your being and your struggles will be met with compassion. You will never, ever be compared, humiliated or found lacking by a crone. However, you will more than likely be kicked, nudged or firmly shoved further along your path! The absolute truth of your being is revealed in the presence of a crone. It can be beautiful, disconcerting, humbling and a revelation! No matter what our response, it is a gift because it takes us closer to the Divine that lives in us, beneath all the stories we are 'running' in our heads about ourselves and our lives.

My first conscious experience of Hecate as crone involved a simple vision. I was sitting in my lounge room, pondering the changes I could sense stirring in my life. It was at a time when those changes felt a long way off indeed and I actually had many years of preparation ahead of me before those changes could manifest in the physical world. I felt somewhat frustrated. I had been doing very intense, long-term, inner work through dreams, therapy and personal healing. To be honest, I was a bit over living in the underworld for so much of the time. I loved the richness of the healing that it brought but I was also impatient for a rebirth. I didn't know it was still years ahead and that the work I was doing was essential for me to be able bear the challenge of being reborn into a new consciousness aligned with how I felt about myself inside. I did know it was taking longer than I hoped!

I had received an email from an old friend from law school who shared a love of travel and spirituality. We had a mutual passion for a trip hop band called Massive Attack and tried to unravel the meaning of their haunting lyrics. In his email he had written of his travel adventures and I was envious. I had not been able to travel since my days at university, when I had lived at home, worked to save money for travel and then took off during the long university holidays. I had sacrificed the ability to do this (temporarily as it turned out) by opting out of a highly paid career in law and into a heart-centred but rather less remunerated profession as a psychic healer! Although I wouldn't have swapped my spiritual vocation for the legal career that would have afforded me money to travel, I was still tetchy about my lack of means as I contemplated his adventures. They were adventures I would have liked to be having! His was such an externally interesting life, for which I felt some considerable longing. His world seemed to have expanded in direct and opposite proportion to the extent to which mine had become internal, still and deep.

He asked what I was up to. At the time, my days felt very small as though ninety five percent of my life was taking place under the surface in dreams, meditations, therapy and inner-healing work in my journal with only five percent of stuff on the surface! I didn't know what to write back to him. I found it funny but also a bit embarrassing. What was I going to say; that I had been having some really incredible dreams and deep therapeutic breakthroughs?

I did end up emailing him back and truthfully expressed that I was in an internal healing process that had me diving into inner depths and whilst that was happening, not much was shaking up in the physical world. His Sri Lankan cultural background (when we were at university he introduced me to the Upanishads, a classical Indian spiritual text) and his mother's avid interest in meditation, had him far more thrilled about my adventures than I had anticipated. Although it didn't completely cure my frustration, his response did soothe it a little.

Except for the frustration that came from time to time that things actually get moving in the physical world, I actually loved the inner-healing work. As painful as it was at times, I could sense how powerful it was and how much good it was doing me. It was also just really fascinating! I was learning so much about the inner worlds, the healing process and the Divine Feminine. It was my spiritual education for the next phase of my work – including this book – as well as a personal healing journey.

I knew at some point the wheel of life had to turn and I would need to rise up out of the depths, taking the wisdom I had won for myself to share it with others. I just had no idea how or when that would happen. I eventually learned not to try and force these things to happen but to trust in divine timing, although I can't say that was an easy lesson for me to learn as I was rather impatient and keen to just get on with things. I still have that tendency at times.

Anyway, it was at that time in my life, while I was sitting on the lounge in reflection one evening, with candles lit and my big, fluffy, orange cat called Leo snoring contentedly on the couch opposite me, that I saw Hecate. I didn't know it was her at first. I saw a black, hooded cloak and felt a powerful, almost disturbing, presence. She was not soft and gentle and it took me a moment to sense whether or not to trust her energy as pure. She tilted her head back and when I saw her face I gasped and dropped all resistance and uncertainty about her. Her eyes! They were utterly mesmerising. I have never since seen anything like them. They looked almost translucent, as though they were crystal-clear, icy-cold lakes that lie below pure snow-capped mountains. Those eyes felt endless. They looked at me without looking and saw everything. I could look into her eyes and see the entire world. Her eyes were not just eyes, but gateways of vision, and were filled with peace and completely unobscured perception. I knew she could see past, present and future without any distortion. I will never forget that feeling of absolute and utter peace in her stunning eyes. She withdrew a few moments later, just fading away. She had not said a word and I did not say a word but I knew without doubt that it was Hecate.

She had come to me with a wordless message I only understood years later. She would protect me as I was guided towards a crossroads. In the year following her visitation I was going to make a series of choices that would set the wheels of my life in motion. I would need all the learning I had gained to see me through it and sometimes it would be very challenging, but I would be protected and honestly shown what needed to happen and when. I would also have to trust in divine timing, and that if I was meant to enter through a particular doorway, it would open to me at the right moment. She was more than a silent witness to my path. From that moment onwards, she was the guardian of the great transitions I would be making for many years to come. I learned to trust in that process, and in her, so that the leaps that I took were greater and greater.

Hecate gave me another gift that day. Again it was one I didn't understand until much later on in my life. It was a gift of understanding that comes with crone wisdom. The crone is understated. In a culture of flash and people needing to be sold to, teachers sometimes feel pushed to explain how wonderful they are in order to attract students who in turn find it hard to trust in the subtle currents of feeling and perhaps find it easier to respond to those who market themselves with a great deal of confidence, the crone can be underestimated.

However, no matter what our public profile may be, it is the silent inner work that cannot be broadcast that is the terrain of the crone. It is rarely visible unless another enlightened heart happens to look within and see what is taking place there. The crone sees and speaks wordlessly from heart knowing. It is subtle, pure and more powerful than the most compelling, over-the-top display of spiritual power or ability. The crone moves in the dark spaces where she is needed. Her power is truly great but not all will recognise her, unless they have benefited from her assistance and even then, conscious recognition may or may not come. Nonetheless, her work continues to support the greater good.

The gift I received from Hecate is knowing that whether or not all of who and what I am is recognised by others, it just is nonetheless. It is the same gift she will bring to you when it is needed. Although I may feel chronically underestimated by others at times, even at lots of times, Hecate's gift is that I never, ever make the mistake of underestimating myself based on another's perception of me. I know what the Divine is capable of, in me and as me, and this sustains me, my inner world and my sense of my true nature. When that is recognised by another it is a wonderful, treasured gift, but it is just the icing on the cake.

A portion of the spiritual work I do is invisible to many. There is a part of me, the crone within, which is okay with this. That work brings me into loving devotion and bliss, as though the bond with the Divine that is deepened through such work is a secret, sacred tryst. It will be the same for most, if not all, healers who work at a soul level. Spiritual work is more than physical actions and conscious wording; as important as they are, it is much more than that. The invisible energy behind the words, the touch or the gaze is where the action really is. The crone empowers us to honour the parts of our path that are completely private, internal and held in sacred confidence between us and the Divine. We all have these parts of us and as we grow they become the source of the radiance and love that can be witnessed by the soul and benefits the spiritual progress of humanity, even when the physical body cannot quite fathom it.

MICA (SYNTHESIS)

I became a bit obsessed with Mica when I was working as a psychic at a crystal shop around the corner from the townhouse I shared with my boyfriend in Glebe in Sydney's inner west. I was in my very early twenties, had just moved in with my first boyfriend and was beginning my career in the metaphysical field. I had a natural ability for the work. When people asked me how long I had been doing readings for and I replied about six months, they were shocked. Most people thought I must have been doing it for ten years or more and often left a tip. Despite that natural ability, I had a lot to learn about working in the metaphysical profession and working in that store was a good place to start.

There were many crystals and many psychics coming and going. Some, like myself, generated a reasonable client base and stayed put for a while. Others came and went. I met many different personalities and learned that a lot of people who are drawn to this field are not necessarily well themselves. Some of the psychics and healers I met, particularly later on in my career, had done a lot of inner work and self-healing and were genuinely able to guide and assist people from a clear, loving inner spaciousness. Although people like that were plentiful enough, I found they were not necessarily typical.

In my early days as a psychic, I often found that I was contending with psychic attack out of jealousy and sometimes downright vicious hatred (which more than likely masked intense fear) from others who wanted to work as healers in the store. Despite the orientation of the store towards healing and crystals, there was plenty of bitchiness, gossip and cheap shots to contend with whilst working there. It was actually a very toxic work environment and even though it was a way for clients to find me when I decided to leave, I actually felt very relieved. The store closed down for good some months later, which was quite possibly for the best.

Apart from the memories of meeting and helping some special people and learning how to work amid negative energies, I also gained some beautiful crystal pieces bought at a discount! One of the pieces was a large cluster of mica that really helped me cope with the toxic environment in that healing centre. It also supported me on my journey and in my healing work with all sorts of energies, some darker and more disturbed than others.

My higher guidance recently suggested that I clear out my book and crystal collection for the first time in twenty years. As mentioned in Chapter Two on Lakshmi, I sold and then donated over two hundred books and numerous crystals. Afterwards, the piece of mica I had put out for sale remained. Although some people picked it up and admired it, no one had purchased it. I was not sad about that. I realised it was meant to stay with me a little longer and I scurried to put it back on my bookshelf in my healing room rather promptly after the sale ended.

I believe that crystals do choose where they want to be. I have heard stories of crystals being stolen and the previous owners saying, "Well, they obviously needed to be with that person." I have always thought that was such an amazing attitude and one that would truly attract more beautiful stones into that person's life.

Not long after I nestled that piece of mica back into my healing room and got a little re-attached to it, a long-term client came for her monthly mentoring appointment. At the end of her session she mentioned her regret at not being able to attend the sale as she had wanted to add a crystal to her collection. I knew of her work and supported it completely. She is a talented healer, in deep connection with divine love and has a very pure heart. Even as I am writing about her now, I can feel her soul moving through me in waves of love. When we work together in person and I take a moment to tune in to her energy, I can sit there for quite a while as it is such a beautiful energy to tune in to! We both have a chuckle at how powerful those moments of initial connection are and how long they can take as neither of us are too keen on breaking out of the bliss we are in so that we can get on with the work that involves things like talking!

I felt drawn to show her the piece of mica, she fell in love with it and purchased it. My brief, unexpected pang of loss was quickly healed when she said, "I know exactly where I am going to put this, in my healing room in front of my statue of Kuan Yin." Knowing that my mica friend was going to a lovely, pure-hearted soul to be watched over by Kuan Yin made it much easier to part with her.

Their highly reflective surface means that mica clusters can show up every speck of dust. Unfortunately, they are also a bit tricky to clean without breaking the delicate flakes off. Cleaning this stone requires a gentle touch, otherwise it will simply break, flake and fall apart in your hands.

Mica can be found in various colours, including the beautiful lilac coloured mica known as lepidolite. The mica that we are using in our work with Hecate, is the bronze coloured mica which is sometimes called muscovite. It forms in wafer thin, semi-transparent and highly light reflective sheets or layers, almost like filo pastry. It is rich in minerals and is often one of the fundamental ingredients in luxury mineral make up (perhaps where the Crystal Angel of Mica has teamed up with Ishtar or Lakshmi for a moment).

The effect of the sheets is that soft, shiny blades, flakes, columns, or even rosettes, are formed depending on the shape of each particular piece. It has a sheen to it, as though it carries a light within and reflects external light back to you. Even in dull light, mica exhibits a subtle radiance that is just beautiful.

Mica carries the energy of synthesis, which is the ability to pull together different energies, experiences and information and create one coherent understanding. Its reflective quality is said to allow us to see our own shadow as well as the shadow in others. When working with light it is important to be able to recognise and have compassion for the parts of us that are based in fear rather than love. If you hold a strong light within, you may unintentionally bring up issues for healing in others, just as connecting with greater and greater degrees of divine light brings up issues for healing in us as we journey on our own path. It is a continual shedding of that which lies between us and the conscious experience of ourselves as divine beings. It can be hard to accept those parts of us that we don't easily love or that cannot easily believe they are worthy of being loved. That is why they tend to remain in the shadow of our awareness, hidden out of sight.

Mica combines with the generative force of our own spiritual growth to bring whatever we need to deal with to light so that we can keep growing. We can then choose to love that part of us. Supported by Hecate, we can compassionately accept that we are doing our best and are not perfect, but rather perfectly created for our life mission. The soul chooses flaws and quirks just as much as it chooses talents and skills, to best honour our path of divine growth. One of my clients has an expression she uses often, even in the midst of a crisis and living on a farm in Western Queensland she has known a few. In the face of drought, flood or whatever else she is handed, she says, "It's all good." With mica, we start to learn that *it's all god* or Divine, no matter how it first appears to be.

Mica brings issues into consciousness slowly but powerfully over time. It also helps to clear blockages and release energy from all of the chakras. It works on the entire nervous system which links the physical body with the energy body. If you have a tendency to collect psychic material such as thoughts, moods or feelings from people or places around you, no matter how much you protect yourself, then mica is helpful. It assists the body to discharge what isn't needed. When combined with adequate restful relaxation, mica gently encourages a discharge of energy. You might feel a bit funny as stuff is released, but a bit like a hangover this is a sign your body is clearing out toxins. That off-centre feeling will pass soon enough and you will be clearer and more energised after your rest.

Perhaps the most powerful property of mica is psychic protection. If you have a tendency to pick up the energies of others, it will happen far less and be processed far more swiftly with mica around that. The psychic protection aspect of this stone is grounded in its insulating physical properties. Mica is actually used to insulate appliances! On a psychic level it helps create a shield against jealousy, anger and violence. I have encountered quite a bit of this on my path and although I have learned to accept that everyone has their own response to love as part of their individual journey, I find it helps to build up my immune and nervous systems to deal with any reactive responses to me or my work.

Fortunately I get far more loving responses than anything else and I am very grateful for that. However, the crystalline energies are an invaluable support for any of us in the public eye particularly in fields of leadership and spirituality. The hand that feeds sometimes get bitten. We have to be realistic and sensible in our work, even when we do have a practice of coming from love. I often remind myself that even the Dalai Lama, one of the most spiritually evolved beings on the planet, is subjected to criticism and attacks. Yes, people do make those sorts of comments about him sometimes. It leaves me speechless with shock when they do. Once I recover I send thoughts of loving gratitude to him and feel a smile broaden my lips as his soul multiples and returns that love to me almost instantly. So I figure if he isn't immune to coping with criticism then it is highly likely everyone is going to cop their share of negativity from time to time. Perhaps more so, as we learn to hold more light within our being. Mica helps strengthen us to stay focused on truth and not get caught up in the pain of another manifesting itself in such an attack.

Mica brings synthesis because it helps us see truth. It clears the chakras which allows us to tap into our inner truth with less obstruction or distortion from the energy of others. From this place, we are able to integrate what we have learned, work out what is needed and take steps forward with intention when opportunities are created or presented for us to do so. When a particularly ugly side of human nature is being shown to you, whether it is within yourself or perceived in another, you can always know that a step towards the light is imminent. Synthesis draws together that which is seemingly inconsistent and finds the underlying truth. It has always been my experience that learning about healing is also learning about wounding. Mica helps us understand this and work with the apparent paradox more easily.

If you are one of those new world servers that are attracted to many different paths and modalities and wish to combine them in some unique way, mica can help you find the points in common without losing the fundamental integrity of each modality. Most teachers who have advanced on a path to a considerable degree will tell you that synthesis is not a good idea, to choose one path and stick to it to gain results. I can understand the value of this. I can also see the urge in particular souls to drawn things into unity. When it is unconscious, we can end up with a bit of a muddle. Sort of like if you get over enthusiastic in mixing your paint palette and you just end up with mushy brown. Or was I the only child that did that in art classes at school?

Anyway, with conscious integration or synthesis, the parts remain intact. Rather than losing the individual characteristics of the various parts trying to make them one, a greater understanding of the place for each part in the greater whole emerges. I share this with you because you are reading this book and it is a synthesis of goddess consciousness, crystal healing and ageless wisdom so it is likely you are going to be a part of that synthesising soul group. You will be looking for a way not to be overwhelmed by all the courses, options, topics and journeys that are available at this rather unique time in human spiritual evolution. You will be searching for a way to walk your path but not miss out on the various options available to you.

Mica helps us with this integration. It can take time and we have to surrender and trust, but it will happen without leaving us feeling scattered, unintegrated or chasing several paths all in different directions. When I was a little girl I wanted to be a singer, a teacher, a martial artist, a healer and an actress. Also a writer and a librarian. And an astronaut. And that is just the short list!

As I look back over my life, even at the relatively young age of 39 as I am writing this book, I realise that the gist of all those things is in the mix of my life, just not in typical ways. I get to travel about the cosmos (just in spirit rather than a rocket!) and see from a vast perspective (which is what always appealed to me about being an astronaut anyway) as well as teach, sing and dance in my spiritual playshops and retreats. I also access the universal mind for guidance (which is the most fantastic library anyone could imagine). In my journey to learn how to manage my energy for healing, I have been taught some incredible lessons by various chi gung masters in the martial arts. The performance aspect of sacred theatre is now arising in my work with the Divine Circus (you can find out more at www.divinecircus.com). As incompatible as those desires seemed and as much as I despaired over how I could cram the dreams of fifteen or more lifetimes into one, in the end all the different threads were synthesised into the one journey. Now that doesn't make it easy for me to answer the question, "So what do you do for work?" but it does make that work interesting and fulfilling.

I also know that my own development will continue to evolve and integrate many more threads over the coming years. This is synthesis. I thought I had to choose one path and drop everything else to gain some mastery in it, so that is what I did. What I pleasantly discovered much later was that all the interests I thought I had to sacrifice would come back to me without force because the power of synthesis in my own divine nature is strong. I always want to find a way to lose nothing by bringing everything together.

Quite likely you have this streak in you too and I share this with you so you will keep hope and not worry. Your entire nature wants to be born, and even if that seems diverse and impossible, like you would have to live seven different lives for that to actually happen, it actually can happen in one lifetime through the healing power of synthesis if we are willing to take the journey with trust. Mica helps us with this. So does making a choice to honour one path, which eventually, leads us towards the fulfilment of all paths when our soul is allowed to have its way and we trust in its power of synthesis.

MANIFESTING THROUGH CHOICE

Choices were difficult for me at times because I was so open minded I didn't want to say no to one thing in order to say yes to something else. Then after trying to do everything, there came at a point in my life when the choices were taken away from me.

It was the beginning of the phase I mentioned above when describing my vision of Hecate. I was forced to dive deep into my inner journey and felt quite disabled in the physical world for many years. As I entered that phase, I had a vision I didn't understand where I felt I was at the bottleneck of a journey and couldn't rush through it with everything, but would have to be squeezed through and only eventually released into an experience of freedom. It was a prediction really.

My natural head-in-the-clouds ability to talk with spirit and feel completely and effortlessly connected to the higher worlds was shut down. Instead, I felt like my head was plugged into the earth like a turnip. I couldn't channel, I couldn't tune in and all I could do was vegetate. Well, that is what it felt like. In truth, my head-first orientation was shifting to connect with the wisdom of my body so that I could get on with serving the path of love in a more embodied, less solely mentally driven, way.

It was hard. I wasn't used to it. The choice was 'taken away' by my soul, but really I had chosen it when I said I wanted to fulfil my divine destiny. I just didn't consciously know what my choice would entail. It was just like what I say to clients who are wondering what on earth is going on, and their guidance tells them their prayers are being answered. It might not look like it, but whatever is happening must be necessary for those prayers to manifest themselves. Ah, we didn't know exactly what we were asking for! Nonetheless, it is for the best.

So that one choice, to do my inner work with dreams and the body, led me into a very narrow pathway for the better part of a decade. Those that know me recognise that I am naturally an expansive spirit. I like to explore many topics and interests and I like to do many different things. All in service to the one love of course, but from as many different angles and methods as possible! So I sing, I dance, I chant, I write books, find art, write oracle decks, make music, channel, do healings, work with crystals, play with goddesses, use colour, sound and crystal bowls for shamanic rituals and group dance journeys and so on.

I have plenty of irons in the fire, most of the time. Recently, my agent jokingly commented that he was talking to his dog (Hecate again!) about how he had only just got his head around my current product list of what was published or in line to be published, when he got copied in on a flurry of emails between my publisher at Blue Angel and myself about ideas for new products. My manager despairingly confided to his dog that he wondered how he would ever be able to keep up with it all. Fortunately he does seem to be able to. Perhaps Hecate, via his dog, is helping.

So you might imagine how I felt at being so restricted and restrained. During those years of divine incubation, I was able to inhabit a deep underworld place of dreams and meditations and not much else. As it turns out, I was being hatched, but at the time it seemed my choices had narrowed down to one pathway – intense therapeutic inner work – and I felt I had to take it. I had absolutely no clue of the variety, diversity and expansiveness that was waiting for me on the other side of that narrowing pathway. That was the bottleneck in my vision, but I didn't understand any of it at the time.

In narrowing down to one choice, I believed I was saying no to so many things I wanted to do and that was very painful for me. It felt like I was sacrificing much of who I was. I did it out of spiritual necessity to honour what was being offered to me. To be honest, what else would I do but take that journey? Even in my moments of shying away from what is asked of me, I always know I'll get on and do it anyway.

On the other side of that choice was so much more than I could have imagined. I say this to you to let you know that making a choice will lead you into your destiny. Even if that choice seems to be letting things go or creating loss. When the choice feels truthful for you, irrespective of what you believe the effects or consequences of that choice may be, then you will be led into your divine destiny.

HEALING PROCESS

This healing process is to help you make that choice from the depths of your soul, so that you can flourish, make your decisions at the crossroads of your life and recognise that the synthesizing ability of your own soul is calling you to make a choice so it can continue to do its work, pulling all the strings of your life experience into one gorgeous, useful, brilliant tapestry for you to continue to live, weave and share as sacred art with the world.

The Process

Have your mandala and/or crystal with you. Find a quiet space where you can relax and have some privacy if possible. Turn off your phone or computer for the duration of the healing process. Give yourself permission to genuinely take time out for your own healing.

When you are ready, say the following, "I call upon Hecate, the ancient crone, the ageless one of unconditional love, she who guards the threshold, the crossroads and the gateways. I call upon your loving protection and wisdom. I call upon the Crystal Angel of Mica, the healing spirit of light and synthesis of my own higher self, and the guidance that loves me unconditionally. I receive your luminous presence completely into my body, mind and soul. So be it."

Close your eyes and imagine, sense or perceive that you are descending down a spiral staircase made of shiny, reflective metallic sheets of mica. It shines even in the darkness as you descend into a deep, open black space.

Within that space, you see a distant figure in a vast, flowing, black cloak with a hood draped over her head. Notice that many paths converge around her, meeting at the point in the centre where she stands.

If you wish, make an offering to this figure by sending love or placing an object, relationship, situation or set of life circumstances, symbolically at her feet.

When you are ready, she will lift her hood as you allow her to gaze at you in the knowledge that she sees all of you without judgment. She will help you make your next choice and take your next step on your path, even if your mind is unsure whether you are at a crossroads or if you know you are but are confused, frightened or uncertain about how to proceed.

She holds up a shining golden key and places it in your hand.

She steps back and shows you the multitude of doorways before you. Allow yourself to be drawn towards the door that feels right for you. If you are uncertain, allow her to firmly push you towards the door that is right for you now.

At the door, place the key in the lock and turn it. The door opens for you and you step through it, on to the next phase of your journey.

Hecate watches you and you sense her presence with you, protecting, guiding and allowing you to make your own way, with trust.

When you are ready say, "I give the Crystal Angel of Mica and Hecate who loves me unconditionally, permission to clear my energy field of any impediments that would hold me back from fully exploring my divine path or that would prevent me from stepping through this crossroads in my life onto the next pathway in my journey, now. I also give full permission to those unconditionally loving beings to offer me whatever protection is needed to ensure I take the journey that will best fulfil my divine life mission. Through my own free will, so be it."

Close your eyes again and relax. Take at least eight deep, slow breaths in and out while visualising, sensing or feeling that your awareness is spiralling back from that sacred space into your body in the here and now. Feel the air on your skin, the temperature of the room and the heat or coolness in your feet.

In your own time, just open your eyes and place your hands in prayer at your heart centre to acknowledge your healing practice.

Notice what opportunities, inner nudges or outer encouragements come to you in the days and weeks following this exercise. Don't be afraid to act. Trust in what life delivers to you. Also trust in your own power of discernment and intuition. Keep your mica or mandala near your bedside for at least three days after this exercise to assist with integration.

7.

MATANGI (DIFFERENCE)
HELIOTROPE (INNER CHRIST)

MANIFESTING THROUGH QUIRKINESS

The dark green goddess smiles at you. You are one of hers. You don't fit into the typical mould, you were born to break it into pieces, allowing for a more authentic way to be. She showers you with gifts and in that which is cast aside, you find treasures and are released into great fulfilment, prosperity, love and wellbeing.

MATANGI (DIFFERENCE)

I have always felt like a black sheep. Born into a long line of rebellious women, doing things differently seemed to run in my family. My mother, my grandmother and my great-grandmother were always ruffling feathers, doing things their own way and were rather ahead of their time. As a result I grew up believing that women were naturally capable, dynamic, independent and empowered. It never occurred to me that it would be otherwise. During childhood, I felt happy just being myself, with all my quirks. I was sensitive, loved trees, the ocean, nature, dancing, singing, music, reading, playing, had a tendency to stare at the sky in awe and had a vivid imagination that made all things possible.

It wasn't until I began pre-school and encountered the socialisation process that came with the education system that I was hit with an overwhelming sense of fear and anxiety. I realised I was different to those around me. I watched some of the more popular children lie, cheat, steal and bully others without any sense of recrimination or remorse. I was absolutely flabbergasted! I distinctly remember being lost for words and was too shocked to speak, when a classmate in the first grade told a barefaced lie to our teacher, blaming me for something she had done. I understood why she had done it – to avoid getting into trouble for taking a puppet from the classroom toy box. But I couldn't believe she would try to get me into trouble to avoid the consequences of her actions. I had no idea what to do in the face of such behaviour.

I struggled for most of my schooling years with a deep and unrelenting anxiety. I hated the violence of schooling, the psychological and occasionally physical aggression from some of the teachers and some of the students. I hated the system and the punitive, authoritarian approach and looking back, my schools were probably more free-spirited than many! I have always had a healthy respect for spiritual authority, but school uniforms and rules just seemed so pointless to me. However, I did want an education and tried my best to get the most out of my schooling experience. Once I was done, I couldn't wait to taste freedom. Although I would miss seeing my friends for hours every day, I was ready to leave school behind. To finally be able to walk out of those gates and leave it all behind, once and for all, felt like heaven. I was exhilarated!

I went through the same process again at university before I decided enough was enough. I went into therapy to deal with what had become depression and anxiety, and began to chip away the layers of pain that came from not fitting in and feeling judged, ridiculed and shamed for it. As I started to let go of that painful history and felt more comfortable being myself whether it was acceptable to others or not, I attracted a whole bunch of other black sheep who didn't fit into the norm either! Suddenly there were many people to play with and I made new friends. The more I knew myself, the more the friendships I chose were nurturing. It took time, patience and a willingness to let go of toxic relationships over and over again. In time, I found a few precious people who are still wonderful, shining lights in my life, who accept me completely as I am. Being me was so much more fun, energising and anxiety-reducing than trying to be something that I was not. I came to realise that my differences were something to be proud of and I began to enjoy being who I was, that defying social convention could be fun and breaking with tradition could actually be stimulating. I didn't do these things just for the sake of it. I just did my best to live my truths whether they matched with the more accepted mainstream views or not. When I was younger, this was difficult as I have butted heads with authority figures rather consistently my entire life. As I got older and became (higher) self-employed, I was able to use all the parts of my personality others had once found difficult to deal with, in order to serve people on their spiritual paths. It all worked out perfectly. There were just a few bumpy moments on the journey.

In the ancient tradition of India, Matangi is the goddess of outcasts, of all that is rejected by society and considered to be outside of polite and respectable society. In the caste system of India, from which Matangi heralds, these people are known as untouchables.

In our society they would be the nerds, underdogs, homeless, imprisoned, diseased, mentally ill or anyone that doesn't quite fit in. Cultural conditioning has a lot to do with that. In India and many parts of South East Asia, being announced as a guru means you are acknowledged and understood (to a varying degree) to be part of the spiritual fabric of a culture. It isn't out of the ordinary at all. If you are to make the same pronouncement in the West, you may well be regarded with a great deal of suspicion, distrust, considered a cult leader or a charlatan out for financial gain by duping others. Whether that response ends up being an accurate one or completely unwarranted is perhaps only revealed in time. But, you can see that cultural conditioning has a lot to do with our viewpoint. Matangi is the patron goddess for social outcasts in any culture. Who those people actually are will vary in each culture.

She is often pictured as dark green but may also be blue or red in skin colour, and is worshipped by many as a protector, saviour and bestower of healing and prosperity.

My first experience of Matangi came unexpectedly one Christmas morning. Meet the Indian Goddess of Outcasts on the birthday of Christ was rather unanticipated but considering how Christ was a social outcast in many ways, it was absolutely perfect too. That morning I was indulging in a solitary hour of dance and meditation before the social aspect of the day began. I was feeling grounded, nurtured and held in that space, and also quite emotional – in a good way. Feeling a strong connection with the Divine usually does make me feel quite emotional.

At the end of the meditation my hands spontaneously went into a strange posture which I had never held before. With fingers crossed over each other and the middle fingers raised, I sat peacefully for some time. When I opened my eyes and gazed at my hands I was curious as to what was going on.

I Googled the hand position later that morning and discovered it was known as the Matangi Mudra. A mudra is a posture from the ancient yogic traditions of India that allows for energy to flow in a particular direction. It might be created with the eyes, the tongue, the hand and fingers or another part of the body. I have spontaneously felt different mudras, especially in the forms of hand gestures, in healing sessions especially when working with groups. Most of the time I didn't know what they were for until I researched them afterwards. In all my teaching, I had never encountered this particular mudra before so it was something of a spiritual Christmas gift.

Feeling quite emotional once again (I am a water sign and easily moved by feeling!), I began to search for images of Matangi and to learn about her. I had a strong desire to know all about the mysterious being who had entered my body and shown herself to me through the mudra. I was astounded with what I found out. I was delighted to discover that Matangi is a tantric version of Saraswati whom I have a strong connection with (we met her in Chapter Three). Mainstream western culture tends to think of Tantra as sacred sexuality but it is so much more than that. If we think of Tantra at all in the western mainstream, it is quite possibly only because the pop singer Sting once talked publicly about the lengthy duration of his sexual encounters which he said was a result of his study of the tantric arts. That tends to be the beginning and the end of what mainstream culture views as being Tantra.

In the worlds of spirituality, sacred relationship and sexuality and to some extent yoga, Tantra is held with rather more intrigue. There are plenty of workshops and gatherings that claim to be tantric simply because they have a focus on sexuality. To simply exchange the word sexuality with Tantra, even if it is sexuality with a more spiritual or sacred intention, is inaccurate. Of course, that doesn't mean those workshops on sexual healing aren't helpful. If we are going to understand Matangi as a tantric goddess, we have to understand that although she may work with us to heal our sexuality, it is not her primary focus. Tantra is like a form of shamanism in the sense that it is a path dedicated to wholeness. The shaman seeks to know all worlds of existence and to learn to navigate through those worlds for healing. The practitioner of Tantra seeks to know all worlds of existence, not only to navigate through them but to integrate their experience of those worlds so that they may come to recognise the Divine as alive in all things and thereby find bliss and freedom from suffering. To this end, when we begin a tantric path, we actively seek out the rejected, lost, taboo parts of ourselves that we once would have avoided at all costs with the intention of accepting them and eventually discovering the sacredness of those parts of us. This is a path of healing and divine awakening. Sexuality can be a part of that but more often it is about learning to face, accept and integrate other aspects of our emotional and physical experience so that we may bring ourselves to some sort of peace with our fears, such as abuse, poverty, illness and death. Tantra embraces all of life. For most of us there are parts of life that we love more easily than others. Tantra asks us to investigate that which we have turned away from and seek our acceptance of it. It is not an easy path. Fortunately, Matangi comes to those on the tantric path and can assist us. Through her ability to support us as we reclaim the rejected aspects of ourselves and our existence, Matangi plays the role of tantric goddess and wayshower.

The reduction of Tantra to a solely sexual pursuit is reflective of the obsessive focus that western culture has on sexuality. I believe this exists at this point in human evolution for a reason. Despite an appearance of being open-minded about sexuality, with overt sexual images popping up in advertising and music videos, and a thriving pornography industry, western culture is so skewed towards a disconnection from the body and the mind that the only thing keeping the West grounded is its obsession with sexuality. It is a way to keep our interest in the body. Without our cultural obsession with sexuality, the body might be rejected altogether! What a disastrous rejection of the Divine Feminine path of awakening that would be. It would also mean more work for the spiritual evolution of the human soul that is teaching us to connect with the body with love so that the soul has a temple through which to manifest the divine presence.

As more people are drawn onto a healing path that requires them to connect with their bodies – perhaps to heal sexual dysfunction, depression, lack of meaning or purpose, or disease – the split between mind and body will gradually be overcome. This is the next step for the soul to be able to grow and fulfil its divine destiny of becoming god or manifesting divinity. One cannot manifest anything, including spiritual radiance, without a physical aspect. It is the physicality that makes manifestation possible.

It is only when we stop connecting with our bodies with endless demands or perfectionistic criticisms that we can mature into a culture led by the feelings of the heart which we access through being present in our bodies with love. When we are led from the heart, we cannot commit atrocities that we can be justified with our minds. The heart simply will not allow it. Imagine a world where decisions are made primarily from the heart. It is far gentler, kinder, more respectful and sustainable than this world that has been created with decisions that are primarily from the intellectual mind. Of course, everything serves a purpose in divine evolution but at this stage of human spiritual development, the heart is to be led onto centre stage. In a culture that has largely shunned the body, for various reasons – shame and fear being two common ones – the path of Tantra and tantric goddesses such as Matangi support us to reclaim our connection to the body as a sacred part of the divine experience of life.

We are in great need of Matangi's presence. The more we are able to loving inhabit our bodies, the more we can learn about feminine wisdom such as the cycles of the seasons, life, death and the healing power of emotions, through our bodily experiences. As we become familiar with feminine wisdom, we become more open to simply learning and growing through life, with less fear and greater trust. Our spiritual path can then open up and as a result of that, we can live with more purpose and passion. We have more of a sense of who we are and what feels authentic to us so we know what choices to make. We don't have to run around trying to find our life purpose and path. It happens naturally as a part of our healing process as we reconnect with our bodies and our wholeness. This then frees us to let go of a distorted relationship with our own sexual nature. Instead of obsession, and typically the shame, fear and guilt that lurks underneath it, we can experience sexual energy in the tantric way as another aspect of the Divine. We can embrace our sexuality and invite the sexual energy to rise and nourish all of our chakras, rather than just remaining at the base of the spine, in the genital area. (Of course, we can love our base chakra and sexual organs as an expression of the divinity in us too!) We can begin to feel ecstatic sensations of bliss, triggered by our sexuality, but not limited to it. Sexuality and spirituality begin to blend and we can experience a different kind of ecstatic bliss, where all parts of us are held in loving embrace. Now *that* is tantra!

Some years ago, a man in his twenties wanted to see me for some healing sessions. He was good looking, played rugby, was in a relationship with a woman but also was exploring what he referred to as Tantra with a female therapist. When I asked him to explain what he meant by Tantra I was uncomfortable with his response.

Essentially it seemed that he was having sex with his massage therapist, whom was apparently also new to 'Tantra' and they were 'discovering it together' with the intention of eventually experiencing full body orgasms. That was the goal he said he wanted to achieve. There were so many problems with the scenario I didn't really know where to start. It sounded to me like his massage therapist had got tangled up in an attraction to him, and he with her, and one or both of them had seduced the other and they'd ended up in a real mess. The once professional therapeutic relationship had become compromised and turned into a sexual relationship instead. They continued on with the arrangement calling it Tantra and neither not really knew what they were doing.

They had discovered Matangi, by breaking taboos whilst searching for the Divine in what was forbidden but without awareness or responsibility. I suspected he was accustomed to getting his own way and expected that trend to continue. So like a child, he would demand what he wanted from a woman and if she failed to deliver it immediately, he would simply coerce, cajole, seduce and manipulate her until she capitulated and gave him what he wanted. When his massage therapist failed to deliver the desired results, he sought me out as someone whom he thought was more spiritually powerful and capable of taking him further down the path. It was, to use a non-technical term, all a bit icky.

Essentially he wasn't interested in Tantra at all. He didn't actually want to go further down any path. He wanted to stay exactly as he was, with all his defences operating and intact, and to have his particular desire of a full body orgasm delivered to him. I realised he actually had no idea of the potential consequences of what he was asking for. The fact that pushing so much energy through his body when it was so closed down emotionally could have caused severe psychological and even physical harm didn't even register with him.

It didn't matter much because he didn't want to take the journey into his own dark side to find the wild erotic presence within himself that could lead him into the state he was seeking. He was utterly terrified of that presence – without realising it. That presence exists in all of us. We have to breakdown our ego with all its defences to open up to that part of the Divine in us. It is quite a journey and rarely an easy one. So while he desired the ecstasy that the inner work on the tantric path could bring, he had no idea that his trait of controlling and manipulating people through seduction, persistence and thinly veiled aggression to get what he wanted would need to be sacrificed. If he was to surrender into the powerful experience he craved, he would have to let go of trying to orchestrate and control it.

We never got very far in our work together. After a couple of sessions, I realised he was quite happy to see me, pay his money, have me process a huge amount of his negative energy for him so he could leave feeling better and as disinterested as ever in doing any personal healing for himself. I felt like I was not honouring myself or him in the work. It was like going to clean a person's house week after week when it just got dirty again. I wasn't a cleaner, I was a healer. He didn't want to heal, he wanted a cleaner. By that, I mean he wanted someone to make him feel better over and over again, without him having to take responsibility for his own path or do any of the work. Once this realisation hit me, I 'resigned' from working with him. He continued to email me and ask for sessions for some time afterwards, demonstrating his pattern of persistence and attempted seduction. It took saying 'no' many, many times before he finally understood that I was refusing him. He then became angry, quite possibly due to feelings of rejection, which I understood but did not engage with. Eventually he stopped contacting me. I don't know if I was the first woman who ever said no to him, but I expect I won't be the last.

Matangi brought me something valuable through that experience. I gave myself permission not to have to engage with people just because they sought me out. Simple, right? However, my natural tendency is to say yes, often without thinking. Especially if people are asking for spiritual help. I like to 'blame' that disposition on being born in the Year of the Tiger as tiger people are said to leap first and think about the ramifications of what we have done later on. Not the most ideal personality trait, I'll admit, especially when I then have to back pedal because I have over-committed myself or ended up in a situation that I really shouldn't be in at all.

After going through rather enough of those experiences, including the ill-fated attempt to work with the man I described above, I advanced in my ability to trust my gut *and* think before I leapt. I still get myself into various scrapes from time to time, but I have learned to get out more quickly and even avoid unnecessary dramas completely by just saying no! I am not too hard on myself for the mistakes I have made because, if nothing else, they often end up as useful teaching stories for my books!

As the tantric expression of Saraswati, Matangi is akin to her shadow sister or darker version. They share some powers in common. Matangi is also known as the goddess of the spoken word, of wisdom, and music. In addition, Matangi is possessed of supernatural powers including the ability to defeat one's enemies and attract what is needed to oneself. These are rather appealing powers to have at one's disposal.

Matangi has the ability to turn what is refuse, rejected, outcast or judged into something that is sacred. If you have ever been handed lemons by life and turned it into lemonade or used adversity to your advantage somehow, then you are under Matangi's grace. Matangi has blessed those of us that have the knack of taking the worst life experiences (such as abuse, degradation, humiliation, rejection or abandonment) and using them as a catalyst for accessing greater spiritual wisdom, love and power. Where she is present, what is cast aside can become more valuable than gold. My darkest and most difficult struggles end up bringing me into the most grace, spiritual awakening and empowerment. It has happened that way so often that I have learned to accept my path is a tantric one. If I want to open up to more light, it will naturally come to me, but the way will involve diving head-first into my darkness, creating some space in there, clearing out old wounds and learning to love myself more unconditionally. What can I say about that process? You probably know it for yourself. It hurts (at first) but it works.

There is nothing that is denied Matangi's devotees because she claims all that is. She knows that the Divine is in that which is rejected just as much as in that which is accepted. Her power enables her to dissolve shame and judgment and claim the divine energy in everything, even that which is most hated and feared. That opens her, and those that work with her, to an inexhaustible reservoir of energy and considerable divine power.

Her tools are the sword, symbolising discernment and the severing of attachments; the noose through which she can grab us and pull us into enlightenment through her love; and the veena (musical instrument) which shows her connection to Saraswati as the goddess of music and creative expression. These symbols feature heavily in her iconography, as do parrots, which are considered to be her sacred animal.

When we connect with parrots or they seek us out in the physical world or in dreams, meditations or visions, we are connecting with the energy of Matangi for our own healing. Parrots generally teach us about language and remind us to pay attention to our communication skills. They also teach us how to work with colour for healing which is one way we know we are being initiated into the realm of the Divine Feminine. We will often become far more aware of (even quite possibly obsessed with) colour and how it affects our mood, energy and behaviour. Apart from those generalised metaphysical medicines, each parrot has its own peculiar message for us. We can sense that message through their behaviour, the circumstances around the interaction and a bit of internet research might help too.

When I was going through a difficult phase processing grief around the ending of the relationship I have been discussing thus far, I asked for some help to understand what I needed to do to work through it. Although it was only about six weeks after I had left the five-year relationship, I was concerned that I may be getting stuck in the feelings of loss and not moving forward. I had taken many steps forward and was enjoying my new life, but I could also feel a heaviness in my heart that tied me to the past. It worried me and I prayed one evening that I be shown anything I needed to know about it.

The next morning I awoke to find a rainbow lorikeet had shed one perfect, colourful feather on my front door step. I looked at it and noticed a cheeky lorikeet hanging upside down from a branch, dipping his beak into luscious flowers and generally swinging about having a good time. I gazed at the feather. I noticed the patterns of colour and how they related to what was happening in my solar plexus and heart chakras, and how that was mirrored by the yellow and green patterning on the feather. I felt Mother Nature was witnessing me with love.

These particular parrots are about seeking out what nourishes you and enjoying beauty, both of which were key approaches I had been taking since I had stepped into my new life. Instinctively, I had been seeking out nourishing connections with people and developing new friendships within a few days of moving house and was somehow feeling more beautiful within my own being than I had felt in a long time. Perhaps that was because I felt much loved by life and nurtured in my process of change in spite of the challenges and also due to how it had all come together (which I will describe later on in the book).

As I watched the parrot forage through the vibrant, red blossoms, I felt a message come to me from Mother Earth, "Seek out and reside in the sweetness of your heart." Over the emotionally challenging days that followed the parrot's appearance, as waves of grief rose and fell, I would bring myself gently but effectively back to happiness and peace by taking my awareness into my heart and feeling the sweetness there. The energy in my heart felt gentle, kind and serene and I found it relaxing and healing to drop into that place within my being. The parrot and the message it brought me from Mother Earth were reminders to do this to support myself through the grieving process. It was very helpful.

This parrot was also a reminder of the importance of expressing myself. They are chatty, communicative birds and the significance of expression is part of their healing wisdom. I actually began writing this book when the relationship break up reached its culmination. I was packing up my belongings and going through intense moments of emotional and physical upheaval, in between writing each chapter. It was difficult but I continued to write the first draft throughout that month and in the month that followed the break up, as I settled into my new life, I continued with the second draft. Although it took a lot of courage to do this, I also saw it as supportive. Writing is something that keeps me connected to my heart and my truths. This helped me to keep my heart open to my grieving process and to the spiritual worlds that are so present when I write. The parrot affirmed this was the right thing to do. I was a bit worried my grief-stricken state might compromise my writing, but it flowed as per usual. Perhaps too much! This book is quite a bit longer than anticipated.

Thanks to the parrot I felt affirmed in how I was dealing with my situation. I did some further research to deepen my understanding about its wisdom, particularly as it had bothered to pay me a direct visit. I was stunned to find that part of the medicine of the rainbow lorikeet is the ability to recognise your soul mate. I felt I was being guided to be open hearted to genuine relationship and to allow that to heal my past experiences when the time was right. I had been flattered but dismissive of any romantic advances since I had become single again because I felt too vulnerable to get involved with anyone else at a deep level and I wasn't interested in superficial involvements. Although I recognised I needed time to grieve, I also heard the lorikeet's message that I would know when I felt a genuine connection and that I could trust in that connection when it presented itself.

Through that parrot, Matangi had shown up again in my life promising me the grace and protection of her healing presence. That one little feather brought me great comfort and the confidence that I was actually healing, approaching my process in the correct way and had a future ahead of me that included a soul mate relationship that would further support the healing of my heart. I accepted these messages with gratitude.

Matangi is a goddess that brings out the rebellious spirit in us and encourages us to walk our own paths, especially when that means we will be doing things in a way that is different or unusual. Hers is the consciousness of breaking with social norms and defying convention. With Matangi, we begin to learn that nothing is without divinity. We can release judgments and find a level of freedom we might never have thought possible.

This is practical on so many levels. For those working in spiritual vocations, money can often be an issue and not necessarily because they aren't good with money. Often there is a huge block around the belief that integrity, spirituality and earning a good income can go well together. People are willing to pay lawyers or a web designer a high fee, but when it comes to healing their soul believe it should be for free or far cheaper! No one said the priorities in our culture as reflected by financial current 'realities' were sane. However, on the tantric path, we are learning to find and embrace the shadow. In corporate worlds, that might mean taking environmental concerns into account in business decisions. In the spiritual vocations it might mean opening up to financial assistance in the form of sponsorship from those with greater financial energy who have enough wisdom to recognise the importance of what you are doing. Even if they don't fully understand it, they may be willing to invest in your success. It could also mean opening up your own belief systems about money and finances, and asking the Divine Feminine to show you the most integrated and authentic way to experience greater financial success in your life, if that is something that has meaning for you. Tantra, and the tantric goddess Matangi, come to us when we are integrating our shadow and that includes anything we are not quite comfortable with. I believe Matangi's appearance to me on Christmas morning was also letting me know my shadow included the Christ Consciousness, an energy I came to know more and more intimately in quite surprising ways in the months and years that followed. I have written about some of those experiences in this book and in *Crystal Masters 333*. So Matangi appears as a herald of our own divinity. In the shadow it lays, partially hidden, until we claim all that we are and come to know ourselves as completely divine, not just intellectually, but in all of our cells.

Matangi exists in all actions, all things, even within those actions considered unlucky, she remains in utter harmony with the Divine. When I opened an umbrella inside a classroom on the first day of my final exams at the end of high school, people were horrified. How could I do something considered so unlucky on the first day of the exams we had all been dreading since our first day of high school! Some people declared it was bad luck and I would have trouble in my exams. I defiantly rejected that notion and went on to become dux of my high school instead. That attitude is Matangi. For those that create beautiful art out of driftwood or from rubbish at tips, there is Matangi again. For those that sing songs of wisdom about being different, outcast or rejected, there she is again. Freegans, who live off the food that gets thrown away, are Matangi's children too.

After my first personal experience of Matangi that Christmas morning, I started to see her everywhere. I saw her on *Glee*, the television show featuring nerdy students with lots of artistic talent that get bullied by the 'in' crowd at school. That show attracted millions of viewers and as I watched a documentary that charted its success, I was struck at how many people could relate to the content of the show. It seemed that those who didn't fit in to the norm were more plentiful than those who did, and absolutely loved having a program that expressed something of their experience. The outcasts were being recognised and feeling empowered by that. Matangi was making her presence felt.

Then I felt Matangi expressing herself through Lady Gaga, the left-of-centre pop performer who has worn dresses made out of meat, is interested in unusual, shocking forms of visual self-expression and performance, and has legions of followers she calls her 'monsters'.

Then I thought of the Divine Circus, my beloved brainchild of dance music with a spiritual edge. When I began working on that project, it was so different to what I usually did that I had long-term clients asking me if I was still a spiritual teacher! They could see the Ringmaster of the Divine Circus was rather different to the Alana Fairchild of workshops and oracle decks and thought I had gone through some radical transformation. It was another aspect of me but it didn't mean the Alana Fairchild they knew was gone. She still lived and loved and channelled but as well as meditation, chanting and energy work, I had added the Divine Circus and its house music to my spiritual repertoire. When I can sneak in a fusion of shamanism and performance art along with the house music, all the better! The Divine Circus is more like running a yogic nightclub than teaching a spiritual class. However, in both I am working towards the same aim: The liberation of the human soul into love and freedom. The circus just offers a rather different route for people who may not have connected with me through a spiritual book or class but needed something spiritually that my presence could bring to them. So when I was off learning about being a DJ and the structure of house music, I knew Matangi was with me, helping me to help others via a rather unorthodox route. Through Matangi's wisdom I trusted I could bring light through my work as a spiritual teacher in many ways, obvious and not so obvious, and it could all be beneficial.

Like Saraswati, her somewhat less grubby sister-self, Matangi is known as Nada or the energy of sound that travels through the energy lines of the body. For those of us who work with sound for healing, especially in ways that are unconventional or unusual, Matangi will be working through us as the divine voice. For those of us that want to heal through music, Matangi is right there with us bringing the divine light alive through all that we do.

At the most sublime levels, Matangi helps us transcend pollutants and achieve divine liberation. It is said that when the digestion is powerful enough, one could digest a rock! I certainly don't recommend anyone literally tries this but the gist of it is that through the divine power of Matangi one can gain the strength to overcome toxicity and digest the indigestible. This is a metaphor for being able to integrate the aspects of life that are hard to accept with peace and equanimity, moving beyond judgment and into acceptance of all of life as an expression of the divine presence that can nourish us. That is the tantric way.

Matangi's energy also brings the practical gift of helping you to overcome poisons. Given the state of our world, this is useful. The use of pesticides and other chemicals means that physical poisons are rampant in products we use daily. Our bodies endure a somewhat unrelenting and increasing exposure to radiation from various technologies and this can become adverse to our wellbeing. On a psychic level, exposure to the psychological and emotional energies of others is increasing. It wasn't so long ago that communicating from a distance required a telephone or even a letter but now have instant email, online chat, Facebook, Twitter, Instagram and other online social networking communities that can subject users to a constant influx of thoughts, opinions, feelings and intentions. Sometimes the stream of information will be uplifting and helpful. Even if it is helpful, the sheer volume of incoming data can be overwhelming to the system and risks becoming something akin to a poison that drains our life force and wellbeing. Working with Matangi to energetically overcome this state of affairs will help strengthen your energy field so that you can work to change what you can and learn to bear what you cannot.

One of my dear friends has a well-developed Matangi energy in several ways. He doesn't fit into any particular social group, yet he seems to know and be known by everyone that I meet. I can be in a totally unrelated group, and his name will come up unexpectedly. He lives by his own set of rules and isn't all that interested in authority though he deals with it when needs be. He is adored, nearly worshipped, by some of his closest friends, yet it doesn't turn his head at all. He is one of the most naturally non-judging people I have met. He just accepts all of life with its ups, downs, dysfunctional and the functional. He enjoys learning how to build up his resistance to poisons by ingesting plants and allowing his body to learn how to fight off the toxins. I have no idea why he does this. I doubt he does either, although in his quirky way he will have a philosophy behind it. I also suspect it is a strong carry through from a past life as a shaman who worked with the medicinal and poisonous aspects of plants. My best friend has difficulty understanding a word that he says and she simply accepts that he is on a completely different wavelength to most, if not all, of the population! He is utterly unique and in all ways possible lives outside of the everyday world and its way of doing things, yet successfully moves about within it.

When I first met him he was wearing little more than a pair of jeans and a leopard-print headscarf whilst wildly playing drums. He came up to me, grabbed my shoulders, shook them a little and yelled in my ear (there were lots of drums playing), "Hey, I like your dress!" It was animal-print and matched his bandanna. He then jumped around the room in his bare feet and went back to his drumming. He plays the piano like an angel even though he has never had a lesson in his life. We sing mantras together, which he occasionally likes to pepper with swear words. This sends me into fits of giggles but at times it does offend others. He writes music and stories for children about accepting all of life. He is a force unto himself and he is open to every sort of person being their own person too. He is keenly interested in people and doesn't want to change them, he just wants to know them. This quality is very attractive to people who have rarely or never been appreciated for who they are and have felt pressured to change themselves to suit the demands of others. When they are finally exposed to someone who is interested in them just being who they are it can be quite an experience. This is a Matangi-blessed man and I feel very blessed to have the gift of his friendship.

HELIOTROPE (INNER CHRIST)

Heliotrope, also known as bloodstone, is a dark, rich green and actually looks like the skin of Matangi. It is sourced from various sites around the world and is relatively easy to find, inexpensive and often available in jewellery or as tumbled stones. It gets the name bloodstone for the red droplets that colour the stone and are sometimes said to be drops of the Christ's blood upon the green earth.

Christ himself was a rebel. He trashed temples, thwarted authority, got angry instead of being obedient and placid, and was rejected, even scorned and scoffed at by most of those around him. He was difficult. He was mocked and misunderstood. He was also true to himself and sought to serve his divine mission even through moments of doubt.

As an outcast he did not spurn society but understood his role in social evolution would require him to rock boats with new ideas and ways of being. He needed to challenge conventional beliefs and attitudes in order to free the spirits of those who were so enslaved by fear. We continue to work with the teachings of the Christ today, freeing society one heart at a time, into the loving grace of the divine.

There is a difference between having a soulful approach to the role of outcast and having an ego wound that leaves one feeling rejected by society. The difference can be in found in our willingness and ability to engage with the world from a position of empowerment and self-acceptance. I have been on both sides of this. I have suffered the anxiety and shame of not fitting in and being judged and ridiculed for it. I have learned to let go of all that as it is the issues of others, not my own! I am now able to step forward into who I am with power, love, a cheeky, creative curiosity, and a desire to share my gifts with as many people as I can possibly touch with that love, self and uniqueness. I hope I can encourage them to do the same.

When it all comes down to it, there is no such thing as normal. There is only the extent to which we are willing to be differentiated, the extent to which we can handle our individuality and uniqueness, and the extent to which we can accept the parts of us that we all have in common. The need for connection, to belong, to experience love and intimacy, to make a contribution or leave a legacy are important human drives. The differences we have within us are unique tools that enable us to access these common needs and give expression to our divine light. This is the same divine light in all of creation, just expressed through many and varied lamps.

Heliotrope helps us accept that the Christ within, the divine rebel and the ordinary human being are all wrapped up as god/goddess in the sacred animal body, manifesting a unique life experience. It helps us feel grounded in our bodies and open to our spirits.

In astrology, heliotrope is associated with the sign of Pisces (the fishes) which is also the sign for Christ, and with the twelfth house which is the place where everything that doesn't fit into the other houses is shoved! It governs all the taboo topics particularly spirituality and the unconscious, the mysterious and mystical, and places that generally function outside of regular society including prisons, occult schools and mental institutions. The twelfth house is a pretty interesting place in a person's astrological chart. It will often show their hidden strengths and struggles as well as their potential to express the divine within them.

When we work with heliotrope we are learning how to access that which society cannot accept and make it functional. That might seem a bit odd but just think of the way our society feels about daydreaming. Is it functional, lazy or a symptom of poor concentration that will lead to poor results? If we can't even recognise our need to escape the day-to-day world from time to time, we can end up blocking a key ingredient for creativity and problem solving. Daydreaming – whilst not a way to spend every minute of every day – actually does have a valuable role to play in keeping our mind open and receptive to possibilities. The stimulation of our imagination also enhances our ability to access the mystical experience of the divine, which in turn promotes the feeling that life is meaningful, fun and rich. Working with heliotrope can help us find healthy ways to be a bit crazy and to shake things up in our lives. You might not want to make the mental institution more accessible but we have to be able to feel a bit insane when we see world affairs and societies carrying on in a way that is not sustainable. We can't accept it, even if most everyone else tells us to put up with it, to take medication and to stop complaining. Krishnamurti put it aptly when he said, "It is no measure of health to be well adjusted to a profoundly sick society." Nor, for example, do most people want to explore the idea of prison but unless we know where we feel trapped and denied our freedom, how can we decide whether to accept it and work with it intelligently, fight it and break free, or both? Heliotrope helps us find the courage to take back our power, stay true to what we know, and put energy into healing it. Like Matangi, it takes that which has been cast aside and helps us find the benefit in it by turning it to our spiritual advantage.

On a physical level, heliotrope is said to stop bleeding. Soldiers used to carry it with them to heal war wounds. On a spiritual and energetic level, working with heliotrope can help stop the loss of energy from our wounds (such as wounds of rejection). Instead, it teaches us to circulate that energy within for our own healing, to gain strength and find the defiance (perhaps with the help of Ishtar) and sacred rage (with Sekhmet) we need to stand up and be ourselves. If we have a tendency to give our energy (blood usually represents life-force) away and not keep enough for ourselves, bloodstone can help us remember to take care of our own needs too. For healers, this is so important. You have to remain well and powerful! It is important work that you are doing. As tempting as it might be at times, you are not to treat yourself as less important than those you serve. You are a divine light and you need to honour that by caring for yourself just as you care for others. This is something I had to learn. This sometimes painful lesson came through encounters with disrespectful students and similar events so that I would realise I was as worthy of love and respect, care and nurturance, as those I sought to serve.

In taking a healer's journey, we can unwittingly become a role model for others on how to live truthfully from the heart with boldness and love. The passionate devotion that so many have to Lady Gaga and the characters from *Glee* shows how much this is needed and craved by people! It doesn't have to be done quite so publicly or in a meat-dress (vegetarians and fashionistas everywhere can breathe a sigh of relief!) but most often an element of our choice to live truthfully takes place in the public eye because others need to see it and be inspired by it, before they can take the inner journey required to reclaim their sense of validation from others and turn it into validation that is given to the self, from within.

Similar to the gifts bestowed by Matangi to have power over one's enemies (which really means gaining power over the wound through which we have given our power away to another) heliotrope was used in ancient Egypt and Babylon to defeat an enemy. It was said to increase one's strength, which it does by rerouting energy back into our energy field rather than letting it drain or bleed out. Energetic draining or bleeding can happen when we are scattered, unfocused, or getting caught up in the dramas or projections of others, rather than firmly coming back to our own truths, feelings and embodied sensations. A quick way to stop the energetic bleeding and come back to an embodied presence in the here and now is with the help of a piece of heliotrope or by calling on the Crystal Angel of Heliotrope.

Underneath the rejection of that which is perceived as different is fear and sometimes also jealousy. People can unconsciously try to quash that which makes them uncomfortable or would threaten to give rise to unresolved issues about an unlived life. Heliotrope helps us find the strength we need so as not to cave into those projections. It supports us to release misplaced guilt that may have us believing we must carry the burdens of others in a dysfunctional, self-diminishing way, rather than shining our light and inspiring others to do the same. This is energising and revitalising emotionally, psychologically, and as a result, physically. Heliotrope will help us understand how beneficial its protective and courage promoting qualities can be, especially for those of us keen to live authentically, by not rejecting but celebrating our differences. This is the radical unconditional love of the Christ, which confronts but ultimately heals the broken hearts and spirits of the world.

MANIFESTING THROUGH QUIRKINESS

You may want to know how and why certain behaviours will deliver desirable results and, perhaps, be able to perfect a method to replicate those results. However, there is an element to creation that is unknowable, unpredictable and wild. Yes, it operates according to certain laws, but one of those laws is definitely the wild card! For all of its seamless order, at times well hidden behind great chaos, there remains a quirky quality to the Divine. Sometimes it seems downright unfathomable. I feel it in myself at times and see it living in some other spiritual teachers too. Although there is love, it is not predictable. It will evoke unexpected responses, strange detours and odd choices that can lead us to the most wonderful healing experiences! Such an impulse can make no logical sense at all but be a genuine, spontaneous encounter that defies explanation or description. It is just the divine presence, in all its quirky genius, happening as it will.

When we aim to manifest through quirkiness, we are calling on the spontaneity, grace and randomness of a cosmic clown. It will answer our call like an enthusiastic lover, provided we are able to really call to it from our hearts. To this we have to hold absolute trust and be willing to let everything go and just fly on the whim of the Divine. It means that we follow up on leads, whether they seem random or not. I have lost count of the number of emails I have sent out in my life as a result of an inner prompting that started something like this, "Hi, you don't know me … this might seem really odd … but I felt this … and this … and I am just putting it out there!" And, these emails have yielded tangible, constructive results.

Sometimes we just have to be willing to dance a merry dance and take action even though it might not yield the results we hope it will or even better, let go of our attachment to what happens and then take action. We will learn more about why that is so useful when we meet Durga later on.

The more we can do this, the more the Universe can intelligently direct us towards manifestation. The mind may see things logically, in a straight line from A to B. A is where we are now and B is where we want to end up. However, the Divine might see that a straight line is not going to work so well. Maybe the frequencies are incompatible with what you want to manifest. And no matter how much you love broccoli, if you are going to make a chocolate cake, you are probably going to need cocoa! The Divine will guide you to what you need, according to what will work for your sacred purpose. If you need certain relationships to manifest a particular outcome, you'll be guided towards those relationships. If you need to be living in an area with a particular frequency (environmental energies can be powerful and we might need to be living in an area to help balance its light or to receive its particular healing vibration) so that you can continue to grow and serve the earth, you will be moved there.

Such twists and turns might take us to C, D and E before we end up at B. As we trust our impulses and quirky notions to go to this place or talk to that person, it might seem that we are moving further away from our simple manifestation of B! However, the Divine is vastly efficient and practical. Even if we are taking a rather interesting scenic journey from A to B, via C, D or Z, it will be more efficient, effective and helpful than a straightforward A to B. In fact, maybe we don't need to get to B after all. Maybe C is want we really want but we just don't know it yet!

I recently had a client who decided she would try the whole trusting malarkey and see what happened. Typically she was a strategist, powerfully adept at creating a plan and able to carry it out with military precision. She was staying with a family member who was quite the opposite – chaotic, couldn't get to an appointment on time if her life depended on it and unable to plan let alone carry out a plan. Rather than let it drive her insane, my client decided to find and tap into this part of herself. She decided that hidden under her more organised nature there must be parts of her that she didn't consciously register. Her chaotic side must be in there somewhere!

As she opened up to this less familiar part of herself, shedding both plans and frustrations when her sister floated about, she began to do some floating herself and magic happened. She could see that through surrender, they were guided into situations and places that could have never come together so perfectly if they had planned it. It just wouldn't have been possible. After this realisation she was wise enough to see that sometimes her family member's refusal to plan was not very healthy and that going to extremes wasn't necessarily the best approach. She also learned a lot from the experience and was able to trust more, surrender more and allow strange twists and turns of fate to work their magic. Alongside her powerful strategy and intention to create from the heart she was now open to what life randomly brought to her door.

The quirks in life, the kinks in the plan and the doors slamming in our face (as another opens somewhere nearby) are universe's way of naturally correcting our alignment into manifestation. If you watch a person driving a car, they don't just hold the wheel and never move it. There are countless micro-corrections that are made with the steering wheel to help the car stay on course. It is the same with us and the divine driver. The quirkiness and the willingness to do things out of the ordinary, to go a different way, to open up to new ideas and to let ourselves be guided by our life experiences are the micro adjustments to the plan.

It was quite painful for me to learn this over the years. When I set out to do something I could be rather single-minded, laser focused and just wanted things done as fast as possible. I was definitely a one-track mind sort of person. Learning to soften, to become more complex and more capable of allowing multiple creative processes to flow, feed and cross fertilise each other took years of surrendering. I had to learn to move in spirals instead of straight lines. I had to learn how to be patient, rest, reset and play, even when I just wanted to work and get things done. Once I could give myself permission to do that, a better way would be revealed or a whole task would become unnecessary. I realised I was guided by a genius far more impressive than my rather impressive stubborn single-mindedness! It all started with trust and with experience I was able to open up to the idiosyncratic, quirky side of the divine genius.

HEALING PROCESS

This healing process will be helpful if you have a tendency to believe that in order to manifest you have to know how, when, where and how to sort out every possible detail yourself. If you believe you cannot succeed without a plan, this healing will help you let go and surrender into the genius of your path. If you feel that you always have to behave perfectly, appropriately or ignore the path less travelled, this healing will be a great tonic for the rebel in you that needs some love, acknowledgement and permission to be.

Those who repeat Matangi's mantra are said to gain her blessings and gifts and as we have discovered there are many. I have included a simple mantra for her in this healing process so that you can develop your personal connection to her.

The Process

Have your crystal and/or mandala with you. Gaze at it and then say the following, "I call upon Matangi, Divine Mother of rebels and outcasts, who loves with the power of unconditional acceptance, bless me mother, I who am your child, who seeks to live in truth over convention, support me with your prosperity, enlightenment, grace and protection. I honour your divine essence and thank you for your presence. I call upon the Crystal Angel of Heliotrope, the bloodstone of the earth, the Christ energy and the healing power, courage and strength that it bestows upon me now. So be it."

Close your eyes and imagine or perceive that around you there is a field of deep green energy with dapples of brilliant red flashing through it. Imagine resting in that field of energy for at least eight slow in and out breaths or as long as feels good for you.

When you are ready, say the following, "Through the healing grace of Matangi and heliotrope, I declare that I trust completely in the divine genius that flows through all of me, including the parts I have found challenging to love and accept. I now choose, of my own free will, to forgive myself and any other that has ever encouraged me to ignore my rebellious spirit or forced me to do things because they thought it was right, rather than encouraging me to trust in what I knew and felt within my own heart. I choose to forgive myself forever giving my power away and I reclaim all energies now, through the healing field of heliotrope, cleansed and purified, back into my energy field. I release all cords of connection between me and another, in this or any lifetime, so that we all may be free. I choose, of my own free will to trust the rebel within me, to trust in the things that make me different, to trust in my own quirkiness and the quirkiness of the divine unfolding plan. So be it!"

Visualise or imagine that you can sense, feel or hear a divine female voice playing a stringed instrument or any other instrument. The music may be otherworldly or something you recognise. She may be singing too. This is the voice of Matangi.

Allow yourself to receive her sound . . . subtly . . . inwardly. Whether it seems audible to you or not this sound is healing.

Imagine, see, sense or feel the energy of that which is half used, incomplete or cast aside in your life. It might be dreams that you had as a child, unfulfilled relationships, unfinished business, unneeded things that you are holding onto, lost children or animals, books you have half read, projects you started but abandoned, extra weight you are needlessly carrying, a toxin in your body that is causing disease and the list goes on. Notice if there is any other toxic energy around you from unhealthy habits or relationship patterns or anything else you feel harms you, even if there are beneficial aspects or you are connecting with it to help yourself in some unconscious way. You might also see the harmful pollution of the oceans or ravages of industry and the waste that is produced. Stay with what appears for you.

Say the following, "I call upon the genius of Matangi, she who honours all and transforms that which is cast aside, polluted or abandoned into that which is sacred. So be it."

Visualise or perceive that those energies are now being drawn up into a whirling force of light, reeling from a messy, chaotic heap into an upward spiralling energy to be transformed and cleansed as they flow through a large, dark green filter of light. That energy may then turn into something else – e.g. a symbol or an animal – or simply return to your energy field or into the energy field of the earth. Be with whatever takes place.

Finally say, "I bow and honour Matangi, the Mother who makes all that has been unclean, clean again. Thank you for your grace and gifts. May I serve the world in love, as your wisdom shines in every human heart, where it is so dearly needed now, mother. So be it."

Finish your healing process with this mantra, which honours Matangi and helps you to activate the power of her healing consciousness and presence within your body and the world around us. A sounding guide is below.

OM MATANGAIYEI SWAHA

Om (rhymes with Tom) Matangaiyei (MA-TONGUE-GUY-YAY) Swaha (SWA-HAH)

Repeat this mantra at least eight times and continue for as many times as feels good. When you have completed this process, simply place your hands in prayer at your heart and you have finished your healing process.

Notice whether there are things you feel you need to release, reclaim or complete in the days and weeks following this healing process. This is the effect of the healing working its way through your body, mind and heart. Trust it.

8.

BASTET (SENSUALITY)
CAT'S EYE (UNVEILING)

MANIFESTING THROUGH PLEASURE

The rattle shakes and sweet scent arises, sheer veils of silk waft flirtatiously, caught by the light breeze. Movement, colour, scent. A feast for the senses. The body relaxes and positive thoughts generate. She blesses with milk and honey, and holds the power of attraction within her.

BASTET (SENSUALITY)

Bastet, or Bast, is the cat-headed goddess of Ancient Egypt. She governs the realms of sensuality, pleasure, dance and music. Her worship has been dated back to at least 3500BC and her temples, including one in particular at Bubastis (a city in Ancient Egypt), was carved of pink granite. Her ancient worship places are heralded as some of the most beautiful, feminine temples ever built.

Having cats as pets throughout my life (now that's a joke other cat owners will relate to, as we are owned by the cat more often than not) has helped me stay in touch with Bastet when my intellect threatened to quash my more wild and free nature. I remember being envious of my Siamese cat, Tabatha, when I was studying a particularly boring law case in some oversized law book. As I balanced the huge tome half in my hands and half on my desk because it was so heavy, forcing an attempt to study, she just sauntered over and sat right in the middle of it. She shamelessly claimed her right to be the centre of attention. I looked at her and admired how beautiful she was, as was only appropriate, before she climbed off the book and padded her way into my top desk drawer, where she curled up, purred and descended into a lovely long nap. I was so tired, bored, depressed and so in need of a respite into to my Bastet nature, of pleasure and relaxation that I felt an unexpected stab of envy! My cat was expressing what I needed to give myself permission to express. I needed to adore myself and have a snooze! Rather than slog away at something I had no interest in and become miserable! That is perhaps one reason why cats are loved by so many. They can be the symbols of dignity and self-care that inspire us to heal wounds of self-neglect and punitive attitudes towards the needs of our body for play, rest and relaxation.

Her shadow sister or other 'side' is Sekhmet, the ferocious lion-headed goddess we met in Chapter Three. Where Sekhmet would burn down the house, Bastet warms it with love, although both have share a strong, protective nature. Bastet can help us learn to let go of the shame and repression that can keep us stuck in our heads and in fear of what others might think of us so that we can get on with living life to the full.

Bastet is daughter of the sun god Ra. Her stories say that she lives with her father by day and by night transforms herself into a feline to protect him. She is known as the all-seeing eye of Ra, can pierce through darkness and strike wherever needed to break curses and render evil incapable of taking root. Hers is an all-encompassing awareness.

Have you ever noticed that problems are easier to sort out and solutions can just come to you when you are not obsessively thinking about them but are instead relaxing or engaging in some activity that brings you pleasure and joy? To relax into pleasure lets energy flow and shift so that things can happen. We are not limited to growing through struggle, suffering and pain. Thankfully! Life is meant to be a journey of balance and variety. When we are really dedicated to our path and perhaps working through some gritty issue or other, we can forget about our joyful nature. I was in therapy for years before I had a moment of just being happy. It didn't relate to anything in particular, in fact I was sitting in the midst of Sydney-pollution on a road with heavy traffic. One of my least favourite things ever. And I just felt a surge of happiness. I talked to my therapist about it later. She looked a bit surprised but asked, "Well did you think it was just going to be pain?"

I guess at some level I had become so used to constant anxiety and inner work just leading to more painful emotional wounds that I hadn't given much thought to joy. When it began to bubble up from within me, it was a pleasant surprise. I learned how to call joy in for healing and to allow that part of me to cackle, celebrate, dance and sing when she felt like it, irrespective of relationship breakups or other challenges that might be going on around me. I learned to surf the waves of my emotions and found that amongst grief, anger, rage and fear, there was plenty of happiness, joy, delight and playful flirtatiousness. That was me meeting Bastet. I had got so used to Sekhmet, it was a nice surprise to realise her pleasure-bringing sister dwelled within me too.

When we are working with evil, darkness, toxic energy and anything that may harm us in some way, it is easy to become defensive. The difficulty with defensiveness is that it doesn't necessarily make us stronger. Like a branch that cannot bend, with enough pressure, resistance can end up snapping the branch. If we can remain softer, able to move and respond from a place of playfulness, even in the face of toxic energy, we naturally invoke the power of Bastet and are often able to side-step it altogether. The trick is to not fear it. This sounds harder than what it is. With practice, we learn to when toxic or undesirable energy is present and our innate ability to firmly, but calmly, deny its right to take up residence in us.

I'll give you an example. I thought carefully about whether or not to share this example with you because I was concerned it might make some people frightened. However, I prayed to the angels to show me if it would ultimately be helpful to include this experience in this book, did some research and realised that many people were having these sorts of experiences and were genuinely frightened and confused by them and needed help. So I wanted to share this story about a disturbing but ultimately helpful experience I had and how I ended the encounter and shifted towards preventing future encounters from taking place.

So that this story makes sense, I need to explain that we have an astral body. We spoke of the astral field when we met Saraswati earlier in this book. As well as the general astral field all of humanity bobs along in like a great cosmic ocean of creation, we each have our own astral body that is a part of our individual energy field. It is something like a big bubble of energy that is less refined than the spiritual part of our energy field and less dense than the physical part of our energy field (i.e. our physical body). It exists between our body and soul, and as we clear it of unresolved pain it becomes a bridge through which body and soul can unite to bring our spiritual light into our physical lives so that we can live the beauty and love of our spiritual essence. The trick, of course, is to clear the unresolved pain. Our life experiences bring that to our attention and then we work on healing it through our personal journey to greater consciousness.

Our astral bodies contains our thoughts, feelings and desires, those that we acknowledge and admit as well as those we don't accept so willingly or even know exist within us. Part of those thoughts, emotions and desires will be consciously chosen by us and others will just be there, inherited through our family and cultural conditioning. Through your personal work, you will find you will hold far less opinion about the 'right' way of doing things, and become more tolerant, free from judgment, open-minded and less fearful. As your astral body becomes clearer, your divine essence can shine through from spiritual purity into embodied radiance.

The astral body is not limited by time and space. So although your physical body is here-and-now in this incarnation, your astral body contains desires, memories and experiences that relate to other incarnations. This is why, for example, we can be perfectly safe in declaring we are healers in this lifetime, and yet, perhaps, feel terrified that if we do so we will be put to death! The unprocessed fear from another lifetime where that was a real danger or actually what happened can be felt in the astral body, even though it is not relevant to this lifetime. We deal with these fears as if they were real, because once upon a time they were real for us and once acknowledged we can work to heal them and let them go.

The boundaries in the astral field are diffuse. They are not like physical boundaries with clear starts, stops and definition. When you are emotionally bonded to another, can feel their feelings, and are affected by their energy then your astral bodies have merged. You can feel each other even when you are not physically connected. So sometimes in our astral bodies, we will pick up on the issues thoughts, unresolved feelings and even the memories of others.

I had such an experience when my beloved grandmother was dying. At one point I felt her long departed husband connect with her astral body. Half alive, half dying, she looked radiant, lit up by her love for him. I could sense him in the room calling her by his special name for her. Not long after, she died. I was still sitting by her body when I felt and saw her memory of furiously pedalling her bicycle down the street as a young girl with her red hair flying. It was not something she had ever spoken of and it was only later when I asked some relatives about it and they confirmed the 'story' that I knew what I had witnessed was a memory in her astral field. I was still connecting with her even though she had left the body I had loved and known as my grandmother, and was moving on into the spiritual worlds for further growth and development. This was a conscious connection between our astral bodies. At the time, I didn't seek it. I was just sitting with her body, trying to come to terms with the fact she was no longer going to be inhabiting it, when it just happened. When you can make this connection with some skill and accuracy, and discern that it is actually what you are doing, it becomes a psychic ability, to be used however you choose to use it.

When you are awake your astral body is usually attached to your physical body and moves about the world with you having thoughts, feelings and emotional experiences. When you sleep it leaves your body and goes travelling to all sorts of places. The astral field to which it belongs is much vaster than the limited world of our beliefs and emotions. The vaster astral field contains all the thoughts, feelings, emotions and experiences ever had by anyone! There are deceased relatives, memories of worlds long gone and visions of worlds yet to come. There is darkness, suffering, light and love. There are endless possibilities for adventure. So when our physical bodies lie down to sleep at night, our astral bodies do what they need to do to live and thrive.

An astral body might visit other souls and offer healing or go to spiritual school to receive training and help. It might end up in some dark places which we may experience as 'having a nightmare'. It might travel to other lands and witness all sorts of people, places or circumstances. We might remember some of this, or we might not. We might declare it was all just a dream, and some of it will be the workings of our unconscious mind processing our experiences. Some of what we recall, that somehow seems more vivid and real, will actually be the adventures of our astral bodies. If you are psychic, or particularly sensitive to energy, you may remember parts of your astral adventures. I have had clients report on their travels during deep sleep or meditation to other parts of the world to share healing there. Sometimes they knew where those parts of the world were and other times not. I have received emails from people all around the world saying I have come to them in dreams or meditations with an offering of guidance or healing. Whilst sometimes this will be an aspect of their own spiritual nature represented by an image of me, at other times it will be happening more literally and a connection between myself and another is actually made at the astral level. I know I am not the only one who does this! Much healing happens when we sleep at night – especially if we remember to ask for it from the beings who love us unconditionally just before we go to sleep.

I also have been in some very dark places via my astral body at night and I share many such encounters with you throughout this *Crystal Spirituality* series as through those dark encounters I came to recognise and be able to deal with the darkness within the world and within myself.

There are various reasons why the astral body travels, and where it does, when we sleep. As it is primarily motivated by desires and emotions, it will naturally be drawn to experiences that relate to those. That isn't bad; it is just a natural working through of those desires and emotions, with a view to eventually gaining healing that can bring clarity to the astral body. As that happens, there is less clutter of unprocessed thought, feeling and emotion, and more space for the spiritual light to shine through the astral body and be received into the physical body. We will also feel and know our heart's urgings, our inner guidance and our intuition more easily and consciously. The astral body then becomes increasingly flooded with spiritual light and its desires, feelings and thoughts will not only be about money, sex and personal comfort (not that there is anything particularly wrong with those things, it is just rather that we will find a more expansive set of desires as we grow spiritually!) but also about love, service, healing, freedom and so on. If there is spiritual instruction or healing to be given and the astral body is sufficiently developed to be moved by spiritual love as a guiding desire, then it will venture off for spiritual instruction. Dreams of being in school can often indicate this. If you are lucky you might even consciously remember some of the content of your lessons! If not, that doesn't mean learning hasn't taken place. It just means it is happening at a subconscious level, helping you to grow from within.

Whilst we sleep, our physical body goes through the motions of rest and repair and our astral body is healing too, just in a different way (and typically different location) to the physical part of us. We don't have to be nervous about this. The astral body stays connected to the physical body throughout our lifetime. I once woke suddenly and realised I couldn't move. My awareness was in the room with my body, but my astral body, the part of me that would animate and move my physical body wasn't fully back yet. I took in a deep breath, which was sufficient to pull my astral body back into my physical body (it returned with quite a thump!) and I was able to move my body at will again. Normally this isn't going to be an issue. Our astral body returns quite happily to our body and we wake up each morning not ever needing to think about it.

I learned something from that experience that helped me with the story I am about to share with you. So it was useful for me to have had that odd experience. I learned that putting my willpower into a physical action – in that case, taking a breath – would pull my astral body back into my physical body. If you ever feel spacey or ungrounded, it is because your astral body is not fully in your physical body. This can happen if you tend to live in your head or are more of an emotional person, than a grounded, here and now, kind of person. Forcing yourself to do something physical – to feel your toes moving or to take some deep slow breathes in and out – can be a way to ground your astral body back into your physical body. This can be rather important if you are drifting off away from the present moment into some emotion-driven fantasy when you are doing things like driving a car! I have had two separate encounters where people who drove right into my car claimed they couldn't see me. I believed them! I was right there in front of them, but they were hardly in their bodies and I had no doubt that they weren't present enough to see what was right in front of them (me!) at the time.

Before you read on, I'd like to offer some guidance to prepare you for the following story. I will also work through a process that you can do to feel empowered and confident, rather than concerned, about this content. Know that I was able to draw insight, understanding and ultimately more peace from this undesirable experience as it helped me to heal an old wound that I didn't even know I had. When I teach this content in person, I talk to the people in the room and check in with them. I can't do that with you here, but as you are reading this book, I trust you are advanced enough to be able to deal with this information. If you feel fearful or need help, ask for assistance from the beings who love you unconditionally and act on what appears. You might instinctively reach out for a healing session with a trusted guide or wish to re-do the healing process at the end of this chapter. If fear or resistance arises in you as you read this story that is absolutely okay. I have detailed my emotional responses below to demonstrate that no matter what happens, there is a truly radiant spirit within each one of us who is capable of rising like a phoenix from the ashes of any experience. I have witnessed that process of healing in myself and others in situations far more dramatic than what I am about to share and I know that each of us possesses an ability to heal that is divine, natural and powerful.

I am about to discuss dark or demonic energy. 'Demon' imagery is the stuff of horror films but although I have never been able to watch a horror movie without feeling ill (I am far too sensitive to consume horror as entertainment), I am aware that demonic or dark energy is a natural part of life. It is like an energetic version of the creepy crawlies that exist in the physical world, in that we accept they are a part of life but that doesn't mean we want to keep them as pets or invite them into our daily lives.

Demonic energy is an expression of life that seeks to manifest itself on a different path to type most healers, spiritual seekers, activists and light workers are walking on. In the grand drama of life, there are essentially two teams. One is on the path of love and the other is on the path of fear. I have come to understand that our job is to pick a team (Guess what? You're on team love!), and whilst you respect the right of each being to choose whichever team they resonate with, you do everything within your power for triumph for your own team. It's kind of like playing a game of cricket with your family in your backyard. You recognise everyone as family, but you are still going to do your best to bowl out your father and get that wicket! At the end of the game of life, no matter what team we choose, we will all be knocking back divine nectar in some cosmic playhouse in the sky, patting each other on the back in good humour and reminiscing on how shocking so-and-so was playing the villain and how spectacular so-and-so was as an avenging activist and so on. But for now, we have to deal with the reality of two teams, each vying for success in its own way.

This comparison might seem to trivialise dark forces, but ultimately it is important to realise that demonic energies cannot harm you. Realising this will help you stay in your heart and respond to them from a firm but non-judging stance, which is the swiftest and most abrupt way of ending any connection between you. Now, the job of those on the path of love is not to rid the world of darkness, as some may have us believe. That would result in half a world and it's not our job to tell the creator that part of what has been created was a mistake. We are here to walk the path of love, not judgment. Demonic energies are a part of life just as more loving beings are, but that doesn't mean we don't have a choice about the company we keep! We can have a 'live and let live' attitude, without allowing ourselves to be doormats for bad behaviour. Realising it is possible to respect all of life and acknowledge the right of each being to their existence, whilst also understanding that we have the free will to choose how we live our lives will help this make sense to you. I'll explain it further through the example of my story below.

This story also involves sexual energy. There is no unnecessary or unhelpful detail, but it does relate to a brief sexual encounter that I will describe in general terms. I believe this experience came to me so I could share it in a way that would help others as well as myself. I am giving you this preliminary explanation so that you continue to read past the story, to the interpretation and information that will help you feel empowered, more spiritually aware, and able to enjoy an expanded understanding of life. I share this story to help you let go of deeper layers of fear so that you can feel safer and more at peace within yourself and within the world. For sensitive humans on the path of love, this is so important. We are often gentle creatures and realising we have a sacred warrior within who can stand up for us without abandoning the loving nature that respects all of life is most comforting! So, let me share the story, and how I worked through it, with you now.

I was alone in my bed, in a deep sleep, when I became aware of a feeling of sexual pleasure in my body. It was very noticeable, as if sexual activity was actually taking place. As I came out of the depths of sleep into a slightly lighter sleep state, I felt and saw the body of a man lying upon me, on my left side. I didn't know who he was. I did realise it was his astral body (the part of us that travels when we sleep) and obviously he had somehow ended up in my bedroom. Almost as soon as I felt the man, I realised that there was something else driving this encounter, operating through him, almost like he was a puppet. I clearly saw and felt the presence of something I had never seen or thought of before, but I instantly recognised it as an incubus. An incubus is an energetic entity that needs sexual energy, just as our bodies need food and water to survive. The incubus was using the astral body of the man to pursue a sexual encounter with me. I became aware of all of this within a matter of seconds.

The sexual energy felt very pleasurable, but I knew it was not of love, not of my own conscious choosing and not something I wished to continue with or ever have happen again. I was not afraid, but I was absolutely determined to stop it, and quickly.

I was still in a relatively deep sleep and had to bring my astral body back to my physical body so that I could deal with the situation that was taking place. To that end, I tried to shake my head, the only part of me that I could move because I was still half in sleep and my astral body was not completely in my physical body. It took tremendous determination and willpower, but I just focussed on shaking my head. Eventually the intention to do so resulted in my head actually starting to move and the movement started to pull my astral body back into my physical body. I continued with the process by trying to think clearly of my address, a neutral fact that would help me ground my entire being in the here and now where my physical body was lying, partially unattended and receiving unwanted sexual connection. It was hard to make myself wake up, but eventually I became conscious enough to state my address clearly. I wasn't back in my body enough to speak, but I could think.

In my mind, I thought of the name "Archangel Michael" and calmly and firmly declared, "No" three times. At this, my astral self, which felt as though it had been very far away, fully returned to my body. The sexual energy immediately dropped right out of the encounter. I remained calm, neutral and very alert, as the incubus and the astral body detached from me and moved out through the front door. The motion-detector flicked the porch light on, giving me confirmation of my experience, if I had needed one. Despite this being something I previously would have confined to an out-there movie script, it was so absolutely clear and vivid that I did not entertain any doubt about the veracity of the encounter.

Although it was the middle of the night, I sat up in bed for an hour or so afterwards processing the experience. I had to wait until I felt clear and safe enough to go back to sleep without being concerned that when I did fall asleep, and my astral body left to do whatever it was it needed to do, my body would still be open and inviting to unwanted influences.

I thought about Archangel Michael. I had felt him standing in my room throughout the entire experience, from the first moment that I called for him and possibly even before that. He has been my divine protector for years and he is there when needed without me having to call on him. I knew he was standing at the base of my bed that evening. At first, I was puzzled that the encounter did not stop immediately when I said Archangel Michael's name. However, it did stop when I said, "No." Now, I have had some powerful experiences where Archangel Michael has blocked negative energy on my behalf and other experiences where he has urged me to fight it instead. That evening, as I pondered what had taken place, I asked Archangel Michael why he didn't step in to prevent the experience or to end it. He gave me a clear and immediate response, "You were dealing with it. I came because you thought you needed me here, but you didn't need me to deal with the situation."

I understood. He knew I was handling the situation effectively and while it was important for me to realise he would always be there when I needed him, there would also be times when I actually needed to be there for myself. I believe he stood there, to let me know that was I loved but also that I was empowered. I was able to set my own boundary and deal with the situation at hand from a calm and intelligent place within me.

Over the next few days, I reflected further. I knew that demons like this incubus could only enter an energy field with 'legal ground.' This is a bit like the mythology that a vampire that can only gain entry to the energy field of a person who invites them into their home. With dark energies we have to allow the interaction. I had not done so consciously, so permission must have been given unconsciously. I reflected on this and asked what was within my unconscious that was so powerful it could attract something like this that I did not consciously want anything to do with?

Unexpectedly, I thought of Jesus. He had helped me with situations that were outside of my current awareness on previous occasions by teaching me how to find my way through and helping me to grow. I had asked him some months earlier to teach me how to bring my sexual energy into the state of loving divine bliss I knew he had been able to achieve. I idly wondered if he had sent me this experience so that I might learn something. He instantly replied, so clearly that it gave me a shock, that he would never send such a thing to me.

That sudden response prompted an instant awareness of the unresolved issue that had allowed this encounter to happen. Jesus loved me in a way I had not yet been loved in the human world. If I had been loved that way, I would never have entertained the notion that he would send a demon to me, even in idle reflection and even if I could learn something valuable from the process. He would never do such a thing. At a deep, unconscious level, I was not loving myself as much as Jesus loved me. Here was the legal ground through which unconscious permission was granted for something like this to occur.

I wasn't angry at the incubus. It would be like getting angry at a dog for barking or the sun for shining. He was just honouring his nature. I could however decide that I was worthy of enough love that I would no longer accept sexual advances from any being if there was not also genuine love, tenderness, respect and affection present. I didn't deserve to be used and seduced, I deserved to be respected, appreciated and honoured. These were the leftover wounds from my last relationship, and they needed to be healed now. I believe in that moment, I moved more completely into genuine self-love than I had done in the previous years of self-work. Perhaps it all just fell into place at that moment.

I didn't begrudge the existence of the incubus, but I did believe my own existence could become far removed from its grasp. I had the right to make that choice for myself and so I did. I was worthy of the love that is full of dignity, respect and kindness but I had to claim it for myself. I gave it to others so freely. It was time to realise that I had to give this to my own body too. She deserved it! She went through so much in life so that my soul could grow and help others. She deserved so much. Even if that wasn't the case, she was alive and she deserved love for no other reason.

I went through an emotional process of feeling shame, disgust and uncleanness for several hours after the experience. When I was a psychotherapist, I had worked with a few people who had been through sexual assault. Not many, but enough to recognise that these were typical emotional responses that followed a sexually intrusive experience. I wrote in my journal, allowing myself to express these feelings and responded to them, affirming that my body, mind and soul were just as they had always been and that I loved each part of myself.

It is important that I share this part of the experience with you. In my research I saw that this sort of sexual encounter was happening far more often than I would have expected. Sometimes 'written off' as a dream, sometimes recognised as really happening at a non-physical, psychic or astral level, and found to be genuinely frightening. People have been recording these experiences for thousands of years and at some point it was recognised that there had to be some sort of invitation through which an experience like this could happen. That teaching, though valid, can all too easily turn into the distorted and wounded view of someone 'asking for it' – like the ridiculous notion that if a woman wears a short skirt she is asking to be raped. It is nonsensical and I shift from Bastet to Sekhmet at the thought of such a proclamation! However, let us stay on point. In my research there was a lot of confusion about what constituted legal ground for such an experience to happen. Many people believed that being in a sexual mood or masturbating was legal ground through which demonic energy could attach itself to you. This is not true! Sexual energy is a part of who we are and an aspect of the divine gift that enables our body to experience ecstasy as part of our natural divine inheritance as human beings. Ecstasy is not only sexual, it is spiritual, it is what the divine feels like – ecstatic, beyond the mind, bliss. The Divine is not so twisted as to create us in a certain way and then punish us for it. The belief that sexual energy alone is enough to attract an experience like the one I had is based on a wound of shame and nothing else. Bastet will help heal any such wound.

As I purged those feelings following the encounter, I realised I could use this experience to help me move further on my own path of healing and help others do the same. I could take the darkness and help it serve the light. I was genuinely moved by the fear that I saw in others when they realised something like this had happened to them. I did want to help, but I also felt that it wasn't enough for me to explain how to stop something when it started and take the healing from it. I wanted to share a way to prevent it from happening. If something is in our learning, we need to learn it, but there are many ways to learn. Provided we don't come from fear-based avoidance, but accept and trust that life will lead us in the best direction for healing, then there are certainly times when we can be granted a gift of an easier or more pleasant way to heal. That is the grace of Bastet again. I wanted to find a way to empower others to get to the learning that I did, through a lighter method, if possible.

To that end, I did a simple ritual about two nights later. I wanted to honour what I had learned and send out a clear, serene and powerful message. I sat on my bed where the encounter had taken place because I wanted to reclaim that space and render it sacred and safe. I rested one hand on my lower sacrum, just at my pubic bone, and one hand at my heart as I said this simple prayer:

"I am a human being and divine soul. This body is pure, worthy of respect and love, and I dedicate her, her light, her sexual energy, her love and her presence, into the grace of the Christ. May her sexuality be rendered sacred and may she always be treated with respect and acknowledgement of her worth. I cut any cord, burn any contract I have made and withdraw any permission I have ever given, consciously or unconsciously, to any being that would allow for interaction with my body or energy field that is not of unconditional love. Of my own free will, so be it."

It might seem strange to include a story that so strongly features the Christ energy but he serves the Divine Feminine path of love. He teaches us the feminine wisdoms: the power of sacred rage when he trashed temples; the power of a shamanic journey to the underworld and rising again, through the resurrection; the need to honour the Divine as loving through his teachings on forgiveness. Jesus was an initiate into the Divine Feminine and he has much to offer those of us who feel a heart connection to him, irrespective of our religious beliefs.

As I sat in my darkened bedroom that evening, I allowed a feeling of love to flow from heart, out through my hands and into my body, and felt the quiet, unshakeable strength of my soul. I felt restored and safer within myself than I had ever felt before. I felt more love and tenderness for my body, and her beautiful sexuality, too. I felt safe.

The healing ritual brought me closure and peace. The whole experience taught me more about the nature of creation and how to work with it. I hope, one day, to be so in alignment with divinity that there is no need to contrive anything, but for now I am at a stage in my journey where it is wise to care for myself as an individual being. I recognise that all of life is connected at a deeper level, where there is only oneness, but I also realise that in this world, there are mosquitoes or their equivalent – physical and psychic – and sometimes it just makes sense to slap on some mosquito repellent or stick up a mosquito net for a more peaceful and undisturbed night's sleep. In this case, the mosquito repellent is a quick, basic prayer before going to sleep at night. I simply say some version or other of the following (and you can too, using these words, or your own version).

"I ask for protection and healing for the physical, sexual, mental, emotional, psychic and spiritual bodies through my sleep. Through unconditional love, divine protection and grace, and for my highest good, so be it."

In the morning I then ask, "Those beings that love me unconditionally, please help me in all ways today, for my highest good. Thank you." I don't say this prayer from a place of fear, I say it from a place of love, gratitude and practicality!

If you have a child who is plagued by nightmares or the like, a teenager or family member that seems to be in a dark and depressed state, or any loved ones that you want to help, you can say these prayers on their behalf. When it becomes age appropriate, you'll want to teach them the prayer and offer them the opportunity to choose for themselves whether or not to incorporate it into their spiritual journey. Remember that you cannot choose another's path for them, nor control it – even if your instincts are protective – but you can offer goodwill and any information that might be empowering to them. It is up to each individual to then choose for themselves. That is the nature of free will on this planet.

What had been with me and helped me through that night, and eventually led me to a place of greater joy rather than guilt, shame or fear, was my own Bastet nature. I had always been drawn to her through my love of cats, dance, music and play, and had naturally been a very sensual being my entire life. Her naturalness and joy in sexuality mirrored my own experience. Despite being raised in a culture and home where there were some rather mixed messages sent about sexuality, I had luckily managed to maintain a sense of value and appreciation for my own sexual nature. I never believed it would do anything other than enhance my spiritual journey, which was what I valued above all.

Without ever really thinking about it, I knew that Bastet had blessed me and I was able to effortlessly and naturally draw upon those blessings to help me find my way through the unwanted sexual encounter. Her ability to see in the dark and express her power at night enabled me to clearly see and trust my perceptions of the man and the dark entity operating through him, to what was happening energetically even though I was in the darkness of slumber through virtually the entire process. Her joyful acceptance of pleasure helped me recognise that although the sexual energy was pleasurable to experience, that was just the nature of sexual energy. I wasn't afraid of that and so I didn't become confused. Although it was pleasurable, I still had the right to decide if I wanted it to continue or not. I believe this issue can confuse many women, and men, who feel that if they are enjoying a sexual encounter, then they are not allowed to set a boundary if it doesn't feel right, safe or respectful for them to continue with it. Bastet encourages enough self-esteem not only to accept our right to pleasure – sexual or otherwise – but also to accept our right to honour ourselves. This sometimes means that an otherwise pleasurable experience requires a firm boundary to be set by us so that it doesn't proceed any further. It might be that it needs to end for no other reason than it just doesn't feel quite right for it to continue at that time, even if you are not sure why.

With her distinct femininity (she is usually pictured as a slender woman with a cat's head or a cat with a scarab beetle necklace and single gold hoop earring in its left ear), she has no fear of male energy and can be a healing presence when we are making peace with masculine energy, to honour it, without losing connection to feminine values. I didn't fall into fear in my encounter with the dark entity, because I actually love masculine energy. I responded to that unwanted experience of masculine energy from a place of compassion and clarity. "No" was me saying, "I honour your existence, but this is not what I choose for myself so you cannot stay here with me." My body barely moved during the entire experience, but my energy shifted entirely. I went from unconsciously allowing, to consciously choosing from my own feminine centre.

However, I have recognised the fear of sexual aggression from men in various situations. I remember doing a reading for a man once and I was overwhelmed with the sense of fear that he was going to attack me. It occurred to me that I may have unconsciously picked up on the fear projected onto him by women he had encountered in his life. It may have been because he had attacked women and the fear was justified. There was also the possibility that he had an abusive father and had learned to fear his own masculine side. Perhaps it was a combination of factors.

The fear of male energy (in men or in women) as being predatory and aggressive can be hard to get past, even if you haven't had an immediate experience of abuse in your life. This is because male energy is still learning another way to be. Just as feminine energy is learning how to be powerful through being vulnerable and receptive, masculine energy is learning how to be powerful through serving the heart, rather than the ego.

Just as men can be uncomfortable when viewed with fear and distrust, women can feel weakened by such distrust too. Bastet helps heal this situation from both sides. To embrace masculine energy so that it can be enjoyed without fear, requires you to realise you are capable of setting effective boundaries. We can consciously say 'no' but it will not be so effective if we are unconsciously saying something like, "No one listens to me" or "I don't have the right to determine what goes on in my own energy field." When we say 'no' we need to genuinely mean it with all of our being. Bastet supports us in integrating our entire being by helping us find the places where we are saying yes when we mean to say no and seeing into the darkness of ourselves being. Bastet also brings the light of Ra, the light of the Sun, into that darkness so that we can align all parts of us into one coherent being. When this happens, we act according to our feelings and our experience will mirror how we truly want to feel about ourselves. This is Bastet's special blessing of healed self-esteem, self-confidence and self-love.

Known poetically as the Lady of the Rising Sun (Her sister Sekhmet is known as the Lady of the Setting Sun), Bastet carries with her the gift of hope and a focus on what is being born rather than what is passing away. We need this hope when we are embarking upon a task of self-healing. When an issue has been around us for so long, sometimes living without it can seem like an impossible dream. However, anything can be healed. Anything. Sometimes we just need her blessing of hope to continue on the path and do our part of the bargain to attract the divine grace of healing that is required for a shift to take place.

Bastet was particularly associated with the protection of women and children and carries the energy of good fortune and fertility for children and for crops. If you are worried about your child or about conceiving and having a safe and healthy pregnancy and birth experience, calling upon her can assist you and your child. Men can also work with Bastet's energy for their own healing particularly if they wish to heal their relationship to women, the inner woman (the part of the man that feels and desires connection with others) or with the Divine. Far from making a man appear a 'sissy' or effeminate, a man who has a strong connection to his inner feminine is attractive to women who are on a path of self-healing. A woman who has done enough work to be in touch with her own feelings and emotional life, wants a man in her life who is not afraid of her openness or her emotional energy because he is familiar enough with his own. When two people who are open to each other and to life connect in a relationship, whether that be as friends, lovers or business partners, it is extraordinary how much magic can happen!

Bastet's sistrum or rattle symbolises her position presiding over the arts of dance and music. Cats were considered as sacred to her and revered in her temples. I suspect cats all over the world have a very distinct recollection of such treatment and expect it to continue in the modern day! Like many cats, her energy is one of freedom and independence. She expects to be treated with high regard and has a tendency to do whatever she wants, irrespective of the desires of any other to control her. In a culture where fitting in, toeing the line and oftentimes degradation and humiliation are part and parcel of daily life to keep a job and survive, her spirit is utterly essential for the healing of the human spirit – for women and for men! The dignity and grace of Bastet is so important for us to access within ourselves if we are going to live as inspiring and uplifting human beings in this world. Being broken down by endless demands that we be a certain way, perform to a certain standard or meet particular expectations is not Bastet's path.

So, Bastet encourages us to take pleasure in life, to give ourselves permission to relax and to realise that underneath current appearances we are royal. However, this doesn't mean that honouring Bastet will lead to mediocrity or slackness. Genius can flow when we combine passion and purpose with an ability to relax with the grace of nobility. The dignity and affirmation that arises from this can give us tremendous self-confidence to create, to love and appreciate our bodies, and to find our voice and honour its creative expression. This all creates a more inviting space for our spirit to manifest its light and shine it more brightly in the world.

I recently did a Skype session for a Bastet woman. All I kept seeing with her was dance! She had the soul of a dancer. I kept saying to her, "I feel like you need to dance!" Eventually she confessed that she loved to dance but had not made the time to do so for too long. I meet many of these souls in my line of work. They don't always think of themselves as dancers but have a natural sensuality and alignment with the Divine Feminine spirit within them that seeks expression through the free movement of their bodies. That might be through free movement to music in their lounge room, through sensual play with a lover or by being open to the sensual experience of nature. The feeling of the sun or the air, the scent of a flower, the roughness of bark, the coolness under a shady tree, the sound of insects and leaves rustling with the breeze, the feeling of floating in salty water . . . absolute bliss! We can allow our spirit to dance in many ways other than attending a choreographed dance class.

That wasn't the sole reason I felt that her soul resonated with Bastet's energy. She operated outside of the norms of her particular culture, which was very oriented towards academic achievement and intellectualism. She didn't want to intellectualise, she wanted to feel, to express, to play and to be. She was passionate about her path of spiritual exploration and study. She had moved around the world, lived in cultures very different to the one she was raised in and had chosen for herself the lifestyle that felt right for her. She felt relieved that she had let go of her parents' expectations that she thrive in academia and instead chose to pursue a path of shamanism. She loved the wildness of it and the sensuality. She was a wise, old soul with a natural ability to 'get' spiritual teachings very quickly and apply them immediately in her life. She decided she wanted to live with trust, so she just did it. That free and uncomplicated attitude towards life is a hallmark of Bastet's energy. If we have a tendency to analyse every choice we make, down to the tiniest detail, and perhaps stress ourselves out with worry or self-doubt in the process, then Bastet can be a tonic that helps us lighten and loosen up emotionally, mentally and even physically. If we have a tendency to put ourselves down or demand perfection of ourselves, we are definitely in need of some energy from Bastet.

Bastet is a free spirit who teaches women and men how to be free within themselves, to completely accept their sensual and sexual natures, and how to revel in pleasure, beauty and the sensuality of life. She was honoured as a sexually vibrant being with many lovers. She did not bow to social mores and can remind us that our decisions about how to conduct our relationships, and with whom, are ours to make.

She also reminds us of the importance of play, to allow ourselves to really feel alive and to take time to smell the roses (her son was the lord of perfumes). Her festivals were known as great, vibrant celebrations and can be imagined as something like the street carnivals of Mardi Gras. The sensuality of Bastet translated into dance as part of her worship. Dance that is sensual, free and about feminine self-expression can be used to honour this Divine Feminine being and open to her gifts and blessings in this modern day. You might access this through a belly dance class or by swinging your hips and letting your arms flow about you as you sway to your favourite music at home.

I recently taught a series workshops on a tour of North Queensland in Australia. Around mining towns and the beautiful Whitsundays coast, I chanted, sang, channelled and danced my way through many groups, meeting some gorgeous people on their paths of divine healing. At the end of one of the moving meditations (which is my fancy name for dancing with inner awareness) the client who had arranged the entire tour wanted to tell me something. She said one of the participants in the group had commented that she wished she could express herself in dance as sensually as I did, but she would have to be drunk to do it!

I was flattered but surprised, firstly because we were supposed to have our eyes closed and be moving in meditation but also because I am not self-conscious about dancing. I have loved to dance ever since I was a child, so I just close my eyes or smile, hear the music and off I go. Her comment reminded me that alcohol was often a feature at the festivals of Bastet (and Sekhmet) and helped me realise it would have been (at least partly) to help people switch off from their analytical minds and surrender into their feelings. It is similar to how many people use alcohol today. I have never been much drawn to alcohol, quite possibly because I have always been able to drop into my feelings and sensate nature without much difficulty. Although I felt unusual during my teens when my peers were getting drunk to have fun and I didn't really understand why, I later realised that the ability to feel drunk with joy, without having to deal with a hangover the next day was a pretty sweet deal!

Over the years, I realised that this tendency was rather unusual – until I met the Matangi man that I spoke about in the previous chapter. The groups of people I met through him often didn't drink and seemed to be more naturally plugged into the natural world and the energies of creativity and self-expression, sensuality and play without necessarily needing drugs or alcohol to access them. They had an earthiness about them, a connection to nature and the wildness and freedom of spirit that all human beings have within them, that allowed them to experience a natural high rather easily.

Certainly for me, experiencing ecstatic energy was pretty natural and part of my blessing from Bastet I suspect. I used to go out dancing in nightclubs from a relatively young age and was frequently asked by other patrons what drugs I was on and if they could get some from me! When I said all I was taking was water, they didn't quite know what to make of it. Most people who are going clubbing or to raves to dance are seeking an ecstatic experience. In a culture that doesn't quite know how to access this through natural spiritual growth, the answer is usually sought through artificial (and sometimes quite toxic) methods.

Unfortunately these artificial methods of blissing out can end up causing harm, not only physically but also psychologically and emotionally. Whilst some people can manage their use of drugs and alcohol with minimal damage to themselves, there are plenty more who cannot. I saw such a man once who disturbed me deeply. He walked into the crystal shop I worked at briefly when I was first starting out as a psychic. At first glance he was a tall, fair-haired, charismatic man, dressed in black. There was something about his presence that drew my attention. As he turned to look at me, I recoiled and fled, getting as far away from him as I possibly could, as quickly as I could. It was because of what I saw when I looked at his eyes, and I wasn't prepared to deal with it at that early stage in my path. They were absolutely soulless, dark, empty and yet filled with what appeared to be an infestation of dark parasitic energies. I was so repelled by whatever it was that had a hold of him, I scooted out of there quick smart. I was frightened and disturbed by him, but had enough common sense to not approach him and try to explore something I was not yet ready to deal with.

Later that day, before the store closed, I spoke uneasily about what I sensed about the man with some of the other psychics in the shop. Most of them had been doing psychic work for many, many years and had more experience than I did. One in particular, an older psychic who seemed to take a shine to me, told me rather casually that the man I was referring to had done a lot of drugs and was filled with attachments. I had not really heard of such a thing before, though I could understand what he meant because it would explain what I saw. He said that random spirits had entered his energy field when he had artificially expanded it through his drug taking. As he was dissociated from his body through the drug use, his consciousness wasn't able to respond to the spirits to protect his own body and tell them to leave, so they just took up residence. And they didn't want to leave now that they had found a place where they could feed of his vital forces. Kind of like psychic squatters determined to stay put and trash the place until there was nothing left to destroy before moving on to the next vacant body. I can imagine that man must have been in a sort of living hell. Like having an infestation of lice that just kept growing, but inside of him, disturbing his thoughts and his heart.

I don't know what happened to that man. I was not in a place to be able to help him at the time. I feel so sad, as I write about him now, looking back at what I saw then through far more educated eyes. I doubt his mind would have survived that constant vampirism by negative energies. At the very least it would have been so damaged he would have been prepped for a severe kind of mental illness later in life or in future lifetimes. Not all mental illness comes from drug-related incidents or negative spiritual attachments, but some does and I wouldn't be surprised if that man ended up in such circumstances. No matter how lightweight Bastet may seem, we have to hold her with respect. Seeking her blessings without being willing to do the work necessary to attain them is as potentially dangerous as working with the fiercer faces of the Divine Feminine.

We have ventured into some dark terrain here, with this goddess of light and joy. It occurred to me that you may wonder why so much demonic or dark energy would feature in this book and I do feel to clarify that. When we work with the Divine Feminine, our consciousness expands. We become able to bear witness to more and more of life. That includes more light and beauty as well as more darkness. Darkness is a part of life. I don't attempt to understand why the divine creation is as it is, which is unfathomable more often than not, but I do know that if we can trust that each experience can always serve love by how we choose to respond to it, then we will sail through life with flying colours. Of course each person finds their own path, in their own way and at their own time.

Bastet will reach for us when our raging is too great and needs to be cooled or our analytical mind is seeking to drown us in over-thinking, reminding us that perhaps we just need to kick off our shoes and dance.

CAT'S EYE (UNVEILING)

Cat's eye is a stone with chatoyance which means it demonstrates a natural sheen and reflective shimmer. When the stone is cut into a cabochon shape the sheen looks like the slit eye of a cat, but the sheen effect is white and will slide all over the stone as it is moved in the light. The chatoyance or shimmer in natural cat's eye is caused by fibrous mineral inclusions in the stone. When the stone is rounded or oval the shimmer of the fibres within the stone creates a stunning effect. This same effect is lost if the stone is cut into faceted shapes.

It comes in a variety of colours – yellow, grey, blue, brown and white to name a few. The chatoyance or shining effect does appear in some other stones, such as Tiger's eye, but the true cat's eye stone is a distinct crystal in its own right.

There is an abundance of artificial cat's eye on the market and I have expressed a view on man-made versus natural stones in this series already. I will say here that I don't feel as much of an affinity with synthetic cat's eye as I do with the natural stone, but we must also trust in what we are drawn to and allow that to support us. The man-made stone will not harm you. It is just that the natural stone is so very beautiful (though somewhat harder to find).

It can also be rather tricky to tell the two apart.

One of the best ways to do this is to accept that the more perfect and highly chatoyant the stone appears to be, the higher the possibility that it is synthetic. Once you have seen a natural cat's eye the artificial ones will look rather too perfect! The chatoyance effect will seem too obvious and the stone itself might be too clear or even toned, rather than opaque. The natural stone is very striking but more subtle and often features imperfections in the surface, slight bumps or dents which are a sign of its naturalness rather than flaws to be avoided. I was never really drawn to cat's eye for a number of years, because I only found the artificial types and they seemed to lack the energy that would nourish me. When I saw how subtle and beautiful natural cat's eye was, I completely changed my mind about it and felt it was so worthy to honour one of my favourite goddesses, the big divine all-seeing feline eye herself, Bastet.

Cat's eye is known to heal the eyes, the head and supports the opening of the third eye for insight and clairvoyance, which translates as clear seeing. Just as the cat can see more easily than humans in the dark, the cat's eye stone helps us access our ability to 'see in the dark' by discerning that which is not immediately accessible, to see hidden truths or motivations, which is what insight gives us access to. Whatever we may see in that darkness, whether it be ill wishing from another or an opportunity for us to take task with a negativity that we generate within ourselves, the cat's eye has the added bonus of offering us protection whilst we work to heal through what is taking place.

Cat's mouths are generally very dirty and they are able to eat and groom themselves without becoming unwell. They are able to feed off rodents that carry disease and are adept hunters when they aren't lazing about and resting (All that rest probably makes them good hunters by cultivating reserves of energy for when they are needed). The cat's eye crystal holds similar properties to cat wisdom and the healing medicine of the cat as a spiritual totem. If the cat has come into your life in dreams, visions or in actuality (by sitting on your laptop as you are trying to write your book on crystals and goddesses, for example) then you are being given a message about some healing assistance or wisdom that is relevant for you. Cats help us develop the ability to deal with quite toxic energy without becoming contaminated by it. They also help us heal our self-esteem and if we have any doubts about our worth and right to feel gorgeous, pampered and adored, the cat will assist with that too.

Cats and the cat's eye stone are of particular help when we are in toxic situations or relationships until we can do whatever self-healing is required to find our way through and out of that situation into a healthier, cleaner environment.

I had a dream when I was working with a woman who was, superficially at least, very Bastet-like. Beautiful, adored and treated as a goddess, she loved music, dance and was also extremely territorial – like a cat. On the surface she was charming and admiring of me also, and very eager for us to work together. I had yet to heal the wound about self-love and self-respect which I spoke of above, and so I ignored my intuition (and if it had of been a cat, would have been hissing and clawing at her with hackles raised within about five seconds of meeting her!) and proceeded to work with her.

As it turned out, she felt threatened by me, although I didn't realise it at the time. Eventually that became such an issue that she took some actions that were designed to undermine my work by casting aspersions about my character to others, behind my back (as was her way) and generally doing her best to cause me problems. I wasn't aware of the extent of the problem until I finally did listen to my intuition, which presented me with a dream that I couldn't ignore.

In the dream, I was walking with a precious golden cat. It was unusual because it could talk! I knew it was special and needed to be protected. I cradled it as I wandered through what appeared to be a marketplace with many different stalls. I was on my way home. I rather thoughtlessly meandered off my path and for no particular reason into a stall in a side alley. I looked up and perched on a ledge sat a black cat, brimming with hostility, its tail twitching aggressively. It hissed at me. I decided that there wasn't anything in that dark, empty alley worth fighting over and was surprised at the cat's territorial aggression. I left the alleyway and went back to the main path that headed home. The black cat followed me and leapt up at me, trying to claw at my face, and quite possibly attack the golden kitten. I quickly put the golden cat at my back, tucking it into my clothing behind my neck and used a firm but gentle chi gung movement to prevent the attacking feline from slashing my face.

After that dream, several events took place where the person the black cat represented, this woman I was working with for a short time, tried to undermine my reputation and work. I stayed in my heart, honoured what I felt, even though I did not enjoy the nastiness in anyway. Eventually I was able to get well clear of her influence and I found that those she may have poisoned against me sought me out of their own volition some years later. I didn't allow her attitude towards me to steer me away from the value of what I was nurturing as was symbolised by the talking golden cat and relating to dance and music. I just learned to protect it and be more careful with whom I associated myself, rather than letting my natural curiosity lead me where more sensible people would refuse to tread!

When we are working with the feline energies of cat's eye we always have a choice of the level we will operate on. For several years, I lived in a house in Greenwich, a leafy green suburb on Sydney's lower north shore. I nicknamed it the Temple of Bast because for some reason it was surrounded by cats. Apart from my own large, orange (or golden – depending on the light!) fluffy cat, there were at least five or six other cats that considered the property to be at least partially their own. The fights that broke out over territory could be quite amazing and I would walk through the house to find that yet another cat had wandered in and was trying to claim the place as its own. It took a near constant vigilance whilst I lived there to deal with the cats – whom I loved but couldn't house all together and remain even slightly sane. And that was aside from the fact they all had homes elsewhere on the street.

The territorialism of the feline nature is a lower vibrational expression of energy. It is based on the fear that someone will take away what belongs to you. In truth, the only thing that cannot be stolen from you is that which is rightfully yours. No matter how much we want to hold on to something, sometimes we'll just have to let it go and trust. There is that saying, which is a bit of a cliché, but actually true, 'Set someone or something free and if it is meant to be yours, it will return to you, and if it does not, it never was.' Territorial attitudes can be softened and turned into a more internal sense of self-possession with firm boundaries that is assertive rather than aggressive, through working with cat's eye. We can learn to shift from fear-based territorial aggression into an instinctive sense of healthy and balanced self-protection. We will be intuitively informed when a transgression of our boundaries is taking place and be able to deal with it. Cat's eye supports us in the latter approach.

The stone is associated with similar properties to Bastet in the sense that it encourages good fortune, success on all levels, self-confidence and the realisation that whatever one might need to create success is already within. It can bring an abundance of new opportunities so that even if we miss one, we know there is something else for us just around the corner. Sort of like the reputed nine lives or great luck of the cat itself.

The unveiling aspect of cat's eye is not only its ability to promote genuine insight into what lies behind appearances. Cat's eye helps to unveil our golden destiny and all that can manifest for us through good fortune when we take time to attune to its wisdom. Its properties of healing the kidneys and the eyes speak of surrendering fear and anger, and allowing ourselves to attune to our natural rhythms and trust in what we perceive. In doing so we will be guided onto our best path for all that we are entitled to – our complete divine inheritance.

MANIFESTING THROUGH PLEASURE

Earlier this year I travelled to Istanbul, in Turkey, to teach at a yoga conference. I was running dance meditations and channelling through sound and music. I met many, many cats in Istanbul as well. The whole experience was very Bastet.

One afternoon, before I was due to leave the charming Old City and move into the modern and thriving hub of Beyoglu, I decided to venture off to the reputed Turkish baths, the hammam, and experience the ancient custom I was sure I had experienced in past lives.

I didn't really know what to expect from the experience. As I ventured through the uninspiring entrance to the bathhouse, which was not much more than a ramshackle wooden doorway, I was stunned. Somehow that shoddy door opened up into a magnificent marble chamber, several hundred years old and exuding opulence and old world charm. I just stood, gaping at the carved marble ceiling! Fortunately one of the den mothers who worked at the hammam as a bathing attendant, noticed I was a bit lost for words and decided to nudge me along. She was short, stout and had a firm grip, as she grabbed my hand and motioned for me to enter the changing area. She didn't speak a word of English but I could smile and so could she and that was enough.

Eventually I was changed, wrapped in a fluffy towel and a pair of plain black knickers supplied by the bathhouse, with my locker key on an elastic band around my wrist. I stepped into the bathhouse itself, which was an even more spectacular marble chamber with cavernous domed ceilings, perfectly carved with intricate geometric patterns. Skylights created by the carving allowed natural daylight to stream through and be filtered by hot steam of the bathhouse to form fluctuations of soft dappled light. I felt like I had stepped back at least several hundred years in time.

The den mother from outside found me again and I was grateful. I had noted some of the resentful expressions on the faces of other bathhouse attendants and was very appreciative of the kindly and nurturing attitude of the woman I was lucky enough to have drawn to me. She motioned for me to lie down on the huge raised platform in the centre of the bathhouse. It was white and grey marble and heated from within. I did as suggested and felt my muscles relax and my mind feel more peaceful. The den mother began to slosh basins of hot water over me, scrubbed my body with a coarse loofah and finished (all too soon!) with softly foaming, lemongrass-scented bubbles, that ballooned around me until I felt like I was in a light-as-air lemongrass cloud. She then took me over to one of the carved marble cubicles and I sat quietly as she washed my hair with more lemongrass bubbles, sloshing water over me, and patting my head gently, with love.

She gestured towards the deep heated pools where I could dip myself and wash off any remaining bubbles. As I emerged from the pools, my den mother sought me out from across the bathhouse, even though she was in the midst of tending to another guest. Clearly she had decided that I needed to relax! She gently but firmly directed me to lie down on the platform again and rest.

I contentedly gazed up at the enormous domed ceiling, carved in patterns of sacred geometry, with sunlight gently descending through the holes in the roof, softly illuminating the steam rooms below. In this reverie, I felt the presence of the Divine Masculine descending into the sacred feminine darkness of the bathhouse filled with women. It was the most sublime experience of utterly divine sensuality and deep, deep peace. In that moment I felt complete unity between the spiritual, the flesh, the erotic and the mystical.

I walked back through the old city later than night and spent a quiet evening curled up in bed looking at the art book containing all the images I was going to use to write the *Journey of Love Oracle Deck* whilst I was in Turkey. I had received the perfect healing I needed to be in sweet, cosseted surrender to write the messages for that deck which features the art of Rassouli – who's work I had loved for years and years without ever knowing who he was until fairly recently. The oracle was all about the experience of the Divine as the beloved and the journey we take through relationships and the spiritual path to unite with the Divine in a great romance – whether that be with the divine presence, ourselves, our lovers or all of the above.

As I felt so content, safe, childlike and womanly all at once, I knew that I had been blessed in that experience. I wrote the oracle deck within the next couple of weeks. It just flowed quickly from an inspired place and I wrote from a space within me that had experienced the Divine from a place of sheer and utter surrender into the simple pleasure of living in a body, honoured with love in sacred space.

This is the healing that Bastet can offer us whether we are in a Turkish bath house or floating in the ocean or standing for a moment feeling the fresh crisp air on our skin or the tingles of warming sunlight. It is healing through the body's sensuality whether that be sexual or not. It is the healing that allows for the spirit to take delight through a body that is honoured and loved as sacred.

HEALING PROCESS

If you have forgotten to play, because of all the tasks you have set yourself, have forgotten to really feel because of how much you are thinking or you just want to honour your body and receive a healing through pleasure instead of struggle and hard work (a nice change sometimes!) then this healing is for you.

Take the crystal and/or your mandala and if you have an image or statue of Bastet that you love, place that in your space too. You can keep your altar simple or really go to town with beautiful objects, flowers, scented candles and lush music – whatever feels most appropriate for you to honour the sensual goddess. I would suggest music, as there is an option for dance involved in this healing process.

If you don't wish to dance, you may wish to do this healing in the bath. Just make sure you don't fall asleep – snorting up water if you relax too much and go under might not be the kind of sensual experience you are desiring!

The Process

When your altar is ready, allow yourself to relax and say the following, "I call upon Bastet, ancient sister of sensuality, protection, freedom and independence. I honour you with this altar, created in your name. I open to receive your blessings, ancient one of great beauty, grace and pleasure. I call upon the Crystal Angel of Cat's Eye, clear sighted and true to help me unveil myself so that I may see clearly, without filters of shame or guilt, and partake of this feast of life with abandon, joyfulness, pleasure, sensuality, freedom and gratitude. So be it!"

Close your eyes and imagine or perceive the joyful sound and feeling of celebration. If you can, draw upon your favourite memories of birthdays or Christmas or some other celebration that has meaning for you. Imagine the most amazing gifts and loving exchanges with friends, family or other loved ones. Imagine there is an incredibly delicious feast and more than enough love, companionship, compassion and goodwill to share with everyone so much so that it creates a field of loving energy that radiates outwards, like a sun, to touch and uplift even those not immediately involved in your celebration.

In the middle of the celebration is a beautiful table, and upon it a unique, sensual creature dances and moves. It might be a cat. It might be a woman with the head of a cat or a being of light or sound. This is Bastet in whatever form she chooses to appear to you.

She is being honoured and those around her toss fragrant flowers and rich luscious fruits at her feet. She invites you to join her. Do so if you wish, knowing you are surrounded and held and protected by love.

First she offers you a sheer red veil. Imagine you can feel the lightness of its flow as you guide it through the air and around your body. You can actually stand up and move if you wish to dance in your healing, imagining that the red veil is draped over your arms and body, and swishes about you as you choose to move and express yourself. Express the colour red and whatever it feels like for you, knowing that this is a healing dance and doesn't have to look a particular way, it just is what it is for you now. If you prefer to visualise, sense or feel rather than move, simply relax into the feeling of the dance and allow it be an inner dance.

Bastet applauds your dance and then removes the red veil, tossing it onto her shoulders as she hands you a sheer, vibrant orange veil. Again you can feel the weight of the veil as it sways with you as you dance the feeling of orange. It is a healing dance, without reason, logic or choreography. Let yourself express and release as you feel is right for you.

Bastet honours your dance by receiving the orange veil from you. She tosses it over her shoulders, along with the red veil, and hands you a sheer yellow veil.

Throw the yellow veil in the air if you wish. Allow it to fall into your arms or on to your head as you let it slip off your body and into your arms. Spin and move in whatever way feels right with this joyful yellow veil trailing behind you or flying over you. Dance or move in a way that feels like yellow. There is no need for thinking, just for being as subtle or as dramatic as you wish.

Once again, Bastet applauds your dance again. She adds the yellow veil to her shoulders, passes you a sheer green veil and you begin your dance again, dancing the feeling of green. Your dance may become more inward, less energetic or more fluid, or not. Trust what you feel and be with that truth in your expression. Whether you are very still or moving a lot, whatever your body is releasing is perfect for you. Even if you fear that nothing is happening, at an inner level healing is taking place. Have faith, let go and be.

Once your dance of the green veil is done, Bastet adds that to her coloured shawl of veils and presents you with a sheer sky blue veil with which to express yourself. Let yourself dance, move and express the colour of the endless bright summer sky. You may feel open and free, like you wish to fly, or anything at all. Be with your experience until you are ready to hand over that veil to Bastet.

Over her shoulders goes the sky blue veil and she passes you a deep dark indigo veil, the colour of a deep night sky. It might be plain or flecked with silvery stars. Dance with that veil as if you are dancing with the night sky. You may sense visions, energy moving or simply be with the feeling of indigo that the veil bestows upon you. You may even wish to lie down and imagine the veil resting over you, like the cover of night. Release, express and be with that veil.

Finally as Bastet gently slides the indigo coloured veil over her, she presents you with a sheer ultra violet, glowing veil. It shimmers with life force and crackles with the energy of living pure white light with flecks of violet light within it. You dance with it and it dances with you.

Bastet joins you now, and together you dance with all seven veils. Together, you weave and flow and connect with the joy of movement.

When you are finished just sit quietly with your hands in prayer. You may feel emotional. You may feel very still and quiet. Be with what you feel. Bow your head and say, "I honour joy in my life. Help me honour and receive the pleasures of life that I may truly relish all that I am given, and feast at the divine table which you so graciously invite me to join. So be it!"

When you are ready, simply open your eyes.

Listen to your body over the coming days or weeks. You may want to move more, eat differently, play more, be outside more often, take more breaks or plan a holiday. You may want to initiate intimacy or have some laughs. You may even want to wear your most beautiful clothes for no particular reason. Do it. Trust yourself. Let Bastet guide you.

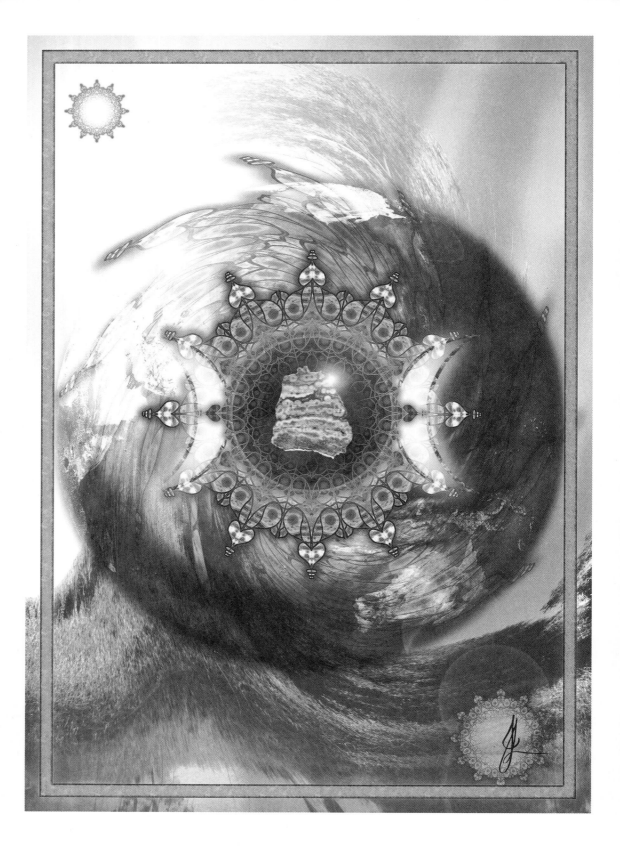

9.

GAIA (WILD GRACE)
OCEAN JASPER (FEELING GOOD)

MANIFESTING THROUGH TRUST

She lives and breathes her creation, expressing it as life in every moment. Unrestrained variety. Endless evolution. Strange. Beautiful. Innovative. The extraordinary genius of the Divine evident in her every manifestation. Through colour, shape, size and form, through light and sound, she gives life. Nothing is too extravagant, nothing is too delicate for her to dream and manifest. She lives through our bodies, and through her, we too manifest divinely.

GAIA (WILD GRACE)

Gaia is the name of the spiritual being that dwells within the body of the Earth Mother through which humanity is born and upon which humanity is nurtured into life. The name comes from the ancient Greek tradition, where Gaia is revered as the mother of creation. The gods were born from her union with Uranus (the god that manifests himself as the sky).

Reverence for the spiritual being of the earth, and her wisdom, is evident in indigenous cultures around the world that have much to teach modern culture about sustainable and conscious living. To those cultures, the earth is not an object, but a living being who should be honoured with gratitude and respect. As we heal our relationship to the feminine and recognise its inherent wisdom and sacredness, our views of the earth naturally evolve too. In terms of environmental healing, we can only do so much through education and advertising to try and evoke emotional responses from people so that constructive action can be taken. There has to be an internal shift in the cultural consciousness towards the feminine from a place of genuine understanding if we are to actually prevent further environmental degradation and become a healing rather than destructive presence upon the earth.

This is deeper than feeling guilt over not recycling thoroughly or feeling urged by morality to give money to starving children, though at a certain level of consciousness, that will 'work' to move someone further along their path. Eventually we will realise we are capable of so much more than this. We are capable of the inner healing of our relationship to the earth, which will then translate into more conscious choices and constructive actions.

A yoga teacher I know recently shared a moment saying that he was watching the shampoo he had used to wash his hair as it floated down the drain in the shower. He thought of that product going directly into the ocean and from that moment he made very different choices about the products he used on his body. Now this is a man who has spent decades getting to know and work consciously with his body – mostly from a perspective of being able to play sport because that is what he loves. Despite the apparently non-spiritual motivation for his journey (i.e. to be better at his sport than anyone else and win all his matches!) his growing connection and understanding of his body eventually led him onto a spiritual path through yoga and into meditation.

Now we could look at how his path started and think it wasn't particularly healing, but in being himself and pursuing his highly ambitious and even perhaps obsessive focus on his sport, something happened. He took a journey. That journey transformed him into a being that could hold a tremendous amount of light in his body and he helps many people through his work and I suspect even more simply through his presence. He is a delight to be around. I sat next to him in a kirtan (chanting circle) once, holding his hand and feeling the light of his being flowing into my energy field. It was a lovely experience, similar to what I felt when I took one of his yoga classes.

Do you think that many people would have honoured him as a spiritual being on an important and helpful journey for human evolution when he was only interested in what would make him a better athlete so he could whip the competition and win? Probably not! He may have seemed self-obsessed and disinterested in the spiritual life of humanity! Yet that was an essential part of his journey to get to where he is now. The soul always takes a long-range view and works towards fulfilling divine destiny by setting up life experiences that will help it manifest its light. Even if those circumstances do not always obviously seem to be relevant to the spiritual life. At some level they will be essential to the growth of the soul. We know this at some level. We just have to remind ourselves so that we don't let the fear of judgment get a grip on our hearts and unnecessarily complicate our journey or the journey of others.

In the case of the yoga teacher, his journey gradually opened him up to a more expanded view of life as something that he was a part of consciously and constructively. He wanted to feel good about his choices, so he made different ones. This happened naturally for him because his physical actions reflected his internal world. He didn't have to try to remember to buy a different shampoo, and forget, and try again the following week and so on. He just did it. The inner realisation led to the outer action. When we try to change the outer action without the internal change, it is harder to sustain.

Most of us know there are simple things we can do to support our environment and help our planet. Cutting back on plastic bags and bottles, recycling as much as possible, choosing eco-friendly detergents and cleaning products, turning off lights, switching to more energy efficient appliances, purchasing organic food from local markets and suppliers when possible, voting with our wallets by not purchasing from businesses or companies that behave in ways we don't respect and by offering financial support to charities that do good works in the world. These things are not particularly difficult to do; they are just new habits to create. If we focus on making an effort to change one thing at a time, we can help the planet.

As helpful as these steps are and however simple they may be, they are not the answer to the environmental disorder of our planet. Environmental imbalances are a symptom of a problem in the human psyche. Treating the symptoms is necessary but it is not the cure. We need to get to the root cause and deal with that if healing (rather than continual treatment to keep symptoms at bay) is going to happen. The problem in the human psyche that leads to environmental problems, by allowing toxic chemicals to be dumped in reefs (for example), is a disconnection from the feminine. The feminine is expressed in our world as life, the Earth Mother and all her creations – including our bodies, the animal and plant worlds and the oceans. It is bizarre that we could be living in the world and be disconnected from it at the same time, but in modern, non-indigenous cultures we tend towards disconnection more than connection. This is often a way of trying to protect ourselves from the increasing stressors of modern living but unfortunately it is turning us away from the world that actually needs our presence in order to heal.

However, a spiritual revolution is taking place and you are part of that. You wouldn't be reading this book otherwise. The revolution is manifesting itself through soul tribes that value life, are compassionate but fierce with passion for a new world. These tribes are incarnating now as the way-showers into a new life in a new world. They are creating this world through art, story, dance, spirituality, activism, compassion, passionate purpose and the craving to do something good, constructive and helpful in the world. They don't just dream about it, they act on their dreams too. These revolutionaries have an insatiable need to manifest their light. This is not from a narcissistic place of 'me, me, me', but out of a powerful compulsion to pull the human race into greater consciousness. They realise their light contributes to the combined light of many souls, creating the radiance required so that others with vision not quite so refined as yet, can also come to see the way forward. Then we can all move forward, together.

This is what is needed. This is the feminine wisdom. We have to move together as a species, as an ecosystem. We are all a part of the body of Mother Earth. You can't pull a body apart and expect it to be well. It becomes well through being honoured and treated as a whole. We need enough souls to tip the balance into new consciousness or enough healthy cells in that greater body so the overall system can be healthy and thrive with life. That doesn't mean you have to get out and awaken as many people as possible by trying to thump awareness into heads that have no interest in it. It does mean that we need to work towards critical mass – the amount of consciousness that can push us out of fear as a species and into love.

Critical mass is significant for those of us on the path of love that may look at the state of the world, and of mass consciousness generally, and wonder how we are ever going to get to where we need to be in order to avert poverty and destruction, and open up to the type of world we know in our hearts is possible for us to create. Critical mass does not require every single person to awaken for a shift of the entire human species to occur. Absolute perfection is not required. What is needed is enough. That is, enough spiritual weight to tip the scale in favour of love. Fortunately for us, the influence and weight of just one enlightened soul is far greater than that of many that operate at a frequency of less spiritual power. Add to this the reality that we are all connected and you will realise that *we just need enough of us to hold a certain frequency of light for the entire human race to be pulled forward.* Exciting, don't you agree? We have to pass this information on to those that can benefit from it. Too many healers become disheartened by the lie that real evolutionary change isn't possible. It is! We must work together. It gives us more energy and passion when we realise that the goal is possible and is within our grasp.

We don't need to disperse our energy into awakening the masses, unless we genuinely feel that is what our heart is urging us to do at this particular time. Awakening can happen for all beings but we must work intelligently for this to manifest. Trying to convert or to illuminate those that are not able to really hear or feel what you are communicating might not be the best use of your time and energy. It doesn't mean that you love such beings any less. It just means that you don't plant seeds in soil that is not yet fertile enough to hold life.

At this time, when we are planting seeds of love, we need to work with those that are willing, eager, and are in love with life enough to care for it more than they fear it. We work with the healers, storytellers, artists, lovers, dreamers, activists, musicians, teachers and therapists. We work with those that want to open to love. As those numbers grow, love will become more present and more will be ready to receive. It is a trickle-down effect!

So we work together. We do not tear each other apart by deciding one modality is better than another or one therapist isn't doing things the way we would do them, as though our way were the only way or the best way for them. There are various healing modalities and therapeutic approaches that don't resonate with me at all. Some I find quite dark and even without much soul. But we are all different. What doesn't work for me could be exactly what another being needs to take their next step. Different people will awaken via different routes. This is fine. When we remember that we are all heading to the one divine source, we can relax a little about how everyone gets there. We can support the journey of others, whatever way is truthful for them, without losing the right to take our journey in the way that is authentic for us.

So let's encourage each other. Yes, you must do your work and even if that work isn't for me, it will be for someone. You are built according to the genius of divine design so there's wisdom in walking your path, just as there is wisdom in walking mine. We can drop the judgment, but be discerning in choosing what will work for us personally and still support each other to take our respective journeys in the understanding that each journey serves the greater human process of evolution. We must firmly and lovingly affirm our own right to take our journey. We need the love and support too.

Then enough of us can move towards love, pulling humanity forward with the weight of our combined spiritual presence. And then we can all choose whether we shall we sink or swim in the ocean of love that will hit the planet like a cosmic downpour, cleansing lower vibrational reality once and for all, and opening us up to a more integrated world where wisdom, rather than fear, is the guiding philosophy.

Loving Gaia means becoming capable of genuine affection for her by healing our relationship with our own bodies, which this book supports us in, through the various healing processes. It takes time, and perhaps we'll feel as if we are taking two steps forward and one back (or even sometimes the other way around!) but genuine progress is possible with commitment, patience and, of course, trust. Fortunately we do gain a lot of help from many great beings when we make a commitment to heal. So when we love Gaia, she will respond to us and help us on our path, just as we want to help her. She teaches us through many methods. Her very body is her scripture. We can learn from her animals, from nature, from the ways she communicates with us, from within us, in every moment. She teaches us through dreams, visions and the signs that live and breathe through her daily. Sometimes she speaks in words that we can hear in our hearts, but at other times, her teachings stir something that is wordless and primal in us and we are fed by her sunrises, her sunsets, her moon phases and her weather patterns – wild or gentle – with extraordinary grace, humour and compassion.

I have already referred to the relationship break up I went through at the time of writing this book. Once I moved into my new home, there were several weeks where I felt as though my life had become very small and quiet. It would expand into a wider social network than ever before only weeks later, but I didn't know that then.

At that time, it felt natural for me to be inhabiting my smaller, quieter world. I spent most of my evenings in silence, gazing out at the beautiful view of the region through the generous bay windows and feeling somewhat removed from life, without being disconnected from it. I did go out to meet new friends as well as old ones several times during those weeks, but I felt as though I was in a liminal space and was even more introverted than usual. Although I was still going through the process of letting go, I was not really in the past. I felt grounded, connected to myself and my body, and was busy with plenty of work to do, but I felt that the new life I was heading towards hadn't opened up to me as yet.

I knew it made sense to be like that for a time. It was part of dealing with the dramatic change that had occurred with me leaving my home, partner and lifestyle and moving out on my own, as a single woman for the first time in several years and into an area that I didn't know very well. I needed time and space to grieve and get my head around what had happened. I wasn't feeling the urge to dance or sing very much. Even my typically vocal cat Leo was quieter than usual. It was probably okay, but I did have some niggles of concern when others were so struck by how simple and quiet my life was. I was peaceful but I wanted to be certain that I wasn't hiding myself away. So I asked for guidance. Is this okay? Is it healthy? Do I need to do anything other than honour the space I am in? Is there a danger I'll get stuck here and miss the chance I have given myself to take a leap into a broader, bigger life because I seem to be heading in the opposite direction, pulling my energy back in and living so small right now.

The young family who lived upstairs in the duplex had gone away for the weekend. As I went up to their back yard to feed their cat, she meandered over to me meowing proudly. Then something caught my eye. It appeared that the cat had left a gift of sorts upon the back doorstep. It looked like a dead rat. I thanked the cat for her offering, saying that whilst I appreciated it immensely, it would be fine with me if she didn't leave anymore for me whilst her owners were away. She obliged, thankfully.

I looked more carefully at the little furry creature, just to make sure he really was dead before removing his body and realised it didn't look exactly like a rat. I didn't know what it was as I hadn't seen anything like it before, but a clear intuition came to me. Bandicoot. I took a careful look at his features, the softer longer eyes and gentler snout and committed it to memory. I gently disposed of his body with a prayer of thanks. Later that evening, I did some research on the bandicoot, starting with an image search to confirm that was actually what the cat had presented. It was. Then I looked up some metaphysical meanings for the bandicoot. I was amazed by what I read. It was an answer to my prayer for guidance from the previous evening.

The medicine or healing power of the bandicoot was about being able to break unhealthy ties with family. I knew this was helping me let go of the man I loved because the relationship between us was not good for me anymore. I was struggling to do so and the simple love in that message brought out many tears, of grief and gratitude.

The healing power of the bandicoot was also about not being afraid to be introverted, and acknowledging that living a quiet life could be grounding, particularly during times of stress and trauma. It also related to the healing power of sand. I had been receiving guidance to spend a lot of time at the beach for cleansing and rebalancing my spirit. I had been doing this and feeling the benefit of it. Bandicoot had supported me in this. I felt profound gratitude for the 'Wildspeak' website (www.wildspeak.com) that had provided me with this information. It was so affirming of my experience. Gaia had managed to get a response to my prayer to me through a number of vehicles, including the local cat and the wise woman who runs the aforementioned website. I was deeply moved.

That night, in gratitude, I performed a simple ritual of respect for the life of the bandicoot that had come to me with that message. Through gentle gonging and singing from my heart, with love, the chant for Mother Earth (included in the healing process below) I honoured the soul of that animal. I cannot even begin to explain the amount of love that I felt erupt in the room at that time. It was the soul of the bandicoot and it was Mother Earth, it was God, in that space with me, responding to the loving thanks I proffered through my simple devotional offering of sound from my heart.

That evening, I was given a healing dream that helped me have the courage to go back and face the unresolved grief and trauma I was still carrying about moving from where I lived for the previous four years. As beautiful as the place I had moved to was, a part of me was in shock and deep sadness about no longer living in the house I had lived in with my previous partner. In the dream I was held safe by a loving angel-man whom I believe represented my own inner-masculine spirit. He guided me through the house, allowing me to confront the full extent of my feelings of loss in each room. Some rooms were very painful to enter into, others not so much. When my feelings seemed too much to bear and I wanted to back away, he would hold me, reassuring me that it was okay so I could be with the feelings until they passed.

I could bear the experience of loss through that dream in a way I hadn't been able to do some weeks earlier, on the actual day of moving, when I was using my energy to simply get through the task at hand and not fall into a crying heap on the front lawn! Perhaps I ought to mention here, to put this into perspective that I was still deeply in love with this man and didn't really want to leave him. I knew that I had to for my own wellbeing, but it was not how I wanted things to turn out.

About a week before I gave my commitment to the new landlords that I would definitely be moving in, and therefore leaving my home and relationship, I was sitting in my car outside the house that I shared with my partner. I gazed at it with the surreal thought that I wouldn't be living there much longer.

A clear message from my higher guidance popped into my mind. "We are asking you to leave here now," they said. They had never asked anything of me before. They had made suggestions and that was it. I knew that I had the right to refuse and choose to remain, but I loved them and trusted in their unconditional love of me. I knew that exercising my free will to stay, would have been going against the natural flow of life and things would have gotten much worse. I knew that their request was a sort of divine intervention for my own greater happiness. Intuitively, I understood that they were saying my time at that house and in that relationship was karmically 'up' and other things were waiting for me. There had recently been changes in occupancy for the houses on either side of the house where I had been living and I knew the energy of the area was changing. My energy didn't belong there anymore. I accepted this guidance but I wasn't looking forward to acting on it, because I knew it was going to feel like I was tearing my heart apart.

This is why I couldn't simply and easily process the experience. It was almost too much for me. I needed that dream. It brought me a grace of healing that supported me in processing an important aspect of my emotional journey. I believe it was the love that had entered the room and my consciousness when I presented my ritual offering earlier that evening that had manifested itself as the healing dream. I woke the next morning feeling deeply loved, honoured and blessed.

A short time after this dream, I asked the angels to help me find a good psychotherapist or counsellor with whom I could work through some of my emotional issues, to understand what was operating within me that had led me into a relationship where I could love a man so deeply, bonding and committing to him with my entire being, when in fact, he was not a particularly good match for me in many ways, though I have no doubt that he loved me also. After I easily found and booked in for a therapy session with a lovely woman who just happened to live around the corner from my new home, I began to contemplate the resolution of my question. Insights began to flow pretty quickly and by the time I was ready to see her, several days later, I was ready for our work together. She offered me an invaluable gift – she really listened to me and reflected back what she heard. As I listened to her, I could hear myself more clearly and a story that made sense to me finally began to unfold. I realised that leaving the relationship was only one part of a far bigger soul healing that was happening for me.

Before and after the therapy session, a vision kept flashing in my mind. I could see a vibrant being of light – it was my soul – and it was almost completely free, but was yet to kick off a brown hessian sack that had been tied around it with old ropes. The sack wasn't covering much. Just a little around one small corner of the soul, but my goodness that soul was determined to be absolutely free and clear. Thrashing about, it kept moving and twisting and turning, finding its way out of that hessian veil. It was almost free! Once this issue to do with respect and honouring myself unconditionally had been mastered, my soul would be free from the old sack that had obscured its light and constrained its freedom. It would be able to burst forth into the world in a new way. It was a strange and powerful vision, and very clear.

As I left the therapy session, I received a clear message from the Divine: "Go to the beach, you need to be in the water and to cleanse this past wounding. It is no longer to be a part of you or your life experience. You need the ocean to cleanse yourself ritually now."

I recognised this as being a voice of love and wisdom. I followed its instructions. I dipped my head in the cool water at Bilgola Beach. The voice returned, "You need to dip your head three times." I did so. I stood on the warm golden sand afterwards, with cool salt water dripping off my body and wrapped myself in a towel. I then realised I had been given a baptismal ritual for sacred rebirth. I had to dip my whole body, head included, into the cleansing waters of the Divine Mother, just like a baby would have water poured over her head three times when she was received into the divine embrace through the Christian baptism ritual. The voice said to me, "This is a birthing place, the feminine energy here is the womb from which your soul shall re-emerge into life." Having gone through a sense of my old life dying, I very much felt like I needed a rebirth! I realised the wisdom of Gaia was speaking through that voice.

In the days and weeks that followed that ritual, I could sense the new life emerging through the gradually softening waves of grief. It was a gentle interplay of new life emerging as the old one began to fade away. Each day I gently took steps to release the old wound, as my soul kicked off more and more of what remained of the hessian sack, loosening the bondage that constrained its full being. I made choices that reflected respect and regard for myself in ways that wouldn't have been possible in the previous relationship. I began to experience myself in a completely new way. It was a beautiful beginning to a new life. I couldn't foresee that new life but I knew I had to come into through absolute trust in the wisdom of life's plan for me.

For those of us that have come to the earth to offer healing, our love for Gaia can be very great indeed. The more we struggle with being on this planet and remaining true to our nature, the more we love her at a soul level. Those of us that carry a very different frequency within us to that which is already established upon the earth, can find life challenging in a far deeper way than it is for those that are less sensitive. I have created a meditation CD called *Star Child* for these kinds of souls and the *Crystal Stars 11.11* book that follows on in this *Crystal Spirituality* series is dedicated to those souls who not only want to learn about working with the energies of the stars for earth healing and advanced soul awakening, but for those souls who feel as though home is amongst the stars and find it hard to be here on the earth whilst remaining true to who they are.

The earth has a special relationship to those of us who know ourselves to be healers, shamans, lightworkers, spiritual channels, star children, artists or environmentalists. That is, those of us who feel that healing the planet and human culture is somehow within our soul plan and heart truths. She will empower us but also move us to where we need to be. Sometimes this is an inner experience, in that we grow through our life experiences and become more fully ourselves. Sometimes it is quite literally an external relocation, in that one minute we are living somewhere and the next we feel we truly must travel to a particular location or live elsewhere for a time.

The energy field of different places around the earth offers us a completely different experience of life, which can trigger tremendous leaps in personal growth. I love teaching around the world because I not only get to work with different groups of people from different cultures, but the experience of working in other countries is palpably different for me. When I was a little girl, my mother used to talk about her tennis career – she was a rather good tennis player. She said that playing on a grass court was so different to playing on a clay court that it was almost like a different sport, let alone a different game. Having worked in the raw energy of Australia, the refined, intellectual energy of Holland, the effusive, sensual energy of Ibiza, the ancient energy of Greece and the chaotic melting pot of polarities that is Istanbul, for example, I can honestly say that this work is so very different, depending on where you are on the earth. The effect of this is twofold. It benefits our own wellbeing, drawing different energies into our system, but it also brings our energy to the place upon the earth and the communities connected to that place, and can help nourish or rebalance them too.

I have had the vision of lightworkers and other healers of the earth as something like white blood cells that are moved intelligently about the greater body of the earth, and focused in the areas where they are needed. For star children who are drawn to working with higher frequencies of consciousness and channelling them into the earth, the metaphor is more like being a cosmic acupuncture needle being plugged into the earth's energy body to release blockages and get things flowing in balance.

This is the wild grace of Gaia. It is wild because it doesn't pander to our fears. It is real, instinctive and honest. It moves us to where we need to be, when we need to be there – internally and externally. The grace is the love within that wildness. It wants us to live, to become all that we can be and to thrive with life. Gaia is life. Anything that has to end through her grace – a relationship, an identity, a friendship, a life – is ended so that life can be furthered. The challenge in accepting her wild grace is that it requires the complete surrender of our notions about how we think things should unfold or be, and letting go of any attempts to control or direct her will. We have to learn to receive rather than take. I am sure it is no surprise to you that we receive so much more when we stop taking, but as a culture, many people are still learning what the difference between receiving and taking actually is. It is a difference that becomes very clear as we connect with the feminine wisdom that Gaia embodies. When we take, it is not rightfully ours and therefore causes imbalance, in our world and in the greater world around us. When we give and receive more freely, balance is restored and sustained. Wellbeing results from balance. Disease from imbalance. This applies to our bodies and the world.

I had a dream many years ago of being in a strange and beautiful place on the earth. An ocean was at my feet and as the tide drew back, a perfect lyrebird feather was revealed. I instantly recognised that it was a valuable and precious prize, and bent down to collect it when a lyrebird swiftly grabbed my finger in its beak. I was not to take that feather. I didn't fight off the bird, I just drew back, surprised but respectful of its message, even though I wasn't exactly sure what that message was.

As I worked with the dream later on, somewhat puzzled by the meaning because I had always felt that the Divine gave to me so freely and abundantly, I learned a valuable lesson in abundance and respectful living from a physical perspective and a spiritual one.

The wisdom offered to me in that dream was that in the realm of the Divine Mother there is nothing to be taken. It is not right. We will be given what is needed, in great abundance, according to her wisdom. If something is withheld from us, whether it be for just a moment, or a seemingly long time, matters not. We are learning not to see and take, but to be open to receive. That is the feminine way. Lyrebird is often about listening and receiving all that is around us, integrating it, and then releasing a true voice. It is not about forcing or deciding. It is about allowing.

That dream, like so many of my dreams, was a predication of what was to come. During the years that followed I began to develop my soul voice – the true nature of what I was to share on this planet. That process, as indicated by the dream, happens in its own timing, according to a higher wisdom that may or may not be obvious to us at the time. As long as we learn to listen to that wisdom, and not apply our ego to try and override it (the finger that the bird gently but firmly bit, was the second finger on my right hand, traditionally associated with the ego) then we shall be in harmony with the greater natural processes.

I have had this experience with people too, most often in context of coming to me for spiritual healing. Let me start by saying that most often, those that I work with lovingly receive what is offered through me, and are incredibly grateful for all that they receive. These are the ones that flourish on their path, experience genuine growth and help others as they themselves benefit from their own journey too.

Then there are others that have what I could describe as a sense of entitlement. These are the people who are yet to deal with their inner child, who have kept a sense of deservedness that overrides the laws of nature. They expect to have their needs met by whomever they decide should meet them, whenever and however they decide that should happen. Woe betide if you don't deliver! Great rage can result, along with psychic attacks, emotional abuse and scathing criticism. Being involved with people like this can feel like you are being simultaneously worshipped as their idol and cast in the role of slave to their fluctuating needs.

I had a client like this once. And I mean once! After the experience I had with her I realised I could no sooner genuinely assist her than stand on my head, spinning whilst performing the arias of *La Boheme*. It just wasn't going to happen!

She came to see me for a psychic reading. She was referred to me by a friend of hers who was a lovely man who had come for a psychic reading several years beforehand and had raved at how accurate his session had been. I told her that I never claim perfection in psychic readings, accuracy depends on a number of factors, some of which are completely beyond my conscious control, however, I would do my best and offer her what came through. She agreed to this and booked in for her session.

I talked to her about a pattern that she had of 'biting the hand that feeds her' and how it was a self-created pattern of dissatisfaction that had the effect of pushing people away from her, keeping her angry, isolated and frustrated, even whilst she thought that she was just looking for 'quality in customer service' and relationships. What she was doing was building bitterness. She seemed to hear me and on we went with the session.

When the session recording didn't work, there was hell to pay. She threatened me with various courses of action that she was going to take and I was struck by the irony that she was acting out with exactly the response I had warned her against. I also found it rather ironic that the reason she was so angry and trying to attack me was because she placed so much value on what I had given her in the session, which she now felt had slipped out of her grasp because she didn't have the recording to fall back on. I understood but I always noted up front that the recordings were not fool proof. I had some recordings that were so bizarre – sounding more like high pitched dolphin sounds than human voices – that eventually I stopped offering a recording service altogether and just invited clients to record the session, if they thought it might be helpful.

It also struck me how keen the Universe appeared to be for her to overcome the issue I had talked to her about. Conspiring with the failure of her session recording (her friend who came for a session immediately before her had no problems with her recording at all) presented an immediate opportunity for her to really learn how to overcome the issue, if she so chose. She did not so choose. She sent me a barrage of emails articulating various threats and completely ignored my suggestion that she treat the failed recording as an opportunity to overcome her tendency to demand perfection and write people off, and to be open to the idea that perhaps there could still be something worthwhile to be found, even if circumstances didn't turn out exactly as she had hoped. She demanded that I do another session for her free of charge. Apart from the fact that you cannot just 'repeat' a session, there was no way I was going to invite someone who was so aggressive towards me and so unwilling to take any responsibility for her own feelings back into sacred space with me. Agreeing with the practical advice of my mentor at the time, who was shocked at how toxic this woman's behaviour was, I refunded her session fee in full and told her not to contact me again as I would not work with her.

Here was a situation where something was offered, but the poor woman was so entrenched in her own rage that she couldn't receive it. She tried to take what she thought she deserved, but what she was actually being given, if only she would have received it, was the healing that would have taken her out of her pain. She didn't see it like that though. We usually don't when we are in great pain. That is why we need trust in Gaia and her experiences. I'll be the first to admit that the experiences Gaia presents to us for our own healing and happiness are not always easy, but I know enough of her wisdom to accept that there will be a point in the future where I will look back at what I went through with understanding, appreciation and gratitude.

The irony with those that try to take is that no matter how much they get, it is never enough. There will always be something more that they desperately need from you or whomever it is that they have decided is supposed to give them what they want, whether that be a person or the world in general. The reason for this is that they can't receive, so they never feel nourished and fed. If we have a tendency to eat and eat and not ever feel really full, or to shop until we drop but never really feel satisfied enough to enjoy what we have and say 'enough is enough,' or if we spend time with people but just end up drained rather than enhanced, then we are taking rather than receiving, or in the latter example, being taken from, rather than received. We need the healing wisdom of Gaia to help us learn to receive, and also what it feels like to be received – which is very nourishing. It is only when we learn how to receive that we come to understand how very different it is to taking. One comes from trust, the other from a place of lack. When we come from trust, we can choose to receive from life, surrendering our control and judgment and allowing ourselves to be moved by a greater intelligence than our ego.

It also feels like a more abundant and enjoyable way to live. Living through taking is quite destructive to the soul. It will serve our growth for a time, no doubt, but eventually the heart won't want to continue to live in that way and will seek out increasingly dramatic ways for the pattern to stop. Sometimes we might end up with financial constraints or in a depression that makes nothing seem worthwhile taking. We can't be liberated from it until we receive something genuine. The divine healing grace has to descend into the empty vessel of our being, and we can do nothing but wait for it. Or perhaps we are physically stopped, like a woman I knew of once who knew she was supposed to take a rest, and refused. Eventually she broke an arm. In her plaster cast, she decided that she would start painting her house. She fell off the ladder and broke her other arm. She decided at that stage to rest, before she ended up breaking her legs too. She was not allowed to continue to take, to control, to force, to demand. She had to learn to surrender. Finally she took the increasingly obvious hint! My wish for all beings is that we may learn the lessons of surrender and receiving with as much mercy and as little harm to our bodies and souls as possible.

Please know that we can still ask for what it is that would move our hearts. We are not being asked to be free from desire. Our desire and passion can move us towards fulfilment and healing. What we are being asked to do is to trust in the timing, in the 'who' and in the 'how.'

About fifteen years ago, I lived briefly in a beautiful little townhouse in a gorgeous suburb of southern Sydney called Oyster Bay. I used to walk around the natural bush land areas that were dotted around the suburb. How at home I felt with so many trees about me! I was in heaven.

At the time, I was doing some very intensive emotional work. I was also working with animal totems, as I have done instinctively pretty much all of my life. I wanted a sign that I was going to get where I wanted to go. I was spiritually ambitious at the time. I probably still am but I have a very different attitude towards myself and my own spiritual growth these days. Back then it felt like my spiritual growth was essentially comprised of a series of tasks that I had to check off and get accomplished as quickly as possible. These days my spiritual growth feels rather more like an interesting meandering adventure with a few hill sprints and the occasional (and much appreciated) leisurely scenic walk down the hill on the side. To be honest with you though, I would say that my closest friends probably think I am still as ambitious and driven as ever! I beg to differ, however.

Back then, I was all systems go and pushing my way forward, or so I thought. What I really wanted was a spiritual gift to let me know if I was travelling along my path with sufficient speed. I asked for such a gift. I knew that the Divine would answer me. I hardly experienced it as separate from me. What I didn't say aloud, but undoubtedly the Divine knew because it was stamped all over my heart, is that I wanted my spiritual gift to be a crow's feather. The crow as a totem had meaning to me at the time, and I believed when I was finally granted such a feather, it would show that I had passed a particular spiritual test that I was doing my best to successfully master.

Now of course we all know (!) that when you pray for something you *do not* get to determine how that prayer should be answered. If we did I would have asked for my declaration for abundance to come via true love, as falling head over heels with a billionaire whom adored me would be a much easier path than the more spiritually arduous task of tackling my fears one by one and learning unconditional trust. Of course I can acknowledge that if I had of got my own way, I wouldn't have learned what I learned, nor grown spiritually as I have grown, but that doesn't mean I wouldn't have asked for it anyway! I am human! I wouldn't have minded the luxury! I wouldn't have been able to fulfil my spiritual tasks in quite the same way though, so I suspect there is some intelligence in that little 'condition' of how the Universe answers our prayers being up to the Universe to decide.

I knew that. I didn't ask for crow's feather, but of course, I wanted one! During one of my regular walks, I decided to stand in the middle of the small are of bushland near the townhouse where I lived and speak my desire for a spiritual gift aloud. "Please show me," I asked, "what I need to know." I may as well have added "and let it be a crow's feather," but I didn't, not out loud at least.

As I walked happily through the bushland, I noticed a kookaburra that appeared to also be noticing me. The inner child in me, always somehow more alive when in the bush, decided to follow him. A game began. He would fly to a tree just a little in the distance and I would follow. He would fly again and I would follow. This continued on until he led me out of the bushland and down the street, back towards my home, via a different route to the one that I had taken. I was a bit disappointed to be led out of the bush – until I looked down. As he started laughing on his branch, I noticed that underneath the tree where he sat, there was a feather. Poking up from the ground, it shone, reflecting a vibrant blue shimmer in the sunlight. My breath caught in my chest as I respectfully walked towards the feather. It was a beautiful Kookaburra feather. As he laughed his head off and I dealt with the mixed emotion of it not being a crow's feather (close, but no cigar!) and the beauty of what was actually given me, a healing happened. I let go. The kookaburra, I only later realised, was telling me to lighten up and laugh more. Everything would be okay. I was being too intense. I needed to approach my journey in a different way. Tapping into my abundant sense of humour would help me get further than trying to plan how my journey would happen. I gave up on my crow feather and treasured my kookaburra feather, and the many others that randomly found their way to me, or me to them, over the months following that experience.

A year or so later, having moved house, I was with my then boyfriend and we were walking through Centennial Park in Sydney's eastern suburbs. I loved to go there and feed the ducks. My boyfriend and I found their antics to be so funny. We would make up little songs about them and sometimes the ducks would come and sit next to us, as if they thought we were just other ducks, albeit of an unusually large size. We would all just 'hang out' together and feel quite in tune with nature. It was lovely. As we strolled through the park that day, I suddenly dropped his hand and stood, stunned silent. Before us was a field of grassy-covered hills, and in it were about a hundred crow's feathers! They were everywhere! I had never seen anything like it before or since then. Obviously there had been some bizarre crow shenanigans going on, which led to the feathers sticking up out of the ground all over the place. Crows sat happily around the feathery fray, in the trees, on the grass, talking away to each other, seemingly oblivious to the chaotic array of their shed feathers on the ground beneath them. I felt like I had stumbled into the remains of a wild crow party. I laughed. I had softened over the year that had passed and become more willing to just be in the process of my growth, and now here was confirmation that I was indeed progressing. I allowed myself to feel which feather 'called' to me, and with gratitude, it went home with me and ended up on my altar. I couldn't help but feel awestruck. That partially spoken request was answered, at the perfect time and in a rather more dramatic way than I could have ever imagined.

We have an effect on Gaia, just as she does on us, we are in a relationship with each other that can become increasingly responsive and healing. To keep things in perspective, which my dream about the lyrebird certainly showed, she is not to be ordered about! She knows and she works according to far greater rhythms and cycles than our minds can fathom. We only need be face to face with her great storms or implacable weather patterns to understand that her power is truly impressive. She is billions of years old and a very vast being. The wisest approach to our relationship with Mother Earth is to recognise that we can make an offering to her through our contributions to the greater good in whatever way we are suited to do so. We can be open and grateful for what she gives us, and learn to become more conscious of the parts of us that can be in lack and fear, and therefore believe that they have to grab, take, claim territory or hoard. These behaviours do not honour her as freely as an attitude of trust can. We are all learning. That is just as it is meant to be. These parts of us don't need judgment, just discernment, awareness and compassion, which helps us continue to learn and grow, surrendering into even greater loving relationship with the divine Gaia.

Gaia teaches us, communicates with us and loves us. She is aware of our presence and our vibration because she is a self-aware being, and we function as a part of her divine ecosystem. Although we can experience the sheer power of her nature as raw and wild, in the Buddhist tantric tradition, which seeks to bring mindfulness to the experience of the body, and absolute acceptance of life just as it is, the earth is known as Loachana, a female buddha of great serenity. In the ancient traditions of India, the term for the great supreme goddess is Parameshwari (Param meaning supreme and Eshwari meaning goddess or Divine Feminine). She is both filled with wildness and grace. I will share with you one of my favourite chants to Parameshwari, whom I refer to as the Earth Mother, in the healing process for this chapter below.

Her wild grace manifests in dedication and devotion to our 'waking up'. She reaches to us lovingly every single day through our life experiences, even the ones that aren't particularly easy to accept. Trusting in our life experience, in what is being presented to us at the earthly level can be confronting, but it is also where our body, spirit and the Divine all meet together. It is grace because it is supportive of soul liberation. It is wild because it is beyond logic, and emanating from the natural instincts of a truly great divine being, moving us in great leaps at times, rather than small logical steps. Her evolutionary process is intelligent and creative, and we are just as much a part of that process as any other creature that lives within her constantly evolving field.

OCEAN JASPER (FEELING GOOD)

Wandering through a crystal warehouse in Sydney several years ago, I came across a rather extraordinary looking globe. With banded swirling patterns of dark, forest green and light grey, mottled with tiny yellow dots, it reminded me of a planet. Our planet!

I grabbed it (clearly forgetting my dream teachings of not taking, for a moment at least) and felt all gooey inside. Its energy was beautiful to feel – comforting, grounding, peaceful and strengthening all at once. When I weighed it and realised it was so reasonably priced for what it was, and was told that it was jasper (I have confessed in earlier books to being a jasper junkie) I decided there and then that it was meant for me. It has happily lived in my home environment ever since, so it seems that yes, it was meant to be a gift for me after all.

Also known as orbicular jasper (for the tiny orbs dotted across the stone) it is mined from one spot from the North West Coast of the African Island of Madagascar, and only at low tide (hmmm, reminds me of my dream!). Orbs appear not only in crystals – as tiny circular formations – but on the etheric plane too. The etheric plane is where the chakras and crystal angels dwell. It is the energy of the physical body and is therefore connected to it. It is like invisible wiring through which spiritual electricity can flow so forms, such as our bodies and other animals, can be alive.

The etheric plane can be seen clairvoyantly by some. If you have ever sensed faeries – and you'll know it if you have, they are wild, cheeky, little things and there is nothing else quite like their strange and beautiful presence – then you are sensing the etheric plane. The beings that live on the etheric plane are just as alive as physically manifested beings like us, but they vibrate at less density and therefore appear to be less substantial and are not tangible to our regular five senses. Beings such as faeries, crystal angels and orbs aren't always visible with the naked eye but will often show up in photographs and when they do it indicates that a lot of life force is present. Often they will appear in natural areas where there is a strong concentration of energy, such as pure bushlands and water sources.

While I was running some healing rituals during my recent tour in North Queensland, the husband of one of my clients took photographs. He wanted to see if the influx of spiritual energy we brought through caused an effect in the earth energy field where we had been working. He took photos at various times throughout the tour. After two particularly powerful workshops, the orbs that showed up in his photographs were plentiful and large. We enlarged the photographs on the computer the next morning and were able to see the most extraordinary details. A pixie-like face showed itself in one. A Celtic cross design was in another. I was quite fascinated. So was the photographer/husband.

The orbs in ocean jasper remind us that the earth is a living being, that the material world is a living thing and that even if we can't see it at the time, life is still working its magic. This is good to remember when we hit those times in our lives where we are working on ourselves but nothing seems to be happening in the physical world. Just keep going! There will be a time when the energetic translates into the physical, but we have to have patience and trust. And most importantly, we must not stop doing the healing work. Energy work is real. It has an effect even if that isn't obvious at first. As the effect accumulates, manifestation will eventually take place.

Jasper is more generally a truly earthy stone that demonstrates much colour, variety and beauty, just like Gaia herself. This particular type of jasper usually includes green, grey, yellow, red, white and black tones. Sometimes it will carry hues of pink or blue as well, though that is less common. It can feature druzy (a fine coating of tiny crystals) in green, although in the specimen I am looking at as I write this, the druzy is a glistening soft grey colour, glinting out from the cracks in the stone.

It is harder to come by these days and it is reportedly mined out completely. However, if you are meant to work with it, a piece will come to you or you will strongly connect to the Crystal Angel of Ocean Jasper. Whilst geologists were searching for the mined out ocean jasper on the island of Madagascar, they found a new type of jasper which they named polychrome or desert jasper. Some believe that desert jasper is the next evolution of ocean jasper. They are both beautiful stones to work with, with slightly different energetic properties. I wrote about polychrome jasper in Chapter Seven of *Crystal Angels 444* to connect you with the spirit of divine play. That chapter and the included healing processes (now also available for easy download through my website) will also support you in your work with ocean jasper, if you wish to delve deeply into this 'feel good' topic for your own healing.

Ocean jasper lifts negativity and helps us become more capable of accessing feelings of gratitude and goodwill within ourselves and towards each other. This increases our immunity, improves our overall wellbeing and promotes peace and accord in social environments. It is a wonderful stone to have around if you live or work in a situation where there are lots of different energies or personalities, perhaps with a tendency to come into conflict with each other.

The soothing nature of the stone promotes emotional healing and helps us to come into our hearts, where we can connect with the soul of the earth and allow her to communicate with us through our deepest feelings, intuitions, art, dreams, meditations, dances, walks in nature and relaxation. Because of this, ocean jasper can help us find our way forward, to walk the most authentic path available to us, to make choices that feel aligned with our hearts and to experience more wellbeing, inner peace, internal security and a truer sense of self-worth.

The orbs on the stone are very protective. Whether you sense them as divine 'eyes' or symbols of the interconnectedness of life, the dual action of ocean jasper allows us to feel both more connected to all that is happening in life, personally at a human level and transpersonally at a spiritual level, locally and globally. On the other hand, we are being looked out for and protected by the Earth Mother individually too.

Over time, this stone encourages us towards optimism. It does so gently and realistically, creating an urge to be positive, to speak affirming and loving words (because the choice to do so is available to us at any given moment and those words are best delivered to ourselves at times). It generates goodwill and a sense of good feeling. In a culture where competition and dominance are still thriving, though perhaps becoming more recognised as outmoded forms of behaviour, ocean jasper helps rebalance this win-lose attitude with a win-win mentality that is intrinsic to genuine spiritual growth.

One of the most powerfully healing attitude shifts we can have on the path of life is to be willing to believe that there is compassion in everything that happens. Divine love is in every speck of this manifested reality. Sometimes it might not be immediately visible, but to have a sense that somehow, even if we can't see it, all of life's circumstances are moving each and every being according to a rhythm of love, is very healing. It helps us look for the good and the Divine in all places and things. We don't have to understand it; we can just trust it.

After witnessing this enough times and being blessed with the realisation that even a difficulty will be an expression of divine love and benevolence that is urging a soul towards enlightenment where there is utter peace and bliss, something profound happens within us. We become more trusting of life and therefore have less need to try and fix its course. This can diminish anxiety and stress so much! We might have to face challenges but we do so with the knowledge that there is love happening through it. We don't have to worry about what will happen because we know that whatever happens is what is needed for our divine healing, so we trust in it. Ocean jasper gently but firmly dissolves the filters of fear, negativity and distrust so we are empowered to see more clearly, and in that, we see love.

It helps to generate a field of positive energy and relaxation. From this place, the body can more readily heal itself, emotionally, physically and psychologically, so that the mind can slow down and release repetitive patterning. With chronic stress this patterning can become quite frantic and have a negative impact on the immune system, leaving one feeling as though they are fighting off something all the time. That 'feel good field' helps one make clearer, more helpful decisions, and feel more connected with the body and the heart, through which the divine self speaks to us from within.

MANIFESTING THROUGH TRUST

It is so much easier to trust when we fundamentally believe that we live in a benevolent universe that is supporting our divine growth, loves us and is guiding us daily. One thing I say to pretty much every client, in pretty much every session is, "Call on the guidance that loves you unconditionally every day." This simple, quick action empowers us to be in a field of divine grace and assistance that is incredibly powerful and helpful.

Having that support is like being part of a team that is all working towards the same goal, and with the ability to cultivate good feelings and relaxation from within, comes a far deeper ability to trust in divine love and realise it is real, it is powerful and it is doing its job! When I had to find a new place to live recently, I had an opportunity to see this in action. A whole series of events, I could not have imagined and did not foresee, contrived to move me to a lovely suburb I had never heard of before.

I have already spoken about the recent ending of my relationship with a man with whom I felt a profound karmic connection. In many ways we were quite possibly the least compatible people on the planet, and therefore unlikely to be destined for a harmonious, long-term union. Nonetheless, or perhaps because of that, we loved each other deeply and with great passion.

We met when I was in my twenties, at an astrology class where we instantly felt a deep connection. At the time, I was in the process of breaking with my first long-term boyfriend with whom I had been living with for five or so years. Only six weeks after the break up, I had a 'rebound' relationship with this other man. After six months of our emotional intensity, I tore myself away from him to focus on healing my heart from the first relationship. I realised that although I was very drawn to this new man, I really was in no state to be entering another serious relationship without doing some self-healing.

Then one day, after having no contact with him whatsoever for several years, I suddenly couldn't stop thinking about him. I decided to search for him on LinkedIn, a site which I rarely used and hardly ever thought about. The idea was so out of the ordinary, I just ended up thinking, "Why not?" and just did it. His profile popped up. It was so strange seeing his picture again. I emailed him with just, "hi." He emailed back with an interesting story. His ex-girlfriend had only recently put his profile up on LinkedIn. He wasn't really that interested in doing it, but she suggested it for some reason or other and he agreed. He had also only recently been standing in his garden, looking up at the sky and saying to the Universe, "I am ready to have another relationship, with someone really cool, like Alana." We emailed back and forth, met up again and the relationship was back on again, after more than five years of not exchanging a single word, as simply as if a light switch had been flicked.

We dated for a year before realising we wanted to live together. I don't know if you are aware of the Sydney real estate market, but even our combined finances couldn't manage to cover the sort of home we wanted so that we could live together with an office for him and a work space for me to see clients. He looked at every possible real estate site, becoming more and more disheartened at the cost of living and trying to minimise what we were asking for, whilst I enthusiastically declared that the Universe wanted us to be together so a solution would come forward. I would urge him, "Stop trying to sort it out and remain open-minded so that you don't block something from left of field!" He indulged my optimism a little, but continued with his search in his own time, ever the practical down-to-earth man to my mystical womanliness.

Sure enough within several weeks, a house became available which suited us perfectly and was financially viable. It was a massive stroke of good fortune, available due to another series of circumstances. I was grateful for the place and the generous terms through which it was made available to us, every single day of the several years I lived there. However, during that time I struggled with the fundamental incompatibilities between the way my beloved was and the way I was, and the conflict this caused even when we were doing our best to accept of each other. We were just not a good match in many ways that really mattered for long-term happiness. The more I grew into myself, the more I opened up to new talents and increasingly creative and dynamic ways of expressing my spirituality, the wider the chasm between us grew. I knew this would only continue no matter how deeply we loved each other, but it took me a long, long time to accept I was going to have to give up the relationship and move on. The grieving process took me years. Throughout the last year of our time together, I felt an almost constant mourning for our relationship and what could not be between us. Even so, during that time, I struggled between the human love I had for this man and the soul love within that was urging me to move on.

Amidst all that emotional turmoil, I realised I was going to have to move again. The Sydney real estate market still being what it was, I wondered how everything was going to work itself out. I asked for guidance and promptly felt drawn to email a woman I had studied Chi Gung with for several months, about a year and a half earlier. We hadn't spoken since then, or even much during the course, but we did connect at some level when we were studying together and in the few short chats we did have, we recognised in each other a gentle kindred spirit.

So out of the blue I emailed her saying, "Hi, I know we haven't really been in contact in over a year, and this might seem like a really weird email to receive, but I don't suppose you are aware of a place for rent up where you live?" She responded (of course!) that she and her partner had just decided to look for a place to buy and they would be moving out of their current place when they found it.

I felt a bit dumbstruck with wonder. Could the problem that loomed so large in my mind be so effortlessly resolved? I left it at that and got on with my life. I figured that when the time was right, I would get the nudge. In the months that followed, as it became harder and harder to stay in the relationship, I despairingly sought out somewhere else to live through less inspired, more typical channels such as Internet searches and asking friends to keep an ear open for anything that might come up. I got blocked at every turn. I knew the Universe was telling me to stop trying to figure it out but I felt I should be doing something to help the process along! I wanted to balance my faith with some real-world action.

Instead, I went on the working tour of North Queensland (also mentioned earlier) and even with all the energetic demands on me, I felt that there was a lightness of spirit and a peacefulness in my heart that helped me let go of any concerns despite the sadness I felt about having to leave my partner.

During my teaching, I was blessed with some personal initiations into a deeper relationship to the Earth Mother. It happened naturally and unexpectedly in the midst of my workshops and I felt strengthened by her. She spoke to me directly upon several occasions. That relationship became particularly strong when, on the last day, I dedicated the opening of a medicine wheel on the property where I was staying in service to the Earth Mother. The group that gathered was beautiful and the photographs of all the orbs flying about that spot on the evening afterwards suggested that the nature spirits enjoyed our work as much as we did.

During my free time I was able to visit Eungella, an absolutely stunning mountain top rainforest, and see platypuses (which I have been obsessed with ever since I was a child – even just saying their name makes me giggle), turtles and ducks. The spirits of the trees felt so good, cooling and ancient. Those moments in nature with the couple I was staying with, who themselves were so at home in nature, was a true tonic for my spirit. I easily gained ideas for another oracle deck and meditation CD and I felt in harmony with life.

After that tour I spent some time with my best friend, which I mentioned in the chapter on Saraswati. As we talked, I felt a clarity and renewal of determination to be wildly open to life and put my clear intention into manifesting my next step. However, I did have a concern. I knew how heavy and sleepy I could feel in Sydney where the energy was quite dense, especially compared to the spaciousness of North Queensland where I found it easier to think clearly and maintain a higher vibration without much effort. I realised that if I was going to move, I might as well make a smart move and live somewhere that had a natural healing energy and make life a bit easier and more pleasant for myself.

I held some concern that I might not be able to sustain my high-frequency attitude once my plane touched down in Sydney again. How was I going to deal with seeing my partner? I knew a part of me was going to be so happy to see him and yet here I was having to make this choice. I wasn't looking forward to going home at all.

As I sat on the plane, preparing for take-off, I prayed for assistance and fell into a nap. I was jolted half-awake by the announcement that the plane was preparing for descent into Sydney and I gazed out the window. In the fields beneath me I saw what looked like an eagle, patterned into the grasslands. Eagle is a totem that has come to me on several occasions when I was being asked to rely on my strength. I felt like Mother Earth was telling me something. Quick as a flash I heard guidance speaking to me. They said, "We have given you all that you need, you have taken initiation, you have been drenched in divine light through your work on this tour and received healing through nature. The time to act is now and the rest is up to you."

As painful as it was to put the separation from my partner into full effect, I began to do so as soon as we met at the airport. We worked through it as best as we could. We both knew it was for the best and we still cared about each other enough to want the best for each other. With a renewed determination, having not heard back from the woman I knew from Chi Gung training, I began my house hunting afresh.

I spoke with the ex-girlfriend of my soon to be ex-boyfriend's brother and we decided to look at some places to live together. The first one we went to see was an apartment at number 44, a number typically associated with the angels, and up for rent by a place called Angel Land Realty. Yes. Really.

I went to look at the place and felt it was somewhere I could feel safe. As I was feeling so vulnerable and heart-achy at the time, that was important. Later that day I realised my cat was used to having a yard and would struggle with the tiny outdoor areas. Not to mention that lying in the garden was one of my favourite ways to relax and connect with nature. Living in an apartment would feel like living in a box!

The next morning at 11:11, I received an SMS from my potential flatmate about another place. (11:11 is a typical number pattern that signifies new beginnings and divine intervention. If you are interested in number patterns like this, I have written a book called *Messages in the Numbers* to be published by Blue Angel.) This one had a yard. I was amazed at how quickly my clear realisation had set something else in motion. Still it didn't quite feel right. Something was missing. I realised it was a heart connection. I hadn't connected emotionally with either of those apartments. I was so focused on just moving on because the transition was proving to be uncomfortable and painful that I hadn't acknowledged one of the things that was so important to me – the sense of love and belonging to a place.

There was another problem. My potential flatmate was still very much involved with my soon to be ex-boyfriend's life. He and his friends still went to her for massage therapy and she still saw his mother and wanted to stay in touch with her ex, his brother. She seemed to have no intention to step out of that circle of people. Apart from that, her business was located around the corner from what was soon to be my ex-home and subsequently all the places we were looking at together were spitting distance from there. If I moved in with her, I was going to find the break up more difficult to process because there would be so many reminders. I wondered if it would feel like starting afresh at all. It was going to be hard enough as it was. Did I really want to make it harder on myself by not making a clean break? If I was going to put myself through this, I wanted to do it completely so I could start again in a completely new way.

I thought again of the Chi Gung lady and the home she would soon be leaving. Suddenly I realised that her duplex in Bilgola, at the very edges of the greater Sydney area, far from where I currently lived and where I had no known associations would be supportive of my healing. It was a slightly more expensive choice, but it was manageable. I could live on my own, grieve in my own space and live my own life. It seemed like the best choice.

That same afternoon, after months of no contact, I received an email from the lady from Chi Gung saying that they had just found their new place and would be moving out in a matter of weeks. She invited me to come and have a look at the home, which I did. As I drove out to the Northern Beaches on the outskirts of Sydney, wondering if this was the most impractical decision ever because it was so far away from the city, but I felt peace and calm. I found her street easily, which let me know I was relaxed in the energy of the area (when I stressed, I tend to get lost easily) and as she showed me around the place,

I felt love in my heart. There was a tiny grotto with a small fountain near the outdoor deck, which made me instantly think of Mother Mary. There was forest within walking distance, beaches only a few minutes away and views all the way to the heart of Sydney with many trees and shorelines.

Best of all, a big red butterfly flew right up and hovered in front of my face for several moments while I was there. That was my 'sign'. My nickname is Red and the butterfly has been a totem for me. At dark times in my life it heralds the promise of new life. It has never let me down. The woman who was living there told me the place had been blessed by a Buddhist monk and that the people who lived upstairs were on their own healing path and were lovely to be around. The only obstacles in my way were in my own mind. I wasn't required to go through an interview process or provide references or financial records. The owners were happy with a simple recommendation from their current tenants, happy for me to bring my fluffy cat along, and happy for me to move in when I was ready.

However, there were some concerns about the place. The major one was it up for sale and I might have to move again in three months. Also, I really had no local knowledge and no clue what it would be like to live there. Despite those uncertainties, my heart said yes and I decided to trust that it would work out how it was meant to. If I was meant to be there, I would be there for however long that was meant to be, and if not, something else would come up.

Moving here has been healing in so many ways and although it was not an easy transition, the love, support and friendship that I have found here has been amazing. I have been able to heal in a way I know would not have been possible if I had remained in Sydney proper. Relieved doesn't even begin to describe how grateful I am that I took the leap and made that choice. Despite the uncertainty of what my next steps would be, the longer travel distances and the painful grieving process, that decision allowed for greater happiness than I had felt in many, many years. It wouldn't have happened without trust. The decision made no logical sense on many levels, yet at the heart level, I trusted it because I could recognise that the choice came from love, not fear.

After I had moved in, one of the owners told me that some weeks earlier she had been at a woman's group where the facilitator had got out a deck of oracle cards. The group had used them and the owner really loved working with the cards, having had a powerful experience of her own. She asked the group facilitator who had created the deck and was presented with the box of the *Kuan Yin Oracle* that I had written. The owner was amazed. The facilitator expressed her love of my work (thank you!) and the owner shared that I was about to move into the area, to the duplex at the front of their house. I had to smile. It seemed that my beloved Kuan Yin was weaving her magic, making my way easier, along with Gaia's wild grace.

HEALING PROCESS

This simple healing process can be used at any time you are struggling to trust. You will know this is happening if you believe a certain event has to occur before you can relax or that you can only take a step if you are certain it will turn out in a particular way. If you are having less vision or insight into the future than usual or feel that you are entering a phase in your life when you are being asked to let go of your need to know and just grow, then this will help you too.

The Process

Start by having your crystal mandala and/or crystal with you. You may wish to have a natural offering to Gaia of a piece of food for use in the ritual, preferably something with a high natural water content like fruit or raw vegetables, that are washed and able to be eaten at the close of your ritual. If you prefer not to have food, you can have a small glass of clean drinking water instead.

Say, "I call upon the unconditionally loving being, Gaia, Soul of the Earth, Mother and Buddha of Serenity and Enlightenment. I choose to lovingly accept your wild grace and thank you for your blessings of abundance, protection and of life itself! I call upon your Crystal Angel of Ocean Jasper and the energy of good feeling, relaxation and optimism. I trust in your love, your wisdom and your divine healing now. I surrender into your divine pathway for my soul light to shine as bright as possible, in service to love. So be it."

Close your eyes and breathe in and out for at least eight breaths. If you can, imagine that any issue or concern you are feeling is beginning to drain out of your body, soaking into the earth beneath you. What is a big issue to you is comparatively small to her. Imagine sending love from your heart along with whatever you are releasing and allow the Divine Mother to transform it through her compassion into peace.

Imagine that rising up from the earth you can sense or perceive a beautiful angel in dark green robes, with wings made of shimmering crystal and a peaceful, happy energy. Just being near that angel, who loves you unconditionally, feels really good. Imagine the energy of that angel can create a smile in your heart. Feel your heart relax a little.

Stay with that peaceful feeling and breathe in and out. Imagine that your heart feels lighter and lighter, whilst at the same time feeling grounded, secure and safe. You feel cool and relaxed.

From deep within the earth, a beautiful soothing voice rises up and says, "Trust in me beloved one, all is working out perfectly."

Stay with the feeling of peace and trust and when you are ready just put your hands over your glass of water or food. Say, "The blessing of the soul of the earth, Mother Gaia, flows through my hands now and into this offering. Thank you!"

Allow love, peace and that good feeling to transfer from your heart into your food or water. Feel peaceful and relaxed.

You can then sound this mantra (sounding guide below) at least eight times or however long feels good. Imagine its sound travelling into your food or water. It calls on the divine spirit of Mother Earth and her gifts of attraction, abundance and clear insight that cuts through illusion and into absolute reality, in service to her divine plan of liberation for all beings.

OM HRIM SHRIM KLIM PARAMESHWARI SWAHA

OM (rhymes with TOM) Hrim (H-REAM) Shrim (SHREEM) Klim (KLEEM) PARAM (PAR – as in parrot, AM as in I AM) Eswhwari (ESH-WAH-RAY) Swaha (SWA-HAH)

When you are ready say, "I thank you for your grace! I accept it willingly so that I may better serve your divine plan of love and freedom for all beings."

Then slowly eat your food or drink your water.

When you are ready, you can simply place your hands in prayer at your chest and bow your head for a moment. Then you are done.

If you find yourself falling back into old habits of worry or distrust, be kind to yourself and simply say from within your heart, to the Divine Mother Earth, "I trust you" and reconnect to that loving sense of peace within.

10.

KALI (REVOLUTION)
BLACK OBSIDIAN (DEFLECTION)

MANIFESTING THROUGH TRUTH

She dances. Open mouth, vibrant red tongue, gleaming white teeth. Her eyes roll back in her head in ecstatic bliss. Her black skin shines and her wild hair fans out around her in disarray. Skulls and jasmine blossoms are littered at her dancing feet. Her third eye is open wide and sees all. Electric blue jolts of lightning spark from her body and she is alive with divine force.

KALI (REVOLUTION)

Kali is a force to be reckoned with. In India, the culture through which she emerged into human consciousness, she is held in great esteem. There are those in the East, and the West, that absolutely adore her and those that are absolutely terrified of her! She is something of a polarising agent. If you really connect with her, your response will not be mild, for she is a dynamic divine force that attracts and repels.

I am one of those that adore her. Still there are times when I find her violent dance of transformation to be shocking to all of my sensibilities. I don't love her because she necessarily brings me comfort, I adore her because I trust her completely. She dances into my life when big transformation is needed and I couldn't do it without her particular power to throw me into a chaos where I simply have to let go and grow. I know she has absolutely no interest in preserving ego, so she is always going to tell me what I need to hear for my own good from a place of pure love.

Sometimes I don't want to hear what she tells me because of the pain involved – as was the case with releasing the relationship I have talked about in this book. At one point, I actually saw her dancing and feasting on the remains of the relationship, tucking into all that energy as though it were a tasty feast. It was a somewhat barbaric, shocking and repelling image but at the same time, she was the one I trusted to be able to consume it. Only Kali was strong enough to wrestle it away from me because my attachment to the situation at the time was very deep, very karmic and very strong. It was going to take a lot of her wrath to set me free. It was an exceptionally painful process and there were times when I didn't know if I could bear it, but she did her work, absolutely, cleanly and with great thoroughness. There are no half measures with Kali. She does something utterly and to the end. So in the final analysis to become completely free from the relationship in question she was the one who helped me get there when a softer approach was not potent enough to shift my attachment.

Kali's job is to annihilate false ego that no longer serves the evolving path of the divine soul. We learn through the upheaval brought about by Kali's presence in our lives that is designed to dislodge ego traits that the soul has to grow strong to overcome. It is the fuel for the divine fire in a way. Yet there are times when the ego has become too entrenched and the soul needs help to shift a stubborn pattern. This is Kali's specialty. The ego doesn't want to let go, and so it is often a painful process. This is why Kali is met with reverence by those who are actively on the path and willing to bear the pain that genuine growth will give rise to from time to time. It is the same reason why she is approached with great fear by those who are aware enough to realise they are serving ego and are not sure if they will be able to truly stand her ferocious grace. Then there are others who have no response to her at all as they are so sound asleep in false assurance that they don't realise there is a wild black goddess crouched, like a panther with claws flexed, waiting to pounce upon them at any moment – at her own leisure, of course – and shear their attachments clean off!

When Kali has struck, there is no doubt about it. She is anything but subtle. The great Indian saint, Ramakrishna, whom we will meet in *Crystal Saints & Sages 777*, adored the black mother. He was so surrendered into her that he was able to know her and share her wild, inexplicable wisdom so well. He knew her to equally be the force of creation and of destruction by realising they were both one and the same dance.

The soul actually delights in this process, not from some sadomasochistic place, but from a recognition that this is what it is to truly be alive. The soul craves variety and transformation, which is perhaps one reason why the path of the soul is never boring! It can be gentle or deeply confronting and everything in between, but it is never the same. Although sometimes when we are working on an issue that seems intent on repeating itself into all eternity until we 'get' it, we may wonder about variety being the spice of our soul life. Nonetheless, it is the ego that likes things to remain as they are, preserving the status quo or shifting it only so that we gain more power. Kali eats the status quo as a light snack between meals. The ego, with its desire for control will be thwarted at every turn by Kali. But this happens only when we are ready for it. It might sound bizarre to say that the ego has to be ready to be sacrificed, but it is the soul that needs to be anchored enough to the body so that it can withstand the breaking down of the false self over time, without the body and mind shutting down in absolute terror and becoming catatonic (and likely therefore to be of rather less use to the soul in its evolutionary path). Kali loves the soul. She is like the big sister on the playground that keeps an eye out for it and takes care of any bullying, but she'll also be quick to call you on your stuff too.

The iconography of Kali is powerful. She can be pictured with anywhere from four to ten arms or more. She is often depicted with a kartika or small curved knife in one hand and a severed human head in the other, representing the false ego that resides in the realm of the unawakened mind being lopped off.

Various spiritual tools have found their way to me over the years which I use sparingly when called for by the souls in question. Usually I am embodying Kali when I work with these tools. I was preparing for one workshop by chanting Kali's mantra (shared with you in the healing process below) and when I felt her power build through my body, I raised the kartika over my head, calling in her electric blue lightening for healing of the group energy during the day. I had a Lemurian quartz crystal in my other hand to help bring in the ancient earth energy and honour the feminine wisdom so it probably looked and sounded rather dramatic. There were glass windows opening into the studio where the workshop was going to take place. One of the participants turned up early and saw me in what must have appeared to be a most startling posture, chanting wildly, head back, arms in the air holding a knife and a crystal – he was a bit disturbed! Nonetheless he girded his loins and didn't run away. After I had worked with two or three people in the workshop group with the knife and directly with Kali's powerful energy, he confessed that he had turned up early, got a bit of a shock and wondered what on earth we would be getting up to that day. He was relieved that the workshop, though powerful and somewhat challenging at times, hadn't gone in a rather different and more disturbing direction!

Kali typically also carries a sabre and at least one other type of sword, which I use to cut karmic cords of attachment in more powerful group healing sessions and sacred rituals. The staff she may also be pictured with is a symbol of her authority and connection to the Divine Masculine principle of eternal light and truth. She is also associated with a conch shell through which she calls us to her at a soul level and she can also hear the call of the souls that are in need of her fierce love.

I have loved Kali devotedly, for many, many years. Even before I really knew anything about her or the Indian tradition at a conscious level, I just resonated with her from my heart. Her darkness didn't frighten me. I knew somehow her fearsome image was one of love. Though I didn't turn her tigerish nature into that of a kitten, I just knew that hers was an extreme version of 'tough love'.

I worked with a teacher who also loved the Indian tradition for about a year. When she gave me the spiritual name, Kali Amma, I was not surprised. I kept the name even when I no longer worked with that teacher because it felt truthful and useful to my soul.

I have some students who like to call me by that spiritual name, rather than Alana. Either works for me, though if a student is calling me Kali Amma, they are bravely saying to my soul, "Hey, I want growth over comfort, I'll accept the Divine in whatever way it wants to come to me – I am ready!" That doesn't mean they are going to get clobbered on the head. They might receive a loving gaze or touch, but equally their life may descend into chaos for a time as a new level of divine presence seeks to manifest itself through their willing being. It is not I that decide all this, but the divine love that flows through my soul in the form of Kali, when and however she wishes to do so.

I once gave a client a Kali mantra to do for his healing. He had experienced a lot of darkness, especially around his sexuality. I could see that he had unconsciously called some deeply humiliating and destructive experiences to himself through the various sexual practices he engaged in and the types of relationships he poured his energy into. When I told him what I saw, he didn't deny any of it. He just agreed with me. I hoped that honesty and awareness meant he was ready to receive healing. I didn't give him a Kali mantra for the more typical reasons such as being deeply devoted to Kali or ready for an advanced path. I gave him that mantra because he really needed it. He held so much darkness within and I was concerned for his psychological wellbeing over the coming years if he didn't do something to arrest the negative flow of energy he was unconsciously generating inside himself. I gave him a Kali practice because she was vast and dark enough to absorb the ill effects of his actions. Rather than absolve him from responsibility, I hoped that her intervention would give him a reprieve, and that the brief respite would give his soul a chance to breathe and experience the purity of his being, free from the onslaught of darkness he called to himself through his life choices. I hoped that in experiencing such a moment, he would realise he did not have to live the way he was living, and liberate himself through his power of choice.

I trusted Kali to deliver this to him, but he didn't trust me or her quite that much. He went home and Googled the mantra I had given him and nervously emailed me. He didn't like what he read about it causing problems in your life as you open up to spiritual enlightenment. He was scared. I explained how Kali worked, but gave him a gentler mantra to use in case he couldn't bring himself to trust in Kali. I don't know what he chose. He has not as yet been back to see me and I get the feeling he will not be returning to me.

When I surrender myself to Kali, as opposed to Kuan Yin or my divine soul essence, I become a different energy. It doesn't happen very often because certain situations are required for it to be useful rather than downright destructive. You don't use a sledgehammer where a chisel would do, and likewise, when you need a hacksaw you don't use a bread knife.

The students who receive Kali need to love me a lot. However, that love is not about me, it is about the strength of the heart connection between us being more powerful than their adherence to their ego. That is asking quite a lot of someone. There has to be unconditional trust. When I am working with someone, I want soul liberation for them. I don't claim to know how that will best be served, but I do trust in the purity of my divine connection and that what is best for that soul will be what comes through. The person I am working with also needs to trust in the purity of my agenda with them so that Kali – or whomever else – can flow through me, into their field. Sometimes it feels amazing, but it doesn't always feel so great. It might bring up anger, sadness or ecstatic bliss. Some people have been so absolutely disturbed by the intensity of the energy they have just had to walk out of the class (I always give attendees full and conscious instructions to do this if necessary before we start). Others who just want to dive right in to it, may find it very hard to come back to their bodies once they have gone in so deep to divine presence. The transformations I have seen in the select group of students who have known me long enough to trust and love me unconditionally even when they have been exposed to Kali's energy still amazes me. It is like seeing a raw diamond polished into a precious gem.

Learning how to work with this energy in the most constructive way is quite a journey. It is like learning to work with high voltage electricity. My body has suffered a lot as I have experimented with pushing the edges of what I can call through. There were periods in my life when I would get sick after every big workshop because the amount of energy I was calling through was burning out my electrical field with. Electricity, of course, can burn as well as illuminate. Someone asked me how I felt after a particularly intense workshop once, and without thinking I said, "Like I have just had my hand plugged into an electrical socket." I was extremely unwell afterwards. So much so that I went to the doctor, who did a lot of tests because my symptoms were very intense. Finally however she had to declare, absolutely puzzled, that there was nothing wrong with me. In trying to solve the mystery, the doctor asked probing questions, but I didn't feel (rightly or wrongly) that she was quite ready for me to say, "Well I had too much divine electricity powering though me in the workshop I just taught and without realising it, I overdid it and blew out my solar plexus chakra." The pursuit of consciousness and divine presence is a double-edged sword. Like vitamins or sunlight, love is good for us, but it can be harmful to think that more is always better. I have been experimenting and studying different techniques to learn a way to minimise harm and still be able to open up to greater degrees of divine electricity. I am still exploring the possibilities, but what I am finding most useful thus far is to take the growth process step by step as I learn to finesse the qualities of the energy so that it is less damaging to the human body.

On my recent journey to North Queensland, the client who organised the tour for me, opened her eyes in the middle of a guided healing meditation and stared at me while I was embodying Kali. I was singing and had my eyes closed because when I do open my being up to embody Kali, it is an intense, ecstatic experience. My eyes tend to roll back in my head and I only see spiritually rather than physically for a time. This client hadn't connected with Kali before and didn't know anything of her. Certainly when such an embodiment happens it is a natural process, not something that I cause or anticipate, so I hadn't described to the group that this process may take place.

She came up to me in the break and told me that she had seen something she had never seen before. She didn't know why she felt drawn to open her eyes and look at me during the exercise. She just instinctively felt she should do it and when she did she got a bit of a surprise. It wasn't Alana that she saw, it was Kali. With many arms! She was shocked by the vision, as well as by her ability to have the vision. She hadn't known anything about Kali before, but she well and truly knew her in that moment of vision.

Kali blesses us by activating our spiritual gifts and is known to bring great blessings of protection, prosperity and wellbeing to those that love and honour her. She is known as the goddess of enlightenment. She is unflinchingly honest (which perhaps explains why Vivekananda, a student of Kali devotee Ramakrishna, once said that anyone who knew anything about becoming enlightened wouldn't want to touch it with a ten foot barge pole). Despite the rigours of the path to enlightenment, which Kali governs with no half measures, she is unstintingly generous with her blessings, or boons, as they are known in India. However, she can only give to us to the extent that we are able to become empty and receptive to her. That means that for what we gain, we will have to let something go. What we are gaining is soul and we are releasing that which has got in the way of having more divine presence in our lives. Although we can know intellectually this can only be a good thing, it doesn't mean that it is easy to accept at the time.

An example of this happened not so long ago when I was on a teaching tour in Europe tour. For several years, a long-term student of mine had been suggesting that I come and teach in her home country. I already had a client base from that country and the thought of seeing people I had been doing email readings for over the course of many years made me very happy. I loved meeting these beautiful people. Many never really understood how a woman from the other side of the world who they had never met or spoken to could know them so intimately and deeply as to write the things I wrote in their sessions. Many of them said that once they met me, they understood. I just felt a lot of love in that community and enjoyed being in it immensely.

My first tour running workshops there had been so successful that we decided to sustain and grow the community that had gathered by me coming over on an annual tour to teach and offer healing sessions. In the lead up to the second tour we worked hard – over Skype between me in Australia and my client in Europe – to clear fear around the gatherings and bring people into their hearts so that if their soul was telling them to come to the workshops, they would not allow their minds to talk them out of it with any number of excuses! It worked well because I could see from a soul level and she was connected with the people who were coming (a good percentage of them were clients of her healing massage practice) and she knew what was going on for them personally, so together we worked on creating the best foundation for the next tour.

In the year that passed between the first tour and the second, I was working hard on my own consciousness and growth as per usual. I changed and grew a lot in that time. Every year I change and grow, that is just what happens with this work. It's a bit like losing weight though. When it's happening, you might not notice that much, because you live with yourself and the changes are gradual. However, if someone hasn't seen you for a while the change can seem very dramatic to them. It was like this with my spiritual growth that year for the student who was organising the tour in Europe.

I am extremely honoured when someone offers to host and organise a tour for me. It is an enormous amount of work and I don't have time to do it myself. These days, the only way I get out and about to teach in country towns and other countries is if someone else has taken over the job of arranging it. I also appreciate that it can be difficult to be around my energy for extended periods of time. It is pretty strong, even when I am not working, and that can bring things up for people. Whilst I have had people say that mine is a calming presence and they never wanted me to leave, it can equally be a presence that shakes things up and is extremely uncomfortable to be around (depending on whether Kuan Yin or Kali is in the house that day, so to speak, and I might add, whether the person around me wants to honour their soul or their ego).

I have a tendency to assume that if someone is motivated enough to organise a tour, then they are also going to be motivated enough to do their personal work, which is absolutely essential when working at an intense energetic level. My energy tends to amplify things, so it's even more important to be willing and capable of dealing with stuff that comes up if you are going to be spending time with me. It's the same for me when I am in certain situations where the energy is powerful and I am affected by it, I have to deal with what comes up for me too. I had a client recently tell me that she felt like she had gone ten rounds with Mike Tyson after sitting quietly on a lounge and talking with me in her hour-long session. She released a lot. I could feel and see it as it was happening, and she had the urge to go to sleep afterwards, which I encouraged her to do as soon as practicable. She would process more by resting for a couple of hours so that she was clearer and ready for the good stuff that was on its way to her, than by spending the next few days struggling to let things work through her.

People who have worked with me for many years and wanted to organise a tour for me would understand all this, or I assumed they did. That was ridiculous of course. People might be very interested in the idea of working with me and all that they imagine it entails, but they might not be at all interested in what is required of one to walk the path alongside me. I gained that wisdom through rather painful hindsight.

Anyway, over the year between the first tour and the second I was energetically gaining power and strength far more than I realised, because I hadn't really had anything to compare it to. I was just doing my daily work so it seemed like small increments to me. I noticed shifts but they happened so steadily, it felt organic and not too shocking. Until I returned to Europe the following year, and Kali, instead of Kuan Yin, decided she would be the star of the tour that year.

I was not conscious of that switch in Divine Feminine presence until the plane landed and the tour organiser who was meant to pick me up at the airport, had overslept, not thought about peak hour traffic and casually texted me after I had been wondering about the airport for some time that she had slept in and was going to be late picking me up. This was after a twenty-plus hour long flight from Australia.

Perhaps because I was so tired, perhaps because Kali had nominated herself as the supervising guide for this tour, or perhaps because of both of these reasons, I felt a flash of sudden rage burning through me. My feet felt as though they plugged right down, deep into the earth in an instant and I had a moment of realisation. "Oh no!" I thought, "This is not going to be fun!" Then a huge booming voice within me declared, "She's not ready for me!" It was an absolute knowing, and I felt helpless, frustrated and cranky. I had committed two months of my time, devotion and energy to this tour. I had left my loved ones at home, was ready to get down to business and I was relying on someone to help me who couldn't even be bothered to set an alarm clock to come and get me on time. I thought about the regular healing sessions I had freely given this woman in the year-long process leading up to the tour. And she wasn't ready for me. Not on that morning when I stood waiting and exhausted at the airport, and not during the months that would follow.

It took considerable self-control to keep this process internal, because what I felt like doing was tipping my head back and absolutely roaring in wild frustrated rage, pulling my hair, gnashing my teeth and so forth, in a performance worthy of any great tragic piece of sacred theatre. Very Kali! This would undoubtedly have been a combination of entertaining and terrifying for those passing by at the airport arrivals lounge. Kali had certainly made her presence felt and I wondered, with some trepidation, what that was going to look like over the next two months.

The rage began to build in me until I felt the extent of it far surpass any human level of frustration that I could have mustered and tip into the realm of the Divine. If this client wanted to work with me and claim all the benefits that such work brought to her, but wasn't willing to do the work through choice with the gentle urging of Kuan Yin (which is how she had experienced me up until that moment), then she was going to get Kali instead. It wasn't a consciously formed strategy by any means. I was realising it only as it was happening. I recognised it as divine will.

As I tried to get my head around all of this, I wondered if there was some deeper significance to why Kali was appearing at this time. Apart from delivering a divine rap on the knuckles to my unsuspecting client to shake her out of her complacency, I was pretty sure there was something else to be learned and it was quite likely for me!

It took me some time to understand what was happening for me, but this was the kick-start to a process that changed my life quite profoundly over the years that followed. The incubus experience I described in Chapter Eight was a part of this personal healing process, as was cleaning out my client list and leaving my relationship. Part of the healing I needed to do for myself, was to renounce any claim laid on me by others that was not absolutely respectful and from love be it professionally, personally, spiritually, sexually or in any other way. I had to learn to honour my own being, my body, my time and my energy, in a way that was more careful and caring. I had to place more value upon myself and not allow people to take from me, even if they didn't mean to do it consciously. In my life I had let many people get away with treating me in a less than desirable way because I had compassion for them – they weren't conscious of their behaviour and didn't know what they were doing. However, I had to have compassion for myself too! I could be as giving as I wanted to be, but there would be no more giving to those that didn't want to receive from me, but wanted to take from me, control me or treat me as though I was at their personal disposal. I needed to respect myself enough not to allow that behaviour anymore. In breaking free of that pattern, which had been very unconscious, I really needed Kali to bring it to my awareness so I could shift it once and for all. I would then be able to reach and help others from a far deeper and more expansive place.

Some weeks into that tour I was given clear guidance that this was the karmic completion of my involvement with this client and the school we had been building together. This was something of a revelation to me because I had worked with this client for more than ten years and trusted in her wisdom. When I realised she had slipped into the pattern of helping others, believing that 'she was the teacher now' and that somehow this meant she didn't need to do her own spiritual work to the extent that she used to, I felt disappointed, angry and sad.

I came to see that she had unconsciously placed me above her, on some sort of spiritual pedestal, and now wanted to be on the same level she had once reserved for me. Rather than remembering we are all divine humans with individual life paths and issues to work through on our way to awakening, she seemed to think I was somehow above all that (I am most certainly not!) and she wanted to be above it too. She wanted to push me over on the pedestal she had placed me on, to make room for herself to stand up there too.

This was coming from a self-esteem issue that was amplified by the increase in my own spiritual energy and made things bigger and more intense (for better or worse!). As she hadn't done her work to the extent that I had hoped, she hadn't grown enough to be able to keep up with me and the effect of my energy upon her was like an overload of electricity through a circuit that wasn't able to stand it. I worried that I was going to burn the house right down, so to speak, which is pretty much what ended up happening.

Of course, she had every right to choose the rate of her journey. Just because I was hurtling along that year didn't mean she had to gallop with me, or even that the quicker pace would have been better for her. Sometimes taking time to integrate and rest is just as important as the times when we are taking big leaps on our journey.

However, the sticking point was that she wanted more. On the first tour she had simply organised and hosted the tour, and she did so beautifully. This time, amongst other things, she also wanted to teach alongside me. I wanted her to have what she wanted. Provided that she worked for it! A sense of entitlement says that we just 'get' things because we want them, irrespective of whether or not we have taken responsibility for what we want to receive. Perhaps we might feel that we have done enough to deserve getting what we want, so we go about trying to claim it for ourselves, but spirit doesn't work that way. When we do the genuine, inner work of surrendering to spirit, we are given much more than we could possibly ever take for ourselves. It is the difference between receiving and taking that I spoke of earlier in this book.

I understand how jealousy of others on the spiritual path develops. I used to envy my first spiritual teacher for how easy, carefree and spiritual her life seemed! By comparison, mine was not much fun and I physically ached to live with more freedom. I fantasised about what it must be like to live as she did. She had her struggles and was graciously upfront about them (a trait which I continued and I believe is helpful to my students too). I understand how one could come to resent the success or power that they see in another, wanting it for themselves. It is a part of them saying, "Hey I resonate with that quality! I want to express it too!" We can turn such resentment, envy or jealousy into something constructive by deciding to do whatever inner work we can to open ourselves up to receiving more. If we do not do the work, it can remain a lower-vibrational energy that manifests in the belief that if someone else has it, we should have it too. The only inner process taking place in such an attitude is the inner child throwing a tantrum.

When we see something we want, our desire is not bad. I have been there many times. There were many years where I was cut off from my voice, out of shame, judgment and the criticism I had received over the year. When I heard others sing openly with emotion, I was filled with longing. It was a longing from deep within me, to simply be able to sing my divine experience, straight from my heart. I do this now as a part of my work, however, it took a long time to get to this place and I never demanded or expected it would happen. When it did, it was a lovely healing blessing and liberation for me. It happened as a natural result of awakening. I didn't know what the pain that arose in my heart when I heard another sing would turn into as I grew. As it turned out the pain was my own heart not being allowed to let the voice out. Once I began to let it out, the pain left me. When I hear someone truly sing the divine presence now, tears can stream down my face and my heart will break. But it isn't from the pain of that once active repression. It is from being moved by the divine presence.

Now I was blessed with another level of fulfilment of my own being. It happened through divine grace, that mysterious and loving face of the Divine that we cannot control, direct or fathom. We can only work on being open to its presence in our life. I was willing to go through a process of awakening that was often exceptionally painful and challenging in order to be able to receive more of the divine presence. I didn't know how it was going to manifest. I still don't! It can unfold in rather surprising ways. However, over time I was gifted with a life that was rather different to the smaller, constraining one I lived when I began working with my first spiritual teacher. I didn't expect that neither she nor anyone else would simply hand it to me because I really wanted it. I understood that I had to grow into my divinity, learn to stop trying to make it happen and allow what needed to be to become. It took decades of inner work and because it is a continually evolving journey to grow our consciousness, the process continues also.

The path for another might not be so arduous or might be even more so. The point is that imagining we should just get granted what we want when we want it from a place of ego, rather than receiving what is rightfully ours through the descent of grace into a heart that has been broken open to receive, is nothing more than childish fantasy.

Unfortunately my client didn't get the difference and to be blunt, it really pissed me off! Kali's fury poured through me and I longed for her to wake up. If she didn't, our dreams of the school growing, for her to grow as a teacher and for both of us to work powerfully together from a place of purity, couldn't happen. And I had really hoped these things would happen. Add to this that Kali wanted me to wake up too. The following two months were an intense time for both of us.

We were no long well matched. She couldn't meet me where I needed to be energetically to continue to do my work and she wouldn't allow her love and devotion to me to be stronger than the grip of her ego so that I could pull her out of entitlement and into surrender. The process would be extremely painful, but it would have got her closer to what she actually wanted and what I wanted for her too. It would have succeeded where demands could not.

However, our continuing to work together was not karmically supported. That meant the frequencies of our paths were diverging and were no longer compatible anymore. This realisation was difficult for both of us. Rage regularly erupted from within me, as I tried to deal with feeling like she expected me to mother her, be her best friend, grant her spiritual power and acknowledgement and generally fill any other unmet needs she had. When had I transferred from respected teacher and friend to enslaved mother with the job of serving the unmet needs of this woman's inner child? I was furious. However, it was quite possible that nothing much had changed, except for me getting a kick up the behind from Kali that meant I was just no longer able to stomach the old pattern.

I also felt a lot of compassion for my student, but I just couldn't bring myself to indulge the unconsciousness that I perceived in our connection anymore. It wouldn't have been kind or compassionate to do so, for either of us. Even though it was certainly a tough love approach that presented itself as the alternative. I had to trust what was happening, as difficult as it was for both of us. As I dealt with my own pain in the situation, I was very emotional. I would cry most nights, with my head on the floor, offering the whole messy situation up to the Divine and asking that I be blessed with an ability to be detached from outcome, so I could just surrender and let whatever needed to happen, through divine grace, to happen. I knew that was going to involve me allowing Kali to move through my actions and I wanted it to be from a place of detachment and purity because although I accepted that my client needed shaking up, I did not want to arrogantly assume that I knew or should decide how, when or to what extent that needed to happen.

When it all came down to it, I knew I could not continue to love her ego and play nice by trying to softly and gently guide her as I had always done. The alternative was to love her soul and let divine will flow through me unimpeded by my own cautions about being too hard with her, and let karma unfold, pushing her to choose between surrendering the ego or trying to bolster it up. I had to choose whether or not to let my own issues with behaving so out of character get in the way of allowing divine will to flow. My sacrifice was my own resistance at coming into the divine flow. I made the sacrifice, and for the coming weeks I went about responding in a way that was extremely out of character for me. I trusted it because I knew that my ego wasn't guiding it. In fact, my ego would have preferred to keep the whole situation in peace-loving mode by talking myself out of what I was perceiving in favour of just doing the best in the situation without ruffling feathers. My soul, through which Kali was making her presence felt, had a far more direct approach and because I trusted her, I just allowed it to happen.

In a practical, worldly sense this meant I ended her co-teaching duties immediately and pushed her back into the position of student. When she tried to assert power at an ego level, claiming the right to control something, to take over some part of the teaching process or to do healing on another participant in the course rather than focus on herself, I blocked it. Personally, I couldn't have cared less about some of the issues she attempted to control. I am not interested in micro-managing those I work with. I like to give people a task and let them attend to it with their own creativity and initiative. However, the word 'no' was flowing from my lips nearly constantly, blocking her every attempt to control or assert herself at an ego level. Kali was there and she wasn't budging.

The more spiritual light this student gained in connection with me, the bigger and more unwieldy this pattern became for her because her ego was claiming the light for itself and using it to grow whilst the soul was slowly starving. This woman has genuine healing gifts, a truly beautiful heart and has the potential to do great good in the world. She had already helped many people. But her ego was taking the credit for it and a monstrous distortion of her genuine light was taking place as a result. If it continued in this vein, she would eventually undermine her own healing path and she would unintentionally come to harm the people she sought to help through her ego's arrogance and superiority. Underneath it all was a lack of self-belief and self-worth, and I had compassion for her journey and her dilemma. I genuinely hoped that Kali's presence in our second tour together would benefit both of us.

In the onslaught of Kali that arose for the next two months, she was denied my friendship and approval at an ego level. This was not from meanness or rejection, but from the loving intention that she be thrown back into herself, so she could stop avoiding the pain within and begin to deal with it, rather than seeking to fill it with me. I faithfully served her soul, though her ego thought I was being horrible, and she accused me of losing my gentleness, becoming harsh and not serving love anymore. I didn't agree with her estimation, but I could absolutely understand her point of view.

Another student who received an enormously powerful blessing through Kali during that tour agreed with her estimation of things for the three days after she received the blessing from me. At that time she was in utter hell, as everything was pushed up and out of her karmically. She emailed me, wishing she had never met me and saying that receiving personal attention and a blessing from me was the worst thing to have ever happened to her. After those three days she was then feeling amazing, reborn and deeply cleansed from issues that had threatened her existence for many, many years beforehand. Her husband was amazed by the transformation, and she was ecstatic. She then emailed to say that she was so glad she had met me and it was the best thing ever. This is how it can be with an encounter with Kali. The ego fights it whilst the soul rejoices. At the time it is rarely pleasant or easy, but the liberation Kali brings to us is sweet nectar in the longer term.

Coming back to the student who organised the tour, it was hard for both of us. I didn't enjoy thwarting her ego attempts to claim power and it was painful for her ego. At the end of the first day of this process it wasn't a surprise that she psychically attacked me in a particularly vicious way. I didn't feel anger, though I was certainly gasping for breath and doubled over in physical pain for about ten minutes until I could clear the attack. What I actually felt was understanding and compassion. I didn't take any of it personally. It wasn't personal. I knew it was her ego acting out. It was her power drive taking over her divine connection and I knew it wasn't who she was, but more about what a part of her was doing in reaction to a personal growth crisis. I also sensed that what was happening between us was an expression of divine will. I realised that karmically she was being given an opportunity. By refusing to indulge her acting out of her power drive, the divine will flowing through me was supporting her soul to push her ego to give up and surrender into something greater than ego. That something was love. This surrender would open her up to the greatness she desired, but it would be greatness of soul, not the illusion of it in the ego's eyes.

There were some moments where it looked like this dramatic 'Kali intervention' might actually result in an incredible healing for us both. I spent hours with her, explaining what was taking place as I saw it. However, the ego grip was too strong and although she could receive what I was saying when I was saying it, only minutes later she would feel confused and angry again and say to me, "Can you repeat what you just said because I could understand it at the time you were saying it, but I have already forgotten it!"

She hadn't done the work so she was not ready to receive what was being offered. She just wasn't ready to face the pain within that would be there waiting for her to deal with when she finally let go of her ego grab for power. Because of that she couldn't give up her criticism and attack of me – psychically and by email later on. This was a way to blame me for her pain and avoid getting into what was really going on within her.

I didn't appreciate that action, but I understood it. I too had only just begun healing the issues that were coming up for me at that time. I had to realise that the behaviour of others was only a symptom and this pointed to the issue within me that needed to be healed. I trusted that when she was ready to take responsibility, she would, just like me or anyone else dealing with something difficult within that needs to be healed in order to progress on our life journey. I knew that the Divine Mother would support her through the appearance other healers and teachers that would undoubtedly cross her path in time. It became very clear to me that we were done. I couldn't help her anymore because she had received as much of the Divine through me as I could possibly offer to her. Our path together had drawn to an end.

I learned quite a bit about the love of the Divine Mother through that experience. Her light face is easier for most of us to recognise and accept. It is gentle, soft and forgiving. It asks nothing of us except to receive her love. My client didn't understand why the dark face of the mother came through for her during that time we spent together. She wanted the light face of the mother, the gentle face. She said that the dark faced pushed her away from me, but the soul is not pushed away by love. Her ego felt pushed away and reacted in judgment. The light face wouldn't have served her. It would have indulged her. The mother is not about indulging the ego, she is about loving the soul. We only fear her when we don't understand and accept this. The dark face can be harder to accept, and often the Holy Mother treads gently with us, urging us along softly rather than cracking a whip to get us moving. However, there are times when the darker face of the Divine Mother is genuinely going to serve the soul more than the light face will in that particular moment.

When a child is exploring the world and comes perilously close to the edge of an abyss, a soft call from the mother may do little to prevent danger. The child wants to see and know, what is over that edge and continues on. The fierce compassion of the dark mother arises, like a tigress protecting her cubs, and she roars at that child to stop. The child is shocked, hurt, frightened and feels rejected and uncertain. What is this fearsome rage? Why has the gentle mother become so cruel? She doesn't love me anymore! The child doesn't realise the danger, but the mother does. She responds as needed to arrest any further steps towards irreparable harm to protect the child.

The Divine Mother is expressed through the soul and the ego is the child. The Divine Mother serves the soul so that it can integrate with and heal the ego. Its job is to gain divine mastery and shine its light and love purely and without distortion, to shatter the illusions created by the ego and thereby revealing divinity.

If we can learn to distinguish the responses of the ego from the responses of the soul, encounters with the dark face of the Divine Feminine make sense and are received in a different light – as an expression of the great mother's compassion. Yes, even her anger is received as compassion, fierce rather than gentle, but compassion nonetheless. This is what I saw and realised when Kali was munching away on the remnants of the relationship I mentioned earlier. I was in agony. My ego wanted to grab the bits that she was stomping over and chewing upon gleefully, and hold on to them for dear life. Yet I knew she wouldn't lead me astray. Although it was painful, I knew that the death of the relationship would ultimately serve my soul and was in service to life. I knew my soul was being liberated through the process, even though at another level the price of that liberation was going through some deep personal pain.

The Divine Mother is always in service to your soul. Her compassion, be it gentle or ruthless, helps your soul grow stronger than the compelling fears of the ego that keep us stuck. The ego may be hurt and fearful during an encounter with the mother, like a child in a tantrum, but the soul rejoices as it grows in power. Sometimes divine assistance is needed because the soul cannot dislodge a powerful ego on its own. We all need such help at times. It is not usually pleasant to be the ego at the time as it can feel like the force of life is conspiring to stop us getting what we want! In time, as the soul grows and supplants old ego patterning with its own vibration, we come to understand that even the challenges (sometimes especially the challenges) in life are an expression of the mother's love and we become grateful in a way that brings us more peace of mind and less resistance to life.

The Divine Mother works according to karma. What is given is given because of karmic grace. Sometimes those that appear to be so worthy are not given much at all, and those that do not appear worthy are given so much. But it is all just perspective. Divine karmic grace determines all of it based on numerous lifetimes and a vast perspective. Return on one's spiritual investment through good works and service may come much later in life or may come in a different form than expected. There are always karmic laws of grace in operation dictating the how and why of unfolding life circumstances. This doesn't mean that only 'good' or 'pleasant' circumstances are the vehicle through which grace is delivered, though they often are. Grace can be delivered through the challenge that is going to cause such growth in you that you can fulfil your divine destiny and experience tremendous joy in the longer term.

The mother works through that grace, always asking for more for her children, but she doesn't control karma. She attempts to soften it as is helpful for her beloveds. This means that she will sometimes be able to work out some karma for her children, provided that they can still learn what is needed to grow. She wants all beings to be free. That is her only agenda and this is why she is so trustworthy.

So sometimes anger from her will replace the need for an abusive encounter with another later on. It is gentler, although the ego may not think so because it hasn't had the other experience to compare it with – yet the mother knows. Through her grace she provides a safe space where an ego can work through its power issues, for example. The ego may fight her and even send an attack against her but she will absorb and process it with love, rather than reacting and returning it amplified according to karmic law, which is what would occur if it was unleashed in another situation with a less awakened, less compassionate being.

This is what happened between my former student and I when she psychically attacked me over those two months. It was an expression of loving wisdom of the mother, flowing through the relationship the student and I had with each other that allowed that student to witness her own ego and do something constructive about it, without inviting the further negative reaction. If she had done what she did to someone else, they would have attacked her back in defence and the whole issue would have escalated.

In that situation the Divine Mother knew the power issue could resolve more quickly if the soul had a chance to reveal it to the ego without the added complications of karmic return that would have left the ego in even more darkness and made it even harder for the soul to grasp the ego and help dislodge the old suffering with its light. The ego may not recognise any of this and judge the mother, not realising she has evoked the attack from the ego to help it be free of its power complex. This also happened with my client. The ways of the mother are subtle, powerful and filled with love. Yet the ego may despise her at times for it, often whilst the soul is in deep gratitude for the assistance in its spiritual growth, as it edges closer to freedom. This same wise fire is applied to all her children. There is no favourite child, all are loved equally but each is treated according to what they are capable of receiving and what will best serve.

In the gale force power of Kali's revolution, when the raw chaos of change and transformation unleashed, it can be hard to remember that we are being blessed by unconditional divine love. The student that has a lot to offer is blessed with her grace. The one who is willing to take the faster path – which is rarely the easiest path – to divine self-realisation calls in her ferocious compassion. Those on the edge of something that is becoming too much for them to deal with may experience her divine intervention move them away from further unnecessary pain with some force. To endure those times when we are in the direct divine dance with her, we have to have access to enough awareness that we can at least attempt to have trust, to help us bear the experience until we emerge in a state of cleansed grace at the other side of it.

BLACK OBSIDIAN (DEFLECTION)

Obsidian, like Kali, is a powerful stone and not recommended for the faint-hearted. Black obsidian is known to be one of the most powerful, if not the most powerful form of obsidian available. I rarely use it in work with others, choosing usually the somewhat gentler blue obsidian that I spoke of in Chapter Six of *Crystal Angels 444* instead. Sometimes, however, when we are working with huge energies of transformation within ourselves and our planet, we need the 'big guns.'

Those drawn to read this book are going to be a part of the new teaching program happening for humanity on the planet at this time. This is especially so for those who relate to this chapter in particular. You will be the ones that can really handle working with the dark feminine and black obsidian will be very important for your soul support, as will Kali.

The planetary teaching program of which you are a part is restoring the dark, denied aspects of the feminine to their rightful place of love, acceptance, and appreciation. That includes the fierce side of compassion and the sacred rage that erupts when the ego is trying to dominate the soul. As acceptance of the feminine is restored, decisions that are no longer appropriate for the evolution of our planet and human culture can no longer be supported. These are the decisions that would destroy our natural resources rather than cooperate and coexist with them. The environment will be allowed to heal because we will be living within it more intelligently.

This sounds simple, and it is, but that doesn't make it easy. Evil exists. I define 'evil' as counter-evolutionary intelligence. Even though it may make no sense to us, it is actually part of creation and the divine plan. We neither have to deny its existence nor become obsessed with it. We can simply accept the existence of forces that pull away from wholeness (or evolution) as well as forces that pull towards wholeness and evolution. It is the friction created by these two actions that creates the fuel for growth, if we are powerful enough to bear the tension and make wise choices for ourselves. We explored this idea in the chapters on Lakshmi and Bastet.

There is a constant interplay of these two forces within us, within the world and within all of manifest creation. Of course, there is a field of divinity that is transcendent of duality, where all is simply one. When people say evil doesn't exist, they might be talking of that supreme reality, where there is no duality in operation. However, the existence of that supreme reality doesn't cause this reality to cease to exist! More so, it doesn't stop us from needing to operate within this reality. To access the supreme reality where consciousness is simply one, we need to engage with the reality in which we find ourselves for our soul growth.

We deal with what is happening in the here and now, in order to grow. That means dealing with apparently opposing forces, and doing our work. We can accept that all of life is an expression of divine creation for a higher purpose that we may or may not understand (probably not, most of the time, and that's fine) and get on with being what we are. If the forces of life expressing themselves as you tend towards goodness and evolution – and reading this book, they most likely will – then you need to find a way to work with counter-evolutionary forces that are opposing your work. You will need to find conscious ways to do this that will support your life-creating nature, rather than draining or distorting it into something it is not. Becoming as angry and fearful as the energies seeking to obstruct your work is not the way for a person on the path of love to have victory. Being honest about one's emotions, working through them and always coming back to the heart as the guiding force behind all our choices, is the way to spiritual and physical victory. There is no genuine physical win if the heart has to distort itself to get a result.

Now just to clarify one further point, darkness doesn't necessarily equate to evil. Kali appears to be dark, but she is of the light. She serves life. The negative influences or evil that I am speaking of are the forces that actively seek to block your evolution and obstruct the support of life. They may or may not appear to be evil. Sometimes they wear appealing faces, promise the perfect body or wealth, if only you do this, or buy that, and so on. Regardless of appearances they either want to lull you into the false sense of security that keeps you from genuine empowerment, or they want you to be frightened. If you don't know what you are supposed to be frightened of, all the better, because then you can't confront it and realise you don't have to be afraid after all. Those darker forces want to divide, conquer and undermine our ability to love.

I understand that this can sound like a melodramatic, childish plot of good and evil – the stuff of movies. Yet these are natural forces of life. That is why they are so compelling to our psyches because at some level we relate to the battle, within us and around us. This section of the book is not about promoting childish reactions or fear, but about encouraging a mature spiritual approach to working consciously with the battle so you can become even more empowered in love through your experiences.

The tricky part for those of us that feel in our hearts that ours is the path of love, is to not try to be constantly nice, sweet and good in order to avoid falling prey to evil. Our dark emotions, such as anger, hate, fear, doubt, grief, sadness and anxiety, can be made to serve life. If we respond to those feelings with compassion and acceptance and allow those feelings to come and go as a natural part of being an emotionally awake and responsive human being, we might even learn some wisdom from the experience of having all those emotions!

In serving life, we are not seeking to eradicate darkness. We are learning how to take love and use it intelligently to bring all parts of our being onto the light path. Then, even evil can be made to serve life, because we can use its presence to become more skilful at healing and finding ways to bring ourselves to compassion eventually and always. Now that is something special! That is the power of light and evolution. It doesn't require us to fear evil, but it does require that we acknowledge its power. We also need to be in touch with our own power, intelligence, skill and compassion in order to use that power to our advantage, to serve the evolutionary path. Every aspect of life can be made to serve evolution or to counter evolution. Attempting to control evil or to turn it into love is not the way – it is how we choose to deal with it, how we approach it and how we work through it that determines the ultimate outcome in this divine experiment of life.

Those of us doing this work are dealing with some very real, very negative forces on a daily basis. You might encounter them in people trying to block your work in an obvious way or through psychic attack from people who are easily manipulated by their own ego's need for power and admiration, especially if they believe that someone else getting either of those things means that they get less. Now this might seem like small potatoes, and sometimes it is, but it can accumulate and make you feel sick and tired when you don't need to be.

Black obsidian helps to deflect such negativity and protect your energy field. If you have ever seen a child in full-fledged tantrum, you will know that a lot of power can come out of a thwarted ego. I have been on the receiving end of it more often than I have cared to be, but have undoubtedly given as good (or not so good!) as I have got over the course of my lifetimes thus far. Even when sometimes such actions aren't intentionally malicious, they can still cause damage.

Fortunately we have so many divine beings to help us. I have written this series so that you can feel empowered to claim your divine power and path, and enjoy yourself as much as possible whilst doing it. It is a rather interesting journey!

Black obsidian is one of those 'divine beings.' It helps to minimise the negative effects of attacks. Like Kali, it is considered to be so black that it absorbs everything, including even the vilest negativity. If you are one of the souls here to help restore the feminine, you are going to encounter some rather vicious opposition to your work. It might be in human form, or it might be in the form of a darker energy interested in blocking human evolution, which sometimes operates through human beings, and other times on an energetic level, but with 'real enough' effect in the physical world. So if the light is to be served, we have to grow smarter and more powerful to deal with these energies, and we have to deal with them.

Evil energies can be clever and seductive. They might promise so much light but the light they promise is not the divine light that burns with passion in life but the deathly light that takes us away from life. The false light is that which appears to promise so much but what it delivers is an emptiness that is devoid of love. Chasing that false light might cost you years or lifetimes of genuine life experience. In the clutches of addiction or the chase for perfection, real life passes right by you, unnoticed. For the soul that is hungry for life and growth, it is like slowly starving whilst a veritable feast of opportunity and experience passes right under its nose. If we are too scared to feast, that is, to run the risk of trying something outside of the narrow confines of illusory control, then we remain vulnerable to the prey of false light.

Fantasising about the life you want to live or just trying to escape the life you have, rather than doing all that you can to heal, grow and live, is to fall prey to counter-evolutionary forces. The false-light that they promise is always just that little bit out of reach, and that is part of its allure really. It's the fantasy that doesn't become a dream to prompt your bold action and growth, but rather an escape from doing anything other than living life. If you are lucky enough to grab hold of the false light for even an instant, you will realise that there's nothing there. As soon as you try to hold it, you will realise it is nothing of substance because there is no life in it. The lure of the false light is about the chase. The more we chase the less energy, time, attention and devotion we have to give to our real path of soul growth. The more we are fearful, anxious or separated from our heart and soul, the more we will want to chase some distant dream in fantasies without taking real-world steps to bring that fantasy to life. In that sense, the operation of evil is at its most clever when we feel like we are hamsters running on a little wheel that never gets anywhere, on the promise that one day, the path will suddenly have taken us somewhere worthwhile. Those that are natural visionaries, that typically tend to be future-oriented in their thinking, have to be careful that they remember to honour their visions by taking steps in the present moment, lest they unwittingly fall prey to false light and lose their footing in the physical world.

As you journey on your path, there will be times when you will be drawn out of the daily world and into your own growth. You might feel less involved in life for a time. You may have a grand vision and be moved by the heart, daring to wonder, could it be possible? That is healthy and natural, and temporary. That is very different to switching off from life, from your experiences and from living, in an unhealthy and counter-evolutionary way. Temporary withdrawal from everyday life to receive a vision or to be in intense personal growth will always have the underlying feeling that it is in some way preparing you to meet the world again in a more powerful and cleansed way. You might not know how, but in your heart, you will feel it isn't seducing you into blissful worlds of no pain, whilst your body is falling apart and the world is rotting around you. Genuine spiritual light doesn't take us out of the pain of growth, it brings us bliss, yes, and sometimes it can be exquisite, but it empowers us to stay present to what is happening and sometimes that will entail great pain.

Sometimes life is really hard to handle and we just want to escape for a while. This is understandable and forgivable but if it becomes a habitual way of existing, then we are going to suffer for it because trying to soften the bumps and bruises to our ego can mean our soul will be denied the opportunity to really live and grow. We have to find a way back to the truth of our soul journey and our divine life mission, and black obsidian helps us have the strength to cope with the demands of this. Don't get me wrong, there is a huge sense of joy and love on the divine path, but it is not without its deep challenges. To fall into light chasing and constantly seeking only the pleasant experiences or spiritual highs without honouring the agony that the ecstasy will also open us up to, can all too easily lead to spiritual addiction. This can end up leading us away from the world, onto a counter-evolutionary path, into worlds of false light that starve rather than nourish the soul and thereby avoiding the path of love that is about serving life and bringing our spiritual light into service in the world.

Every time we grow spiritually, we are asked to shed another layer of attachment to further enable our divine light to manifest itself. To shed that attachment whilst still absolutely loving all that is, rather than cutting ourselves off and pretending not to care or imagining that only the light exists, is hard. We have to accept and remain present to all that is and do our best to love all of creation, even those parts that are actively fighting our growth. This is quite a spiritually advanced task, but it is our job as servers of life.

The idea that evil might not always appear evil, and that such forces can try to seduce us with false light might seem surprising but it is endemic in our culture. It is what fuels anorexia, constant perfectionism, an inability to turn off one's mobile phone, the endless marketing of countless products, the fame-obsessed young thing that seeks out the fame of reality TV and forgets how to live. This false light is particularly rampant in modern advertising and affects generation Y and younger generations profoundly. They have wonderful skills in technology, but this can easily be turned into anti-relationship and anti-body by counter-evolutionary forces and it can work against the plan for divine connection, rather than enhance it. Personally I feel that technology can be used to enhance our connections with each other, if used with love and awareness, and is an exceptionally powerful tool at our disposal. But like any power, it's what we do with it, how consciously we work with it, and with what intention, that determines whether it generates more love or more fear in the world.

I directly experienced the evil, counter-evolutionary force that seduces through false light when I went through a series of extremely violent and terrifying dreams of psychopathic assassins in various guises keen to murder me. They were unstoppable and it was only through spiritual intervention and my own keen commitment to working on my relationship to my own body and the physical world (helped by the love I had for crystals) that enabled me to not be destroyed by my own rampant perfectionism that barely concealed a life-hating, death-loving destructive side that lurked in my own shadow. I still have to be careful that my love affair with the light is directed towards its expression in the physical world, because that is what is needed. I can fall prey to imbalance when I don't temper my near constant creative drive to produce with enough rest for my body. This is the same part of us that says if we can't do something well, or perfectly, then don't do it at all. Or that creates something but refuses to share it with another because it might not be the best thing ever. Or that is humiliated and angered beyond all means if one of our children doesn't behave perfectly in accordance with how we would like.

Black obsidian shows us where we are doing this, and helps us find the sacred rage within that will yell out from the depths of the body, "I am not less than the light, I am the temple to receive the light, cast me not aside and honour me instead, for without me there is no life and even light shall cease to exist!" Quite a statement of truth! Black obsidian grounds us into the body and in doing so helps deflect counter-evolutionary interference, except where it will help us learn and grow, to the extent that we can handle it. We are always loved with unending care and our spiritual needs are tended to with precision by very skilful spiritual masters.

Evil doesn't only operate within a glittering package promising false light. Interference in the work and healing of those on the path of love can arise in a less appealing package. The fearful, devouring, castrating forces that sap our energy, give us a tendency not to care or make it too hard to grow, encourage the belief that you aren't good enough or getting enough done so why bother. This can be powerful but we just need to respond with compassion and question any voice or belief within us that doesn't feel like is resonates with love. We always have a right to do this. Always.

You might have noticed that evil likes to dwell in extremes. It urges us to do all or to do nothing. Passionate people who are a bit extremist themselves (like me – I don't just decide to write one book, I decide it will be an entire series!) have to be vigilant to hold our own personality traits in check. We want our passion, for example, to serve our path, to support us, to give us energy and to not burn us out as we set an ever-higher bar to jump over in a mistaken quest for perfection. We need to develop skills that will bring us back into balance. Black obsidian helps us to do this through grounding but also by gifting us with the truthful insight of where we are not honouring our soul path. This insight is not always pleasant, but it is helpful and constructive.

I recently had a Skype session with a beautiful Dutch woman who was experiencing darker aspects of interference that black obsidian can be rather helpful for. Our attempts to connect with each other met with so much to-ing and fro-ing that was months before my wonderful admin angel could set up an appointment! Then there were problems with payment. Then with scheduling again. Then when we finally locked in a time and the payment had cleared and we were both available to connect and talk to each other at the same time, her computer just shut down and began downloading updates. She didn't even touch a button! If it wasn't so incredibly bamboozling and frustrating, it would have been hilarious.

It took about fifteen minutes for her to get back online. During that time I did some rather fervent prayer and healing for her and called on her angels to assist in clearing this most bizarre series of obstructions. When were finally able to connect, I talked to her about the field of chaos around her. I could see it wasn't a manifestation of her own or that an imbalance in her spirit was being played that out in the world around her, for she was well-adjusted and fairly balanced. I recognised the work of darker forces and even felt them enter my mind during the computer breakdown and tell me I shouldn't be working with her as it wasn't right. This proved to be utter nonsense. When we finally connected again, I had called in a lot of divine protection and our work was beautiful, funny, from the heart and touching for both of us. Nonetheless, those forces were there around her and they were very real.

During her session, I asked her about how she felt about the chaos around her. Was she aware of it? She validated what I had said immediately and told me a story of what happened when she was going to see another healer. She couldn't find the room in the building. She couldn't get the call through to the therapist to clarify the location without the phone dropping out. When she finally made it to the right place, all of a sudden there was the invasive noise of window washers right outside the therapist's window. The unusual and constant interruptions caught the therapist's attention and they discussed it quite deeply.

These sorts of interferences are from darker forces. Their job is to put you off your path. They create obstacles, take over your GPS (yes, this has happened to me!), cause chaos, get into your mind and create fear or doubt. Often this will create doubt about whether or not you should see a certain healer, which is very different to having a clear, neutral knowing from the heart about whether someone can help you on your path at this time or not. Such interference generally makes the journey from thinking about an appointment to actually having one unnecessarily long, complicated and confusing. The more powerful your healing is likely to be, the more effort will go into negative interference to distract you from getting to that appointment! Those most afflicted by this interference are the clients who have a lot of light, a lot to gain and a lot to offer but either haven't yet discovered the necessity of calling on divine protection and unconditional love each day or are in the midst of learning how to work more consciously with darker energies!

Before my admin angel began working with me, I instructed her on the necessity of calling in divine protection so that I could help her manage the difficulties I suspected someone working to support me on my path might encounter. Whenever she forgot, the wheels would start to fall off. Her computer would stop working. Client's messages would get lost or confused. Time zones for international bookings would get confused and so on. Fortunately it would only need to be a brief blip before we would realise what had happened and she would get back on the prayer bandwagon and call on her higher guidance. In the meantime, the angels are extremely helpful in correcting mistakes. I could always sense when there had been interference or chaos around her or one of my clients. I would pray and wait. I knew it would get sorted out eventually, and it always did. Prayer and working with crystals can minimise these instances and stop them from getting out of hand. However, we do have to do it for ourselves. We have to learn to ask for help from the guidance that loves us unconditionally.

Having stones like black obsidian around can help create this field of protection permanently. Even at the times when you get rattled for your learning, it will help. Note that no divine being who is genuinely and unconditionally loving will ever stop you from learning, but where possible they will absorb any hard knocks that are unnecessary for your ultimate education.

When you work with Kali, black obsidian or both you are being brave. You are also being honest about the dual nature of this manifest reality, whilst remembering that it is ultimately all about love. We do have to deal with the here and now and that means coming to terms with darker forces, and learning how to intelligently respond to them without worrying or getting into fear (because that really isn't helpful or necessary). Some people who I have given the Kali mantra to work with are nervous, even though it is only given when it is rightfully suggested by the heart. Spiritual work should and does work. It is meant to effect change. Black obsidian will help you to dissolve whatever is in the way of your growth and you will find it strengthens you to move forward.

The field generated by black obsidian also helps us to see into the stickiness of projections. These are the thoughts, feelings, expectations and demands that others energetically fire at us on a daily basis. It can be obvious when it is spoken, but most of it is invisible and inaudible – at least to our physical eyes and ears. An example of a projection is that a good spiritual teacher is always gentle, never gets angry, is a strict vegan, never criticises slow drivers in front of her on the roads (even if she immediately apologises afterwards!) and lives in perpetual divine bliss so that she never feels pain or suffers for her own path of growth. As you may have guessed I have used myself as an example here, so I can tell you that those projections do not hold up in reality, but lots of people no doubt carry them. When I don't seem to match up to someone's idealised projection, they might decide I am not a true spiritual teacher or they might become angry with me. On the other hand, they might instead decide that they need to revise their projections!

The more self-aware we become, the more we will recognise and call back the projections we have cast on to others. In doing so, we allow people to be more complex or even contradictory without feeling utterly compelled to try to stuff them into a stereotypical box or to judge them for not fitting. We can also extend the same respectful courtesy to ourselves and dispense with ideas of how we should be so that we can learn who we actually are. When we can do this in relationship with another, demands and expectations are replaced with genuine connection and intimacy, which can be deeply healing and fulfilling.

Black obsidian helps us see the truths behind the projections both within ourselves when another doesn't behave as we think they should, and within others when who we are doesn't match up with how they think we should be. If someone tries to correct our behaviour, tells us how we should be or tries to manipulate us into matching their projection of who we should be, then we may react and feel criticised or unloved. Black obsidian will help us see why we are attracting this 'projection' into our experience and know whether we need to engage and learn through it. We might immediately feel it isn't about us and let the experience go. If a relationship can't shift along with you and keeps trying to pull you into dysfunction, perhaps it will also mean stepping back or letting the connection go altogether.

At a psychic level, black obsidian opens inner vision and hearing that in turn helps us gain perception at a higher level. Through this higher perception we can more easily accept various divine assignments that might otherwise seem just too illogical to support. For example, deconstructing my involvement in the school I had helped to build for two years might seem illogical, but with divine insight I realised it was the most compassionate and wise course of action. So, I accepted it and how it needed to happen, which was actually quite abruptly and completely.

When you are working with or wearing black obsidian you will need to cleanse it with pure water regularly. Just ask for it to be purified and for anything that is released to be sent into the endless black void of Kali, for the greatest good, then rinse it under flowing pure water for as long as you feel it is needed. It doesn't have to be for long. If you feel that the water is not reaching in to the stuff stored deep in the stone, bury it in the earth for a few days, then rinse it and it will be ready to work with again. If you like, you can also use the Kali mantra in the healing process below to cleanse and charge the stone for healing work. It is a powerful combination.

MANIFESTING THROUGH TRUTH

You have probably heard the expression, 'the truth can set us free.' As I have mentioned, some clients get nervous about working with these energies and I can understand why! However, there is a great and compassionate mercy in all of this. Those that love Kali and have worked with her energetically through meditation and prayer, such as in the healing process below, may at times report rather violent encounters with her on the inner planes, as though her 'savaging' them in some way was part of her gift. However, there is a line between her gift of healing destruction that serves life, and the unresolved sadomasochistic tendencies of human beings, originating from a fundamental humiliation or rejection of the self at a young age. Then the experience of the Divine is received through that filter and experienced as destructive or punishing of the self. That is not what the Divine is about. Healing with Kali is about liberating the self, not being humiliated or destroyed. As any rejection wounds heal, the experience of Kali, whilst hardly likely to be as soft as the touch of feather, is experienced as less aggressive towards the self and her destructive actions are seen to be more about circumstances or situations so that life can continue to flourish. It is about destroying the bondage that constrains the self, not self-destroying. Those that love Kali are often able to do so because they have experienced a lot of darkness in their lives and are at some level, typically emotionally or psychologically, familiar with it. In loving her we have to remember, that she serves light. Loving her is not about remaining forever in darkness. It is about learning to grow through it.

There is truly no need for fear here, just for a soft heart. Come to Kali as a child – not childish or demanding – but sure of your own innocence and her love for you, and with a willingness to trust in her ministration of your soul. Likewise with the Crystal Angel of Black Obsidian and you shall find the truth that will set your heart free as your soul blossoms into greater joy and fulfilment.

HEALING PROCESS

Those that come to Kali from the heart know that her strikes are precise, only ever to the intensity required and delivered with a mercifully swift blow. This is the revolutionary power of Kali and of black obsidian as well. Together they can work quickly and turn a world on its head with one snap of her divine fingers. However, the preparation for that moment will have been served with love. It happens as and when one is ready for it, though with such powerful energies it can feel like it is taking us beyond our edge. When it is genuine – and this healing process will take you to a place that is genuine – it is not beyond what is best for your soul but what is going to most compassionately, honestly and beautifully serve it. If you enjoy the healing process below and want more, I have also recorded an entire CD of Black Madonna meditations dedicated to the Mother Kali.

The Process

Sit with your crystal and/or mandala and have a black candle lit if you wish.

You might wish to have a mantra playing in the background, like the Black Madonna track which features the Kali mantra on my *Voice of the Soul* album, or *Mantra Dance* DVD, or you may wish to have silence.

Sit and gaze at your crystal or mandala and say the following, "I call upon my higher self and the guidance that loves me unconditionally. I call upon Kali who loves me without condition and upon the Crystal Angel of Black Obsidian. I surrender with loving trust into the truths that best serve me now, delivered with mercy, compassion, swiftness and divine love, so be it."

Imagine that all around you is inky blackness, high and wide and moving in all directions.

Relax and breathe in and out at least eight times.

You sense that this blackness is a living being, swirling, constantly moving and expanding.

Imagine that it can absorb anything from you that is not for your highest good. Imagine you can breathe out and let go of anything that you no longer need – whether you understand it consciously or not.

Then imagine that you are aware of an endless spaciousness in the centre of this blackness and send the following mantra into the blackness. See the space open up and expand with each repetition.

OM KRIM KALIYEI NAHAMA
(Sounds like OM CRIM CAR-LEE-YAY NAM-A-HAH)

Repeat anywhere from eight to eighty-eight times or however long feels good. If it feels too strong at any point, stop immediately. Know that as you do this mantra, stuff will be leaving you and you may feel waves of nausea or other emotion as it does so. However, it will pass.

When you are ready to finish just say, "I thank you for your continual field of grace and protection so that I may dwell in your fierce compassion and serve life. So be it"

Then simply bow your head to your hands in prayer and if you have a candle, extinguish it. If you have worked with a physical crystal rather than the mandala, keep it with you for the remainder of the day, evening or even overnight, and then cleanse it using the suggestions above.

Be gentle with yourself in the days that follow this healing process. It will work deeply and move energy. If you are going through a difficult time or experiencing any form of psychic attack or physical violence, you may use this healing process daily or as needed to build your energy and allow it to support you as you take steps to seek out further help from healers, therapists or legal advisors, to assist you on your path to the dignity and respect you deserve.

11.

RHIANNON (FREEDOM)
AMAZONITE (INTEGRITY)

MANIFESTING THROUGH RESPECT

Dressed in golden robes, riding a white horse through the mists, she is freedom embodied. She loves, she trusts, she honours without questioning herself. She commits to love and serves love. From her grounding in unconditional love, she is always free.

RHIANNON (FREEDOM)

Rhiannon is a Welsh goddess. Her stories teach that she was fae or of the natural world of faery spirits, the same world in which the crystal devas or crystal angels dwell. She rejected offers of marriage from other faery beings and sought out a human husband instead. As a result of this choice, her life took some interesting turns and many adventures took place.

We can interpret her choice literally, or as a symbolic reference to our own spiritual nature that seeks out a human – our body – to marry or unite with in order to experience love. Rhiannon's story, on one level, is the story of human spiritual awakening via the power of the Divine Feminine.

It is said that she charmed and tested her prospective husband by riding through the mists, upon a white horse. Transfixed, he chases her upon his own steed but although his horse is more powerful, he can never catch her and the distance between them always remains.

The spiritual being within us might be invisible, inaudible and intangible to the powerful physical body we are blessed with, and yet, is it not even more powerful? Is it not able to inspire the human being to dream, to dance, to create and to yearn for greater love?

Rhiannon laughs and tells him that he must wait for her at a sacred Tor (a mound the Celts believed was an entrance way to the worlds of the nature spirits) in one year's time and at then she will marry him.

When our spiritual awakening is deepening, as will happen throughout our journey, our physical body is not in control of the process. The self of the physical world cannot just lay a casual claim on the Divine and say, "Okay, manifest now divine presence!" Even though our spiritual nature wants to love and be loved by the body, to become one coherent being united in sacred marriage that brings Heaven to Earth, there are rules. The human being needs to have a genuine yearning for the spirit. In *A Midsummer Night's Dream*, Shakespeare wrote that 'the path of true love never did run smooth.' The spiritual path, which is certainly the path of true love, is challenging for the human self. The human has to grow and evolve, sometimes through great pain. If there isn't great love, a great yearning desire to sustain the passion for the path through all its challenges, then the marriage will not occur.

A year of waiting speaks of a complete cycle. In our own sacred marriage between our divine spirit being and our sacred human self, we go through crises of commitment and deepening of intimacy and love, just as we do in a marriage between two people. It doesn't matter how much time each phase takes, but it will take the completion of a cycle before the next experience in sacred marriage can take place. You can imagine as different levels of connection and closeness between two people. A marriage of minds might begin where you connect on an intellectual level, enjoy conversations, the exchange of ideas and feel very much in sync with what you each think and believe in. Then you might have a marriage at a more emotional level, where you come to know the flow of feeling that is the particular emotional ocean that surrounds your beloved, what moves them, what frightens them, what inspires them and what fills them with passion and joy. Then at another level you could have a marriage of bodies, where you become physically and sexually intimate with your beloved, learning to really just love their body. You'll feel that you want your partner to be kind to his or her body, to love it and treasure it just as you do, and your partner feels the same way about your body. You may physically feel it when something isn't right with your partner's body. Although you know you are both separate, there is a sense of oneness and when something isn't quite right for your partner on some level, you are keenly aware of it, as though there is a crinkle in your otherwise smooth field of oneness and relationship. Of course sometimes things happen and it will be a surprise to you both, but you'll still recognise a growing closeness between you.

These are different depths of intimacy and connection. There is ever-deepening connection and intimacy possible between our spiritual and physical natures as these parts of us learn to recognise, understand, love and appreciate each other. Our ability to love increases as we move into a healthier and more passionate marriage between these parts of us. Each increase requires a cycle of growth through which certain lessons are mastered, so that we can love more. This is symbolised in the year of waiting. An entire cycle must pass – whether it takes us eight weeks or eight lifetimes – in order for the marriage to take place, either for the first time or at a deeper level (like a renewal of vows).

Wisely, Rhiannon's beloved does indeed wait and returns for her hand in marriage, one year later.

There was quite a ruckus over the match from both sides, as a marriage between the worlds of the nature spirits and the humans was out of the ordinary, to say the least. I would compare it to the huffing and puffing that went on when my grandmother (Italian) decided to marry a man who "chased her until he was caught" (according to my grandmother). He was Lebanese. The Italians didn't understand why she didn't just marry a nice Italian man. The Lebanese were horrified that the upstanding pillar of their community was marrying outside of their culture. The numerous challenges from relatives somehow seemed to strengthen the determination of my grandparents not only to marry, but to keep their relationship loving and dedicated to oneness in all that they did. They faced the challenges around them, of which there were plenty, from a position of being in complete accord with each other. There were many demands placed upon them culturally and they faced them together, with humour often enough, and without allowing their love to become contaminated by the opposition that they faced at times. For Rhiannon and her beloved, it was much the same, but on a rather more epic scale. They didn't just have immediate family and some cultural issues to deal with, they had entire worlds up in arms about their union which was breaking new ground, changing the way the worlds interacted with each other, and certainly making those that would prefer to maintain the status quo extremely uncomfortable.

During her marriage to her human husband, Rhiannon endured trials. When she did not bear an heir to the throne for two years, she was criticised, viciously gossiped about and chastised by her community. When she finally did bear the child, those who wanted to undermine her hatched a wicked plan. They killed a puppy, smeared its blood on her during the night whilst she slept deeply, and stole her child.

You can perhaps imagine the depths of her horror and despair the following morning to find that her baby had been taken from her, whilst at the same time she was condemned for murdering and devouring the child.

What is born of the union between spirit and flesh, between divine and human, is the royal heir. This is the divine destiny of love that the spiritual presence within us has come to manifest. It might be a life's work or a vocation of some sort. It might be artistic self-fulfilment through art or music. It might be raising and loving a family, biologically or in other ways. It might be the fulfilment of particular dreams that have deep meaning to your heart. Our destiny is to completely and utterly be the divine being, that is, the love made manifest through the sacred marriage of our spiritual essence and the body.

There are forces that don't want that birth to occur. We have mentioned counter-evolutionary forces, those aspects of life that are against growth. Whether consciously evil or unconsciously harmful, within us as the voice that says our art is never good enough or around us in the voices that say you can't possibly be successful in a field you dream of working in, we contend with these forces on a daily basis. These are the gossiping, sabotaging, undermining attitudes and actions that we need to recognise, hold with compassion and adamantly refuse right of entry into our heart.

When birth – the manifestation of love – does take place, it is like a divine child is born. That might happen many times in our life. It happens each time we take a significant step on the path and through every moment where we don't collapse under criticism or fear and simply stay centred in our hearts instead. We feel the flow of divine power within us as love. We are free to be ourselves and be of love, and there is nothing anyone else can actually do to stop that. Wow! That is a moment of powerful realisation and that is a birth in itself – of divine love into the physical world. It might not seem visible, but it is exceptionally powerful and real. It can send the forces that want to deny love and life into desperation to kill off that birth. It would mean that they could lose their grip on the world – a grip that is based in fear and the illusion of disempowerment. They don't want to be loved 'out of the game' so they react, often with horrifying intelligence.

When Rhiannon was accused of killing and devouring her own child, a situation was set up. She could be judged by others if she was made to appear guilty and shameful. If you have ever felt guilty and shamed for something you know you didn't do, then you will have experienced first-hand the power of negatively projected emotion. It's often seen in political campaigns based on mud slinging. 'Writing off' (as we say in Australia) your opponent and making them seem like an idiot is based on the idea that if you sling enough mud, some of it will stick. Of course, it is without any sense of responsibility or integrity. The aim of it is to put a negative spotlight on someone else rather than letting the spotlight stick on you and reveal your essence. Darker forces don't want to be revealed, they want to be powerful and they gain a lot of power by operating through the unknown, rejected parts of the human psyche, where they can fester away and plant seeds of doubt, unnoticed. Counter-evolutionary forces don't give a hoot about how they achieve their means, they just want to succeed in undermining the royal heir, of killing off what has been born, of murdering love. Attacking Rhiannon and saying it was her own fault was their first poison arrow. The second was the abduction of the child. The child lives in hiding and ignorance and will eventually return and redress the imbalance, for love cannot actually be killed. No matter how many attempts are made, it is fundamentally powerful. However, it can be rendered less visible, less obvious or hidden under an onslaught of darkness, at least for a time.

The young dog that was killed and had its blood smeared upon the queen Rhiannon shows us the nature of darkness, that any life will be sacrificed in its pursuit to put an end to love. Dogs often represent loyalty and instinct. The psychological and emotional manipulations of those that wanted to kill off the love in the royal court were able to turn the community against the innocent queen. If you have ever felt your own hope and optimism become tainted or been sent into a state of hopelessness, despair and distrust because of the negativity of others or the fear that exists in the media, then you have experienced the murder of the puppy on a symbolic level for yourself. The puppy represents developing loyalty to love and an instinct for truth. Eventually, that vulnerable puppy will grow into a ferocious watchdog who would snap at the hand seeking to harm it. An example of how this symbolism might pan out in reality, would be someone or something trying to poison your love or hope with doubt or fear, and you being able to recognise it, keep it at bay and stay true to your inner knowing of love and trust.

It takes time for that inner watchdog to grow. Sometimes those that we serve might turn against us in criticism. That is the murdering of the puppy. They may say we are wrong and to blame for them turning against us. That is the smearing of the blood. Rhiannon bears this with dignity, never doubts her fundamental innocence and never makes the issues of the other about her even when they impact upon her. This allows her to overcome vengeance, bitterness and resentment. This is the pathway through which we can avoid giving the darker forces the upper hand.

On a more general level, for artists or creative people in any sense, we cannot allow the reactions of others to dictate how we feel about our art or creativity and what we are bringing to life. We might be accused of killing off our voice, selling out, losing our spirit or of not honouring our original vision by evolving and expressing ourselves in a different way. We may simply be misunderstood by those who want us to behave according to their expectations rather than authentically as we are. We could be subject to manipulation and power games in a work or personal situation where people are jealous and want to undermine us.

There can be all sorts of ways that the blood of the dog is smeared, symbolically speaking. According to the teachings of Rhiannon, it is how we respond to it that matters. She never tries to outsmart those who attack her. There is a saying that you should never get down and wrestle with a pig in mud, because the pig actually enjoys it! For those on the path of love, we have to learn how to respond to life in a way that is authentic. This does NOT mean pretending that all is love and light, not fighting for what is true, nor does it mean flinging mud right back and sinking down to the same level of the attacker's consciousness. We lose our power that way and it is highly unlikely that it is going to feel right and authentic for us to act in that way anyway. It does mean fighting with intelligence.

We can get angry and tap into Sekhmet or Kali to allow their fire to cleanse us into a place where we can come from purity and compassion, and act from a place of wisdom. We don't always have to be gentle, but Rhiannon teaches us that we are successful on our path when we are truthful, and in that truth, we don't need to react – even to the most vicious attack. We do need to honour the purity of our being. Then our responses can be pure and empowered by spirit, whether they are fierce or quiet, because we have nothing to prove. We are fundamentally unharmed because we realise it is about them, not us. We just deal with our part of the story, and they are left to deal with their part. We may be able to touch the attacker with our compassion, and that is part of our gift to the world, the attacker is on their own journey and what they do with that compassion (accept or reject it) is completely up to them and that is as it should be.

Sometimes this is hard to do, and that is alright. Rhiannon's human husband lost faith in her and was confused by the circumstances in which he found himself. This happens to us at times. We can lose faith in our spirit because of all the drama and suffering going on around us. There are plenty of scheming forces that put a lot of energy into making this happen, even above and beyond the natural ups and downs of healthy, loving growth. It is easy to get caught up in the drama of life. Rhiannon represents the eternal, unflappable free spirit within, that we can always return to, no matter what.

Rhiannon was punished for the crime she was told she committed. For four years, she was chained like a horse at the entranceway to the kingdom and told that she must announce her crime to anyone who visited the kingdom and carry them on her back from the entrance way to the court.

When we are in the throes of counter-evolutionary forces attempting to overcome the love in our being – through jealousy, fear or whatever other impulse – we might feel as though we are being locked out of our rightful kingdom. For years it might seem as though we are denied access to the sacred life we feel we are meant to be living by divine rights. We might have to endure being shamed. This is the healer without the confidence to heal, the singer who is terrified to sing, the lover without a beloved or the writer without a story or a publisher. You might know that inside you are pure, but feel as though you are stuck under layers of shame, doubt, fear, anger or judgment. Oh to break free of those chains and be restored to the kingdom that lay so tantalisingly close-by, and yet apparently so far from reach!

We might feel as though the only way we are going to get back to that kingdom is to tell our stories of shame and doubt, as though they were real, to all who pass by. Spiritual teacher Caroline Myss calls this 'woundology.' This is the tendency some of us have to become our stories, to believe that we are the survivor, the victim, or even the perpetrator. We are not any of those things. We are not even our processes or our pain. Those are merely experiences we encounter on the path to wholeness as we work through of the ups and downs of love in our sacred marriage of body and soul. Each of us is a divine human – at first, a human becoming and eventually, a human being! However, if we forget our true, innocent and pure nature, and think of our experiences as who we are (i.e. the doubts, the grief, and so forth), then we might feel chained and forced to retell our stories over and over, just to feel that we are alive somehow. If this is happening for you, then at some level you believe in those forces that have smeared you with lies, judgments and deceit for whatever reasons of their own. In these scenarios, we can falsely believe there is something wrong with us and we must go about declaring it to try to find a way to heal it. This can be part of our journey in life until we come to the realisation that perhaps we are fundamentally okay and just need to make peace with our past. Feeling and releasing whatever lies unresolved within our bodies is what the healing processes in this book are about. Clearing out will unveil the truth of your being.

There is a time frame in Rhiannon's story. Four years. Four as a number refers to completion and wholeness as in all parts of us – body, emotion, mind and spirit. On the path, we have to come to a place where we accept the truth of our purity on all those levels. When we have gone through that initiation and found the ability to honour the purity of our nature, no matter what experience has taken place or what charge is laid at our door, then we are truly free. The way the world responds to us is then able to shift.

Rhiannon endured her situation without forgetting who she truthfully was. She impressed many others with her quiet dignity and integrity. Word got around about this regal woman and her harsh punishment. Eventually word reached the man who had adopted a baby, he had found abandoned and crying years earlier. The kind and gentle man put two and two together and came to find the goddess queen. Once the true story came out, her son was restored to his rightful royal position and Rhiannon was freed from her chains and recognised once more.

After years of enduring public humiliation, Rhiannon's pure spirit touches enough hearts that the truth is able to find her and order is restored through divine justice with merciful grace. Love triumphs, through patience and the refusal to give up on our own inner truth, regardless of the circumstances in the world around us. Sometimes we have to experience being misunderstood, denied, shamed or unfairly persecuted. Those of us who have been on the healing path for a long, long time – and if you are reading this, you are one of those souls whether you consider yourself a beginner or not – will have been subject to at least some adverse reaction to our light. Out of fear, or the hate or jealousy that can come from fear, we will have had to endure. It may have happened in this lifetime, or we may be recovering from past life wounds and be learning to have the courage to stand up and be truthful, to come out of the spiritual closet, as I put it, and let the world know who we truthfully are.

Rhiannon's time to shine and be restored to her true place of dignity comes without effort on her part. She does not try to force justice to be served. She stays true to herself and balance comes through a series of events over which she has no control. She maintains her equanimity through the whole process. This does not mean we are not supposed to have emotions, human doubts or struggles. The human part of us, represented by her husband in this teaching story, does lose faith and succumbs to the lies and gossip for a time. However, Rhiannon, representing our spirit, is the part of us that always knows what is true and is free to love and be compassionate, no matter what. It is this part of us, that Rhiannon helps us to access. The forces of truth always win, eventually. Rhiannon helps us stay comforted and strong in the knowledge that by holding our vibration at such a level we can more swiftly affect events with our frequency than by forcing things to happen or resisting what is.

Rhiannon's capacity to forgive those around her might seem quite amazing to us. She could do this so easily because she never took on the issues that were so unfairly put upon her. She never lost herself in the process, she endured it as a part of her rocky road to happy marriage and because of her incredible inner wisdom, she wasn't made bitter. May we all have such grace! Or at least regain it swiftly when we stumble into resentment or bitterness in the event that we do take on something that isn't ours to carry – the wounding or pain of another, or society at large, perhaps. Rhiannon forgave her husband his flaws, whereas another goddess would perhaps not have been so understanding and genuinely compassionate. In Ishtar's story, when she returns from her ordeals, and sees her husband kicking up his heels, sitting on her throne and partying while she has literally been to hell and back. She uses the powers she acquired in her dark sojourns to cast him promptly off her throne and into the underworld ... perhaps with a view that he might grow up. Rhiannon's wisdom offers us a different take on divine justice. She is utterly free. She has no need to assert or direct karma. For those of us that prefer to remain in our hearts and leave the rest up to the Divine, Rhiannon reveals that this too can be a wise approach. The kingdom was eventually restored and thrived, despite its rather shaky beginnings and Rhiannon maintained her freedom of choice, dignity and integrity throughout the entire process.

This doesn't mean that we cannot feel or that we ought not to feel. Rhiannon's teaching is not about forgetting to be human. It is about the process that we go through to truly be able to let go, not bear a grudge and forgive. This is the true freedom that comes from realising that nothing has ever changed our fundamental purity. No experience, no attempt by another to shame, judge, abandon or betray us – no matter how terrible the circumstances may be – can ever influence that part of us. We might believe it can, but Rhiannon shows us that nothing can taint our fundamental purity of being. When we remember this, no matter what happens, we are free.

Rhiannon's spirit was alive in Nelson Mandela; a powerful soul who believed in the fundamental dignity of humanity. He was a powerful teacher of freedom and he spent decades of his life, one unbroken period of twenty-seven years, incarcerated for his anti-apartheid politics. His writings show us that attempts to chain and confine us, can give us the determination and focus to ensure that our spirit will not be broken, but instead become even more powerful. He saw prison as means by which to persevere and test his commitment to life and to develop patience. He taught that becoming bitter would make one a prisoner. His responses, rather than his circumstances, gave him his freedom. Mandela was an exceptional, beautiful soul, touched by the grace of the Divine Feminine. That same grace flows through Rhiannon and into our own hearts.

Rhiannon is entrancing by her very nature. She holds the qualities of feminine grace and an unbreakable spirit that can never be tamed by anyone, no matter what situation is impressed upon her. She is light and also substantially powerful. She is the creative, free spirit within us that seeks to manifest itself in the world. In her wisdom stories, it is a human husband that she wants. It isn't that she sees her future husband, falls in love and chooses him at first. That happens second to her decision to seek a human mate. There is another layer of interpretation to be found here. Fae energies exist on the etheric or energetic plane. The human plane is the physical world. For us to manifest our spiritual light, our creativity and our essence in the human world, it must connect physically. If this does not happen, we remain trapped in some wonderful world of fantasy, where all is possible. It may be shining and beautiful, but it is not real in the sense of making a concrete offering in the world. For many that are strongly connected to these worlds, there is an abundance of creative ideas, but a difficulty in following through and bringing them to life.

Rhiannon's teaching stories show us how to attain this sacred marriage, which brings the free spirit within us into the physical world where it can inspire others and bring about the healing of wrongs and injustices without compromising our integrity or lightness of heart. If you have a passion to really live your spirituality, visions and dreams in the physical world, to have your inner and outer worlds match and to really walk your talk, then Rhiannon's journey is a part of your particular soul journey too.

In her teaching story, Rhiannon accepts what happens as part of the course of life. She never once resists, but nor does she lose the knowledge of her own heart and is therefore never consumed by false guilt, shame or anger. She knows her fundamental nature, her innocence and her desire to be in the human world. She gives up the energetic world to become physically manifest and to bear her son who is her divine offering to the world through her sacred marriage. It isn't easy, but it is necessary to the final manifestation of a happy, restored Kingdom where the spirit and the human live in perfect harmony (after their rather dramatic and challenging earlier phases of relationship).

Rhiannon's fundamental values never change, in all phases of the creative process. Where there is a 'delay' in conceiving her child, she is criticised and questioned over being a genuine queen, but she doesn't give in. This teaches us that sometimes we have to wait for our creative efforts to bear fruit. I know that I have held, and still hold, much more creative energy within my energy field that is incubating and waiting for its moment to be born than what has already been realised. It can be challenging at times, knowing that more books and even more oracle decks are waiting in line within me. Music, meditations and visions for other projects have been growing in an energetic womb within me, some for years, but each must wait until the energy becomes available and the timing is right for their birth in the physical world. The larger creative process involves the assistance of some wonderful people like publishers, designers, editors, managers, distributors, marketers, admin angels and the like, who all help to bring the creations to the people they can help. It is a huge undertaking, but it all starts with one idea.

Rhiannon does bear a son, showing us that no matter whether we are under pressure to produce, to have our products earn an income, to be commercially viable, to be artistically different or any to fill any other external (or internal) demand, we can learn to trust ourselves above all. At times the creative process itself can be so powerful and tricky, that Blue Angel Publishing and I have collaborated on *Sacred Rebels Oracle* with guidance for living your authentic, creative life. It is dedicated to awakening and supporting you to live uniquely and to express your creativity, so that you can actually create a beautiful life path just as Rhiannon was able to do.

AMAZONITE (INTEGRITY)

Amazonite is a beautiful soothing stone of blue-green, which can range from very vibrant to quite soft pastel tones. It often has inclusions that appear opaque white or show a soft grey or yellowy mottled effect. This stone restores balance, helps soothe the energy field, the mind and the heart, and in doing so helps to release blockages. It shifts stuck patterns from a place of peaceful inner orientation, much like Rhiannon, without force but with great effectiveness.

It helps us see both sides of any story, to find the masculine and feminine perspectives in a situation and to bring them together. It is a restorer of inner peace that helps us tap into spiritual freedom and the light of our heart.

If you have been in darkness, grief, or unfair circumstances for a long period of time, combining amazonite with stones like danburite (see *Crystal Masters 333*, Chapter Twelve) will help break through the muck and debris, and deeply restore your awareness of your spiritual purity and integrity. That awareness is always within you, but sometimes we need help to budge the stuck emotional energy that can feel a bit like sludge or tar. We don't often realise just how much is there within us until it starts to come out and we feel so much better for it. I have seen and felt this with clients as they release old energies – they can feel it too – as though sludge is pouring out of their chakras! They didn't realise it was there until it was gone and suddenly they have more energy and feel lighter, clearer and more like 'themselves' than before. The healing process at the end of this chapter will help you in a similar way. As this process takes place, you will be able to be yourself, in truth, no matter what situation you find yourself in, how much intrigue is going on around you or how much of an effect that is having outside of your control, upon your external reputation. Remember that truth will always win. Amazonite supports you in remembering this and keeping the faith, from a place of nourishing inner peace.

A cleansing stone energetically as well as physically, amazonite dissolves negative energy and helps purify the nervous system so that it can heal itself naturally. It generates a positive field of energy that can also boost the immune system and minimise the draining effects of electromagnetic fields generated by mobile phones and computers, for example.

The stone heals and supports healthy functioning of the throat and heart chakras, which are integral to our ability to exercise integrity. When the heart and throat work together in harmony we are able to know and honour our truths by speaking and expressing them through our choices or by intuitively tapping in to our hearts in order to know which direction to take. We can, over time, heal our life through making decisions that gradually bring our inner truths and our outer actions into alignment with each other.

This can ask a lot of us in terms of change. We might have to let go of situations where we have compromised ourselves and that might take some strategic decision-making and a great capacity for trust if that scenario was a security blanket for us in any way. Amazonite helps us remember that we are strong divine lights and that no matter how frail we might imagine ourselves to be, we can manifest through clear heart-felt intention in order to attract the right situations, people, opportunities and pathways into our lives at the right time. It also helps us have enough self-knowledge and integrity to take the risks involved in acting on those situations when they do come our way.

Amazonite doesn't repress our anger, but helps to redirect it into constructive channels. It can be a force that makes us stop and check in with our truths. Are we living the way we want to or letting our emotions push us unthinkingly into reactions and self-defeating behaviours like addiction or other self-sabotaging patterns such as self-directed anger or self-doubt? If we catch ourselves doing this, the gentleness of amazonite doesn't inflict shame upon us but allows us a moment of recalibration in which we can shift to our true free-spirited self once again.

If you are transitioning out of situations that are chronically toxic, such as abusive relationships or working environments, you can find support in amazonite. It encourages us to come back to our truths and find courage and positivity, while we do our inner work and have patience as we seek the best way to move forward. Amazonite is not about rushing towards what should be, but about dealing with what is, as best as we can, as we consistently move towards greater authenticity in our life choices.

This can give rise to anxiety, as we might not be able to see how it is all going to work out when we think about taking steps towards a different sort of life. Amazonite helps soothe away that mind-created anxiety. We don't have to know how something is going to happen in order for it to happen. We just have to ask for divine help and trust, act when necessary and have patience when action is not yet possible. With amazonite building a healthy connection between heart and mind, and supporting that through journaling, art or any kind of honest emotional self-expression, we will come to know very clearly when the opportunity to act has come, or when we have to wait because we are not quite ready to take the leap yet. Our feelings will tell us. We won't need to question whether our patience is masking an unwillingness to act from a place of fear. We will trust ourselves to know when it is time to move on.

If we do not know what our truths are, it is impossible to be in integrity to them, let alone have the power to back them through our actions and choices. Amazonite empowers us to be able to come into integrity with ourselves and allow the light of our hearts to shine forth into the world, to shift even the most impossible situations through the power of our frequency and undistorted vibration. When the throat is clear, the power of the spirit to manifest itself from the heart out into the world is made so much more powerful. Amazonite is a very supportive helper on that path of healing.

Amazonite has been referred to as a stone of hope. That gentle but powerful state of being is what happens when the heart is open to the Divine and the wounds of another are not allowed to poison us and lower our vibration. We realise that we are free to be who we are, in love, and suddenly so much happiness becomes possible.

MANIFESTING THROUGH RESPECT

Like power, respect is often a misunderstood term. It cannot be created on demand, though those in positions of authority (as opposed to genuine empowerment) might confuse obedience based on the fear of losing one's job, for example, with respect. Or perhaps they don't care, but it doesn't really matter. What matters is that you access your own experience of respect for yourself. It is only when we genuinely respect ourselves that we can find a healthy respect for others.

Respect is not about bowing down to another, or placing another over you in some way. Nor is it about being less than or handing your power over to another. Respect is about acknowledging the fundamental worth of yourself and others, and the right that each being has to walk their divine path, make their own choices (whether you happen to agree with them, or they with you) and the right of each being to access compassion and divine love, if only they will open to it.

You can respect someone without liking them. To offer respect to another being is an expression of love. It might not be an expression of love in the more typical definition of the word, which is usually held to mean having a preference or particular affection for someone. To express love in the form of respect means that you recognise the right of that being to exist and to be free. Respect is an acknowledgment of our own divinity and the divine light that dwells in each being. It does not require us to agree with the choices of others, but it does require us to support their right to make them. Likewise for ourselves, respect is what affirms our right to exist as independent, divine beings. It is what affirms our right to healthy relationships, a nourishing life and choices that supports this.

Respect for life is not about trying to control it, but about honouring it, doing our best to deal with the challenges it presents from a position of knowing that if life is delivering it to us, then something in us has called it forward and we can handle it. It is part of our life journey. When we respect ourselves we put time and energy into the things that matter to us. We don't demand perfection of ourselves or others, but genuine effort and a willingness to do our best and live up to our divine potential. We will also have compassion for ourselves in those moments when we get stuck in self-doubt.

HEALING PROCESS

If you are struggling to assert your own inner freedom and light, to live in accordance with your internal values rather than to the sometimes overwhelming pull of external forces, then this healing process is for you. If you have been struggling with a lack of acknowledgment or genuine recognition for who you are and what you stand for, this healing is for you – and yes, you can feel this way amongst those that say they love you, but don't seem to take your needs seriously or respond to them with respect.

If you need help to take the next step on your path of personal empowerment and spiritual growth, to shed old traumas and trust in your ability to attract what you need, at the perfect time, through your divine frequency, this healing is for you.

If you are willing to do the emotional healing work needed to make your energy clear enough so that your internal divine frequency can be broadcast into the world of forms powerfully enough to create physical expressions of your inner light, then this healing is for you too.

If you have had a tough day at home, on the telephone dealing with customer service people who have no interest in customer service, in court, at the office, in the world, subjected to nonsense in the media or on the radio or television, and are generally feeling diminished, tired or less than human because of it, then this is for you too dear one.

Please find some peace and quiet for yourself to complete this process if you can.

The Process

Have your crystal and/or mandala with you. Say out loud, "I call upon Rhiannon, free spirit and wild horse woman of divine freedom who loves me unconditionally and the Crystal Angel of Amazonite. I ask for your loving assistance and healing now, through my body, mind and soul. So be it."

Visualise that you are lying in, or near, the most beautiful turquoise or green-blue waters imaginable. The water is pure, free from any pollution, tropical and just the right temperature.

Allow yourself to float in, under or by the side of these waters. Let them gently and peacefully lap over you. There is a little movement in the water, but it is unhurried, lulling and serene. The sun is shining softly. You might be in the shade of a coconut tree, in a cave near the ocean, or lying on soft, white sand.

Out of the water beautiful blue-green angel arises and showers you with light. You breathe in and out, with your eyes gently closed. You feel whatever has been troubling you shift into perspective and you sense your ability to deal with things grow as you feel more calm, strong and centred.

Stay with this process for as long as feels appropriate.

When you are ready, you notice a bright white cloud swirling in the sky above you and the gentle pattern of horse hooves sound subtly forth. You see a goddess in golden robes mounted on a white horse. Her hair is flying in the wind as she rides towards you. She has a smile on her face and she knows you. She has known you for long before you remembered who she was.

She tells you that everything is going to work out and reassures you that you must trust.

She tells you that she loves you without condition and will help you find the strength to be in touch with your inner light and that you can never lose that, no matter how trying the circumstances in your life seem to be.

She tells you that divine justice will always find its way and you have nothing to be ashamed of or guilty about. Nothing!

Now, let her take you into the peaceful pure light of her heart and feel how the light in your heart is the same as the light in hers. Let yourself acknowledge this now. If you feel resistance or doubt or any emotional response, just notice it, let it come and go and accept this is part of your process.

When you are ready open your eyes and say the following, "I now empower Rhiannon who loves me unconditionally and the Crystal Angel of Amazonite to protect and rebalance me, to support me in aligning with my divine integrity and in living my life in absolute trust so that my purest frequencies can emit clearly and powerfully from my inner self, into the world of forms to attract perfect opportunities, support, assistance and intervention of grace. With respect, may I live my divine path and serve the path of love from a place of deep serenity and inner peace. So be it."

When you are ready, close your eyes, place your hands on your heart and breathe this prayer in and out for at least eight breaths.

Then, in your own time, just open your eyes once more.

Notice what you feel and honour your growing need to express yourself, even if it is only through journaling, in the days and weeks following this healing process. If something or someone no longer feels like a worthy investment of your time and energy, act on that. Respect yourself enough to honour your true feelings by listening to them and responding to them with action. You deserve such loving attention.

12.

FREYA (UNTAMED)
AMBER (AGELESS)

MANIFESTING THROUGH ZEST FOR LIFE

Naked, but for a cloak of falcon feathers, she soars. Unquenchable thirst for life, she chooses to be fully alive. So she laughs, weeps, argues and desires. Her golden radiance reveals an ageless beauty that soothes the souls of those who have suffered in war and restores them into love for life.

FREYA (UNTAMED)

Freya is wild. A Norse goddess of beauty, war and fertility, she is passionate, untamed and enthusiastic in her pursuit of life experience. When she wants something – such as the beautiful amber necklace that she sees and desires as her own – she will stop at nothing to obtain it. She will simply not be thwarted! She refuses to be bartered around as a prize by the male gods and as for her lovers, well no god is out of bounds for her renowned sensual appetite. She brings a lust for love, life and pleasure, as well as an appreciation for beauty in its many forms. She appears as a beautiful feminine being, often scantily clad or in provocative poses which represent her sensuality and passionate, free-flowing energy. She is revered for her sexuality, not humiliated or shamed. When Loki, the trickster, accuses Freya of having made lovers of every being in the court, she is not silenced and answers back as good as she gets. She is completely comfortable with her own nature and does not hesitate to truthfully act upon her feelings, and this is accepted and honoured in the land of the gods.

She uses her powers of beauty, strength, protection and magic, not only to freely obtain what she wants but to protect and nurture women, children, and also the men who pray to her for assistance. She is not considered to be selfish or destructive, but a force of good in the world and a patron goddess of healing. Cats are sacred to Freya and two felines are seen pulling her chariot through the sky and are often considered her messengers. Their spirited independence, sensuality, self-centred and yet warming, healing presence are not unlike Freya herself.

Freya possesses a magic cloak of falcon feathers, which gives its wearer the ability to fly. She is said to use this cloak when she visits the underworld to gain prophecies so as she can rise up again to spread her messages. Because of this cloak, Freya is considered a goddess of shapeshifting and transformative magic, and another of her totems is the falcon, known as a messenger that holds the ability for higher vision and protection. This aspect of her iconography ties her to Isis, who also holds these powers.

Her sensuality and boldness are not the only things that mark Freya as a goddess of depth. She also governs the realms of war and death. She is something like Bastet and Sekhmet combined into one. She chooses who will be slain in war, giving her a karmic aspect, like Sekhmet. She takes utter delight in making love and the pleasure of sensuality, like Bastet. Freya is a complex feminine creature, of unchecked sensuality and openness to all of life, including death. She is benevolent, self-centred, passionate and protective.

On a recent tour of North Queensland, I noticed something intriguing. We did a lot of driving and covered thousands of kilometres as we ventured out to mining towns, tropical destinations and more. Wherever we went in our travels we were watched over by falcons. They constantly hovered over us as we drove. It got to be something of a joke, so persistent was their presence, but I knew at a deeper level we were being protected.

During that time, Freya was there with us. I didn't realise it until afterwards. Goddesses can be like that, showing their presence in hindsight rather than being blaringly obvious at the time. As well falcons, my time in North Queensland also blessed me with significant interactions with a cat and an invisible but powerful guiding hand that helped those that I was working with tap into their sensuality through movement, music and guided imagery. There was healing – for me, as well as for the students in my classes.

When Freya connects with us, we are going to be challenged on any beliefs we have that what is good for 'us' somehow competes with what is good for 'them.' Freya does not discriminate between gain for self and for others. She is utterly open and generous by nature, does not pull back from what she wants nor does she put limits on herself to obtain it. She doesn't do this out of self-obsession or narcissism. She does it from a place of being completely open to life and of accepting of all parts of herself.

Freya's energy is not about taking, but about being honest and open about our desires. She defies the traditional rules about sexuality and in doing so can help us find our truths.

For those that don't relate to monogamous relationships or prefer to explore their sexuality by experimenting with different paradigms, even those that are generally shunned or misunderstood in mainstream cultures (e.g. open marriages), Freya is a patron protector.

When running dance and music events with a spiritual twist, I often meet people who are in the polyamorous community. The members of that community are keen to explore relationships of a sexually intimate variety, outside of the more commonplace monogamy. Whilst I personally prefer monogamous, committed relationships, I support all people in finding what works for them for their own emotional growth and sexual healing. If there is respect and accord between all involved, then it can be conducive for personal growth for people to be free to choose what will suit their relationship needs. The polyamorous community is typically very motivated to get out and about to meet like-minded people. The events that I run, and sometimes attend as a participant, are open to everyone irrespective of their relationship preference but there are usually at least some of the polyamorous community present.

I have been approached on numerous occasions by members from that community with an invitation to connect more intimately. Whilst open relationships do not personally hold an appeal for me, I am intrigued by those that are exploring relationship dynamics through such an approach. My understanding, from the outside, is that polyamory is about being present and intimate with more than one partner in an open and transparent way. What is interesting to me is that there are different levels of consciousness at play in the men from that community who approach me, although on the surface, they are offering me the same thing – an open, rather than monogamous, relationship.

Some people, often but not always men, claim to be polyamorous, but aren't really interested in multiple relationships at all. They are just interested in having sex with as many different partners as possible and any relationship beyond that is not held with much importance. They may use the term 'polyamorous' to make it sound as though they are offering a legitimate spiritual, sexual and emotional connection that could bring depth to their relationships. However, simply using the term to describe their relationship orientation doesn't mean they are taking an actual journey. People who describe themselves as polyamorous but do not possess some emotional maturity will have little regard for intimacy, depth or commitment.

It's pretty obvious within a few minutes of meeting such people just how much or how little regard they actually hold for you, instead of just seeing a body they would like to sleep with. They might speak as though they hold great awareness, but when it all comes down to it, they can act like kids in a candy store.

Recently I was at a café in deep conversation with a friend. It was an incredible interaction, as though we were floating in the divine ocean together. I felt uncommonly nourished by the encounter. Suddenly, we were interrupted by a young, vivacious couple. Friendly and good-intentioned as they no doubt were, the deep communion with my friend was brought to an abrupt halt as they boldly inserted themselves into our conversational flow. My friend and I politely interacted for a short, but revealing, exchange.

During our interaction with the couple, the young man said he was polyamorous. Quite a conversation starter! He talked about himself and explained how his sexual openness was about his journey in life. I might add that this was in no way related to the conversation my friend and I were having at the time. This is not bad, but perhaps you agree, it IS rather amusing! He was friendly, flirtatious and a nice looking man. I wondered how the girl sitting opposite him, whom he declared he was sleeping with but not committed to, was feeling about his open declaration of that fact and his equally open interest towards myself and my friend. She was extremely friendly and bubbly in personality, but I couldn't help wonder what the relationship was doing for the self-esteem of either of them. Of course, only they could know that for certain. As my grandmother always used to say, 'One cannot know what goes on behind closed doors.' She meant that the dynamics of a relationship might always be a mystery to those on the outside.

When I complimented a piece of clothing the young woman was wearing, she immediately offered it to me. I didn't know how to respond except to politely decline. I didn't want to take the shirt off her back (or the tights off her legs in this instance). She then offered to rummage around a bag of clothing that she was carrying, to see if there was something there that might suit me. I declined that offer also, saying I already had enough clothes and was actually cleaning out my wardrobe, so she had no need to give me anymore! The young man promptly suggested that I take out a market stall with the young woman and sell my clothes with her. As I mumbled yet another polite refusal (no time, but thanks anyway), the young woman asked outright for my number so that we could stay in touch. She was extremely keen to connect and although I appreciated her friendliness and interest, I also felt an instinctive need to slow things down and set some boundaries, to get to know her a little before launching into the intimacy of a deeper connection.

When the young man started asking questions that were obviously geared towards finding out my relationship status, I panicked a little. I was very newly single at the time and certainly did not want to put out any message that I was open to a relationship with him. At the same time, I didn't want to be rude or to lie. I felt under pressure but not really knowing how best to deal with the situation, apart from being polite and setting boundaries, I made an unnecessary dash for the toilets to get some space instead! When I returned, I didn't sit down again. My friend had also claimed a visit the bathroom, so when I returned, I found myself in the even more awkward situation of standing and waiting for her while our new acquaintances sat and continued conversation. When the man expressed an apparently irresistible desire to play with my long curly hair, I smiled but remained standing. When my friend finally returned, she also remained standing. Together we said our goodbyes to the couple and continued our conversation whilst walking along the nearby waterfront.

They were a polite, friendly and enthusiastic young couple, but their intensity for sharing personal information, their eagerness to immediately connect and their active interest in us becoming a part of their lives, in various ways, was uncomfortable for me.

Less than a week later, I saw these two people at a mutual friend's party. The young man made eye contact with me the moment I walked into the room. Whether that was because he recognised me from our previous interaction, I cannot say because I didn't pursue further interaction with him. I didn't feel he was actually interested in me. He was certainly interested in what he would experience in an encounter with me, but that is something quite different. I was thankful for the previous encounter with him where he had been so upfront about himself and his journey, so that I had that clarity and could avoid any unnecessary entanglements or misunderstandings.

The young woman then came up to me and began a conversation. She introduced herself and asked my name as though we had never before met. I thought back to how uncomfortable I had been with the sort of strained intimacy she had tried to create between us less than a week earlier. Offers of her personal possessions and active attempts to set the ground for future connections, which suggested some genuine feeling of connection with me, were apparently completely forgotten. I wondered if, perhaps, she was purposefully pretending not to remember me as some kind of assertion of power because I had declined her many offers. Perhaps she was so dissociated and lacking in presence that she genuinely couldn't remember sitting down and engaging in enthusiastic conversation with me, attempting to give me her clothes, watching her sexual partner flirt with me and demanding my telephone number. Or perhaps those things were so completely ordinary for her, that she really just didn't remember me at all. Either way I was struck by how open and interested in making a connection both of them had appeared to be, and at the lack of substance in that appearance. That was my reality. Perhaps theirs was very different.

We all have our own journey to take, our own way of journeying and it isn't for me to say that one is right or another is wrong. I don't judge these two people but feel a lot of compassion for their search for themselves and wish them all the best in finding their way, however might be best for them. However, I did feel an emptiness in their apparent wildness as it did not – for me at least – seem to touch the heart. It was like piling a plate full of food from a buffet and wolfing it down, perhaps with appreciation for the variety and abundance on offer, but still not really tasting anything. We might even wolf down so much that we can't digest it or have it nourish us. When it's too much, we can end up sick and starved instead.

I have a friend who has fallen for this sort of emotionally immature man who proclaimed he was on a polygamous path. He promised her a relationship but without commitment. How you actually have a relationship without a commitment to love, respect, being present and so on – whether the relationship is monogamous or polyamorous – I am yet to understand but the gent in question appeared to think it could happen. It didn't however, and the involvement ended messily for my beautiful friend. She felt used as he moved on to someone else. He was spared any need for ill-feeling about it, because he was upfront about his supposed polyamory and therefore his behaviour was somehow acceptable, rather than immature and dismissive.

That may be what men of a certain level of consciousness consider to be polyamory, although I suspect others who explore it with more depth may define it rather differently. Of course, there are lessons for all involved, however accepting that we are learning something doesn't mean we also have to accept emotionally destructive behaviour in our relationships.

Sometimes the lesson is simply that no matter how spiritually evolved someone claims to be, we are best to look not at their words, but their behaviour in determining whether we want to progress into relationship with them.

Other men have approached me, and even though they were not offering a monogamous commitment – something which is important to me – they were so present with me and so willing to connect at a level beyond the sexual that I realised they were proposing something substantial and reverent. For them, I could feel that polyamory was about having more than one relationship, not simply more than one lover. Even though it wasn't a monogamous commitment, in their own way, an offer of commitment was still being made. Although I did not follow up on these offers, I was respectful and appreciative of the more mature intentions and respect behind such advances.

I could sense Freya alive and well in these more mature, polyamorous men. They were about loving. Yes, outside of what is typically considered to be the best model for a marriage, and outside even of what I have chosen for myself as the most nurturing relationship dynamic for me, but genuinely loving nonetheless. One man in particular, just through his friendship and his genuine appreciation of me, helped me feel a great deal of trust and faith in the emotional depth and presence that some men can offer. This was something I had previously hoped for, but had not yet experienced. Getting to know some of these men and women, and sensing the difference between those trying to score notches on a bedpost and those offering a non-monogamous but loving commitment to be present in their relationships, helped me understand Freya at a whole other level. This doesn't mean that devotees of Freya have to be polyamorous. However, I do feel that she shows her face through the emotionally and psychologically mature members of the polyamorous community.

Of course Freya's taking of many lovers does not have to translate in a literal sense. Freya can be just as active within the consciousness of someone who tends towards monogamous relationships. Perhaps that person expresses their craving for diversity not by taking many lovers, but in pursuing many passions. There are many ways that we can express the passion within us. It might be through creative work, a constantly evolving healing journey, or an openness to new worlds and cultures through learning new things, meeting new people and travel.

I once met a man who politely declined my invitation to have coffee together. We were law students at a community law centre, doing volunteer work as part of our legal training. Despite the fact that we got along like a proverbial house on fire, he made it quite clear that he had enough friends and didn't need any more. I was disappointed because I thought he was great fun, but was also a bit turned off by his attitude, which couldn't have been more different to mine. Perhaps he was monogamous in his friendships! Whether or not that is the case, I certainly love meeting new people. There is always a sense that just around the corner, whether it be in another country, at another evening of dance or at another drumming circle, a kindred spirit awaits and together we will bond as we naughtily laugh at something we are not supposed to joke about.

Everyone expresses their passion for singularity or diversity in their own way. The more creatively fulfilled I am with projects on the go that I feel passionate about, and the more friends I have that I feel a genuine connection with, the more satisfied I am in a monogamous relationship. I can find the variety I crave in life through my creative work and the passionate depth, intensity and intimacy I desire through a committed personal relationship. And, my relationship to the Divine is where I can love the one and the all simultaneously. I genuinely feel love for those whom I meet and work with, yet it is really the Divine expressed as those human beings that I am loving. That is Freya. Loving the one and the many with equal passion. You may find a similar approach works for you, or you might find something very different. Freya doesn't mind. Whatever works for you, is what is best suited to your growth and development.

However we want to approach it, Freya supports us in discovering what works for us in relationships and in our expression of passion in life. She teaches that we don't have to confine or limit our passion for life, but we do need to be open to finding authentic ways of expressing it.

If the demands of society or your primary relationship are making you feel too small, Freya will call to you. She might call to you through a passionate attraction to someone outside of your marriage. However the calls comes, the way you respond is always your choice. You might be able to understand the deeper, hidden meaning in the attraction and seek out a fuller life for yourself in ways other than acting on your passion for another, for example.

Working with the energies of Freya, or any goddess for that matter, is not about mimicking their divine behaviours in a literal sense. We don't look at the goddess and try to be like her. Working with the Divine Feminine is more about integrating their spirit in a mature and functional way within our own psyche. We find the essence of their consciousness – with Freya it is the freedom to love from an open heart without restraint – and bring it down to earth into our hearts, our bodies and our lives, in a way that feels truthful, authentic and helpful for us.

Freya also empowers us to have relationships that are not based in power or ownership. She is always a free agent unto herself. She loves freely, expecting respect in return, and it is given. She is a warrior, a lover and is most passionately herself. When we drop the power games in relationship, intimacy can happen. This is what takes place when two people are more interested in knowing and loving each other, than trying to turn each other into what we want them to be. When Freya's spirit of self-expression and passionate love fills a relationship, there is freedom. We can stop posturing, defending our egos and trying to be good enough or to catch a mate. Instead, we can become present, be who we are and actually learn who the person sitting opposite us really is.

Freedom doesn't spell the end of genuine relationship, it marks its beginning. By owning the freedom to be oneself and allowing your partner to do the same, we can begin to experience the healing and energy enhancing qualities of loving relationship. Two people who choose to be together create a field of spaciousness in their relationship which can give them room to breathe, and to grow. It takes a big heart and plenty of self-esteem to love in such a way. Yet, if you feel connected to Freya or attracted to her nature, this is part of what you are here to learn and experience in this lifetime. Far from creating superficiality, freedom in partnership allows each person to become more of themselves and the opportunity to share more of that self with the beloved. Freya loves many, but she also loves deeply. When she loses her husband, she weeps for him. The tears that touched the sea turned to gold and those that dropped upon the earth turned to amber.

These precious creations, born of her tears, are gifts from the goddess. Gold and amber teach us that through great loss we can acquire something of great worth – wisdom and a heart that chooses to remain open to life, no matter what. This wisdom and openness generate a boldness, bravery and willingness to experience life with a youthful zest that Freya certainly possesses. The transformation of her tears into precious metal and stone also symbolises her blessings of prosperity and abundance. Through her openness to life, and our openness to her, great blessings can be bestowed and received.

Gold and amber are sacred to her and form her most precious possession, a stunning necklace called Brisingamen. The necklace was created by four dwarves with such intricate workmanship that it glitters like the stars in the sky and mesmerises Freya. It is said she desired it so much that when the dwarves said she had to sleep with them to obtain the necklace, she had no compunction about doing so. On the surface, this might seem like a questionable behaviour, but remember with the Divine Feminine, we have to see not just the surface, but through the eye of the heart. So what does this story mean?

Dwarves are creatures of the earth. They are known for their talent in creating beauty and generating wealth. They are the means by which ideas are grounded into reality and potential is transformed into tangible, real creations in the physical world. Without dwarves and the earth element that they represent, the divine world of ideas, beauty and inspiration would not be able to come to life in the physical world.

The number four represents grounding, earth energy and creation. It is the wholeness of us – mind, body, emotions and spirit. The four dwarves represent the earth element and the skill of manifestation – the ability for something exquisite to be created when all aspects of ourselves come into balanced relationship with each other.

The necklace they create is Freya's destiny. It is her presence made visible in the physical world. It is a representation of her soul in connection with the world. It is her light made manifest. That is why she responds to it as she does. It isn't some passing whimsy that causes her to desire the necklace and be willing to do anything to obtain it. It is a spiritual need to fulfil her light and bring it to the world. Sleeping with the dwarves to obtain the necklace isn't a random act of audacious harlotry! Although, if Freya wished to engage in such an act, I suspect she would do so freely and without a second thought. Nonetheless sleeping with the dwarves is an acknowledgement that to fulfil her spiritual nature, she needs to have a completely open and accepting relationship with the earthly world.

Freya is associated with Fehu, the rune for property, cattle and gold. Again we see Freya's divine connection with the earth and the abundance that can come to us when we allow our love and passion to interact with the world. If you work with runes and often draw this one, then you have a strong affinity with Freya whether it is conscious to you or not.

In our modern culture, when many of us are afforded greater freedoms of choice than ever before, Freya guides us to not fall prey to the glitter. AS a child, my mother would tell me, '*All that glitters is not gold*.' She was talking to me about one particularly shiny, pretty girl at school who was behaving in not so shiny, pretty ways towards me. I couldn't understand how someone so apparently lovely, popular and pretty could be so different on the inside. It was a lesson in discernment between substance and appearance. This seems simple enough but as a culture, we are often seduced by the glitter instead of seeking out gold. This simple lesson can be more difficult to practice than one might first expect.

Freya is not about the glitter, she is about the gold. She is about what is real, whether that be multiple relationships where you are present and intimate and committed to respect and love with all of your partners, or one partnership where you are committed to each other. She teaches us not to stuff down meaningless excess because we can, but to engage voraciously with life and all that it offers with presence. That is the untamed self. It doesn't shy away from presence and real engagement, sticking to the surface of things. It doesn't talk of love and walk in fear. It lives truth and loves.

AMBER (AGELESS)

Amber is one of my favourite stones to wear. It is not actually a stone per se but fossilised tree resin, some of it from ancient forests dating back hundreds of millions of years. It can be dredged up from the sea and in the Baltic region, where amber sources are naturally concentrated, winter storms can toss nuggets of amber straight out of the ocean. Imagine standing at the ocean's edge with your arms raised in joy towards the crashing waves when a piece of amber hurtles from the sea and lands in the palm of your hand!

Natural amber ranges in colour from pale, golden yellow to almost black. It is mostly rich yellow or orange in tone, though occasionally red or green hued amber can also be found. There is a natural blue amber, which is sourced in small quantities from a different type of tree. Under normal electric lighting it appears to be the same as regular amber with a yellowish tone, but when it is held in sunlight or ultraviolet light, it has a fluorescent blue sheen and is very striking.

Butterscotch amber is amber that is not transparent. It is light weight, like regular amber, but opaque with varying tones of pale lemon to deep, dark yellow. Its milky appearance is prized in the Arabic worlds and personally I find it quite beautiful too.

Transparent amber often features inclusions such as plant or animal matter, or other organic materials, sometimes obvious sometimes indistinct within the resin.

Single and large pieces of amber can be reasonably expensive and sometimes large, but inexpensive pieces are actually broken shards that have been cast in a plastic resin and sold as 'reconstructed amber.' Bonded amber is similar but with less synthetic bonding agents used and involves one or two pieces joined together. It is advisable to purchase from a reputable dealer and to ask before purchase if it is natural or altered in any way. If it is marked as natural Baltic amber, for example, then it will the natural stone with only mechanical changes to the stone to work it into a wearable piece of jewellery, for example. If it is marked as modified amber, then it is likely to have been treated to heating to intensify its colour or alter its degree of transparency.

You'll know if a piece is for you, no matter how natural or modified it is, because you'll like the way you feel when you hold it.

Recently I was on a little shopping adventure, looking for some beads that my Vedic astrologer said would be useful for me to work with. I knew of a store in Sydney's inner west that was likely to have these beads. It is a jewellery store that also houses various fabrics, beads and statues from the East, most prominently from India. The familiar soothing scent of incense met me as I entered the store and asked about the beads I needed. As I went to look at them, a cuff with several pieces of butterscotch amber caught my attention.

With remarkably little thought, considering it wasn't exactly a cheap piece of jewellery (it isn't exactly a low-price store!), I decided to purchase the cuff as well as the beads that were the point of my excursion (or so I thought!). I put the cuff on immediately and felt a field of protective energy and wellbeing around me. I loved it. I knew it was for me.

It was only afterwards that I consciously realised I had felt an instant recognition with the cuff in a similar way as Freya had 'known' her amber necklace, Brisingamen. Something in that cuff spoke of the strength of the feminine warrior, something I related to as I was revelling in independence and freedom having just left a long-term relationship. I was discovering myself again. The cuff was not just beautiful, it was symbolic of something in me that was blossoming into fullness. I felt bolder and more like myself, than I had done in some time. I felt Freya with me. She was reflected back to me in that amber cuff, as the self I was becoming more completely. The cuff symbolised an important part of my divine destiny. No wonder I loved it instantly. I was not required to sleep with four dwarves to obtain it, although I did have to honour the earth element, just as Freya did, to obtain the meaningful jewels. The journey that had lead me to the cuff had involved leaving my long-time partner and grieving the relationship with many tears. It also involved an assertion of my economic independence as I had to part with a hefty sum of cash. I also had to believe in what I felt when I saw that cuff, in my own strength and in my own self claimed more fully than ever before. It was a powerful moment that only deepened my regard for amber as a healing substance.

Amber has been used as medicine for thousands of years and also as a healing oil, perfumed incense and even as a flavouring for some liquor. Amber, as a note in modern perfume, is created as an ode to the warm beauty of the crystal, often with benzoin (a type of intensely sweet smelling resin), vanilla and copal (another very sweet scented resin used as incense) as ingredients, rather than amber itself which is actually rather subtle in fragrance.

In folk medicine amber was used as a tonic for courage and strength and to heal the throat. It was used to drive away negative spirits or energies, and amber maintains these properties in crystal healing today. When we work with the throat chakra we are healing our ability to discern, to sort the glitter from the gold and to set priorities so that we can work on what really matters to us. Freya, with her amber necklace worn at the throat chakra, can help us with all throat chakra related matters including self-expression, self-determination and personal sovereignty. Combined, we could say this is an ability to define, honour and possess oneself as a divine royal being.

Baltic amber contains succinic acid, which is known to have a positive effect on the immune system, on clearing toxicity from cells and promoting wellbeing. This acid has been used in anti-aging pharmaceuticals as an antioxidant due to its ability to restore energy balance at a cellular level, inhibit the degeneration associated with the aging process and promote feelings of youthful vitality and wellbeing.

Similarly, it also holds properties of emotional, psychic and physical protection against anything that would drain and diminish the body's energy field. This includes blocking and repairing the negative effects of electromagnetic radiation from technological devices. When worn directly on the body or in the energy field for long periods of time the stone builds up its own electrical field of negative ions. Negative ions are the invisible healers that promote wellbeing, heal the body and encourage natural pain relief and an improved appetite for life and enhanced sex drive. They are responsible for that rush of feel good energy when we near an ocean or other body of water. Negative ions create positive energy and enhance that sense of agelessness that amber can bestow.

Despite its strength, amber is a stone that sensitive people can wear for long periods without being overwhelmed or drained. This is just one more reason why I particularly love it. It generates a field of positivity, warmth and optimism that brings out our sunny nature, enhances self-acceptance and boosts fertility and creativity. Overall, it is a joyful crystal that for all its effectiveness and strength is a gentle healer.

MANIFESTING THROUGH ZEST FOR LIFE

Life is a responsive intelligent expression of universal creative energy. When we are in love with it and open to it, it dances with us, flirts with us, responds to us. Sometimes this is enjoyable, sometimes challenging, but those with a genuine zest for life relish whatever comes their way.

I work with a very special woman who is like this. She has been a client and student for more than ten years, and we have a close spiritual bond. I have often experienced just how delightful she is from the perspective of the Divine when we work together, as though I see through God's eyes exactly how much he is enjoying coming to life through her, as her. Her enjoyment of life, her utter surrender into all of it (the good, the bad, the exciting, the dark and inexplicable), her relish in doing so and her determination find nourishing wisdom from every experience, is so very Freya. She is intense, kind, articulate and expressive and changes the energy field in a room when she enters it.

I love having her in groups that I run. On one level, the obvious closeness and intensity of our spiritual connection inspires others to want to move closer to me and that opens their hearts to allow me to do deeper work with them. Apart from that, she inspires people with her willingness and sheer zest for life. She energises the people around her. In a group setting dedicated to consciousness, this is appreciated greatly. In other situations where she might ruffle feathers and promote growth that is not desired, she is not always so appreciated. Nonetheless, she is herself in all situations and whatever comes her way. Despite her fundamentally joyful and exuberant nature, she has had some truly dark life experiences in life and has treated those as an opportunity to discover and be more of herself. She treats life as the grand adventure it is. That is true zest for life.

Zest doesn't mean that we are always 'on' as sometimes we will be relishing the quiet times too. It is about being present and really engaging. If you have ever complained about the coldness of winter, only to find yourself thinking of it rather fondly in the heat of summer, then you know it isn't always easy to remain present to what is with openness and acceptance – although sometimes we look back and wish that we had!

HEALING PROCESS

If you are feeling a bit blah, lacking in inspiration or excitement, wanting some more spice in your life, needing some adventure or the courage to accept the adventures and invitations that are starting to come your way, then this healing is for you.

If you feel as though you have lost your sense of wonder and appreciation for life, like life has become an unending series of chores to be checked off a growing to-do list or that you are so tired from all the demands on you that you haven't laughed, or felt sexy, romantic or inspired for far too long, then this healing is for you too!

If you can't relate to any of that, but you just want to connect more deeply to the ageless beauty of amber and the untamed radiance of Freya, then this healing is for you also.

The Process

Have your amber and/or crystal mandala with you. Please find a place where you can feel free to express yourself. Some privacy can be very useful for this work as it will allow you to feel safe in your space and open to work more deeply.

Say, "I call upon Freya who loves me unconditionally and the Crystal Angel of Amber. Be with me beloveds, bless me with your golden grace, your healing energy, your loving protection and all blessings of happiness, abundance, prosperity and vitality. So be it!"

Close your eyes and imagine you are bathing in a beautiful yellow and orange sphere of light. The sun shines through it and it is soft, golden, hazy and glowing vibrantly. You might rest in that light, or play or dance in it. You might get up and move around physically to sense the golden light all around you as though it was sweet and vibrant honey. You may choose to sit quietly and rest in the energy.

Do this for at least eight breaths in and out.

When you are ready, notice a chariot led by two large cats above you. See their fur, their eyes, their ears and colour. You may be drawn to the cats or repelled by their energy. Whatever you feel is fine. You see that the chariot they pull through the heavens holds a golden goddess wearing a falcon-feather cloak and a shining gold and amber necklace. Her eyes are stunningly clear. Her necklace gleams in the light, glowing at her throat. She rides towards you. You feel a wave of her energy as passion, love and boldness.

Allow her to come to you and sweep you up into her chariot as you travel across the sky together. Feel the thrill of the journey with her. Let go of any anxiety or fear and just be open to the feeling of freedom.

She places an amber pendant around your neck. Feel the weight of it at your throat. She looks into your eyes with her direct gaze and transmits an unspoken knowledge. Know that you have been blessed by Freya in this exchange.

She gently sweeps you out of the chariot and rides back into the sky.

Place your hands very lightly at your throat and say, "This blessing is received. May it vest me with divine timing, mercy, protection and grace. So be it."

When you are ready, simply open your eyes.

You may wish to sleep with the amber mandala under your pillow for the coming evening, to help integrate your blessing, which will apply to whatever part of your journey is most in need of Freya's protection, strength and passion.

13.

MAYA (VEILING)
RUBY AURA QUARTZ (PRESENCE)

MANIFESTING THROUGH REALITY

She is the cosmic artist, the storyteller, creating tales on the grandest scale. She creates the roles and casts the souls who can best learn from those passing identities, but now and then, when grace descends, she pulls back the curtain and reveals the truth. Reality peeps out from behind the sacred theatre of the world and life itself is seen without filter or veil, in shocking, beautiful glory.

MAYA (VEILING)

When I first began serious explorations of the metaphysical world as a young woman this lifetime, I was passionate about applying what I was learning at a practical level through my life decisions. This approach to life was received with mixed responses from those around me. When some of my family members became fearful that I was stepping out of their world and into a world they couldn't understand and hadn't really experienced for themselves, they would sometimes respond by becoming dismissive or angry, masking their fear, I believe. They would demand that I "come back down to the real world."

Being rather stubborn and single-minded, I didn't for a moment consider that I could forget what I knew and pretend I lived in the world they believed was real. With a healthy sense of irony, I also realised that the worlds I was seeking to become conscious of, and to live consciously in connection with, were far more real than what people mistakenly referred to as the 'real world' anyway.

In the spiritual traditions of India, Maya is the goddess and the phrase used to describe spiritual delusion. Maya has been taken to mean 'illusion' in the modern Western world. However, this is not the most accurate translation and has actually caused some difficulties in being able to work with Maya in a healthy, loving and nourishing way.

When I was first contemplating the nature of Maya, it was along the lines of 'this table is not real, it is made of energy.' Now that may be true at one level. Essentially, the physical forms in the world are energy vibrating at a level of density in which they appear to be solid. Yet, that isn't really the heart of the Divine Feminine teachings of mother Maya.

It wasn't until I began really working with greater awareness of the false light, mentioned earlier on it this book, that I began to understand Maya in a more meaningful way. The false light might appear to be spiritual but is in fact turning away from the world and chasing fantasies without any view towards grounding them in the earthly world where they are needed. That false light can manifest itself in excessive spiritual practice, as much as in other addictions, including perfectionism. This teaching came to my awareness in a series of terrifying dreams of psychopathic assassins that were determined to murder me.

Through these dreams I was confronting the terrifying parts of my own psyche that were not connected to or wanting to serve life. A part of me held a murderous, psychopathic attitude towards myself and my life, but as it was so deeply hidden from my conscious awareness I could only sense it through my dream life. It took me several years to understand those dreams and what they were actually teaching me.

The two years of my explorations was spent growing strong enough within my heart to actually be able to contain and release my feelings of intense terror, and not have to shut off from them because they were too much, thereby pushing them back into my body again. That series of dreams and interactions, whereby I experienced great terror over a period of years, helped me learn how to deal with it. Although I certainly didn't feel like I was doing any learning at first. I just felt overwhelmed by an intense mix of fear and horror, and I couldn't do anything with it apart from bear as much of it as I could. When it became too much, I forced myself to abruptly wake up from the dream. Archangel Michael, whom we met in *Crystal Angels 444*, was with me in those dreams. I mentioned a particularly powerful example of his divine protection in Chapter One of that book, but there were also times when he would simply stand by and urge me to fight off the forces for myself, which is ultimately what I needed to learn how to do – if only to realise that I (and anyone else who wishes to overcome fear) am quite able to do. Sometimes we have to go through the process and learn that for ourselves. Of course, we are lovingly supported by the spiritual worlds until we are ready to be in our own power completely. There will be times when the Divine steps in on our behalf for protection, and that is perfectly fine and healthy.

What was happening at a deeper level only became clear to me years on, when I was coming towards some degree of mastery in that challenging process. I was actually learning how to handle intense fear without shutting off from it but by allowing it to be fully felt, witnessed, and responded to with compassion. In working with my dreams and processed their messages, symbols and feelings in my journals as much as I could. Over time the fear was released and I became more able to deal with the next level of teaching present in those dreams.

When I was no longer cowering in fear from those parts of me that were anti-life, I could remain present and learn something about how and why they existed within me as well as how to deal with them constructively. At first I couldn't relate to the idea the psychopathic energies were operating within me, as part of me. As a healer on a path of consciousness, I did accept that I had a destructive and negative side that could unconsciously undermine me, or even others at times. However, vile, destructive, violent and cruel energy that created absolute atrocities was not something I knew how to find consciously within myself. The dreams brought it to my awareness and taught me that this was the part of me that fed on false light. It was completely disinterested in the wisdom of nature, in the limitations of the body, in patience, seasons and cycles, surrender and trust, relationships or connection. It didn't care about life in the least. This psychopathic energy was like a crazed, brilliant, fierce, intelligent lunatic on a drug-induced high without mercy or compassion, as relentless as some deranged Energizer Bunny filled with the energy and power, and absolutely devoid of heart, emotion or feeling. It was the mind disconnected from the heart. It was utterly and absolutely terrifying, and very, very real.

Sometimes dreams indicate extremes to get our attention and really bring a point home to our awareness. I certainly didn't feel I could ignore these figures in my dreams. I was waking up with panic attacks in the middle of the night from the sheer terror of encountering them. No, they were not to be ignored. It is said that God works in mysterious ways. The mystery of the divine instruction behind these dreams was that I learned a lot more about how to love life, what was real and what was not. This is the wisdom of Maya.

Those psychopathic energies were the part of me that wanted only light and wanted everything to be done yesterday. It didn't want the body and got annoyed if it was tired, hungry or needed anything that would disturb me from doing what my mind was intent on doing at the time. It was the part of me that eschewed needing a break or a holiday and felt as though I should be able to operate at high speed, high flying, high energy, high intensity constantly. It drove me to over-exercise, under-eat, run up sand hills, do boxing and gym training for hours on end six or seven days a week, and eventually saw me collapse in tiredness and chronic fatigue. I was doing all of this so I could love my body, but because I was unconscious of the psychopath at work within me, I was mercilessly flogging and killing my body bit by bit by creating excessive stress and negative health conditions under the guise of fitness and attractive appearance.

Eventually my body and unconscious mind fought against the destruction and urged me to eat, and to overeat, in an attempt to ground and block the relentless doing, pushing and striving of the psychopathic self. All that self-directed aggression couldn't go unchecked. My being tried to balance it, but because I didn't understand what was going on at a conscious level, I just ended up at war with myself rotating diet and over-exercise with overeating and barely being able to move while I overcame the exhaustion. Add to that cycle the criticism of those around me if I put on any weight, and the equally unsolicited comments when I lost weight. Apparently my weight was a topic very open to public scrutiny, even though I don't recall ever asking for anyone's opinion on the matter. All in all, I was angry, frustrated, tired of fighting myself, confused and wasting an enormous amount of physical, emotional and psychological energy to that pattern.

The dreams came to help me wake up and budge me out of a pattern that had dominated my emotional and psychological energy since the age of thirteen, perhaps longer. Two and a half decades on, I finally understood the need to let go of the struggle, the plans and the control, to get out of my mind, to listen to my body, and to balance activity and discipline with kindness and compassion. Over time this new approach brought results on a physical level, with my body changing, my wellbeing increasing and my naturally high energy levels being directed into more constructive channels such as creative and spiritual work. It took a long, long time and lots of patience. It took becoming conscious of that psychopathic tendency to seek perfection, absolute control and domination over my body and my life and being willing to challenge it from a place of love. Sometimes I would slip and fall back into old ways – all too easily – and at other times, I learned to further relax and be more loving. It was an extremely challenging wound to heal that was not just about my body, but my entire approach to life, spirituality and the earthly world.

As this happened, I began to see that the psychopathic nutcase in me was not just trying to kill off my body, but my spiritual growth as well. It was so devilishly clever and intelligent that it took me some time to see it and to realise that despite its subtlety, it was very, very powerful. If it was allowed to take root, I would fail to manifest my life path and to really help people in the way they needed to be helped. I could still become well known and successful by physical world standards even with that psychopathic energy operating within me – there are plenty of people who fit into that category. But, I wouldn't be able to get to the real grit of what I was supposed to be doing on this planet at this time if I didn't go through this particular spiritual learning.

The sneaky spiritual sabotage that this part of me tried to set in motion was based on a belief that the physical world wasn't real, but illusion. This distorted understanding of Maya held that only the spiritual was real. It meant that all the struggle and suffering in the world was a delusion, and therefore it didn't mean anything because one day people would wake up and realise only the light of the Divine was real and all the physical world stuff was some kind of fakery.

In the chapter on St Germain and the Violet Flame in *Crystal Masters 333*, I talk about healthy transcendence and when it becomes unhealthy. The sneaky spiritual sabotage of the psychopathic consciousness within me – within all of us – wanted to move me into unhealthy transcendence, so that I turned away from the world in the believe that only the light mattered and all else was merely distraction. That teaching supports the notion that those on the spiritual path don't really need to do anything in the world to change it, because it isn't real anyway. So we can just withdraw from what is going on, and move into the light towards enlightenment.

These are the workings of the false forces of light. They are especially insidious because they seem so innocent on the surface of things. They can be soothing as it is much easier not to engage with what is happening on our planet and the struggles going on in the hearts of people if they aren't real anyway. These were the dream killers that wanted to kill my body. They wanted me to forget about having anything to do with this physical world and to retreat into the world of false light, believing it was the end of the path. It wasn't the end at all, but a pitfall to avoid on the greater path!

The lure into false light is sort of like a spiritual anorexia. If it is allowed to take hold it slowly starves the soul of real, embodied experience, and the ability to grow through life which are the very things that lead us to enlightenment, divine power, compassion and the genuine ability to help others on the path. I believe that those who actually go through a physical experience of anorexia are learning how to deal with this false light syndrome, and those that go through binge or overeating are unconsciously trying to counteract a false light addiction and, in some way, to stay grounded. There are more conscious and healthy ways to deal with this sickness in our culture, but eating disorders are often a first response to the illness and its effect on particular individuals who are here to help heal it.

As we become more powerful, more intelligent and more aware of the tricks of the false light, we can outmanoeuvre it. This is how we get a voice and are able to use it. Otherwise, no matter how much talent and potential we may have within us, or how much love lies in our hearts, we are powerless to support the divine awakening happening on this planet.

Some of you will not relate to this as much because you will already be quite an earthy type in that you are grounded, connected to the physical world and wanting to reach for the light. Part of the reason you were drawn to this book will be because you have already sensed that the Divine Feminine is the bridge between the body and the light. Others of you, especially those who consider yourselves to be star children (*Crystal Stars 11.11* is especially for you) with a natural tendency to feel more comfortable in the non-physical worlds, and a feeling that the earthly world is rather foreign, difficult to navigate and be present to, may relate more to lure of the false light I have been explaining, which is essentially the 'shadow' of the light bearer. It will also be why you were drawn to this book – to healthily bridge that light with the body, because you certainly don't want to sacrifice your connection to the light in order to be here in the physical world. No matter whether we are more earthly and learning to become sensitive to spiritual energies, or more ethereal and learning how to become embodied, our ultimate goal for spiritual progress is the same – to discern true light from false and unite that true light with the body.

It was with some horror that I began to realise I had accepted some of the teachings of the dark side of the light as truth, such as that life in the physical world is a distraction to be overcome or at best a school to be used for learning and not worth much else. I also realised that by invoking some rather dramatic and intense emotional states, my dreams were helping me to wake up and come to my senses. I was being invited to become far more present to how I was living, or not really living, as the case was at the time.

Throughout that stage in my life, I had moments where I craved to be free of the constant struggle within myself. I didn't know if it would ever end. I couldn't change it on my own because I didn't know how. I needed to be guided blind through whatever process was necessary to heal.

Sometimes we sleep so soundly that we cannot be jolted by quiet invitations to wake up. We actually need more powerful prompts to move us along. They don't feel good at the time but they are what is needed to break free of whatever has held us in an invisible but intractable, regressive grip.

I still remember the drama of my mother trying to wake my brother up for school. He had an extraordinary ability to sleep through anything, including my mother's increasingly frenzied nagging. Until one day, she simply filled up a bucket of water, went into his room and tipped it straight over his head! It had the desired effect and got him out of bed. Additionally, I don't remember there being quite as much drama in the mornings afterwards.

Sometimes we need the equivalent of a bucket of cold water over our heads to jolt us out the comfortable, unconscious desire to remain who and where we are. So out of compassion, our higher self will evoke a crisis that we cannot avoid by retreating into our minds to really pull us into presence.

I was fortunate to have reached a stage in my path where I understood the power and authentic reality of my dream life and had the ability to work with it consciously for personal growth. Had I ignored those dreams, the energy would have progressed until it was in the world of my waking life, increasing in intensity and possibly trauma, until I paid attention.

This is how divine messages work. They start of as a dangling carrot (perhaps as a dream or a heart-felt desire) and we can follow their lead, or we can ignore them until we get whacked with a stick! When we are in crisis or trauma, we are getting a wakeup call that is ferocious with compassion. We have already contemplated the notion of ferocious compassion in the chapters on Kali and even Tara, and I will speak about it further in the chapter on Durga, but for now, you can know that whatever is happening in your life or your body is not a punishment, but a desperate call to truth and reality. Sometimes we just need a push rather than an invitation. It is mother Maya, in her own inimitable way, seeking to set you free through her initiation process, also known as life.

Her initiation process and the freedom it ultimately bestows, brings us to a state of intensity and awe that is unlike anything we could cook up for ourselves by believing in our own stories, emotional dramas or suffering. You see, the stories we participate in, are not the reality. What we experience through reactions to life is not the real stuff. Life is real. What is happening is real. Our responses to it – when they are conditioned by unresolved past pain – are not a reality. Mind you, our reactions are not to be dismissed, but honoured and worked through so as they can be healed and released so that a more immediate, spontaneous responsiveness to life can take place.

When rushing towards what we think is spiritual involves denying the body and the world or labelling it all as ego, we are being seduced by false light. All that physical stuff is *real*. It is the Divine Mother living, sitting, dancing, breathing and being, right before us. As us! She is everywhere. If you want to see God you only have to open your eyes and look. I am experiencing a rush of powerful emotion as I write this. Her body is right there in front of me, as the tree. She is my body. She is living and breathing as my furry feline companion, which is how she comes to me with comfort and reminders to play. She is the soothing music coming out of my stereo and the wind that is bathing Sydney in unexpected coolness on this summer's day. The delusion is unconsciousness vision that sees the tree as just a tree, a cat as just a cat, or at a darker level believing those things aren't real but nothing more than distractions from the real divinity.

Maya is leading us into reality via her intricate web of spiritual initiation through life experience. Reality happens behind all the mind-stuff that we project on to life. Maya leads us to the ability to put our scripted reactions to life to rest as each one is a result of unresolved pain from this or other lifetimes. As we accept our life experiences and are guided through healing, we are eventually able to be present, spontaneous and bear witness to life as it is. Rather than reacting, we can receive. Suddenly, what we might have once believed was a distraction from the spiritual path shows itself to be divinity incarnate. It can be so unexpectedly shocking! Startling! As well as mesmerising, mysterious, utterly confounding, absolutely hilarious, cheeky and erotic all at once.

In *Crystal Angels 444* I spoke about seeing God in a dog on the street and of how powerful the moment was for me. I expect it was oddly amusing to outside observers, as I stood dumbstruck in the middle of the street, looking at a small, black dog and seeing God. It was as though he had flashed himself at me from some cosmic trench coat, grinned cheekily and swiftly transformed himself back into an ordinary dog on an ordinary street on that ordinary afternoon.

This is the gift that Maya brings to us, if we are willing to take her journey. Her web of life experience, delicately, violently, compassionately and thoroughly denudes us of the veils of ignorance and the mistaken or partial belief systems that would prevent us from realising the divine all around and within us.

This is the gift that the psychopathic obsession with perfection tried to make sure I would never gain. The more energy I was seduced into expending in my constant battle against life, the more distance I was putting between myself and the realisation of what was right in front of me, waiting to be discovered! The real, living, breathing, spiritual being that is God hides behind scanty veils, and when we learn to accept life and work with it for healing, we will catch the feisty, mother Maya in the midst of removing those veils, layer by layer, before our eyes.

So whilst our projections and beliefs about the world can be brought to consciousness and worked through for healing, when we are blessed with those moments where we experience God directly, there is just ecstasy. We prepared for such moments over the course of many lifetimes. Sages, saints and other spiritual masters know this. When you strip away the layers of beliefs and reactions, life isn't revealed to be nothing more than illusion. Life shows itself to be the Divine in action. Beneath the veils there is only the Divine there and it is love. These aren't just words. It is a real, living experience. The human response to divine love is utter bliss. It is an ecstatic, rapturous emotion that makes us blubber like fools or drift into utter serenity and satisfied fulfilment. We don't have to reach for that response, when we can receive divinity, it just happens and in those moments we want for nothing. When we are experiencing the Divine we are absolutely complete and whole. I have not experienced anything I can even begin to compare it to – it would be like trying to illuminate the sun with a candle.

However, there is another reaction to this knowledge and experience of embodied divinity. It is one that took me by surprise at first. I had to get my head around the fact that there really are souls in bodies, animals, nature and plants. Of course, that is obvious, but I didn't just think of it intellectually, I began to feel the reality of it in my bones. There are beings who are living and dying. There are people who are blessed with so much, but toss it away. There are people who create magic and extraordinary gifts for the world heart, out of apparently limited circumstances through a wealth of inner resourcefulness. These things are real. They are not fake, illusion nor delusion.

When one has a moment of this realisation, life itself leaves us utterly gobsmacked. We could be standing on the most ordinary street, on the most ordinary day, at one apparently ordinary moment, and be rooted to the ground amidst a dizzying array of the most outlandish, flamboyant, extraordinary living artwork! And it will be temporary and swept away, only to become something else entirely. However, in that moment we take in life around us to the extent that we can, because even just taking in the entire reality of a bug on a leaf would mean completely taking in God, the Divine, the Goddess and all of the reality of the creator which is in every blade of grass, every human being and every spinning galaxy. Often the only intelligent response to such an intense, over the top moment is to stand like a bumbling awe-struck fool and let your brain feel completely scrambled, as you grin stupidly and feel like you are being shown a most wondrous secret, hidden in plain sight.

I was once lying on my bed, reading when my large, exceptionally fluffy and puffy, marmalade cat leapt up on the bed and stared at me. As I watched him, I felt the layers of Maya stripped away and I just stared at him, transfixed. I cannot really explain what I felt, but I was so deeply moved. I felt a combination of horror at how this living emanation of the Divine would be lost through death at some stage, reverence for the divine aliveness of this creature and how the Divine Mother didn't just create him, but lived as him, and the mind-boggling extraordinariness of divine creation as a phenomenon itself. The Divine created itself, lived and destroyed itself, to be born again in other form. In the process the experience of loss, grief, devastation, passionate love, deep attachment and yearning, were borne by the Divine, so that this grand creation could manifest itself.

In moments like that, life feels so very raw, fragile, unstoppably powerful and precious. I don't claim to understand any of it, but am merely a witness to it and a participant in it, to the extent that my brain and nervous system can handle. The realisation that the Divine Feminine is not only the creator, but also present in the experience of the creation, living as each one of us, dazzled me. She is totally and utterly within all of life – she cries when we do, she loves when we do, she suffers when we do, she goes through death when we do, and is reborn again and again.

The more we are plugged into this reality, the more the entire experience of it, becomes our entire experience. When the earth is poisoned, we feel poisoned. When she is loved and healed, so too do we feel love and healing. When her species evolve we feel the excitement of new life. When a species becomes extinct, we feel the grief of loss. Throughout our own lives, we are living her and she is living us. That is reality. That is the rawness and realness of life where Maya dances her initiating, unveiling dance.

The Flammarion Engraving, an anonymous image first published in France in 1888, features a man climbing across the world. The Sun shines above the Earth and the man's body is captured within a bubble that wraps around the world. Only his head, his right hand, and the top of the staff he holds in his left hand, have popped through the bubble with much effort. It looks as though he is gasping for a breath, which he can finally obtain on the other side.

This bubble is the thick veil cast by our beliefs and stories that are based on unresolved issues. It is the veil that prevents our immediate and raw experience of life from being one of living divinity. From the inside of the veil, it seems as though the edge of our belief is the edge of the world. As we break through our known reality, there can be moments when we feel like we are going to break through into nothing and quite possibly cease to exist at all. This is resistance to breaking free from reactions and moving into spontaneous receptive responsiveness to life. What if I am not safe? What if something happens I don't like? What if I don't know what to do? What if I end up alone? Or poor? Or lost? That bubble can remain impenetrable for a long, long time.

The testing of Maya brings us closer to breaking through that bubble. She crafts means and life tests. We can continue to indulge our beliefs and cling to them for all their worth (often clinging to them as though they are a worth a lot more than they actually are). In time, we may choose differently. Through faith, personal healing, surrender, trust, sheer defiance and daring, we might choose to open up to what is presented to us and view it with a fresh perspective that will challenge our typical responses. Through personal healing work, we might dare to lie our past pain to rest and dare to imagine there could be something else – even if we don't know what it is yet. When we are more willing to meet life like a child, without preconditioned views and with a readiness to be shown something other than what we believe, then we will see what *actually* is.

However, this initiation is not easily taken. Maya is a relentless taskmaster and so she should be. After all, through her grace we come to the revelation of naked divinity, absolute reality unveiled. In taking her initiation and increasingly opening up to direct living, without the veil of preconditioned reactions, there can be great fear. Maya asks us to let go of a certain familiarity and comfort that we might have used to feel safe in the past. Letting go of what we know is rarely easy. It might not sound like much, but the fear of letting go of what we know is one of the most powerful gravities in the human mind. It can keep people stuck in realities, even when they know it's not doing them any good. There can be so much inner gravity that they cannot summon the strength needed to begin to nudge the edges of that reality, let alone poke a head through the thick, resistant membranes of belief holding it in place.

When you are strong and prepared enough to take the leap of faith into a more immediate relationship with life, you can look back and see the operation of Maya. On the other side, you can see the veil of beliefs, fears, doubts and stories that were used to insulate you within a relationship, a career or pattern of behaviour. You will realise that although the emotional, and belief patterns seemed real at the time, they were nothing more than the bubble we had to break through in order to live a different way.

Astrology teacher, Alan Oken, once described the way perspective changes as we grow spiritually. He said that an advanced spiritual student might realise that he was not the son his mother thinks he is, but actually a divine soul. His mother will continue to relate to him as a son, and even though he knows it is not the higher truth, he can keep his awareness of himself as an eternal soul and relate to his mother as a son, without necessarily believing in the same reality as his mother does.

The realisation of Maya doesn't prevent us from acting in the world, in having relationships, or working through various identities to fulfil our life mission. It actually empowers us to do so with awareness and greater freedom. We become capable of consciously working with the roles we play and to serve our soul path, rather than feeling defined, limited, trapped or victimised by them. This is the ultimate point of the veils of Maya. They push us to grow. It is a bit like spiritual resistance training. The thicker the obstructing veil, the more spiritual consciousness is required to dissolve it and open up our belief systems to create some space within our minds and emotional patterns so that we can push through them and gain a new perspective.

I sometimes compare this process to Superman moving from one planet to another. On his home planet, the gravitational force was so much more powerful than on Earth that he was considered to be of quite ordinary strength. However, when he moved to

Earth with its lower gravitational field, his powers were measurably more impressive. If he had always been of Earth, he would not have developed the strength to move through the gravity of his home planet. In going through that experience, he was able to gain extra strength to serve Earth in far more powerful way.

So it is for those of us on the spiritual path. We are often 'dropped' deep into a consciousness that is weighed down with heavy veils of Maya. Underneath the emotional gravity, the Divine is hidden as if cloaked in Maya's veils. Our divine nature might be mostly forgotten, as we try to break thick layers of fear, anxiety and ignorance. We might sense something isn't right, but not be strong enough to break free of the low-vibration collective belief systems in place and for a time we will need to retreat to the light inside ourselves to show us truth and sustain us. This is the beginning of our journey. Eventually we will have enough trust in that inner light to want to expand it so it is not only alight within us, but shining out into the world as well. We will want others to experience life beyond the veil of fear too.

So we go about growing the light within until it is strong enough to loosen the threads of the veils. The light will begin to pierce through the veil of fear. We then fall under the spell of fear less often. Fear is less constant as it becomes less convincing as a way of life, and so we get stronger and more able to remain centred in love. We recognise the veil of fear, but the light of truth burns a tear in it and we can pop our heads through. Fear exists but we are no longer suffocated by it. Beyond the veil, we start to see new vistas and other ways of living. Perhaps we see other people that are already living that way, too. We are inspired. It is possible! We gain strength and optimism. Our light grows stronger, tearing a bigger rent in the veil of Maya. She might give it a little rip on her side too, to help us along. We push through a bit more. Our hands get through next. We are able to operate in the world in a way that is not dampened and diminished by fear. We give and receive with love and trust. And so the process continues.

When you have been granted an unveiling by mother Maya, you will know without a doubt. Your perspective changes completely. Your life may change considerably, as previously inaccessible door begin to open. You will benefit from her grace, but will have done plenty of work to become a ready vessel for that grace. It is not always easy. Penetrating the veils of Maya is the key to spiritual liberation. All the healing and manifestation work done with the other goddesses and light beings leads towards this work, and helps us to shed conditioning and connect to our innate spiritual wildness. It is the turning of the key to spiritual freedom. So it's heavy going sometimes.

Even when we understand it, it doesn't become easier, we are just more aware of the task required of us. I have had moments where all I could do was sigh at the realisation of what I was attempting to break through in order to grow. Fortunately, the healing work that we do throughout this entire book series grows the light within so as you are able to tear bigger holes in the veils placed between ourselves and our immediate experience of the Divine.

There is always a descent of grace when needed. We have to do our bit, but when we are at the edge of what we can accomplish by our own efforts, the hand of the Divine reaches down, as if from Heaven, and pushes up, as if from the earth, to help us rise beyond our struggles. By that stage we are at such a level of trust (and sometimes fatigue from our exertions on the path!) that we willingly receive the assistance of the Divine. Then, great leaps and accelerations are often possible in ways that were not available to us before.

That hand of grace will find its way to us at the right time and in the right way. It will come to us through reading a book or oracle deck that fills our hearts and shifts the way we have been. Or it will come through a teacher who has enough light to help ignite yours, so that you can shift a stuck perception once and for all. Perhaps, a life circumstance might lighten your load and free you from what held you back in some key area or other. It might take place so subtly that you are not actually conscious of what is happening. However, the effect is not subtle. You will feel it when Maya has withdrawn her veil from your face. The world looks completely different. You know it is the same world that was always there but you see it from a place of spiritual truth and the view is extraordinary.

Grace will never prevent our growth by taking away the work we need to do to learn. It isn't an overprotective mother! It just works to alleviate unnecessary struggle. Pushing through Maya's veils requires heavy duty inner work, often over a long time, but even with the intervention of grace, what strength we gain! We can then help others because we are strong enough to stay in our truth, even in the face of fear and other collective beliefs. We have had to grow strong enough to pop our heads out of the bubble of mass consciousness, and in doing so, we have gained more insight, intelligence and empowerment to support others to do the same.

This is the gift and the challenge of Maya. As we grow, we don't see her as a foe, but as an initiator on the path who gives us the opportunity to become realised divine beings. We see her raw, wild, mysterious and unfathomable beauty as the true nature of the living goddess receiving the light of the Divine Masculine and manifesting this world as a result of their sacred union. As we see what is happening and pierce through the veils to witness their union, we feel awe, ecstasy and reverent presence for the incredible act of divine creation that is our world.

RUBY AURA QUARTZ (PRESENCE)

Ruby aura quartz, sometimes also called magenta aura, is a treated quartz, like aqua aura which we explored in connection with Mary Magdalene in Chapter Six of *Crystal Masters 333*. As I mentioned then, some healers like to work with treated quartz, while some prefer completely natural stones. I generally love to work with natural, untreated stones whenever possible, but there are some exceptions to this, such as quartz that has been bonded with high consciousness generating metals like silver, gold and platinum, the combination of which is how ruby aura quartz is created. The result is a bright, rich fuchsia coloured quartz that is partially transparent, partially opaque, with a high vibrational field and a strong emanation of the Divine Feminine. It is a beautiful stone to work with and even in small pieces it has a powerful presence.

For those who feel a strong lure to the spiritual light that is outside of form (as the genuine eternal light of the Divine Masculine or the false light of perfectionism) and may consequently have difficulty honouring our bodies and the earth with much enthusiasm, this crystal enchants us to fall in love with the divine creation of form. It supports us in sensing and seeing beyond the veils of Maya that may have us believing that God is in the sky and that our bodies, emotions and sexuality are distractions at best or sinful at worst. Ruby aura helps to bring our awareness into our bodies with reverence, so that we can build spiritual presence and light within, burn through the veils of Maya and begin to directly experience divine reality. It prepares us to receive the Divine as an immediate experience. For those that want to speak consciously with the Divine in its many forms of higher guidance, angels, masters, God and Goddesses, ruby aura is an excellent support.

The gold, silver and platinum energies in ruby aura quartz bring the Divine Masculine and Divine Feminine together through unconditional love and light. The result is a stone that supports genuine tantra of the soul, which brings together light (Divine Masculine) and form (Divine Feminine) to create a sacred divine child (the soul). It supports us in experiencing life as a living union of God and Goddess so as we can start to see and feel the Divine everywhere, even in the most unlikely situations, people or events.

As we begin to experience the non-manifest, eternal spiritual light and the manifest world as one, the duality in our consciousness ceases to operate in the same way. Instead of judging things as good and bad, desirable and undesirable, we start to just experience and honour life as the divine path unfolding.

This doesn't suddenly mean that we no longer have ordinary moments. Of course we do! But we also have extraordinary peace in those ordinary moments, as well as the extraordinary moments that shake us up into new worlds of understanding and experience. Instead of our divine parents living in separate houses, they are happily and passionately living together, in a home of increasing harmony and light. That home is our body radiantly united with the indwelling soul, as if an inner light switch was flicked on within every cell of the body. We talk more about that process in the chapter on Mary Magdalene in *Crystal Masters 333*.

Working with Ruby Aura brings the gift of presence that is truly precious. It brings us to life. If we have a tendency to live in our heads because we don't get enough time to exercise or be in nature, or we tend to analyse rather than an 'experience first, understand it later' kind of person, then the gift of presence can feel like the beautiful thawing out of our inner self. No longer frozen in old, restrictive patterns, we can breathe, move and be free, from a place of inner warmth and unconditional love.

Ruby aura warms and opens the heart and the base chakra, allowing us to feel more connected to our bodies in acceptance and appreciation, rather than judgment, shame, criticism or fear. When the base chakra and the heart chakra have an open exchange of energy, we can love and appreciate the physical world and our life within it, and bring more love into the world.

You may find this stone rather stimulating on a physical level and might prefer to work with it in the morning or the middle of the day, unless you are a shift worker or about to go out and paint the town ruby red! It works on healing the legs and feet, the colon, the digestive system and the immune system. It helps repair the body on physical, energetic and emotional levels following any kind of abusive or toxic relationship. It supports one in 'starting again' with more love, self-worth and trust.

As an alchemical stone, born of human and Mother Nature's hands, it aids reconciliation, unification and helps humanity work constructively with nature for the greater good. That in itself is so very healing. We want to be aware of the suffering on our planet, but we don't want to fall into the trap of despair. It can be such a fine line, but if we take on guilt, shame and horror to the point that we collapse under the weight of it, we won't have the energy to actually make conscious changes in our lives.

Those changes might include researching brands and deciding whom you want to purchase from, voting with your wallet, so to speak. I recently had an experience of this quite by accident when I was thinking of purchasing from a large online clothing seller. However, when I Googled for the web address, I somehow ended up with an article on the store's internal marketing plan. It was a short article and intrigued, I quickly read it and learned enough about the company to realise I did not want to support what they stood for and how they went about it. Their internal marketing approach was extremely aggressive with talk of "annihilating the competition" and "dominating the industry." They used the word 'blitzkrieg' which is a term used to describe a technique of warfare. I was so put off by their energy and approach that I decided not to support them with my wallet. I don't reject their right to choose how they want to conduct business, but I maintain my right not to support their efforts!

If we are big souls, we can unconsciously lend a lot of power to people, places, situations and companies with our support – even if we don't consciously intend to. If this is not for the greater good, we'll be given intuitions, signs and nudges from the Divine to let go, step away from or actively disengage from further conscious involvement with particular companies or people. I trust in this and don't need to understand it all, although there are cases like the above example where I do realise what was being shown to me and why. That company didn't just want business success for themselves, they wanted failure to everyone they considered to be competition. I have met people like this in the metaphysical profession. I see what it does and I don't wish to support it, or people who wish to act like that, with my own talents and energy. I once believed that my light would be a good idea anywhere, however, I have since learned that pouring energy into a situation will make it bigger, for better or worse. So, I have become more discerning about when I teach and with whom, not to mention where I shop and which causes I support.

I don't get all finicky and stressed about this. I just tend to trust my intuition and the nudges that I get from the Universe because more often than not, people reveal themselves and their level of consciousness pretty easily. We just have to be willing to be present enough to recognise it and then, with compassion, make a choice about whether throwing our energy into the mix is the best choice.

Working together with people who are best suited to the purpose is a great idea and it is extremely helpful on the path. You will feel as if things aren't quite right if you are working with people who are not well-suited to your light and it can cause more trouble than its worth. So, I encourage you to be discerning, but there is no need to become paralysed with indecision because you don't know all the details. Trust your gut rather than appearances. Ruby aura (and the Crystal Angel of Ruby Aura Quartz) will help you be present to your body so that you can recognise your feelings, intuitions and signs and know when and how to act on them instinctively.

There are people who want to do more than choose where they shop and what they purchase, and also want to give money to worthy causes. Sometimes we find out that the organisations promoting those causes don't support them, even indirectly, or that the 'good cause' provides a front for otherwise untenable behaviour. Andrew Harvey, a spiritual teacher who is very passionate about the divine mother and serving her with conscious action, has a website dedicated to genuine charities and causes that he has verified as being in integrity. If you search for 'Networks of Grace' on the internet, you will find the page and the works he has verified as 'karmically clean' which you can support if you need help finding somewhere to donate your money.

These kinds of action require energy. They also help us feel empowered and positive because we are engaging in the world through love and helping to generate a new field of consciousness through which a new emanation of divine creativity can be birthed. In this new emanation there is more care and connection between human beings and the natural world. It all starts with us, but for us to be able to do anything, we must first become present to what we feel and who we are. In realising that we are genuine divine beings, we can respond to our feelings with empowered action, rather than hopelessness or despair. Ruby aura quartz supports us in this process.

MANIFESTING THROUGH REALITY

Reality can be experienced as raw, wild and intense, but it can also be sweet, responsive, loving and tender. I have found that manifestation through the connection to reality can be exceptionally quick. Making a direct connection to reality – and even just our intention to do so – is like placing a direct call to the head of operations! So, this method bypasses the customer service operators who redirect our call to five different people and then inadvertently disconnect it before we say more than two words and gets us straight to the source that can help. Go straight to this source, to the reality of the Divine beyond fear, doubt or anxiety, is a bold move. It requires us to be daring enough to believe that the Divine wants to take our call (it does!) and that we can send out such a clear intention. Holding that intention is like having all the fluff and corrosion removed from the wiring system that links us into the divine creative field. So, the synapses fire super-efficiently and we are able to draw what we need to us with astounding precision, perfect timing and often a healthy dose of divine humour and loving kindness.

When we manifest with the intention of forging an immediate connection to reality, we are saying to the Universe, "Show me the truth and the way forward. I am more willing to receive you than to stay stuck in my fearful little world of self-imposed and unnecessarily limiting belief systems. I want out! Show me the way of your genuine reality, with mercy and grace!"

When I have done this, it was usually with a healthy dose of trepidation because it really does work and has rarely responded subtlety whether I was manifesting for the smallest or the most significant matters in my life. The answers are not always what I want, but once I receive them, I deal with it and it works out just fine that way. At other times, the answers are just what I wanted to hear and sometimes this is harder for me to believe. I must have a hidden pessimist lurking in the shadows of my optimistic nature! Perhaps I just know how easy it is to hear what you want to hear. Either way, the answers come. Surrendering control and inviting the absolute reality to cut through any attachments or fears we have can seem equally exhilarating and scary, but it is the quickest route to resolution. If other methods of approaching healing manifestation aren't quite getting the job done quickly enough, then this is the way to go.

Please remember that when you are emerging into reality, there will be moments when you, or the people around you, wonder if you are going crazy. One of the paradoxes of the divine path is that the saner you become, the more likely you are going to question your sanity. This is healthy and natural. You might worry about it at the time, but it is best not to. The generally accepted belief systems of mainstream culture are the insanity. To assume that anyone can behave in isolation, as a narcissistic spoilt child, demanding that the world bow to his or her personal whims is utterly ridiculous. To believe that generating a culture of dominance, fear and dissociation is going to make us safe or contribute to the abundance of the world and the flourishing of the human soul is absolutely nuts! As you break out of these ways of being, people around you will question you. You will question yourself. That is a sign that you are coming out of your mind, and into your heart. Trust it. You'll see as you do that there will be others like you, who are taking the journey, and warmly welcome you to join them. In the real, 'real world'!

HEALING PROCESS

If you have a tendency to get caught up in what you think is (or is not) possible, are disheartened by apparent failures to manifest or are uncertain about whether you should even attempt a new project, then you will need help to cut through the veils of Maya and go straight for clear guidance. If you simply want to get out of your mind and into your heart, this healing process is for you too.

The Process

Have your mandala and/or crystal with you. Find a place where you can have some privacy and turn off your phone.

Stand or sit so that you are aware of your feet and legs as much as possible. This might mean that you move your toes and feet for a few moments.

Relax but feel grounded and connected to your legs and feet, which will keep you alert.

Breathe in and out for at least eight breaths or however long feels good.

Then imagine that the energy in your head can become softer and more diffuse, almost like it can evaporate outwards.

See all the energy from your head travel deep within, spiralling down, from left to right, towards the base of your spine, legs and feet. Like a gentle descent of spirit it moves through your feet and connects you to the earth energy beneath you. If you can, feel that your feet are beautiful. Send love and gratitude to your feet. Imagine you can smile at them!

When you are ready say the following, "I call upon the Divine Mother Maya, who loves unconditionally. I honour your incredible power; please bless me with grace. Beloved one, please surrender me into the light of wise perception. Please help me see what is real through merciful compassion and divine loving wisdom. It is safe for me to surrender my point of view and my past beliefs. What has been does not have to continue to be. It is safe for me to open up and invite in reality. May I perceive, know, and trust in what is real. May this discovery be one of merciful realisation, so that I may serve the divine reality with love, empowerment and passionate presence. I call upon the vibration of 888. May the manifesting power of the Divine Feminine, who triumphs over all illusion, shine her loving presence through me, without obstacle. Through her compassionate mercy and divine loving grace, so be it."

Imagine a rich, vibrant, white light, dappled with electric, violet light, flickers and crackles all around you. It may feel buzzing, tingly, cool or hot. It dissolves stubborn, sticky, glue-like matter inside of your head, your body and all the way down to your feet. It is moving swiftly, and expands until it is fizzing and dissolving stuck energy around you too. Feel your entire energy field flowing more freely.

Stay with this process for at least eight breaths in and out. Don't try to control it. Just be with it.

When you are ready, say the following, "I call upon the Crystal Angel of Ruby Aura

Quartz, of Quartz, Platinum, Gold and Silver. Restore this body, mind and energy field. Fill me with your loving presence and healing magenta light so that I may be empowered to engage with reality, from a place of loving awe and divinely inspired action. So be it!"

Imagine that all around you, from within the earth, rays of rich ruby red and deep, magenta pink light fan up and shimmer with flecks of precious gold, silver and platinum.

Imagine that you can move or dance through them. Do this in your mind's eye or actually get up and move about physically. Let yourself be bathed in this healing light.

Stay with this process for at least eight breaths in and out. Don't try to control it. Just be with it.

When you are ready, say the following, "I surrender my belief in what has been and in the way I have tried to impose myself upon the world. I now allow my true path to be revealed, and I am open to know, witness and experience divinity, in its glory and truth, according to grace, mercy and compassionate protection. May I be empowered to step out of fearful ignorance again and again, and to step more deeply into the ecstasy of divine reality."

If you have a particular issue that you want to have resolved through divine wisdom, ask for help with that issue now. Otherwise just finish up by saying, "So be it."

Rest for several moments and when you are ready, simply open your eyes.

You may expect to feel challenged or changed in the weeks following this exercise. Stay true to your heart and know that no matter how rocky things may be, if you don't feel oriented or are unable to work with your old belief systems anymore, it is a good sign that you are allowing yourself to be moved by a greater reality than what you once held on to. Trust in the part of you that assures you everything is going to be alright. Repeat the above process within three weeks if you feel you need the additional support and healing.

14.

PERSEPHONE (VIRGIN)
RUBY (POTENCY)

MANIFESTING THROUGH MATURITY

She, the Queen of the Underworld, with heart of pure light, body of passionate love, able to live and love in the world of darkness below and the world of light above. She reconciles the opposites and is seated in the centre. She brings us the gift of maturity, leading to integration.

PERSEPHONE (VIRGIN)

In colloquial terms, the term 'virgin' is used to describe a person who has not consummated a sexual relationship, however, it is a term that carries a more profound definition on a psychological level. Sexuality has emotional, psychological and spiritual aspects as well as a physical one. Virginity is not about whether or not we are touched on those levels, but actually whether we are capable of being impacted upon, permeated and penetrated by another, without obscuring our experience of our own essential being. It is a divine paradox – can we be our essentially eternal and unchanging selves, while we are constantly evolving and growing.

Contrary to popular understanding, the virgin in our psyche does not pull back from life experiences, sexual or otherwise. This part of us is capable of sustaining a deep and honest connection with all of life – even the darker aspects of our human existence – while retaining a fundamental innocence and purity. This is not lack of experience, but the innocence that comes from understanding that at your heart, you are a pure being and nothing can change that. Any shame or guilt you may feel, are responses to experiences and something to be worked through, but are not an expression of who you truthfully are.

The recognition of this innocence and purity deep within us, allows us to truly live without fear of being tainted. If you are a sensitive or receptive person by nature, this is very important for you to realise. When we understand the purity within cannot be taken from us, we can find greater peace in being alive. This will be especially true if you have encountered abuse in your life in any way, or have found yourself acting in abusive ways towards others. Purity is not determined by whether or not we have sex or have opened up to life in other ways. It is not amplified by avoiding the darker experiences of life. The more we live and the more we grow spiritually, the more we eventually realise that all life experiences – the apparently good and the apparently bad – refine our awareness and distil the innate purity within. This allows purity to grow stronger and more obvious to ourselves and others.

It might seem strange, but it has been my experience that recognising and accepting the fundamental purity of our nature is one of the harder things for many people to do. Even in my own journey, realising my own purity of heart took many years to de-fragment. It was sort of 'stuck' over in the 'spiritual' part of my identity and the rest of me was all a bit too much to deal with. It took me decades of inner healing to be able to accept and integrate much more of myself, including my sexuality, as being part of the purity of my being. It was a process of integration, much of which was supported through the wisdom of Persephone.

I have a friend who is a beautiful man. He is talented, a bit wild and generally very accepting of me, although there have been times when he makes comments about me which I find rather curious. Sometimes I wonder if his comments are more about his own self, than me. Isn't that the way with all of us at times? Life mirrors something and we imagine it is the mirror (the person, the situation) rather than ourselves that is being witnessed. Anyway, one of his curious comments that relates to purity. He and I were meeting, with other friends, for a musical gathering. I was wearing a long white dress. I often wear white. Some years later, my Vedic astrologer told me it was a good colour for me to wear, so I guess there was some intuitive sense of it as being good for me. So, I turned up at my friend's house all in white, and when he opened the door he had quite a reaction. I smiled and he blurted out something along the lines that I was trying to convince him of something. I got his meaning instantly; he was referring to me being pure and in white. I didn't react to his comment because it didn't bother me in the slightest. I knew it was about him not being able to see and love the purity in him that I saw and loved in myself. He sometimes seemed to struggle to recognise it, but I could sense the purity within him clearly enough, even beneath his darker side, because it was who he was in truth. In that moment he acted as though I was trying to be something I was not. Even though he saw me as a wild goddess (he had told me as much and shared dreams that he had of me that indicated this) and yes, that is part of my being, but I also know it isn't incompatible with the pure childlike part of my nature either.

The notion of virginity in a psychological, spiritual and emotional sense is about being able to honour your purity, while our life experiences attend to the distillation of your 'self'. It is the self-possessed ability to know and hold yourself, so that the experiences of life or the opinions of others do not contaminate your sense of self. You never can be tainted, actually. To honour the fundamental purity of your being means that you recognise it is virgin – not out of absence of experience, but because experience is used to strengthen and reveal that self for all that it is – like the pressure upon coal that reveals a diamond. There is no tainting or distortion possible; there is only ever refinement and revelation. Anyone who has fully processed and resolved an experience of trauma that involved some deep shaming, such as sexual abuse or hate crimes based on gender, race or religion, will understand the freedom of virginity at a psychological and spiritual level. No matter what happens in life, you shall always be as 'you' as you ever were and always will be. Anything that happens to challenge that, no matter how damaging it may seem on the surface, it can be made to become nothing more than the pressure used to concentrate the diamond truth of your being, still pure, still intact and always to be so.

So much of the hate and anger in this world comes from a deeply wounded place of fear that you are somehow a bad person. Childhood abuse or trauma, far more widespread than we may be comfortable acknowledging, can shame and guilt a soul into this distorted sense of self from a very young age. The internal scars from abuse, whether from this or other lifetimes, can take time and considerable inner work to heal. I remember the moment, in my early twenties, when I had a breakthrough in my healing work. For such a significant moment, it was a relatively quiet and unassuming experience. Something just flicked in my brain and I had a profound thought, "There is nothing wrong with me!" That was the thought. I was standing on the street at Broadway, in Sydney's inner west, having just left my therapy session. There was pollution, chaos, noise and people everywhere. I was just waiting at the traffic lights to cross the road, and the thought popped into my head as a revelation. It was more than a thought; it was an actual realisation. It changed me. I felt relief and freedom, as an emotional weight lifted from my shoulders. My internal focus shifted from believing I had to be fixed, to realising that I just needed to sort out the externals of my nature (thoughts, emotional patterns and habits) so that the pure internal essence could shine through with less obstruction. That has been the focus of so much of my journey ever since.

As simple as it sounds, getting to that moment was hard. You can intellectually know you are a divine being but to get to a place of complete acceptance at an emotional level can be more challenging because it usually involves feeling and releasing layers of shame that have been dumped upon you and reinforced by your own interpretations of experience over the course of years – or lifetimes. There can be a lot there! Fortunately we don't have to go back to every experience we have ever had. We just need to be able to feel the feelings of shame as they arise through our life journey and realise that once such feelings come and go (which they will) we are still there. We haven't died, the world hasn't ended, and somehow that shame isn't actually who we are at all, because it has been felt and released, and we are still here.

It takes a lot of courage to go to that place and when you are at the cusp of a major breakthrough into accepting your purity, your virgin self, it can feel like you are risking profound rejection and abandonment. I have had the experience myself. During my years of intensive therapy, I had a moment sitting in my therapist's office when I wanted to express that I felt helpless. That was an emotional state that was extremely difficult for me to express back then. I hardly ever felt it consciously and was always telling myself I was in control instead. I felt that my therapist knew exactly what was going on with me, but she patiently waited as I wrestled with myself internally.

I wanted to tell her I felt dependent on her and was scared she might leave me. But, how could I admit to such a thing? I was raised to be independent and pushed myself to act as if I didn't need anybody. All I needed was spirit and myself, and if others couldn't be there for me, well that was okay because I would be alright without them anyway. So tapping into a feeling of helplessness and dependency as though I was a little child, instead of a grown woman, was quite a leap in the other direction. Or so I feared at the time.

As I tried to summon the courage not to shut off from these shameful feelings, I felt as though my throat was burning with hot metal liquid. I could hardly open my mouth to speak. Panic and fear clamped at my chest as the unresolved emotional trauma arose from my body and into my conscious awareness. The urge to speak and be emotionally free hit the wall of my defence mechanism to repress my need for others. I was fascinated and horrified at how physically difficult it was to just spit out the words and admit to my feelings.

When I finally did express myself it was quietly and tentatively. My therapist very kindly accepted my words without judgment and in that instant, I had another profound shift. It was okay to want people around, even to need them! This didn't make me weak, it just made me human. Feeling vulnerable in a relationship was okay too. It didn't actually mean that I was helpless without her, it was just a feeling. In learning how to be present with my feelings and give them a voice, I was another step closer to being able to understand what I needed in order to live a happier and healthier life. To get to that moment though! It was difficult.

I have seen clients in that position with me as their therapist. I have felt so much compassion as they tormented themselves with what they could hardly admit and were frightened to say aloud in case I ran from them in disgusted rejection. Sometimes I have wanted to shake them and say, "Spit it out! I already know what you are feeling and it's just fine!" And, perhaps, that reveals one of the reasons I chose not to continue my work as a psychotherapist!

I know how hard it is. In theory, recognising our purity is not a complex task, but very simple. In practice it can be an exceptionally painful and challenging journey. It is worth it though. There is a fundamental empowerment that comes from being able to recognise yourself as a pure being. We are far less likely to fall into power games, manipulations and other dysfunctional relationship patterns (at least, not for long!) when we accept our virgin nature. We can let stuff go more easily because we don't hold on to it out of false guilt, shame or unworthiness. We don't have to resist or fight against such games, they just no longer gain any traction with us. That is very liberating!

As we come to know our purity, others sense and respond to it – with attraction or repulsion. Inherent in the genuine recognition of our individual purity is that we also recognise the purity in all beings, even if others cannot accept it in themselves. In that sense, it isn't a personal discovery, but a human discovery. It doesn't mean we become blind to the wounds of others – or ourselves – and how they are being acted out, but we don't make them mean more than what they are. We will more clearly see who a person is in essence and what is just the unresolved stuff being playing out.

When we genuinely discover our own pure nature, we may attract darker energies to us as they are often drawn to light. However, this is not a cause for concern. I have shared teachings in this book so you will know how to deal with such matters from a restful and empowered place. If you find yourself in a situation that you don't feel equipped to deal with, help will always be provided. Simply request that the beings who love you unconditionally show you how to sort out the situation at hand and whatever additional information, support or guidance you need will come to you.

The journey to this purity happens through maturity – again challenging the notion that the young are innocent and as we get older we get sullied by life.

Persephone, also known as Kore, is an ancient Greek goddess. In the Roman cult, she was known as Proserpina. She brings us a powerful story of healing and growth. Her journey is one of innocence in the more typical definition of the word – lack of experience – and being opened up to other worlds through a great adventure (or trauma, depending on the interpretation of her myths). From that trauma or adventure, she matures. She transforms from an innocent, young girl to a queen of the world, serving the journey of souls in the darkest realms of existence and in the light.

All advanced spiritual aspirants will take this journey on the path in some form. Her stories relate to the development of the self which happens through growing up. Of course, this is different to simply getting older. It involves letting oneself become separated from the mother in the sense of outgrowing what one was raised in. That means breaking with limitations in consciousness from our family of origin, our culture, our religious upbringing, or our own sense of our place in the world. The more mature a soul becomes, the more likely it is to want to experience a great variety of life experiences. It is not interested in keeping the status quo intact to soothe the ego. It wants wholeness more than it wants comfort.

This can lead us into a rather interesting life. The people around us may not always understand our journey because it involves a departure from what we were raised with. A person raised by gypsy-like roaming adventurers might become stable and settled. A person raised by those that have lived within ten miles of one spot their whole lives might become a global wanderer. If they are challenging their original consciousness, that is. This does not mean we just go and do the opposite of what our family did, as some sort of token of our spiritual maturation process. It is less about what we appear to do and more about what is happening inside of us. It is about being able to question and grow beyond what we have learned.

As a child, natural curiosity abounds. To become mature requires access to the curious child within. Bringing together apparent opposites leads to integration which in turn brings maturity. Integration is the synthesis that happens when we take opposites (e.g. being 'grown up' and allowing the child within to flourish) and unite them into psychological and emotional coherence. If we don't do this, we'll have a splitting off of the parts of us. This leads to the overly responsible person who has a dreary life of adult obligation and then acts out as a child with temper tantrums or making 'out-of-character' choices in rampant spending or excessive drinking and partying when their child-self finally has enough of being denied and wildly erupts. The person may also lack the curiosity and the self-belief necessary for taking healthy risks and really living into their potential. This is not maturity, no matter how grown up the adult seems when they are functioning as the responsible self. Maturity brings together child and adult, so that life becomes more healthy, balanced and fulfilling. The curiosity of the child leads to questioning, yearning for experience and an openness in our nature through which life can reach into our being and stimulate growth. When that is united with the adult, we are empowered to believe in ourselves and take the actions necessary to respond to life and grow by taking responsibility for our actions and their consequences. This constantly leads us beyond what we know, into new terrain. You can age without really living, but those that are mature will be constantly learning, living and growing as if they were still children at heart.

As we mature, we are willing to encounter many experiences, relationships, jobs and emotional states. As we grow beyond the consciousness of our family of origin, we will end up in some unexpected terrain. This has certainly happened to me over the years, in so many experiences of life, love and work that fall well outside the smaller and more suburban world proscribed by my middle class Australian upbringing as a Catholic.

I have worked in one of the top commercial law firms in Sydney. Only a year or two earlier I lasted a whole day in a factory assembly line packing mobile phone SIM cards (I found it tedious and boring to put it mildly). I have cleaned houses (Well, I lasted through one job – I am a reasonably tidy person, but cleaning is not a passion!), sold lingerie (working in retail was not for me, but I loved the staff discounts, so that job lasted a little longer) and worked as a photographer, a marketing person, a psychic, a psychotherapist, a counsellor, an astrologer and more recently as a sacred musician and spiritual teacher, not to mention all the other jobs in between. There is a lot of variety there. The only work that has ever truly touched my heart has been spiritually and creatively oriented, but the other jobs all taught me something useful and were a part of how I learned and grew into who I am today. As for how to describe my job now, I inwardly groan when people ask me what I do for a living. I never know how to describe it well enough to give them a clear picture! Throughout the course of my life thus far, I have experienced feelings of power and status, feelings of poverty and hopelessness and plenty in between. It has been a relatively full experience of life that has not fit within the confines of my upbringing at all and I expect the trend of expanding consciousness will continue. To my view of things, the soul wants to know and love all of life as that seems to be the trend on my spiritual journey.

The virgin within moves us through varying and sometimes difficult circumstances without pulling away. She doesn't fear that her fundamental nature will be compromised, no matter what life hands to her as she adventures into unknown territory. In the process she becomes more wise, whole and accepting of life as experience leads her into maturity. In wealth, poverty, prestige or potentially degrading circumstances, the essential self is always what it is. That is Persephone's power. Her story helps us to understand this process within our own lives.

Persephone is a young girl living with her mother, Demeter. Never far from her mother's sight, she has a rather peaceful and sheltered existence. The advances of various gods, including the sun god Apollo, seeking the fair Persephone's hand in marriage were rejected by Demeter. We don't really hear much about Persephone's say in the matter. Instead, Demeter chooses to hide her daughter away from the world, where she plays alone in fields of grass, through an endless summer. On yet another idyllic day, Persephone is out in the golden grass, when all of a sudden the earth cracks open and a dark hand rises up, grabs her ankle and pulls her out of her world, into an unknown terrain. The hand was that of Hades, Lord of the Underworld. The world changes forever and life will never be the same again for Persephone.

Demeter is inconsolable! She cannot find her daughter who has somehow disappeared despite Demeter's possessiveness and protection. She will not give up her search for her daughter and eventually rumours abound that Hades has abducted Persephone. The endless summer stops as Demeter, the goddess of nature and fertility, is overcome with grief. She stops growing life on the earth, plunging it into an apparently never-ending winter.

Eventually the cries of all the people against Hades, and the constant winter his abduction has caused, elicit a divine intervention that force him to release Persephone back to her mother. He is not without his own boldness and guile however. He wants to keep Persephone for himself. So he tricks her, before releasing her, by having her eat pomegranate seeds knowing that once someone has eaten anything in the underworld, they must always return.

Persephone rises up from the underworld, leaving a besotted Hades behind. Demeter is overjoyed, the natural world springs into life and celebrates her return. The realisation that Hades has tricked her and that Persephone has to return to the underworld for three months of the year doesn't make Demeter happy. When Persephone is with Hades in the world of the dead, Demeter plunges the world back into winter for the duration of Persephone's descent.

This story takes us on Persephone's transformational journey from the virgin who is hidden from male suitors by her mother, in carefree, but ignorant bliss, into a mature queen who rules the underworld and the souls of the dead, and has the ability to rise forth bringing joy to the world through summer and harvest, and to die again, over and over. This power to thrive through life and death marks her as a truly powerful goddess.

Within us, there will have been this virginal child self, hidden from the world and living in a realm of fantasy. The more disturbed our childhood experience was or the more sensitive and spiritually attuned we are, the more out of sync we probably would have felt with the world around us and the more powerful the realm of fantasy would have become, to help us cope with the situation in which we found ourselves. Fantasies might be dark and disturbing or light and joyful. They are a natural outlet for whatever is going on for us as children, and sometimes as adults. Fantasy life can be healthy and even helpful when we are conscious to its purpose and function, and don't hold on to it at the expense of our growth.

Our natural progression through life will chip at and knock our fantasy world about so that we can grow. This doesn't mean we are left without imagination or a powerful fantasy life. It just means that we can relate to the world and the events in it, as they are, in the here and now, rather than avoiding them or clouding them in a way that would undermine our ultimate wellbeing and growth. Fantasy is a part of life. Like anything, it is about finding balance.

If we resist the deconstruction of our fantasies as we grow through life, it may be because there is unresolved trauma hiding under the fantasy. The fantasy of the rescuing prince in a relationship might be based on painful childhood disappointment in one's father, perhaps due to perceived abandonment or betrayal. The negative fantasy that everyone is out to get us so we better pull away before anyone gets too close, might come from a negative childhood experience connected to a mother that was unable to nurture or that used us to meet unmet needs of her own and left us feeling used, exploited and abused.

If we remain locked in fantasy and use it to avoid dealing with life rather than inspiring us to live more fully, we are effectively still within those golden fields of Demeter's overprotective control. It will keep us from breaking through the limitations of our consciousness and hold us back from developing the new attitudes we need to live a different experience.

Our reluctance to let go of the fantasy is a defence against the original pain, but it might end up continuing a powerful pattern of abuse, distrust, betrayal, abandonment, possessiveness or suspicion in relationships that is very tiring to the heart. Sometimes the resistance to the natural way life chips away our fantasies is very powerful, as breaking away from the fantasy would force the confrontation of unresolved trauma, pain or disturbance that was caused by the original wounding. The psyche shut down and tuned out the pain with fantasy. To undo that powerful self-protection mechanism can be very difficult indeed, even when it is no longer necessary. It happens most easily when we can mother ourselves without suffocation or being overly controlling of life.

We need to learn to care for ourselves without trying to prevent any hurts, scrapes or bruises. This means allowing ourselves to take healthy risks. It doesn't mean being careless or rushing into any experience or relationship without intuitive discernment and evaluation. It does mean we need to stop holding on to what we have known so we can go through the process of grief and open up to new life again, and again. It is rarely easy, but it is how we can truly be alive. Otherwise we run the risk of being snatched by Hades and dragged out of our childlike attachment to excessive safety (or the illusion of safety in life) in less conscious ways, such as through disease, accidents or other events beyond our conscious choosing.

The closeness of the mother-child relationship is an important part of this story. It doesn't literally mean that being close to your mother keeps you as a child, although it can do so. It depends on the consciousness of the relationship and the willingness of both parties to relate to each other as individuals, not just as role-playing child and mother. That is a task in and of itself! Often it isn't until a 'child' gets married that the parent will see them as an adult in their own right and sometimes in a highly dysfunctional family system, where allotted family roles don't budge very easily, not even then.

However, the mother relationship in this myth is not only literal. As outlined above, it also refers to our relationship with the consciousness in which we have been raised. The beliefs we grew up with and the people we spent time with are all part of the mother at a symbolic level as are our parents jobs, the cars they drove, the sporting teams they supported, their political affiliations, their religious views and the places we lived, how we lived and where we went to school.

The mother in our consciousness is not only how we care for ourselves, it is also the part that pushes us to belong, to be part of a family, to feel loved and nurtured, and to be loving and nurturing. This can be a healthy and supportive consciousness. If our upbringing was quite free, well-adjusted and emotionally healthy, we will gravitate towards relationships and communities that really do nourish us and help us to grow. If we are still healing this wounding within ourselves, we will tend to attract relationships that are more fear-based and controlling, and end up in communities that diminish our light, rather than support its expansion.

Healthy mother consciousness might encourage us to make life choices based on our inner values that we will have been encouraged to search for and trust in. This is very different to being taught obedience and being the same as our parents is the right way to move through life. The fear-based nature of mainstream culture means the latter is a common experience. On one hand, this means there is more inner-healing work to be done, but it also means we develop strength and skill as we labour to be free, happy, self-defined individuals. So, there is a plus side hidden in this rather challenging situation.

We are all learning to heal the mother energy within. When our mother consciousness is trusting and empowering, we naturally take risks and have adventures in the way that is best for our growth, but if it is fear-based and tells us to stay with what we know, then we are ripe for an appearance by Hades.

Hades is the liberating force who has been cast aside to the extent that we were told to toe the line, not to question, keep our heads down and not make waves. It is also the force that is cast aside whenever we try to keep things pleasant or nice and in particular, unchanging. The more we are in the mother energy in an unhealthy, demanding, dysfunctional or abusive way, whether that applies to us as individuals, to family or community groups, or to society in general, the more Hades will be hidden away in the underworld or the shadow of our consciousness and getting really lonely, and really angry about it.

The healthy part of the psyche seeks wholeness. The Hades part of us seeks a loving connection with the feminine spirit that Persephone embodies. She is not only a fantasy figure, but a goddess with beauty, spirit and lightness of heart. In her maturity, she has great compassion and becomes a guide for souls in darkness as well as a source of joy for those alive upon the earth. The darker parts of us, the parts that have been rejected and wounded, really need that healing presence.

The hand of Hades that reaches up through the cleft in the earth for Persephone is the rejected, lonely and powerful part of us that has been cast into shadow, away from our daily consciousness. It wants to experience wholeness and doesn't care if it has to shake things up to do it. We can enter into a conscious relationship with that part of us through healing work, or we can try to avoid it for as long as possible and then do our best to deal with it when it dramatically arises and forces us to pay attention. Either way, when the time is right, the Hades within us will quest for love.

Ultimately, this will benefit us, as it did with Persephone who gained access and empowerment in a whole other reality. Through her encounter with Hades, she stepped into a new found power in service to many in their time of need. Even when we know this, the process can bring up all sorts of resistance and fear within us or within those around us frightened by our ventures out of the worlds they know and feel comfortable with. If they have their own issues of abandonment, they might even see our personal growth as a personal rejection, rather than valuing themselves as being a part of our maturing process.

If we are in the mother energy in a deeply fearful way, any attempt by Hades to reach for us, or one of our loved ones, will be terrifying and subject to great resistance. As ridiculous as it might logically seem, this translates into a deep fear of otherness which may be expressed in religious and racial intolerance, misogyny and even in the tendency of women to treat men as useless or inadequate. All of these behaviours come from a place of deep fear and they are still running rampant in the greater consciousness of the human collective, as well as deep within many of us as individuals.

Sometimes, despite the fear, people try to connect with the other anyway. A deep desire for relationship and intimacy might remain intact within their heart and they learn to love more than they fear. This is a healthy impulse. If the fantasy realm has been confronted, allowing old trauma to be resolved and the person to become more present in the body, with its instincts and intuitions available, the person will be able to discern between healthy and dysfunctional relationship choices.

I have made dysfunctional choices in friendships and relationships over the years, and each time it was because I didn't listen to my body. I felt what my body was telling me (something along the lines of, "Danger! Danger! Do not proceed!"), but thought, "What the hell, I'll go with it anyway." After doing that several times, and experiencing extremely painful emotional outcomes, I decided to listen to my body from the beginning instead! I have thus been able to avoid numerous emotional catastrophes. I guess it took me a while because I wanted to be sure the intuitive voice of my body was actually worth listening to. Turns out it is.

When one is still operating in a world of fantasy and is not yet ready to confront the wounding underneath it, to come into the here and now, then the ability to be present to the body and its valuable instincts is almost non-existent. I have seen intelligent and highly intuitive women who have suffered through abusive relationships – the underlying wound that attracted them to such a situation not yet resolved within themselves – continue to make the most terrifying choices in prospective partners. Through the thick veil of fantasy, they can cast the most unlikely and dangerous of candidates into the role of prince charming. It's like inviting an axe-murderer over for tea, with the bloodied axe resting on his shoulder, and asking, "Oh, would you like sugar in your tea?" It's not going to end well. Obliviousness and dissociation are not protection!

In such cases, Hades will keep appearing. In my case, I had enough toxic people in my life causing a lot of unnecessary pain so that eventually I just became more discerning and selective about whom I shared myself with and to what extent. My anger and frustration prompted me to learn to love myself enough not to allow just anyone who happened to take an interest in me to get a piece of me, so to speak. Hades popped up in relationship after relationship where I was cast into a world of pain, because I couldn't move beyond what I had learned as a child. When I unlearned that, and taught myself new behaviours, I had integrated my Hades and brought the part of me that demanded I opened up to different ways of being into my heart. It wasn't an easy process, but it was essential for me to grow. He likely has more to teach me, but I hope that I am now more open to learning from, rather than resisting or fearing him.

We don't have to wait for Hades to catch us by surprise. We can look for him within and seek him out by finding the anger to say, "Enough is enough!" and kick some relationships to the kerb. We might then get some guidance or therapy to help us deal with the causes of the patterning so as we can genuinely outgrow it and mature into Persephone, the queen who engages with experience. However, we can also choose to avoid the Hades within. This may cause us to project our Hades on to other people, come to believe that they are the problem and that they should change so that we can remain the virginal Persephone in the field of Demeter.

In my late twenties, I found myself amongst a group of female friends. We all loved spiritual matters, shared a wicked sense of humour, enjoyed expressing ourselves through fashion, and liked socialising and chatting about our love lives. Rather unhealthily however, most of our conversations about relationships actually took place amongst us, rather than within the relationship with the man in question. (To be fair, the women were much more willing to listen and talk than those particular men were.)

I loved these women, they were fun and feisty and we supported each other. I remember one absolutely hilarious Valentine's Day when we all happened to be single at the same time. We dressed up as glamazons and went out to paint the town red. One of the women brought us each as 'valentine' – a photocopy of an Archangel Michael angel card! We walked around Sydney holding up our cards to random strangers, asking if they had seen this man and generally bursting into laughter. At one point we taped one of the cards to a telephone pole and scribbled "WANTED" on the top of it. I don't know if the passers-by realised we were sober and just letting off some steam, but most of them seemed to enjoy our antics. I know we certainly did. It is quite possible that Archangel Michael did too.

However, the laughter and love covered up a deeper sense of collusion in our woundedness. In our own ways, we had learned not to trust men. We wanted love and affection, but due to various childhood experiences, were not certain we would receive it. I am a child of divorce, two of my friends were subjected to sexual abuse by family members, and the fourth member of our group had been subjected to physical assault in her childhood. So, we could be quite distrustful, quick to judge and even quicker to encourage each other to terminate a relationship if it didn't measure up to perfection. Despite that, we all had an ability to endure relationships that were fundamentally painful! It was part of the fantasy – expecting the prince to show up and wanting it so much that you could imagine it, even while you were with someone who was so wounded themselves that they weren't able to relate to you or offer the most basic respect, love and kindness. It was a meeting of wounds, rather than a meeting of people and therefore underneath all the flamboyance and apparent spiritual connection, it was quite lonely. So we turned to each other for comfort and connection.

This continued on for some time, until one day, something in me snapped. I didn't want to play this game anymore. It was tapping into my childhood wounding that had me choose mother over father in the game of divorce and it was very painful to realise I was replaying the false belief that I had to choose a 'side' and connect with either men or women, not both. This meant I couldn't have meaningful friendships with women and a loving partnership with a man. I didn't want this belief.

So I started to rebel against the unspoken rules in the group. It came to a head one day when one of the friends was complaining about the way her employer treated her. We all knew what she was talking about, and we also knew how she contributed to the situation, although no one would have ever dared speak up about it for fear of being disloyal and unsupportive. I both loved and didn't respect that about us. I loved that we tried to be unconditional for each other, but I didn't respect that we couldn't seem to hold the space for genuinely honest communication.

On this particular day, I was hosting an Easter celebration at my apartment and we had all gathered to spend time together. When this friend started up with her story, the other friends immediately took her hands and made sympathetic noises but I couldn't bring myself to engage in what felt false to me. I knew his behaviour left a lot to be desired, but I knew she was no victim either. She wasn't trying to find a way to heal, she was just trying to blame another person and leave it at that. It wasn't worthy of her. So I said nothing. I looked at her straight in the eye and said nothing. It was as if an electrical charge was released into the room and everyone could feel it. I had silently declared war on our past way of relating to each other. The effect in a group of sensitive women who worked with energy was powerful, the group fractured and my friendships with those women fell apart not long afterwards. I was sad, but not about letting go of that way of being in the world. In the years that followed, my relationships with men became healthier and more open and varied. It took time and personal work, but it couldn't have happened if I had remained in that dysfunctional dynamic with those women, no matter how much I appreciated them.

At the time when I was most deeply working on this issue, I had a dream. I was to be married to a mysterious looking man, who was a gangster. I sensed a hidden violence in him and I was very uncertain about him, but he was committed to me and gave me a ring. Shining, living crystal, exactly to my taste and fit, this ring was so perfect for me. It showed me that he had an insight into my heart that surprised me. However, in order to marry him I had to leave my mother and I was hysterical with fear. So much so that I woke myself up!

Letting this dream work itself out has taken years – and is still going strong, I imagine. That man was my Hades. He was calling me to let go of my fear and open up to a different way of being, and perhaps a completely different type of relationship. It wasn't about being safe and clinging to what I knew, it was about being loved and genuinely recognised. The dream was urging me to let go of what is known, to overcome the fear that was an obstacle to the not necessarily safe, but mysterious and uncannily suitable destiny that was calling me. The dream was teaching me about the difference between feeling secure and taking a risk on being accepted, embraced and committed to absolutely.

It was painful and challenging, but also quite wonderful to work with my emotional responses to men more generally as a result of that dream. I had always loved male energy but at the same time, had never held it in high enough regard to truly trust it. I began to challenge what I had learned, and run the risk of trusting.

I met and learned from many new male friends and relationships in the years following. I attracted men into my life who have been extremely beneficial to my personal and professional growth and have improved my life and my ability to do my work effectively in profound ways. They have been nurturing and tender with me in a way I didn't realise men could be. They were also challenging and dynamic, which brought out my self-confidence and strength. I had to work through the fear of being abandoned, betrayed, rejected, and run the risk of being deeply hurt and realised I would still be okay even if that happened. Sometimes I did get hurt, but I chose to learn from these experiences to see what part of me attracted such a wounded man into my life. It was always the part of me that was unaware of my own wounds. When I became conscious of a wound in me and healed it through loving acceptance and kindness, I would cease to be attracted, or to attract, that sort of man. Or if I did, I had a greater awareness of how to deal with the situation without compromising my wellbeing as I had tended to do in the past. I had always been spiritually mature, but through that process of inner healing, I began to grow up psychologically and emotionally as well.

Our relationship to male energy, which is what Hades symbolises, is intrinsically linked to that part of us and of life that pulls us beyond the role of the dependent child and into our maturity as an independent being in our own right. Yet to release the fear of being raped, attacked or otherwise violated is very challenging, especially if you have a conscious memory of those experiences from this or other lifetimes. Even without those memories and even if you live in a male body in this lifetime, you can still be energetically moved by the fear of abuse because at a collective level we are plugged into fear and unresolved past pains, and you may be sensitive enough to be somewhat conscious of that. Releasing such a fear requires us to process those experiences or that consciousness and come to peace with it. This can happen in layers, and more trust always follows the healing of one of those layers of fear conditioning in our consciousness.

It is so important that we do this. It is not only those who relate more to the victim role, but also those who get cast in the role of the perpetrator that suffer. Male clients have spoken to me in genuine, heartfelt frustration and pain of the experience they have when women relate to them from a fearful place and cast them as potential predators. They want love and connection too. Of course, there are men and women who are not in conscious connection with their hearts and would be predators if circumstance permitted. The more present we are in our bodies, the easier it is to sense such people and steer clear, with compassion and discernment. Sometimes this is a karmic experience and we are meant to go through it, heal and find greater empowerment and love. Part of accepting Hades is accepting that sometimes even when we are working hard on ourselves, we will have some experiences we would rather not have. When we are in touch with the virginity of our essential being, we will realise that even those experiences are not going to damage us but give us some work to do. The energy generated by that work burns away the coverings of our true nature to reveal more of its purity.

As women own their maturity – sexually and in other ways by working with Persephone and ruby – the unconscious projection of victim-abuser will happen less and less with men, and the ability to fully feel the body and its instinctual guidance about whom an appropriate partner might be will increase.

However, we are still learning not to fear and therefore shame female sexuality in the mainstream and the projection of sexual predator as though it is a fundamental aspect of masculinity, still takes place. The notion that masculinity could be tender, loving and protective is novel to many women, and to many men too. We are still developing an understanding of conscious masculinity, which is such an important and pivotal shift in human consciousness. Healing the feminine cannot occur without healing the masculine, and vice versa. They are in relationship with each other, not separate from one another. We have to allow for the feminine and masculine to discover each other afresh. I am so passionate about this that I am writing an oracle deck with Blue Angel dedicated to healing the masculine and feminine in sacred relationship called *The Tantra Oracle*.

Through this work, I have also been able to change the way I relate to women. I have connected with blessed women, one of whom is my best (and blondest!) friend, who are able to empower rather than disempower each other and encourage each other to reach for the stars. They know what potential we have, and are empowered enough within themselves not to be jealous of what a friend has, but to be happy for their good fortune when it comes. This is a precious, rare treasure of a friendship. It only becomes possible by confronting Hades, being ripped out of fantasy and confronting one's limited identities and beliefs, and entering into a deeper experience of life, maturing as a person and coming into one's own power. This is the gift that Hades brings Persephone and that the masculine consciousness can bring to the feminine. It is maturity.

RUBY (POTENCY)

Natural ruby is a deep pink colour, sometimes with red or brown tones. Faceted rich red coloured rubies are extremely expensive and usually reserved for jewellery, but unfaceted natural stones can be truly beautiful too, and whilst not cheap, they are far less pricey than prized red rubies.

Ruby brings us into connection with our inner royalty, dignity and energetic potency. That energetic potency might be sexual, creative or physical in other ways. 'Ruby' people naturally have a lot of energy and have a tendency to always be involved in this, that or the other. They have big energy fields and make a big impact on those around them, even if it is in a subtle and refined manner.

Ruby strengthens the base chakra and pumps more energy through the body, in particular the heart and the blood, which one reason it is known as a stone for healing sexual issues, building passion and dynamically attracting love, wealth and success. It is a very powerful stone to work with and it is a stone of truth.

In previous chapters, I spoke of a relationship I had which was not able to last. Despite deep love, we weren't so compatible energetically. Aside from our love for each other, a passionate physical connection and a somewhat bizarre appreciation for funny, animated children's films, we had little in common. We met in an astrology class, but personal growth and spiritual exploration were more of a passing interest for my partner, as opposed to the life-long dedication which they are for me.

As I was still learning to be fully present, I hung on to the hope that he would rekindle his interest in metaphysical pursuits. But, apart from the odd comment here and there, he showed no interest in doing so. I didn't feel he needed to be interested in my work, but I did struggle to relate to someone who struggled to relate to his own emotional life. That was the reality I eventually had to face when I did become present. Nonetheless, before I finally let him go, I did give the relationship a chance.

During those times we spoke about marriage. I told him I was not a traditional jewellery kind of person. One only has to catch a glimpse of the rather massive crystal jewellery I wear to see that I am not a fine gold chain kind of woman, although I can appreciate the beauty of it on another wearer. This got him to thinking. He said that if he was not going to give me a traditional diamond ring (which he would have preferred) he would choose to give me a ruby.

I was delighted! I had not thought of that and when I did, it felt really good. He purchased an absolutely enormous natural ruby (some three hundred carats in size) for thousands of dollars and decided he would have it made into an engagement ring. It was a huge step for both of us, but the power of that ruby combined with the ill-fated combination of our paths this lifetime, meant that it was not destined to become my engagement ring.

That stone radiated an extraordinary kind of light and energy. We were both mesmerised by it. However, after its purchase it stayed hidden away in the house. The truth of our relationship became clearer and clearer. I grew stronger as my personal and spiritual path continued to unfold, and was increasingly sure of what I needed in terms of emotional intimacy and increasingly lonely in the absence of that in our relationship. I was amazed at how much I could love someone who couldn't or wouldn't meet my basic needs for emotional connection and communication without a lot of cajoling. The more present I became to my emotional needs, the more potent I felt and the more aware I was that loving myself and choosing healthy, supportive relationships meant that I was not going to be able to stay with this man. I was heartbroken and grieved for a long, long time, years of which took place when I was still in the relationship.

Towards the end of the relationship, after a particularly painful fight, my partner told me something that shocked me. He said he had dreamed that if he were to give me that ruby, he would need to die. Tears poured down my face and my heart twisted in anguish. I didn't know what to do with the idea that my beloved felt this way. The pain behind that dream was so obvious. He felt as though he would have to die in order to honour a deeper commitment to me and proceed with an engagement. In a way that was true, symbolically, rather than literally. He couldn't remain as he was and become a husband to me. I was his Hades. I wanted to pull him by the ankle into a far bigger world than he had known and it would require his sense of self to go through a transformation that he didn't want to endure. He didn't think he would survive it and I realised I couldn't ask him to take a journey that he didn't want to take. Yet, I couldn't remain while I felt so unmet in the relationship. The unhappiness was poisoning our love and that made me even sadder. The ruby was our crystal truth serum and the honesty it gave rise to pushed me to acknowledge my own needs, to love myself and be truthful with my heart, even if that meant letting it break. I could not hold myself to less than what I was becoming to try to make it work, especially as if it wasn't meant to be more than it was. The love the ruby promoted between us was love of the soul, that knew the truth of our limitations and urged us to be honest enough to free ourselves with trust that the Divine knew what it was doing – even if that meant our paths would be separating. Both of us were to take very different journeys.

As for what happened to that ruby, I don't know. I assume it will sit hidden away in that house, invisibly continuing to work until it fulfils its healing purpose for my once beloved, because crystals choose us and work with us to fulfil sacred karmic contract. When it is no longer to be with him, it will find its way elsewhere.

Now of course, this doesn't mean that working with ruby will end your relationship. In fact, ruby is known as a great love stone. Perhaps that ending was necessary so a new beginning in love could arise for both of us. I suspect that is the case.

Ruby is also a stone of wealth, prosperity, passion and enhancement of our natural attractiveness. As ruby encourages us to love life and to engage with it with a sense of personal potency and enthusiasm, it is also a great stone (ironically perhaps) for heartbreak, whether it is anguish over a relationship or in our great romance with the Divine. As we grow closer in love to the Divine, what we cherish and hold on to gets torn down and rebuilt in new forms, over and over again as we learn to detach and accept the mysterious workings of divine intelligence in our lives. On this path, heartbreak is inevitable.

I am so passionate about the human experience of divine relationship that I have written an oracle called the *Journey of Love* published by Blue Angel. They will also be publishing another book in this series called *Crystal Saints & Sages 777* which goes into the human experience of the divine awakening, with all its funny stories, mystical encounters and dark nights of the soul, in more depth.

Supporting us to access greater self-love, more energy and combat exhaustion on all levels, ruby is a loving stone that empowers us to remember we are potent beings. As such, we can tap into the sensuality, passion and vitality that it gives rise to in us, to claim the divine destiny calling us to it, with boldness and a huge, "YES!"

MANIFESTING THROUGH MATURITY

In this chapter, we have explored maturity as the outcome of actively engaging with our life situation without resistance, temper tantrums (well, maybe an occasional tantrum) or the belief that we are a victim of circumstance, rather than a soul liberating itself through life. It requires a sense of personal potency and capability, and a fundamental sense of our innate value as a divine being who has been gifted life experience to acquire wisdom and spiritual growth.

When we seek to manifest through maturity, we are not asking the Divine to gift or reward us for good behaviour, as a child might try to cajole a parent. Rather, we are taking responsibility for our own power, and our ability to work through our issues and raise our frequency to a place of compatibility with what we are seeking.

This means that if we want love in our lives, we learn how to be loving – to ourselves and others. If we want wealth, we learn how to break the habit of lack and shift to a position of gratitude for the abundance we already have in so many ways. If you are unsure of what that abundance is, I can tell you that you have an abundance of spiritual guidance and wisdom because you were attracted to this book and more than likely are already helping and guiding people along their paths too (whether through a formal role or not). Walking the advanced stages of this path is actually the opportunity that is afforded to us when we have a lot of karmic grace under our belts, so to speak. So you will have an abundance of spiritual energy within you. Now you might be using that energy to journey to the underworld or bear some deep challenges, but you wouldn't be empowered to do that without great blessings of light.

Manifesting through maturity is essentially about manifesting through responsibility for our own level of resonance. This is where we "be the change we want to see in the world" as per the catch -cry attributed to Mahatma Gandhi. In doing so, we become the essential vibration of what it is we want to manifest in our lives. That is a full expression of creative maturity because it rightly places the responsibility for our part in the process in our own hands. The mature heart also knows that the details of how, when and who are best left in the hands of the divine.

HEALING PROCESS

This healing process helps us mature the internal and external aspects of relating between masculine and feminine energies. Healing this dynamic internally will lead to your feelings, actions, passion and plans in life falling into alignment. If you have been feeling a lack of trust in your heart's desires and dreams, this healing will help you learn to rely on your heart with more faith and feel enough respect for your feelings to honour them by listening to them and acting accordingly. As this healing takes place internally at a subtle level, you will feel safer and more loved, irrespective of what is happening in your external relationships (although when we feel like that internally it generally improves our external relationships eventually also).

If you have been struggling to really identify your dreams, or if you know what they are but have lacked the courage of your convictions to take responsibility for them and take legitimate action in the world, then this healing process will help with that.

If you have unresolved childhood trauma from divorce or death, or loss from one of your parents being an addict, workaholic, narcissist, depressive or any other version of emotional wounding that prevented them from being a good-enough parent to ensure your basic sense of safety, love and belonging in the world, this healing process will assist in restoring your inner world to a place of unity and love, creating a sense of inner soothing that will become a healing balm for old wounds, allowing for a new reality to permeate your inner world and eventually, expand out into your physical body, subtly but powerfully changing the course of your physical reality over time also.

If you have been having difficulties in accepting male energy or female energy – in yourself or others – this healing process will help calm the struggle and support the integration of a new and more openly embracing attitude.

The Process

Have your crystal and/or mandala with you and begin by saying, "I call upon Persephone who loves unconditionally. I call upon the wisdom of the ancient ones, the mysteries based in unconditional love and divine wisdom. I call upon the healed masculine consciousness and the healed feminine consciousness, in unconditional love. I call upon the Crystal Angel of Ruby, in unconditional love. So be it."

Sit and sense or feel that you are being bathed in beautiful flowing waves of ruby red light. Allow it to feel nourishing and perhaps sensual, relaxing and uplifting. Imagine your heart is drawing in whatever energy it needs and that the energy is flowing all the way down into your toes, the soles of your feet and radiating softly out into the earth.

Imagine, sense or feeling that a loving king and queen stand before you, with vibrant ruby red heart chakras shining unconditional love to you. Receive as much as you wish.

Say, "I now accept the loving potency of Divine Masculine energy, the loving creative fruition of Divine Feminine energy, and surrender into the manifestation of my own divine soul light in all worlds, including the physical world. Through divine grace, may I be blessed in this task, assisted always, supported and protected by those beings who love me unconditionally. May I have the courage, strength of heart and will, to always support and honour myself as I manifest my soul light. So be it."

When you are ready, just relax or if you wish to, get up and move or dance and do so for at least eight breaths in and out.

When you are ready to complete your ritual, simply place your hands in prayer at your forehead, bow your head and say "thank you." And you are done.

Notice any changes within you and within your relationships following this ritual. If you feel you need help anchoring a change or to keep it unfolding, you may repeat this ritual up to three times in the next three weeks, if that feels appropriate, and not too strong for you.

15.

ISIS (RESOURCEFULNESS)
ISIS CRYSTAL (FEMININE ENERGY)

MANIFESTING THROUGH DETERMINATION

No obstacle can deter her from love, neither war nor death. Her love will prevail. For love, she will journey deep and far. She will emerge victorious for even in war, her heart remains pure, her sight always set upon the truth of love. She will move even Heaven to her cause, in her divinely embodied presence upon the earth.

ISIS (RESOURCEFULNESS)

Isis, ancient Egyptian goddess of life, magic, healing and protection, is also known as the Goddess of 10,000 Names. One of her many monikers is Auset (AWE-SET). If you say this name you will call on her spirit. I used it on the *Isis: Power of the Priestess* meditation CD and when I was recording, singing that name put me into a deep trance, which you can probably hear in my voice when you listen to it. It was an incredible feeling that took me beyond my mind into a place of expansiveness and peace.

It is said that Isis contains all within her being. The more spiritually advanced a being is, the more they contain within them, from a place of unconditional love, without losing their individual essence. Her stories are many and told in slightly differing versions, but the essential tale of her love, healing, resourcefulness and feminine mixture of vulnerability and power, remains intact. I will share the key wisdom story of Isis with you now.

Isis loved Osiris, who was her husband and the King of Egypt. Under his power, all was well in the world. He travelled to share his great wisdom to benefit other communities. Isis ruled well in his absence. Her authority was unquestioned and the loving rule of Osiris continued through her own wise hand. However, there was one who did not share in that love. Osiris' brother, Set, was consumed with jealous rage towards Osiris.

Set built a beautiful box of wood, ivory and other precious materials, to Osiris' exact measurements. Under the guise of offering a gift, Set invited Osiris to step into this custom-made, box. Osiris had no evil in him and suspecting nothing, he did as Set asked. Set quickly nailed the coffin shut, filled it with lead through a small opening and flung it out to sea.

When Isis heard of her beloved husband's fate, she was devastated. She also knew that the dead could not rest without a proper burial, so she set out to find her husband's body. Her search took her to Byblos, where she the queen's handmaids are captivated by Isis' tragic story, beauty and her talent for creating exquisite perfumes from flowers, which they chose to wear.

The Queen of Byblos becomes intrigued and intoxicated by the perfumes her handmaids are wearing and asks how they came by them. Upon hearing the story, she is moved by Isis's qualities and invites her into the castle and to care for her son, the young prince.

Isis agrees. After a time, she comes to love the young prince and decides she shall bless him with immortality. She lets him suckle from the tips of her fingers and each evening, she plunges him into the fire she has built.

Word gets out of these strange happenings, and one evening the queen hides herself in the room to see for herself. Sure enough, Isis readies herself to plunge the child into the fire. The queen panics, bursts free from her hiding space and, in terror, tries to save her child. Isis scolds her, explaining that she was tempering him to become a god, but his mother's actions have now prevented this from being. The queen apologises and offers to help Isis find the lost body of Osiris.

The King of Byblos had already found the beautiful coffin and without realising its history, had installed it within the kingdom. He was so moved by its beauty that he could not part with it. Once the truth is revealed, the coffin is liberated from the royal quarters and returned to Isis. She journeys with it back to Egypt and hides it along the river Nile until the following morning when she can complete the proper burial rites that will free the soul of her husband Osiris.

Set stumbles upon the box. In disbelief and howling rage, he rips it open, dismembers the body of Osiris into fourteen pieces and scatters them across the land.

Isis hears what has happened and is plunged into new depths of grief. She begins searching the land for each piece of her husband's body, until all but one piece are found. The phallus has been swallowed up and eaten by a crab. Using her healing magic, Isis joins all the remaining pieces together and fashions a new phallus from gold and wax. She then shapeshifts, turning herself into a small falcon and fans her wings so fast that the breath of life is blown into her husband's dead body. It is just enough for them to conceive a divine child together.

Osiris is assured that Isis' grief will heal through the birth of this divine child. He is free to leave his earthly body and live as King of the Underworld, protecting the dead. The divine child is eventually born and named Horus. He is a solar god with the head of a falcon. He is noble, wise and grows strong, becoming a lord of war, protection and the sky. He has purity but also street-smarts because of what happened to his parents. He becomes a powerful challenger of the dark lord Set, and a force of good and wise rule in the world.

Now that is quite a story! Isis comes to us with this teaching story in order to share great wisdom, her healing power and her unending resourcefulness. One piece of guidance I am constantly given, for my journey and that of others, is there is always another way. Sometimes my guides pass on this teaching as a simple statement, "Look for the third path." What they mean here, is that we often think things are either black or white, or an outcome is success or fail, but there are endless ways that can happen. We just have to get out of the way and let it happen by engaging with active, passionate intelligence, and never giving up on the essential dream. We must be willing to surrender the details of the final outcome.

For Isis, love triumphed. It didn't prevent the death of Osiris or the evil of Set. It did not protect her from great grief. In fact, the grief was what pushed her to keep going until she could find a way to put her beloved's soul at rest. That grief led her on a journey that taught others magic and the ways of divinity. It also realised the birth of a divine child who would become the saviour of many and the defender of goodness in the world. She was not spared a full gamut of emotional experience and challenge, but the goddess in her – the same divine energy as the immortal soul in each of us – enabled her to turn challenges into victories through great resourcefulness. Every crisis was a step for her divine journey. She resisted nothing, did not even entertain the possibility of failure and just kept engaging with life even as it took twists and turns that broke her heart. Through a passionate, resourceful interaction with her life experiences, she triumphed over jealousy, evil and even death, to bring forth new life.

Hers is the gift of resourcefulness, strength, courage and inspiration. When Isis enters our lives, she whispers the memory of our divinity to us. Sometimes, fed by our toxic celebrity worship and the mass media, we might fall into the trap of believing that to be blessed with the divine is to be beyond struggle. Yet, in the myths and wisdom teachings of the goddesses, we are shown that they too are living and are therefore within the sphere of life with the same struggles, losses and triumphs as us. Their experiences are not so different to ours, but the way they engage in them is. That is their offering to us. Isis teaches us that love will find a way. We must not give up, be attached to the outcome nor be dissuaded if things appear to be going pear-shaped! Love will triumph, but we need to give it a chance to do so.

One of my favourite expressions from the divine is, "I have provisions which you know not of." I love this because it has been my experience that when we are down on our hands and knees (or prostate on the floor sobbing) at the eleventh hour and all hope seems lost, that the Divine brings forth our Horus, so to so speak. This new life is the way forward, the solution, the hand of grace reaching out and offering us resurrection.

Isis carries this resurrection mystery within her. It is a gift of rising out of death, out of great grief and loss, through unspeakable devastation, into a hopeful state of renewal and greater spiritual maturity. With the wisdom of hindsight, Horus is capable of recognising the evil of Set without losing his own goodness and is therefore a powerful defender against him. Those of us that are pure at heart may have a tendency not to expect evil to turn up, and are often shocked when it does. Working with Isis is very helpful as she helps us grow in understanding so that we can become more powerful advocates of love in the world, without denying the existence of darkness. I have also commented on this in earlier chapters, particularly in the chapter on Kali.

In the story of Isis, as she spends time in Byblos and tempers the young royal child in fire, she teaches us something else of value. We learn that through passionate engagement with the fires of life, even when we fear they are burning us, we are being tempered into our divinity. It is the royal child – the soul – that is turned divine. At times the ego may well feel like it is being burned alive as it endures the experiences that life brings to its door and some will challenge the ego until it feels like it is dying. Growth doesn't only come from pleasant experiences, as I am sure you already know from your own experience. The fearful mother energy that we spoke of in the previous chapter, tries to overprotect out of a fear of life to the point that growth is stunted. This aspect is represented by the queen who is frightened for her child, because she doesn't understand that his soul is being born through the strange actions of the Divine Feminine. She only sees the fire and pain at the ego level. Isis scolds her because she wants the mother to allow her son to go through the process of being made divine. This is the same process we are taking as we journey through this book together.

As discussed in the previous chapter, we need to have trust and love to allow that divine journey to happen. I once received a message from the Divine Mother that has helped me to become more trusting of that process over the years. She said she is experiencing every single moment of every single living and dying being – every suffering, every ecstasy, every heartbreak and every triumph. All of it. I was so incredibly moved by the absolute presence and compassion she has for every single life experience of every single being. Of course! She is all those experiences and all those beings.

The journey to our awakening divinity doesn't take us away from the full gamut of experience, it empowers us to be present to it and to deal with it with increasing resourcefulness so that every single moment, whether of apparent light or darkness, may be utilised in service to love.

ISIS CRYSTAL (FEMININE ENERGY)

An Isis crystal is a clear quartz terminator. This is a single clear quartz crystal with a hexagonal or six-sided base, with the six sides rising up to meet a single point at the top. An Isis crystal will also have a face at the top of the crystal with five sides. This will be created from a straight base line, two shorter lines on the left and right which angle outwards slightly and then two longer edges on each side that angle back inwards, meeting at the top, creating a five-sided shape on the largest sloping face.

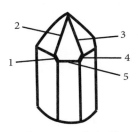

Isis crystals help us access feminine energy. For men and women, this energy can create nurturing, connection and healing, as well as enlightenment, through active participation in life from a receptive, open and accepting position. Receiving life completely and being moved by it, allows us to grow via a feminine path. It isn't the easiest of paths, but then genuine spiritual growth isn't known for being particularly easy. Simple? Yes. Easy? Well, let's just say it is easier than living a lie, killing off your divine nature and as a result suffering ongoing depression, anxiety, despair and hopelessness.

Feminine energy is not just about nurturing within relationship, it is a way of relating that is primarily driven by instinct and intuition, rather than intellect. I had a dream once that summed up the differences between the masculine and feminine approaches to life rather succinctly. A naked, wild-haired woman lay peacefully, flat on the ground, feeling the earth through her belly, much like a snake feels vibrations through its belly on the earth. A modern man stands above her, scratching his head in puzzlement and asks her what she is doing. "Listening!" she responds.

The feminine approach is honoured by wise, enlightened teachers, both male and female, who we shall meet in *Crystal Saints & Sages 777*. Their ways are not often understood by mainstream consciousness as they are so advanced on the divine path. What you will find common to wise ones from all traditions is that they have surrendered any misplaced arrogance based on a disconnection from the Divine. That misplaced arrogance would have someone believe that they know better than the Divine as to what should happen and when. It is such a relief to realise that we are allowed, encouraged actually, to give this up and get on with living life as it is.

Engaging with the actual, rather than the wishful, helps us realise our divine potential more swiftly. This includes all the desires of our heart. It is my firm belief that whatever we desire, no matter whether it is a material possession or a profoundly spiritual desire such as union with the beloved divine, it is an expression of our heart truths. Sometimes those truths are cloaked under an obsession for techno-gadgets, but the real desire lurking underneath even the most apparently mundane, ego driven desire, is for the truths of the heart – freedom, love, empowerment, service and so on. Sometimes the ego thinks those truths can be bought in the form of a car!

As we grow, our awareness develops and our relationship to the material world changes, but everything along the path serves, whether we know it or not – even a passing obsession with owning a Porsche. It is sometimes only through the experience of material wealth that we can come to celebrate it but also know its limitations.

When we can trust in our own desires to lead us along the path and that what we really want and need at a profound and truthful level will come to us in abundance as we surrender into who and what we are, then the feminine way becomes increasingly attractive to us. We have to give up on taking and learn to receive. To do this, we have to trust in the benevolent nature of the Universe and heal our experiences of lack, poverty, greed, being passed over or anything else that has created distrust. The nurturing energy of the feminine can help us feel loved and treasured enough that we can let go of the past and its pain, and step right into the present moment with an open heart. It can take time, but if we just take it step by step, we will experience healing progress.

Rejecting this more feminine way requires that we always have a plan, always know where we are going and how we are going to get there. This is why travel can be such a good teacher on the feminine path. When we consciously choose to take ourselves out of our known world there are so many factors that are out of our control, it is a chance to allow ourselves to be moved by something greater than us – life itself. That can feel tremendously inspiring, exciting and quite possibly downright terrifying at times.

To embrace the feminine means accepting that there will be times when we are gifted with a clear plan and even a clear means of bringing it to life, and then there will also be times when we don't have a clue where we are going and can only take one step at a time. Although our society might tell us this not acceptable, feminine wisdom assures us that it is – when we are trusting enough to allow ourselves to live beyond what we already know because divine magic, the realm of Isis and her healing powers, can really happen! On the feminine path we learn to feel with our belly rather than to see clearly the vista before us from a higher perspective. Of course the latter will come and go, but to honour the feminine path means receiving the higher vision when granted, and not turning away from life and experience when it isn't there to guide us. We trust our instincts and our hearts and do the best with what we have available to us in the moment. We trust that all we need to take the next step, we have within. This approach allows us to really gain some traction, experience genuine spiritual growth and transformation (rather than just change, which shifts external circumstance but may not shift internal substance adequately to provide any real shift in the quality of our life experiences).

We need the masculine energy to be able to put actions into place and to have the strength to move when needed. The feminine approach of trusting surrender attracts the masculine energy when needed. It is then back to the feminine way to evoke internal growth from our life experiences. This is how we become wise. If you have ever seen a person make the same mistake over and over again without seeming to make the connections between what they have been experiencing and the need for change in their own consciousness, if they seem to be living but are not really being impacted upon by life so that they grow, then they are in need of developing more feminine consciousness. Exactly what this book can assist with! The feminine energy within us is the cauldron, the womb, the container, the alchemical part of us that can receive and therefore be acted upon by life.

If we are making huge changes in our lives – leaving relationships or jobs, moving house, changing our lifestyle in other dramatic ways, perhaps moving to another country – then that requires a lot of masculine energy. If you have ever left a job or relationship, but after a promising fresh start you find the same issues repeated in the next one, then you will have experienced the limitation of change through masculine consciousness. It is necessary, but it just isn't enough on its own.

With feminine consciousness, internal growth, rather than just the outward appearance of change, can take place. The alchemy of transformation requires that we allow the breaking down of ourselves, so that a new self can be born. We need to have a psychic container, womb or receptacle in which that can happen so that we feel held enough to allow the process to happen. The 'container' determines the degree of feminine consciousness that we are able to hold. The stronger that is within us – through trust, the embodiment that comes through clearing our issues and allowing the body to become infused with the unconditional love of the spirit – the more we are able to bear the divine fires of alchemy. The more present and connected we are to our bodies at a spiritual level, the more we are able to bear the process of transformation. If we have insufficient feminine consciousness, the body is still packed with unresolved pain and we aren't able to be present to our spiritual light within that body. We therefore don't have an adequate container and cannot possibly bear the transformational pressures that come with the next phase of growth.

You wouldn't decide to climb a mountain without preparation if you intended to be alive and well through the process. It is the same with the spiritual mountain of healing transformation and growth. We prepare ourselves for the task. I am very passionate about the transformational path and with Blue Angel Publishing, I will be sharing an oracle deck dedicated to that path called The Butterfly Oracle. Apart from being one of my personal totems that has helped me through some truly devastating and challenging darkness in my life, the butterfly is a universal symbol for rebirth.

When we want to be climbing the mountain, so to speak, and reaching for the next level in our growth and development, we can call on Isis. She empowers us to not resist the divine fires of life. This lack of resistance is not weakness, but an empowered vulnerability. So many women and men think that being vulnerable means being weak. This is simply not true. Being able to be soft without fear takes a lot of strength. It lends us a power too. In softness we allow truths, insights and strengths to come to us and to act through us because we don't hold ourselves back from anything. Indeed, we can see and know very clearly from a softer place. We don't have to fight against life to become strong and in doing so risk becoming hard, defensive and inaccessible at a real soulful level, no matter how outwardly social and friendly we might seem to be.

I have known a people like that in my life and although I wanted to get closer to them it was impossible. They loved me and I them, but a genuine intimacy and closeness could not often occur between us. When I wanted to be still, present and really penetrate into their being, deep into who they were, they were not able to receive me and would avoid eye contact, withdraw, chat about something else or physically move about thus dissolving the possibility of deeper energetic connection. When it came time for me to really receive them, I could only do so to the extent that they would give themselves to me. Sometimes they did and it was so beautiful and precious to me! I still remember those few moments with so much love in my heart. Mostly however, they weren't comfortable being vulnerable as is necessary if we are going to offer an experience of ourselves to another. So, I couldn't really get anywhere near as deep in connection as I would have wished. Because of this, there was always a sense of comfortableness and even politeness in our interactions, but our connection rarely went beyond that despite sharing years and plenty of personal interaction together.

Of course, this is not bad, but nor did we get to experience the aliveness (sometimes fearful, sometimes exciting, sometimes both) that comes with genuinely sharing yourself with another without holding back. Without the feminine energy the genuine giving and sharing of self wasn't possible, and so I never felt as though we got any closer to or were able to grow our relationship beyond predetermined limits. No matter how much courage, energy, friendliness, talent and awareness these people had (and the three friend I am thinking of as I write this had an abundance of those qualities) my desire to really connect with them and their own desire to create a different life for themselves, was thwarted to the exact degree of their resistance in surrendering to the feminine flow. Perhaps that will change for them over time. We can certainly hope that all of us become more open to life as we grow, rather than turn away from it. But that is always our choice.

Wounded views of feminine energy equate it with being passive, weak and somehow inferior to dynamic activity. If we were shamed and made to feel 'less' because of sensitivity or feeling, and that will be most people in modern culture where feeling is generally considered as a substandard to intellect, then to tap into and find the power in femininity takes a huge amount of courage. Fortunately those of us with enough spiritual wisdom to realise this will have a heart big enough to possess plenty of courage.

Feminine energy actually empowers us with the capacity to dive into life rather than try to bend it to our will. It gives us energy to act. Isis didn't sit about twiddling her fingers, feeling helpless and moaning about her situation, she acted and felt and engaged – and great results came from her determination, empowered by the feminine feeling consciousness of her own heart and her resourcefulness in using whatever skills she had available to her (which included asking for help and allowing others to help her when she needed it). With Isis and the Isis crystal, we are empowered to manifest through that same determination she showed.

MANIFESTING THROUGH DETERMINATION

Manifesting through determination is not about imposing our expectations upon life or trying to thump it on the head like a cave man, until it gives in and does what we want. In a staring contest with the divine all-seeing eye, I can guarantee that we are going to be the ones who blink first. Determination is the power to engage and not give up on ourselves or on life. We will have to give up on getting our way of course, because if we try to live like a two-year old for our entire life, throwing a tantrum whenever life seems to say 'no' to us, we will make ourselves and those around us quite miserable in the long run. We use determination for our divine success, which is a more mature understanding of success. Divine success is the culmination of our divine nature, manifesting itself in authentic perfection, in all worlds, including this one. It is what we truly desire, underneath all the passing fancy, and the nature of our divine inheritance. We are here to live our divine success. We have to be determined to receive it and Isis helps us with that.

HEALING PROCESS

If you are feeling blocked, thwarted, confused or lack the emotional energy to keep going on your path in the face of the inevitable knockbacks and readjustments consistently required of us on the divine path, then this healing is for you. On the other hand, if you find you have a tendency to keep pushing when maybe you need to let go, this healing will help you use your power of determination in the correct way – to keep coming back into alignment with higher will, making micro-adjustments in attitude and behaviour over and over again to stay on the divine path, rather than trying to align the world around you.

Isis' particular power in healing grief and enduring emotional challenges with triumph in apparently inevitable failure means this healing process will help if you are going through a time of deep loss and are uncertain of how you will ever emerge into the light again.

If you want to continue to work with Isis beyond this healing process, I have an oracle deck dedicated solely to her published by Blue Angel called *Isis Oracle*. I have received emails from many people with such touching stories about how it has benefited them – often in rather surprising ways, for Isis is a creative and empowered healer. If you want to do more meditations with her, there is also my meditation CD called Isis – Power of the Priestess for men and women who want to connect with her healing energy. It has also received powerful and positive feedback and you may enjoy the four meditations on that CD in your journey to connect more deeply with this restorative and inspiring goddess.

The Process

Have your mandala or crystal with you.

Say the following out loud, "I call upon Isis who loves me unconditionally, she of ten thousand names, and the Crystal Angel of the Isis Quartz Crystal. I ask for your blessings of feminine healing energy now. I release all negative imprints, conditioning, memories and beliefs that have disconnected me from the powerful healing flow of Divine Feminine energy within myself, in my relationships and the world around me. I enter into the healing fountain of her eternal flow. Through divine love, so be it."

Imagine, sense or feel that you are beholding a beautiful fountain made of quartz crystal. The top of the fountain has a large five-sided face reflecting out pure white light in all directions. Crystal-clear purified and blessed water, bubbles in the fountain and you may enter the fountain to be blessed, cleansed and healed, or sit near it as you wish. Receive as much as you can and allow the movement of the water to naturally draw negative energy and old pain from your body, mind and energy field.

Relax in this process for at least eight healing breaths, in and out.

When you are ready, you see or feel a large pair of white wings and a gleaming golden-white energy that is Isis, before you. She may speak or simply radiate light. Allow her to be with you and trust in what you receive from her – it will be perfect for you at this time.

Finally she says, "You are my beloved and I call you home to me now through light and grace. I shall guide you so that you may serve love and awaken to your full potential. Through my divine protection, so be it."

Be with her and rest for at least eight healing breaths, allowing her light and energy to build a field of healing and grace around you.

When you are ready simply open your eyes, place your hands in prayer at your forehead, bow slightly and say, "Thank you."

You have completed your healing process. Do this again at any time you feel stuck or like you are trying to push for things to happen in your divine creative journey, and are in need of realignment, strength and protection to stay on track – even if that means being patient for a time.

16.

DURGA (MANY ARMS OF THE DIVINE MOTHER) HEMATITE (GROUNDING)

MANIFESTING THROUGH GENIUS

She rides a wild tiger, a great roar emerges from her very bones. Her sound vibrates out into the Universe and her will manifests. She will not be defeated! Her many arms and her many weapons are skilfully employed so that nothing is immune to her triumphant grace.

DURGA (MANY ARMS OF THE DIVINE MOTHER)

Divine figures from various traditions are sometimes pictured with many arms. This is symbolic of their ability to perform many tasks simultaneously and reach many people with their intervention and grace. Over the years, clients have confessed they were worried about calling on higher guidance too much, as it might be preventing other people from receiving the support that they needed. This is simply not true! I am always touched by the sentiment but it is misplaced. Divine love is without limit. It can be hard to fathom this from our human mind, but the many hands of the divine in various spiritual traditions is a way to impart that message at an intuitive, visual level. You could think of it as the ultimate cosmic multi-tasking. Not only that, but the more we call on divine love, the more it can operate through us to assist others. Invoking divine energy is a win-win situation.

It isn't about limited resources but an ever-expanding consciousness that uplifts us and others the more we work with it.

In the ancient traditions of India, the warrior goddess Durga is pictured carrying different weapons in each of her many hands, each tool has its own divine purpose and method of defending evil (or the forces contrary to love) and liberating the soul. Durga can be pictured with anywhere from eight to eighteen arms or more. She is often pictured riding a lion or tiger, with demons falling at her feet in submission, and dressed in red with a beautiful golden headdress. She is known as the protector of the soul and is undefeated in battle. No matter how many people call upon her, or how many demons need defeating, she will be there, and she will succeed. If for some reason, she cannot succeed in her own form, she'll give birth to a fierce goddess out of her third eye (and call her Kali!) and that divine creation will succeed in her place. There is just no getting around it. Durga means victory for the soul, and she will triumph, no matter how fearsome her opposition may seem.

Durga is a solar goddess and unlike the vast darkness of Kali that absorbs all, Durga burns bright like the sun. Her energy is uplifting and energising and when I feel her emanate through me, I feel incredibly bright, light and fearless. It is like there is an explosion of light in the room and the sacred warrior soul within those present is called forth. It is a strong experience, but very beautiful. With Durga I feel that nothing is able to touch her. She is the force of divine loving power that acts upon all and the world bends to her will. She can help us find the divine paradox in building up our personal will in order to surrender it and be moved by the divine power of love. We cannot offer our will to the Divine if we have no will to offer. It is one of the ironies (to the ego at least) of the spiritual path that we must build up our will and strength strong so we can surrender and therefore become truly empowered and effective on our divine path.

Durga is about empowered, active surrender. When we connect with her, we are often very active in the world but feel guided by internal inspiration from the Divine, rather than our own smaller sense of what we think we should be doing. Instead of trying to force things to happen through sheer (perhaps stubborn) willpower, with Durga our action comes from an inspired place. One approach is like swimming towards the shore against the current. Even if it is in a straight line and seems to be the most direct and efficient route, it could take longer, use up energy and leave us too exhausted or too late to enjoy the beach party happening on shore. By working with the currents and heading towards shore more indirectly, we'd get there in better time and with more energy, even if our path seemed to meander. How do we know which way to swim? We feel it. We sense it. We combine willpower and guidance, and when we can trust that nature has a way of getting us where we need to be, we no longer feel the need to fight against nature. Durga might even inspire us to let a passing dolphin give us a ride to shore, which would certainly make for a grand entrance to the party and be an excellent conversation starter!

Along with Kali, Durga is one of the supreme forces not only of getting things moving when needs be, but also of psychic protection through the sometimes volatile process of growth and awakening. In some versions of their stories, Kali was born out of Durga's third eye. In other interpretations, Kali was the vast cosmic void out of which Durga emerged. Either way, these goddesses are intimately linked.

I was at a dinner party some time ago with a group of people, including a mother and daughter. To put it bluntly, their relationship was not healthy. The daughter worked as a healer, with good intentions to serve the light, but was deeply bound psychically to her mother. The mother was jealous of her daughter's skill and because of her unresolved psychological and emotional wounding, believed that the daughter was hers to treat as she wished. She was both incredibly possessive and completely willing to play her children off against each other through gossip and manipulation to serve her own needs to feel powerful and secure. I suspect the mother would have been a very adept warlord in a previous lifetime, or a successful (in a manner of speaking) politician in this one, had her mind tended in that direction.

During the course of the dinner, the mother made a remark about her daughter that was shaming. I can't recall what the remark was, but when I somewhat protectively chose to diffuse its sting with a joke of some kind, the mother glared at me across the table. I remember the malice in her eyes and unspoken outrage that I had dared assume a relationship with her daughter that could challenge her power to shame her. It was as though she had released a poison into the atmosphere.

The evening progressed and by the time we were ready to leave, I felt cramps in my stomach. I knew the negativity this woman leeched into the space had affected me. I spent the twenty-minute drive home, chanting the Durga mantra, (with my then partner looking at me rather strangely) in the hope that it would ward off the pain. It took about ten minutes of chanting for the effect of her negativity and vicious hatred to begin to wear off, and by the time I pulled into my driveway I was free from the negative effects.

My partner was not so lucky. He declared that there was no such thing as psychic attack, and deciding it was just bad digestion, he suffered throughout the night with stomach cramps and was not able to sleep properly, whereas I was fine. I am so much more sensitive in digestion than he is; if it had been bad food, it would have been me struggling and him not at all. If he had been open to Durga, either choosing to chant with me or to receive my chanting, the negativity that was manifesting as stomach cramping (it was a poison that the body couldn't digest) would have been cleared out of him just as it was with me. He would have been spared the physical pain and enjoyed the sound night's sleep that I had been blessed with.

Apart from this sort of healing and protection, Durga brings a special kind of grace to victory. She is the one we call on for impossible situations where the odds do not seem to be in our favour. She is resourceful, fearless, bold and defiant. She is without a consort, which is unusual in the tradition from which she comes. The absence of a partner speaks of her perfectly balanced masculine and feminine energies, and her fundamental wholeness, as well as making her a divine icon for feminine independence and strength. For women who are learning how to feel whole within themselves without sourcing a sense of self or identity from their partners, Durga is very helpful.

Her many arms render her most suitable for those of us who feel like cosmic jugglers, with so many plans, projects, ideas, relationships and more going on at any given time, that we need help not to drop the lot! A dear friend and I often email each other about our ambitious schedules. We each have so many projects on the go and when it all gets a bit too much and too complex, with things firing here, there and everywhere (much to the amusement, awe and occasional bewilderment of our loved ones, managers, publishers and so on), our affirmation is, "I am working with the many arms of Durga!"

It has become something of a mutual catch phrase. It is not just an affirmation either, it is a way of being. I have so many projects in the pipeline and work on different phases of each one at different times, some will be near fruition while others are just starting and there will be more in between. Some projects come to life in a matter of weeks and others take years and years of being patiently held in my mind, heart and energy field, to percolate and grow, before they are ready come to life in the physical world. There is a great deal of complexity in my creative process. Working with Durga has enabled me to let this be without stressing out unduly (well, most of the time!). In calling upon her, I have a sense of projects that are for 'now' and ones that are being developed for years to come.

To many people, this seems very natural for me to do, because that's all that they have known of me. However, it was certainly not always the case. I used to experience so much internal anxiety that one unfinished project or simple task would nag at me until I could complete it, put it to one side and feel some relief. To have anything 'hanging over me' unfinished caused a great deal of stress. I still have a tendency to just get on with things and get them finished, but I also have the capacity to be open to allowing many irons to be on the fire with pots bubbling away. I can stir the ones that need to be stirred and let others percolate and so on. I look at how I live my life now, creatively, professionally and personally, and I am very aware it would have been impossible for me to live and work this way several years ago. I have had to learn and increasingly embody the strength, wisdom and grace of Durga. I share this with you because I know that whatever we think we are capable of is only a tiny fragment of what we are really capable of when we are empowered through the Divine. Durga in particular has a tendency to bring out the boldness and the magnificence in us, and help us find our empowerment.

The many arms of Durga allow us to let the Divine happen through us with increasing complexity. I often say that the Divine is nothing if not efficient. When I talk to a group of people, I speak to them as one. One soul, one group. The amount of people who come up afterwards and tell me they felt like I was speaking to them personally as they could really relate, is a testament to the divine genius. It just works. It is the same with the oracle cards I create by channelling divine energy. The Divine comes through the words, through the spaces between the words, and they work. They help people. I am a part of the process but my job has really been learning how to allow the Divine to be. I believe that is the most any of us can ever learn on this path. The more we surrender to it, the more it can do its brilliant creative work. Those oracle decks are helping people all over the world, in very different ways, depending on what they need and when they need it. I have heard over and over again how spot on they are, how perfect the messages are for whatever is happening, how people cannot believe it sometimes, and yet the magic is there.

It is touching for me to hear and I am deeply honoured by such feedback, but although I feel awe and reverence for the divine power that comes through those cards, I am not surprised because I know that is the way divine energy works.

So, if I have moments of feeling like I am not focused or that there is simply too much flowing towards me and through me at any given time, I call on the divine energy of Durga, and just step into the centre. I know I don't need to control it, I just need to work on being one of her arms, and then I can leave the rest up to her to sort out with her exceptional wisdom.

Earlier on in this book, I mentioned a teaching tour in North Queensland, Australia. During that tour, I visited a mining town that was very fragmented energetically and people were suffering. I was there for a day and a half. It felt like I was there for a week! Time moved slowly and not in a good way. There were misplaced power lines everywhere that were energetically, physically and emotionally draining. The mining around the area seemed to have distorted the natural energy lines that run through the earth as well. While I was there, I felt like I was moving in slow motion, again not in a good peaceful way, but in a sticky, heavy, clogged kind of way. The people who came to see me, all different personality types from different educational backgrounds – men, women, engineers, stay-at-home partners, parents, young newlyweds – all said exactly the same thing. To the point that I felt like I had stumbled into a twilight zone, or was being secretly filmed, it was all so oddly uncanny. They felt depressed, had lost connection to their intuition, couldn't connect with the others in the town, felt isolated and alone, wanted to get out, couldn't tolerate being there, felt low in energy and drained all the time, and that only started once they moved there. It was the same, word for word, in every session that I conducted.

I began to not only understand what they were saying, but to begin to experience it somewhat for myself when I did my yoga practice on the morning following my arrival. I experienced some most unusual symptoms. Rather than being able to plug into the earth and discharge excess energy, as well as draw up fresh energy to replenish myself, the earth energy was so fragmented and diseased that I felt as if there was cut glass in my hands and feet. My bones felt old and painful, like I imagine arthritic symptoms might feel like. Doing yoga was like pushing slowly through hard baked mud. I had never felt anything like it before. It was not pleasant.

The energy for the work came through very strongly in that town. Yet it felt as though we were gifting it to the earth, rather than the earth gifting us with support and nourishment as she usually would. My heart was so moved for these people and for my beloved Earth Mother who needed us to be like acupuncture needles, clearing the blockages. One young woman there was so utterly radiant, loving and wise, runs regular groups and offers distant healing on a regular basis, and I truly recognised as a soul sister. I felt such admiration and appreciation for the work she was doing, not only because of its purity, but because of where she was doing it and in what circumstances. It was harder to do spiritual work there, even though it is one of the places where it is most needed. She did it faithfully however. I knew the light of Durga burned in her heart.

I worked a lot with sound over the day and a half I was there, more so than usual perhaps, because I know it is the most powerful, immediate and potent way to access divine energy in such circumstances. If someone cannot easily access light – because they feel disconnected from their perception or their body for example – the sound will cut straight through that into the truth of their being. During one workshop, I was standing with my hand on the head of one of the students, singing words from the Divine Mother into her crown chakra. I moved on. She later shared that she had opened her eyes when she heard me singing from the other side of the room, because she could still feel my hand on her head. I instantly realised she had felt the hand of the Divine Mother reaching through so strongly during my time there, simply because she was so needed. She had her own arms working steadily with people in that space and she used mine too.

This happens in groups that I run from time to time. People feel the loving hand of the mother, one of her many hands, and think that I am standing there touching them. Often it is when I have been with them and leave, and they still feel the connection of the Divine in a physical sense, but at other times, it happens completely independently of my physical body. This woman literally felt the hand of the Divine Mother on her head long after I had moved on.

She also felt a drop of cool liquid on her foot. She opened her eyes again and looked around, thinking that someone must have been drinking out of a water bottle and spilt some on her, but everyone around her were deep in meditation. What she had experienced was Amrita, or holy nectar. It feels like cool water on us or under our skin, and one drop of it is enough to permanently erase karma in that part of our being. It was quite a bestowal of grace.

The woman who organised the workshops later commented that this participant was able to receive so much grace and direct connection because she really loved us and was completely free from withholding anything from me. I knew I could have asked her for anything, and she would have done it without question. Far from taking advantage of this for personal reasons, so much more divine energy is able to flow through me to such people, that I am able to give them so much more. It just happens. She is a generous woman in the truest sense and she genuinely loves me, as she does many people in her life. It is just her way. An open heart invites in the grace of the Divine to empower us in ways beyond our conscious understanding, and yet we feel it working at a palpable, practical, life-altering way in our daily lives.

However, sometimes Durga is not particularly gentle. I have had moments, occasional I will say, because my nature is gentle unless particularly roused, where the guidance and teaching that comes through is fierce. Sometimes it is called for though it is certainly the exception (for me at least) rather than the rule. I do acknowledge the love in fierce grace, although I feel compassion for those on the receiving end. If it is coming through, then it is needed, but I understand it isn't always pleasant even if it is ultimately helpful. The difference between fierce grace and aggression is enormous. For starters, the intention is so very different. For it to be genuine, fierce grace and not an abuse of power, the being delivering the grace must be completely surrendered into divine love, be fully in their hearts and in a place of compassion. They are not the ones who choose the delivery method of that love, simply the messenger.

I have been on both sides of this fierce compassion, which is at the heart of Durga's consciousness and fire, sometimes delivering and at other times receiving. In the chapter on Kali I mentioned an experience I had with a student that was tough rather than gentle, where I felt I was to deliver a hefty dose of fierce grace whether I wanted to (I didn't particularly!) or not. Although Kali and Durga have a different face, they have tough love in common. However, I have been on the receiving end of fierce grace too. I was going through a very difficult stage in my life, with a lot of demands on me. That I wasn't falling apart at the seams was a testament to divine mercy and my own connection to Durga, the ultimate multi-tasker. However, I wanted to take care of myself and try to set some limits too, as part of my growth was to learn to nurture myself and not demand endless productivity. I needed to learn to be gentler with my own relationships with myself.

I had just enrolled in a Chi training course, as a way of experimenting with how to manage the intense levels of divine electricity that poured through me when I taught, and to avoid 'blowing up' my body with too much power and causing illness. It was very important study, however even at the early stage of a couple of months, I was not keeping up with the studies as much as I would have liked. In terms of time and commitment, the course was not asking too much of me. However, the mental energy required to learn this very different approach to energy work and the personal transformation that was required to do this, felt like one demand on myself too many. I emailed the school administration and asked for suggestions. Could I take a break for a couple of months from training or if not, what other options could they suggest? I thought I would get a pleasant email with some suggested options.

The reply came from the head of the school, an elusive figure who was spoken of with much reverence by the other teachers but who rarely connected directly with a student – especially not one only a couple of months into the four-year plus training program. I was very surprised that he had emailed me back personally. I was even more surprised when I read his email.

The response to my short enquiry was a rather long, somewhat critical, certainly challenging email that bordered on confrontational. His reply seemed completely out of proportion to my simple question. He suggested that I had all sorts of issues going on and really challenged my commitment to the training. I felt this was unfair, misplaced and was really missing the point of my question. I took pause. I knew this man was held in high esteem but I had never met him. Was he as masterful as people suggested? His email was not a proportional response to what I had written. Why? Surely he wasn't sent into an emotional tantrum because of an innocent question from a student? Had the email arrived when he had just about had enough of people not appreciating his work and just lost the plot and taken it out on me? I certainly hoped not!

I felt rattled but remained calm, with occasional bursts of 'What the hell is going on?' I wondered if I was overreacting or misreading his words as can certainly happen with email. I took my time and methodically responded to each of his critical remarks, hoping to bring our interaction back into proportional and helpful terrain. However, the email that came back from him again had another 'bang' of energy attached to it. It almost felt like he was deliberately misinterpreting what I had written and was 'at' me for some reason. I was very confused by his behaviour! I did my best to stay calm, clear and communicative in my response, even though I was really baffled by what was happening and was uncomfortable with how bizarre the situation seemed. I did question the level of consciousness of this man, but I also wanted to suspend judgment and be open (but discerning!) until I could work out what was going on. I believed his teachings were very valuable to my development and I was willing to wait and see what unfolded in this strange, surprising and quite frankly, rather annoying, interaction. I again answered his email, trying to keep a cool head, but promised myself that if I sensed he was indeed unworthy of the respect that others afforded him, I would terminate my involvement with his school.

His next reply abruptly switched into a completely different tone. It was nice, polite and short saying, "Thank you for answering my questions, I am happy to keep you in the school." The energy was now completely neutral, and that was that. I was more shocked by this polite email because all the force of his other emails had just switched off as quickly and unexpectedly as it had switched on. He 'disappeared' and I didn't receive any further direct contact with him. I was bamboozled to say the least.

Later that day, I received an email from the senior teacher in the school, who knew the enigmatic school founder rather well, having trained with him personally. She was the person I had dealt with on several prior occasions and although what she was teaching me sometimes felt quite strange, I sensed her skill and trusted her enough to become open, receptive and allow her to teach me. Without my asking, she explained what had happened with the school founder and his emails to me. I did chuckle to myself as she explained. It made sense.

The founder of the school was a martial artist and energy healer with a high degree of proficiency. He understood energy, how it works in the human body and had developed a technique based on ancient principles and modern understanding, so that energy could be utilised without the burnout and damage to the physical body that could happen when it became strong. This is what I was struggling with and why I had enrolled in the school. I worked with high levels of energy, especially in group situations, and had been struggling with the negative side effects. My body could be literally burnt out by the intensity of the divine electricity coursing through me when I taught. It caused endless health problems and I knew from decades of physical struggle how difficult it was to handle the negative effects of working with high voltage energy.

He wanted to see what I would do when he, to use his expression, 'threw me around a bit.' That is certainly what it felt like he was doing at the time. My teacher said that he asked her not to respond to my email, and he just took over. She said he didn't normally do that, especially to someone so new to the course, and she felt like she was watching him put one of his martial arts students through their paces! She explained that he wanted to see what I would do and how I would respond to the force in his encounters with me.

He said that I completely internalised my energetic responses to others. I suppose he was waiting for me to explode at him in righteous anger, which I rarely do. I hadn't thought of how I handled the situation as internalising my responses, but as I sat with it, I realised that was probably pretty accurate. I had taught myself to pull my energy back in on myself, so that I wouldn't unnecessarily harm others with the force of my energy, and perhaps unintentionally engage in psychic attack if I got angry at someone. I was extremely self-controlled in that way, at least for much of the time, and according to him this did not always have the best effect for myself, and possibly not for the other person either. As much as I knew anger could be useful for me to draw upon to make changes in my life, to unleash it on another was not something I wanted to do. However, he said this approach was causing me harm instead. I needed to learn to discharge rather than internalise the energy.

The information he gained through his fierce compassion was passed on to the senior teacher who very generously, and very kindly, helped me through the difficult time, supporting me and benefitting me with even more personalised instruction. I learned through that process of being 'put through my paces' that I could benefit by making some changes in how I responded to life. I have been working on that ever since, and it is a very helpful learning process. Now that didn't have to turn out that way, of course. It could have ended with me in a strop, making judgments and rejecting the entire process, but I had enough experience with fierce compassion to at least take pause and wait and see. Fortunately in this case, that is what is was, though I have seen other people lay claim to divine authority for what is quite simply, abusive behaviour. Either way we can choose to turn it into an opportunity for healing (remember we can choose to make the darkness serve the light through our divine intelligence). In the case of an abuser, our relationship might be better kept short term!

Either way, the only way we get to understanding is to be open to letting go of our personal reactions and to trust. We can then grow through our emotional responses and use them as sign posts for inner healing. When we are willing to suspend our judgment of people, events and circumstances in favour of seeking out the divine perfection lurking within, we are calling on Durga. We are putting our evolution above our ego comfort, for the moment.

This does not mean that we accept abusive behaviour as a way to 'smash' our ego and give our soul triumph. It does mean that we surrender our immediate judgment and seek discernment and that we move out of fear and into love, to suss out the bigger picture. We need to be willing to be open to the possibility that there may be a higher wisdom at work than what our emotional reaction first tells us. We don't dismiss our experiences, but nor do we believe they are the only truth. We strive to heal through them by asking, 'How am I being asked to grow spiritually here?' Be open to the possibility that the wounding we believe we have experienced at the hand of another may be our own soul trying to get us to grow. Instead of abandoning or avoiding our personal pain, we can use it as breadcrumbs to lead us to our own divine soul by staying open to the possibility that there is growth rather than injustice at hand. By looking within, rather than reacting externally without reflection, we can make wise choices about how to deal with a situation. The results might be the same (e.g. the ending of a relationship), but they may be very different indeed, depending on how we deal with the process of being challenged and whether we react as victims or believe that we are being given an opportunity to become empowered.

Through my encounter with the mysterious founder of the chi school, I learned that the person I needed protecting from was not so much him as it was myself! I had to learn to discharge rather than hold and internalise the energy through my work. I learned something valuable and it gave me the impetus to continue with the studies and apply the wisdom with more understanding. Nothing like a bit of immediate experience to get a point across! I already knew I needed more learning, but this interaction showed me why I needed it and how to put it into practice more effectively.

When we work with goddess energies, our energy grows stronger. This is both a blessing and a challenge. In writing this book I have been shown where I have great power as well as where I need to unlearn behaviours and open up to love in a more conscious way, including how I love myself. It has been a beautiful, painful undertaking and part of the process of ending a relationship, moving to a new town and opening up to new friendships and ways of being in the world that feel more liberating, enjoyable, easy and natural for me.

Take your time reading this book, especially if you go deep. Do the processes, allow the consciousness behind it to really permeate your being and you will be transformed too – to the extent that is helpful for your soul journey. As that takes place, your shakti will grow. Shakti is the name for life force and Divine Feminine energy in the Indian tradition from which Durga, Kali, Lakshmi, Matangi and Saraswati all come. Shakti is a word that describes our power and our effectiveness in the physical world. Shakti can be loving or not. It is neutral, it is energy. It is what we choose to do with it through working on ourselves and becoming increasingly pure of heart and surrendered to the Divine that dictates whether our shakti (energy/power/action/talents) will tend towards the increase of love or fear on this planet.

When someone has a lot of shakti, they move people, they get things done. They can be very charismatic and powerful in the way they are able to manipulate people with lesser shakti. It is the case of a stronger force overpowering another. This is one reason why, if we want to serve love, the more we grow in power the more surrendered we need to become. It is very dangerous to remain locked in the ego stance of believing that we know best for people. As we grow, our opinions will hold more sway, not because they are necessarily wise, but because the energy behind them is increasingly powerful. I have seen a couple of really talented healers, with a lot of wise knowing in them, fall into this trap. They believe that because they see a lot it means that they see all. But we don't know what we don't know! If we can know that we don't know what we don't know (confused yet?) then we will be on the path to true wisdom. Part of that true wisdom is the realisation that we are given free will as human beings for a reason. To use it! There will be plenty of people who might want you as a healer, a friend, or a spiritually empowered person (in their opinion) to tell them what to do or how to live. However, to do so isn't necessarily helpful.

Assuming the right to tell people what to do is a mistake for a number of reasons. Keep this in mind if you find yourself falling into this trap as a healer, especially if people seek you out as their personal oracle! Also keep it in mind if you have been on the receiving end of such behaviour from anyone in your life – whether they are trying to help or not – who believes they are supposed to guide you or tell you what to do.

For a start, we can't actually know what another should or should not be doing. We'll have our opinions perhaps, but beyond mere opinion, no human mind is going to be capable of understanding the unfathomable divine genius at play in each being. The best the human mind can do is become pure, open and surrendered to love.

Secondly, if we do go about giving advice or setting ourselves up as the one to tell others how to live and what to do, we are not only creating a rod for our own back by creating dependent relationships, but we can end up pulling people off their paths and away from their own truths through the magnetism of our energy or shakti. If we are doing that, we are not serving love but have unintentionally stepped onto the dark path of counter-evolution. It doesn't matter if we think we are pushing someone into something for 'their own good.' Even if we say we want liberation for all beings, if we are not completely surrendered into the divine, without an opinion about how things should be, then we are not serving love. It's as simple, and as tricky, as that.

Add to this trickiness that just because someone has more powerful shakti, it doesn't mean that the soul of the person being overpowered is less evolved. Sometimes dark beings have a tremendous amount of shakti. Cult leaders come to mind as one example. Hitler is a fairly classic example of a being with a lot of power and an ability to manipulate and create in a very powerful way, but from a place of fear rather than love. Just because someone is powerful doesn't necessarily mean that they are wise.

We can all grow our shakti. It happens naturally and in a measured way when it is approached not for its own ends (which is likely to be come from a lust for power) but as a by-product of our spiritual growth. It is important that we allow ourselves to grow in power course, especially those of us on the path of love. I spoke about power in the first chapter of *Crystal Angels 444* because it is such an important issue. To have an evolved soul with much wisdom, but too little power to be able to stand firm and be present in the physical world where that wisdom is needed is painful for the soul in question and a loss for the world that needs that loving light to be shone bright enough to be registered consciously. We need those on the path of love to be powerful enough to have a strong, surrendered voice as an alternative to the strong, fear-based and ego-driven voices that exist in our world. It is not always easy to be one of those alternative voices, and sometimes it is downright depressing when you realise you need to be the light when someone is unconsciously promoting darkness. Especially if they are in your beloved metaphysical field, let alone those in advertising, finance, real estate and media. We need empowered lovers of the Divine on the path. The work in this book will take you into greater empowerment.

Those with greater shakti simply have more energy flowing through their being because their chakras are larger and more open to life. I have met some beautiful, pure souls who are actually very reluctant to open up to life. The *Crystal Stars 11.11* book will focus more on such people because they are very important to the spiritual evolution of humanity and hold far more power than they realise. Their empowerment is so very dear to my heart because I know what good they can do in the world. They can learn to build their power to match their wisdom and love, and become truly illumined beings capable of doing much good in this world. And they'll have a lot of fun doing it too. Feeling inadequate to the task of manifesting your own soul light and talents is not much fun at all!

One of the best ways I know to build shakti is to commit to your spiritual and inner-healing work. The spiritual work opens us up to divine love and the healing work clears the chakras so that the divine love can be well received. The healing processes in this entire series, my meditation CDs and my oracle decks integrate these two arms of healing which lead us further along the path of love. That's all we need. Divine love is alchemical. It changes us, leads us to wholeness, and as that happens, we are initiated into greater power through the growth of our shakti and our kundalini energy awakens.

Kundalini energy is a particular type of shakti or life-force that lives in the human body. In the Indian tradition it is said to be a coiled serpent, sleeping at the base of the spine. On our journey of consciousness, over many lifetimes, the kundalini is eventually awakened and begins to travel up our spine. It moves through the chakras and along two energetic lines that intersect from the base of our spine to the third eye, as well as through a central channel in the spinal cord, which is called the 'sushumna.'

As the kundalini begins to flow, chakras naturally open and are cleared out. We can experience this as our 'stuff' coming up. Eventually the chakras are free enough from unprocessed emotion to become receptive to divine energy, as there is space in the energy field to receive it. If we do conscious healing work with the body then the light that filters through the chakra system eventually filters through into the physical body via our nervous system. It takes time, but it happens naturally, just like water works its way through obstacles, clearing them out and nourishing the landscape left behind. Although the clearing out process is rarely much fun, there are other experiences that come with activated kundalini that are more enjoyable. These include the opening of divine talents, healing abilities, clairvoyance and an increasingly direct and immediate experience of the Divine. Our energy – including our sexual and creative energy – is enhanced and we can become more energised, vital, compassionate and wise beings. However, if the kundalini doesn't quite rise up beyond the lower chakras towards the heart, we may just become more power hungry and even sexually obsessive! This is something to be aware of as a caution. But remember too that all things do come, in time, including a fuller flow of kundalini that is ultimately balanced, helpful and allows our shakti to serve love and contribute to the unfolding of loving divine will upon this precious planet.

It is important to know this is a natural process. Kundalini is trendy as an idea in spiritual circles and I have seen people try to awaken it using all sorts of strange breathing and dance techniques. The truth of the matter is that typically the last thing we need is more power! Growth, healing, awareness and so much more come first. So, these people were already dealing with issues around ego and control. More power drawn into that situation would have been like giving a kid having a tantrum a loaded gun. Perhaps the Divine Mother will grant an activation of kundalini as a learning experience in those sorts of situations, but I can tell you it would be an experience of fierce compassion and tough love if ever there was one. Their kundalini was already too active in the lower centres, and not yet reaching the heart. To just bring more power into those lower chakras (which is all that would happen until the block in heart was cleared and the kundalini could rise up through the chakras towards the crown) would have exacerbated the issues they were already working with.

We are given more power when we are ready for it. We don't have to go after it as though it is a hidden prize (tempting though that can be). That is why I am cautious with exercises that are designed to specifically make kundalini rise, rather than those that are about preparing for its natural activation (such as the healing processes in this book). In my experience it is wiser to clear the way, and become open and receptive to greater power naturally, through trust in life and by engaging in our life experiences. However, that is the way of the heart and of course, if we aren't consciously connected there yet, that approach will not be available to us. I have seen some people with a lot of spiritual talent, who have awakened kundalini in a way that does not engage the heart. The young man I mentioned earlier in this book who used his psychic skills to seduce women is one example, but I could mention others that are far more dramatic than that. Awakening kundalini doesn't necessarily mean there will be spiritual wisdom. As we journey, we will sometimes have more power than wisdom. Eventually however, we will find the balance and wholeness that is the eventual destination of the feminine path.

I was singing at a dance gathering run by someone I didn't know well. Eventually I had my own painful dose of tough love and fierce compassion, and realised I had better become more discerning about whom I worked with, but prior to that . . . I was standing in a circle with facilitator and participants of the class, with our thumbs pointing up, huffing and puffing away. I felt like so foolish and wondered what on earth all this carry-on was supposed to achieve. Later I realised it was supposed to be a kundalini raising breath exercise. Perhaps it could be effective, but all the same, simply coming into the heart would have attained far more.

I believe in divine timing, as you know, and divine grace. Both of which are received in a surrendered state. It is up to you to find the paths that feel right for you, but I can offer you this: If you are involved in groups that are playing with kundalini, rather than earnestly working on themselves y and allowing it to awaken naturally, tread carefully. Kundalini is divine fire and it can set the heart ablaze with love or it can burn the chakras out if they aren't ready to receive it. If we try to plug a device into a circuit and the voltage levels are not compatible, we can damage the device. Our body is the device in this metaphor. We have to find a balance between opening up to growth and trying to force growth to happen. If you want a safe way to prepare for its flow, the work we do in these healing processes will support you in. I have also created a chakra meditation CD through Blue Angel which is powerful, but balanced and designed to open you up in accordance with your soul journey rather than to force kundalini to rise before it is naturally prone to do so.

The movement of kundalini will be obvious if you are sensitive to energy. The side effects of kundalini rising are often not so subtle and include emotional and psychological pain as well as inexplicable physical pain. People who do regular meditation – one way to open up to kundalini flow reasonably safely – often tell me of strange pains that only pass in time. I experienced this myself when I had a stabbing pain in my back, but only when meditating. It took several months but eventually it was released. I sensed that the kundalini was moving through my heart at a new level at the time. As that happened, old pain (perhaps from having been literally or figuratively stabbed in the back in one incarnation or other) was pushed up into my awareness and out of my body. Eventually the rising energy was strong enough to overpower that pain and force it out. My heart could then open further and the energy could continue to rise through another cycle.

Kundalini is not a one-hit wonder. It moves in cycles, ever growing and expanding. That is why it is good to be discerning around those who claim to possess an awakened kundalini. Many of us have this to some extent. But the trick on the spiritual path, as with life perhaps, is that you don't know, what you don't know. A few experiences of kundalini might be mistaken for a full kundalini awakening, but more than likely, that is not the case.

Another experience that can come with awakening kundalini is an intense type of natural high and bliss that can leave people laughing uncontrollably for hours. I remember a woman who had highly developed upper chakras and not so developed lower chakras. This meant she tended to become spaced out very easily, was extremely sensitive to spiritual energy, but often found it hard to ground herself. She found her way into a dance class I was running with my best friend at the time. After about twenty minutes of intensely chanting the Divine Mother's name, she was so filled with shakti that her kundalini starting buzzing. She began running about the room and didn't stop until the end of the class some considerable time later. She laughed, spoke of love and just couldn't keep still. She was like a blissed-out child on a sugar high! Although we did our best to ground her, she would have none of it! She wanted the spiritual high and stayed with it. She became sick a few days following and I have no doubt it was because she had too much divine energy in one hit. Her body was trying to clear out toxins, became overloaded in the process, and became unwell to try and deal with it all. When kundalini awakening is more balanced, we can still become filled with energy for hours on end, but the 'come down' will be softer when we learn to ride the more moderate path rather than chasing the highs and then having to deal with the compensatory lows. This comes from working with an experienced teacher (and listening to their guidance!) and learning how to monitor your own energy field. We learn that with experience and practice, and by honouring feminine wisdom as taught in this series, especially this book.

Awakening kundalini also tends to stimulate latent spiritual abilities along with it and this, combined with the bliss energy, can have people lusting after the awakening. This means pushing for it, rather than accepting it as something that happens naturally along with your growth. I have been witness to all this and more. I will share some of my experiences with kundalini because I want you to be able to recognise them when they happen in your journey, and to make sense of things that may have already happened for you, and overall, to not be scared. Kundalini is wild, but it is divine. It has its own intelligence and provided we come to it with respect, rather than arrogantly trying to force it to our will, we will be able to manage the awakening process without getting into too much trouble.

In trying to bend it to our will, we are setting up a karmic learning for ourselves that will eventually teach us humility and reverence. This can happen in any number of ways. I have seen it in action with people who have truly difficult kundalini awakenings that take them out of healthy, challenging but containable spiritual growth, and to varying degrees, into disturbed states that border on mental illness and render them incapable of functioning. It can take years of therapy and physical healing practices to undo that damage and I am not even certain that all such damage at a physical level can be completely undone, in all cases. If the imbalance is severe, and there is little regard and understanding of the feminine principles of patience and cycles, it may take healing over lifetimes for the soul to truly recover from the harshness that the 'spiritualised ego' wrought upon life so that life was required to lash back with some tough love to redress the arrogance and promote more wisdom. ('Spiritualised ego' is the quest for spiritual enlightenment that comes from the desire for power, status and influence, rather than the genuine desire of the soul for divine union and service.)

I don't mention this to alarm you. I mention it to make it clear that there are no short cuts and that the apparently faster way on any path is not necessarily the most direct way, because we have to go back and learn what it is we missed in our efforts to get ahead. I have a lot of regard for people who value spiritual light enough to want to build their powers and become more effective in their work, and I have a lot of compassion for how easily the ego can get caught up in this. I don't judge – I have been there myself so I can hardly be precious about it. I just share the knowledge in the hope that you will gain some helpful awareness about this part of you that is still largely misunderstood in Western new age culture. And so that you can relax, get on with your work, and let it just happen.

In my late teens, I struggled with food allergies and health issues. Looking back they were a result of a body overloaded with unprocessed emotion. This impacted my vitality and my immune and digestion systems were not working optimally. Those things improved later as my emotional healing journey took place, in really rather dramatic ways, but at that time I was yet to benefit from the inner-healing work in a physical way. So, I went to an alternative healer to find a way to work with my physical ailments.

Acupuncture was part of my healing journey. Though I recognised it as powerful and potentially effective, my first experience of acupuncture was not pleasant. As the needles went into my neck and shoulders, I felt the most extraordinarily strange sensation of what seemed to be hot, blocked coils of wire creaking in my neck! It eventually became so unbearably painful that I had to have the needles removed. I was experiencing the flow (or in that instance, obstruction to the flow) of energy in my body. Energy flows through us constantly and is obstructed to greater or lesser degrees depending on the state of our emotional, psychological and physical wellbeing. This energy is called chi in the Chinese tradition and prana (a type of shakti) in the Indian tradition. I have always been able to feel energy, but I didn't know what it was at the time. I was quite bamboozled by the strong, unpleasant physical reactions to the treatment. I didn't know that energy could feel so very physical and tangible.

I intuitively understood that unblocking energy would require emotional and physical healing. I consciously began doing emotional healing and spiritual development work in the years following that first experience. Over time I shed emotional blockages and became more energetically open because of this. This process was sometimes very pleasant and at other times, not so much.

One evening as my partner quietly slept beside me, I suddenly awoke with the disturbing sense of not being able to feel my hands. It was not as though they had gone numb, it was like they weren't there! I sat up in bed and strong pulsations of energy began to tingle through me. It was like 'pins and needles' but much, much stronger and very unpleasant. The sensations powered through my chest, arms, but especially in my hands and I worried that I was having a heart attack of some kind. My then partner eventually registered that I was having a silent, though intense experience and woke up. He was rather aware at that level. He would feel my thoughts at a quite intense level and sometimes when we were falling asleep, he would suddenly say, "Stop thinking Alana! Your thoughts are keeping me awake!" We often played telepathic games together, like two spiritual nerds, because we were very plugged in at that level. Anyway, as he sat next to me, looking at me having this bizarre experience, all sorts of thoughts flew through my mind. Firstly, did I need to go to hospital? Secondly, what the hell was happening? Thirdly, would it ever end?

I didn't go to hospital. The sensations ended about twenty minutes or so later. It was a very long twenty minutes. I believe my heart chakra was clearing and opening at a deeper level. I sensed that my energy field was being opened up, and the channels along my arms and hands were being cleared so as I could perform healing work and the divine transmission of energy could flow more freely from my heart through to my hands. I had experienced a lot of grief in the early days of this lifetime, and I needed some help clearing it out and unblocking my heart. So, that is what happened. I started doing hands on healing work with people a short time later.

A year or so later, I needed further energetic support on my journey and I decided to give acupuncture another try. Despite the discomfort of my first experience, I felt acupuncture was an exceptionally powerful healing tool – in a skilled practitioner's hands. A friend recommended her local doctor. His surgery wasn't a particularly spiritual or inspiring place to be getting acupuncture, however, I didn't have a lot of money, the doctor bulk-billed the treatments and my friend reported good results. So off I went, wondering what, if anything, would happen, this time.

I sat in the doctor's shabby, messy clinic room, with a little TV blaring and a waiting room filled with patients who were happy to talk and treat their waiting time as an opportunity to socialise. It was not uncommon for him to be hours behind on his appointments, so his rooms were always jam-packed. He jabbed a few needles here and there, and left me to sit in the room for twenty minutes, while attended to his other patients in a second clinic room.

I sat in the room, staring at the drab surrounds. I am highly responsive to beauty, so being in that physical ugliness wasn't doing much for my mood! I closed my eyes and tried to tune out the TV and the noisy conversations from the waiting room down the hall. After a few moments I began to feel very nauseated. I thought I was going to be sick, then all of a sudden I heard a powerful hissing and clicking sound. It sounded like a wild rush of energy – almost like an ocean wave. At the same time, the sudden impression of golden scales slid behind my eyes. I could see them shimmering, flowing, bending and curving. I could only see a small portion of the scales but I instantly knew it was an enormous serpent like energy that was moving. It was absolutely huge, even wider than my physical body.

As it moved, and the sound gushed and rattled through me, I felt sick, dizzy and utterly mesmerised by what was happening. The movement of the snake quickly progressed towards the top of my head where it stopped abruptly just beneath the top of my crown. The inside of my head somehow felt like it was bigger than the room. The snake tried to force its way out through my crown. The power of its upward flowing momentum caused it to pound at the top of my head, as though it was held under a trap door and wanted out. It felt and sounded so violent, like someone determined to kick a door open. Bang! Bang! Bang! I could feel and hear it pounding at the inside of the top of my head. I flung my eyes open, gasped and the process ebbed away. I still felt sick and dizzy, and just focused on trying to breathe normally back into the present moment, without throwing up.

I had again experienced my kundalini shakti. It was not a nice, little snakelike energy that wafted through the chakras within my body. It was huge, almost more powerful than I could cope with and determined to bust through whatever was blocking my crown chakra from opening to it. Given how much nausea I felt in the process, I expect the block being cleared by my kundalini energy was some type of fear lodged in my body.

Not long after that my spiritual path deepened and I began working in a more powerful way with people, channelling my first ascended master meditations which were published by Blue Angel many years later.

I often dream about snakes when kundalini is active. It isn't always evidenced in such dramatic physical episodes, though of course it can be. I have seen clients have spasmodic fits as their kundalini powered through them, and others that have become so still they cannot move. I have felt both of these experiences myself. However, the effect of its movement can also be very subtle.

When I was going through the challenging situation with the client mentioned in the chapter on Kali, I used a more vigorous yoga and meditation practice to keep me as pure and surrendered as possible through the process. I did this because I felt I needed it to help keep me present and grounded, and not get caught up in Kali's roaring energy. During one my meditations, I had a most sublime, subtle and beautiful kundalini experience. It was almost the exact opposite of how I had experienced it previously, when it was wild as a tiger. In that instance, the kundalini was like subtle, sweet ascending nectar. It was light, pure and I could feel it rising in the centre of my spinal cord. Although the spinal cord seems like a small space physically, the experience was very spacious. I felt utter bliss as the energy rose. It was somehow silvery and light and so refined. As I floated in that state I felt completely at peace. I didn't know for sure what I was experiencing until the word 'sushumna' popped into my head towards the end of the meditation. I Googled it later, and found a helpful webpage explaining sushumna as naturally awakening column of energy that runs up inside of the spinal cord, as part of our overall movement of kundalini.

Some weeks later I went for a break at a yoga retreat in Ibiza, before concluding that tour with a few intense spiritual workshops on the European mainland on my return. On the retreat, it was easy to do each spiritual practice because we were so looked after. I didn't have to get myself anywhere to do yoga because it was offered at the retreat. I didn't have to go and buy food and cook, because that was done for us. I could meditate, dance, walk, play and relax and it was wonderful. I did end up facilitating some dance journeys when I was there, unexpectedly so, simply because the energy in Ibiza was so wild and feminine that it made me want to dance. I figured that if I was going to be dancing and singing in the main room of the beautiful building where the retreat was being held, I might as well invite others to join in if they wanted to. All the participants ended up dancing, singing and meditating with me more than once during the week-long yoga retreat. It was not exactly a holiday as I thought, but beautiful nonetheless because it just flowed that way.

During my time on Ibiza, my meditations were different. The energy of the shakti or life force in Ibiza is very strong. Different parts of the earth have different shakti or energy. Australia is quite raw and Europe is quite refined in places. Sometimes the shakti or energy of a place is rather organised and masculine and in other areas it is quite unstructured and feminine. Greece and India are two places I have visited that have a more feminine shakti, for example.

Anyway, I could see why Ibiza, was considered (at least by some) to be a place to party and have a lot of sex! The moment I stepped off the plane from mainland Europe and onto the island, I felt all my energy drop out of my head and into my sacral chakra with a pleasant 'thump.' I felt grounded the entire time I was there, and intuitive in a very easy, naturally flowing way. If I wanted to go somewhere or find something, it just happened. Which was rather helpful because the street signs on the island have arrows pointing in all directions! So if you want to get to San Raphael, for example, the street signs will give you so many options on how to get there that the sign is rendered rather useless. It was a point of some amusement for a while, and then I realised the island is just like that – all flow and you just get to where you need to be.

This and the fact my energy field is very affected by the earth energies of wherever I happen to be, meant my meditations were more like spinal adjustments in chiropractic sessions. My spine clicked and cracked physically with the sheer force of energy flowing through it, even as I sat perfectly still. That can happen in Australia of course, or anywhere in the world, but it was unusually strong and constant in Ibiza. My kundalini was moved by the greater kundalini of the earth there, and my body registered this as a different experience of meditation, mood and being. This happens to people whether they are consciously aware of it or not. I am sure it is one reason why so many clubbers venture off to Ibiza for the summer and why the island attracted so many 'hippies' to set up shop there, many of whom are still there, living a life of flow and naturalness.

A year or so later, I was off on another adventure, this time to Turkey. A group I was teaching was made up of yoga practitioners who had done plenty of work on themselves, and a young man who was relatively new to it all. He was a DJ, had a good heart, and I recognised a purity in him spiritually. He was also the only man in our group and therefore rather brave too! During one workshop I used chanting, where I sing mantra and transmit divine energy through my voice. As I sang, I felt a lot of energy flowing through and I moved about the room adding subtle touch for the transmission of divine energy and support of the body when needed.

For whatever reason, this young man was deeply affected by the experience. He went into mild convulsions and his body froze in an awkward position. I could see he was going to fall over so with the help of another participant, we gently laid him down on some cushions, with his arms locked into an awkward postures and his fists clenched. As I gently stroked his hair out of his face and looked into his eyes to calm and assure him he would be okay, I could only see bliss and love in his eyes, not fear. I allowed him to rest, but at the closure of the meeting, he still couldn't move his arms! I knew he would be able to again and as we were on a residential retreat for another day or so, I would be close by and the situation would be well handled if, for some reason, fear took over. However, he was not fearful at all.

It was a few hours before his body returned to normal. He came up to me later and said, "Your voice dropped from the sky into my head and I felt love." He then shared that a fear he had been carrying his whole life, about losing love, had just left him. It had somehow just been freed from his body and he knew it would never return. That is kundalini arising. That is grace. It happened through me but it was not something that I made happen. It was an expression of divine compassion, fierce and tender in this instance. He was ready for it and it came to him.

Kundalini is part of the bridge that opens our everyday consciousness up to divine consciousness. I couldn't write a book on the Divine Feminine and not mention it, because it is at the heart of her manifestation. When we are touched by her hand, kundalini moves. After all, anything we seek to manifest is secondary to the ultimate manifestation of our lifetime, which is our divine becoming.

HEMATITE (GROUNDING)

Hematite can appear as beautiful blood red and brown crystal formations or as shiny, smoothly polished tumbled stones or spheres of dark silvery grey crystal, which is heavy for its size. It is a stone that feels cool to touch. Rich in iron oxide, even the dark grey stones resonate with the frequency of red. It is grounding and healing to the base chakra. We might think of red as a hot energy, but it is actually the ultraviolet frequencies that are hottest, and red as a frequency can be quite stabilising rather than heating. Hematite has been discovered on the red planet, Mars, which has a nice poetry to it. Astrologically, Mars is associated with strength, courage for battle and passion, all of which correspond to the metaphysical properties of hematite.

Hematite is sometimes used in love magic as it is considered an energetically magnetic stone. The natural magnetism in hematite is subtle though. The strongly magnetic jewellery that is sold as magnetised hematite, which some market as being ground and reconstituted hematite, is actually an artificially produced compound. It is sometimes called hematine or magnetised hematite, but it has a very different energy and feel. Visually, it appears far lighter and shinier than hematite and energetically it is completely different to handle.

Hematite is a protective stone, and helps us drop out of our heads, into awareness of the present moment. For highly sensitive, receptive and creative types, this is rather helpful to stop us spending so much time chasing one idea, and the next, that we never get a chance to see our ideas through to completion.

If the stone is drilled, the high content of red iron ore that comes out looks almost like the stone is bleeding. It is a visual representation of the healing potency of the stone and its connection to life force. Hematite helps generate life force and the connection to the physical, earthly world that we need to bring things through to completion. It supports us in engaging with the physical world by nurturing our sciatic nerve and our blood, whereby life force and energy can flow from life into our bodies. It can help us manage our kundalini awakenings too, so that they are more balanced and integrated into our bodies.

On the psychological level, it helps us ground and focus. When there is a lot of complexity in our lives, we need focus and grounding to prevent us being overwhelmed. If you have ever had so much to do that you lost your ability to be efficient and effective, and perhaps found yourself standing in one spot wondering what to do first, then you will know what being overwhelmed can do to our productivity. Completely bring it to standstill!

The more the Divine flows through us, the more we can be vehicles for the will of Heaven in many and varied ways, even without being completely conscious of it. Just to be able to be in the simplicity of the moment is so helpful. We can have great complexity flowing through us, without having to identify with the complexity. We simply need to be in the moment and tend to what needs our attention in each particular moment. That approach can take quite a bit of emotional and mental (not to mention physical) discipline, but hematite supports us with this.

As a stone for the mind, it helps us still our thoughts enough to get a sense of what is happening within and around us. The reflective quality of grey hematite helps us see where we are getting in our own way, to calm down, to become heavier energetically and to settle our energy so that we can tend to one step at a time. Which is all any journey, even the greatest journey, requires. The protective and grounding qualities help counteract jitteriness and distraction. We can see if there are saboteurs inside or outside of us, and be protected from their interference so we can get on with living our lives, and have the courage and optimism to trust.

For women and men who need more strength and courage, hematite increases energy in the belly and helps us draw upon the power of the Earth. For those that need to cool down and adopt a gentler, more yielding way to be, hematite balances the yin energy – feminine, cooling, receptive energy – thus allowing for one to be both strong and surrendered.

From its heaviness, it can provide the centre point from which polarities are balanced. So much of our stress comes from slipping out of balance. If our life has many factors to deal with, then balance can be even trickier to maintain. Just sitting with a heavy piece of hematite can help us feel grounded and back in our centre again.

Hematite is particularly helpful for those with restless minds, always filled with ideas or lists of things to be done! Supporting the health of our nervous system and spinal alignment, as well as the balance of fluids in the body, the mind finds a more soothing temple to rest in when our bodies are in a greater state of wellness and balance.

Hematite is also helpful for overcoming compulsive and addictive behaviour, as it releases negativity and helps dissolve negativity coming at us from outside sources. It is that negativity that we often struggle to process and convert into useful constructive energy (and we try to release it in addictive or compulsive behaviours instead). Hematite helps us learn to discharge energy, releasing it rather than re-routing it through our systems only to have to purge it later in ways that might not always be so constructive or in tune with our body.

The more our body and mind work together, in balance, supported by the earth energy, the greater our ability to handle the real electricity of divine energy becomes. We can then allow it to guide us from within, and sustain us as we open up to the multi-faceted life path that is our divine destiny.

MANIFESTING THROUGH GENIUS

If there is one thing I have learned through working with the Divine, it is that divine intelligence is absolutely brilliant. It is sheer genius. The way solutions are presented in win-win situations, that work on countless levels for all involved and somehow provide the perfect measure of challenge and support, no matter what level of spiritual growth each person may be at, is absolutely flawless and astounding. The more I see and know of the divine, the more stunned into awestruck silence I become. And I am not one who is typically lost for words. Its healing genius is breath-taking and absolutely, completely, without exception, trustworthy.

It is the last part that we probably find the most difficult to accept. However, trust is essential for that genius to be unleashed. The more willing we are to trust, the bolder the divine will become in utilising our gifts and talents in the world. It isn't always the most talented who are moved forward, but those that are ready and willing to be moved! Trust, and the willingness that comes with trust, are considerable contributors to our path of spiritual growth.

For a long time, I knew all this in my heart, but not from seeing and experiencing it in profound ways for myself. That heart knowing became increasingly powerful as I had the life experiences to confirm it. My heart didn't need any reinforcement but my mind certainly benefitted from it. In every small step of trust that I took, I found absurd, wonderfully funny and perfect solutions that would lead me forward, like breadcrumbs on my path. In time, I was taking steps without thinking about it, which I would never have believed myself capable of taking without a lot of pain and struggle in the lead up. I still have my moments of course, where I sense a step before me – that seems like a mighty leap – and I have to remember to breathe deeply and trust. But I recognise that this is part of the process of growth and nothing more meaningful than that.

When we are accepting of divine genius, we become more curious than anxious. I often find myself wondering what the Divine has in store for a particular situation rather than whether or not it will work out. Things will work out. The divine genius is the 'how'.

To really receive the Divine and learn to know its ways with utter trust, we have to become empty. There is a story I love about a man who went in search of a monk revered for his wisdom.

He travelled for a long distance and eventually found this wise monk. They sat down for tea together and as the monk poured the man his tea, the man talked at length about himself and his problems and why he was seeking the monk. On and on the man talked, and on and on the monk poured until the tea was streaming out of the cup, onto the saucer, onto the table and down onto the floor! The monk was offering the man a teaching, but the man was so mentally full, he was overflowing. He couldn't receive any assistance until he stopped filling himself up with declarations of his woes. To receive the tea, he had to learn not to overfill himself. We need to be careful when we seek out the Divine so that we don't forget that we are here to receive. We need to become empty, to open up and let go. If we have already decided should be and how, then there is no room to receive the gift of tea that we have asked for. So, when manifesting through genius, we must remember to let go, and let god – and goddess!

HEALING PROCESS

This healing process will benefit those who are multi-tasking, or who have big dreams that they want to manifest which will take numerous steps and stages to bring to life. It helps us let go of the anxiety, stress and fear of failure that comes with the assumption that we have to 'do it all ourselves'. Sometimes the biggest effort is not in the practical steps that we take over time, but actually in trusting enough to let go so that we feel intuitively when we need to take a step and when it's time to be patient and know that life will show us clearly when it's time to act again.

If you have felt overwhelmed by the sheer extent of your visions or dreams, or just by life, or the content of your own mind and fluctuating emotions, this healing process is a deep cleansing which will assist you in being able to more easily and effectively set correct priorities in your life (those being the ones that lead you to wholeness rather than into overload or overwhelm).

The Process

Have your mandala and/or crystal with you.

Say aloud, "I call upon Durga, the sacred warrior mother who loves me unconditionally. I call upon your wild wisdom, your divine genius and your powerful success! I call upon the Crystal Angel of Hematite. I call upon the vibration of 888. I call upon success and manifestation according to the highest divine laws of love. So be it."

See, sense or feel that you are resting in an ocean of silvery grey shining light. That ocean of light pulls heavy metals, toxins, old patterns and karmic debris out of your system through the back of your energy body. Imagine you can sense or perceive the gentle extraction and dissolving action of that sea of light as your energy field, body, mind and soul are cleansed and strengthened.

That ocean of silver grey light becomes rich red earth beneath your feet now. Feel the vibration of the earth beneath you, almost like you can feel her energy flow and her heart beat through the soles of your feet. Allow the love in your heart to expand until your heart opens like a flower and sends energy down through your body, out through your feet, into the earth.

When you are ready, say, "I would like help to manifest the next level of my life path and divine destiny through divine genius. Through mercy, grace and compassion, so be it." If you have a particular issue that you want help with, mention that out loud now also.

When you are ready, begin to speak this mantra:

OM DUM DURGAYEI NAMAHA

OM (sounds like Tom) DUM (sounds like DOOM) DURGAYEI (DOOR-GUY-YAY) NAMAHA (rhymes with Yahama).

Say it at least eight times or as many times as feels good. Don't worry if the language feels strange because you are not used to Sanskrit or that particular prayer. It actually means, "I call upon the wild divine grace of She who cannot be defeated." You can say the prayer and know that it will call her energy into your being.

If you have fear or attachments that are leaving you as you take this spiritual medicine into your body, you may feel some nausea or tiredness. Just try to go with it but don't overdo it. If you have been sick, are emotionally stressed out or hormonally imbalanced, do less repetitions of the mantra, or just relax instead. Listen to yourself. Sometimes less can be more. These are powerful prayers and we need to build up to working with their energy. The more sensitive we are, the more responsive we may be to divine energy and the less force we need to get things moving. So be attuned and trust your sense of what you need.

Once you have finished your mantra, relax and soak in the energy of the sound.

You may perceive, sense or feel a vibrant golden goddess riding a tiger, dressed in red and gold, and wielding many golden weapons in her many arms. Allow her to use her weapons in your situation, on your life path, to clear obstacles and lift you into the next step of your life. Allow her to give you whatever you need – perhaps even one of her golden weapons – to defeat obstacles and move forward on your spiritual path.

Stay with what you see, sense and feel and in your own time, surround yourself with rich emerald green light with flecks of gold, healing and protecting your energy.

When you are ready, simply open your eyes and bow your head to your hands, in prayer position at your heart.

Over the coming weeks, repeat this exercise and mantra if you intuitively feel drawn to do so. You can safely do eight repetitions or more of this mantra on a daily basis, especially if you are feeling challenged in some way in your life.

You may like to do further work with Durga through my *Inner Power* meditation CD available through Blue Angel and on my website.

17.

XI WANG MU (IMMORTALITY)
STROMATOLITE (STEADFASTNESS)

MANIFESTING THROUGH PATIENCE

Grandmother from whom all the wise ones descended. She smiles and knows. Deftly she determines who shall live and who shall pass, who shall be well and when sickness shall serve love. With endless wisdom she draws forward the ready ones, into enlightened bliss.

XI WANG MU (IMMORTALITY)

A truly ancient Chinese shamanic goddess, Xi Wang Mu (SHEE-WANG-MOO or SEE-WANG-MOO) is incredibly gentle and exceptionally powerful. Her name translates as grandmother in the spiritual sense, as heavenly mother and as Queen of the West.

Upon the tip of the Kunlun Mountains in Western China, at the meeting place of Heaven and Earth, she dwells in a beautiful garden, veiled by clouds. In her garden there is an enormous cosmic tree, which bears her peaches of immortality. Those sacred peaches ripen once every 3,000 years. The great tree is a sacred ladder which shamans and mystics use to travel between Heaven and Earth, to know the divine and bring wisdom, healing and spiritual energy back from the heavenly worlds into the earthly worlds were it is needed. Could anything be more beautiful?

Fifteen centuries before Christ, and before even the old spiritual philosophy of the Tao existed, she was known. Named as the Queen Mother of the West, oracle bones dating back to 1500BC have been found with her name inscribed upon them. With the inception of Tao, several hundred years before Christ, Xi Wang Mu was integrated into the way and is described in the ancient texts as being a woman who attained the Tao (or mastered life), and therefore had become immortal.

From that moment onward, she was divine. It is said that no one could know her beginning or her end, for she has attained oneness with life and is limitless. She has become ageless, a pure radiance of life itself, burning immortal love. The Tao is unknowable, indescribable. We could very loosely translate it as the way of life. It is the highest spiritual wisdom and state of being. To attain the Tao is to enter into divinity in such a way that one can never lapse, return or do anything other than be divine truth, wisdom, love and being. It is the end of the spiritual journey, from our perspective at least (though at a higher perspective I suspect there is no beginning or end, but let us leave that discussion for another time).

The Queen Mother of the West holds the power of Heaven and Earth, of harvest, prosperity and also spoil, epidemics, disease and their cure. She is described in ancient teachings as having the power of sound. Sometimes it is described as roaring, other translations say her sound is clear and melodic. Her singing moves and excites the spirit of all beings. Shamans who work with voice for healing, such as myself, often use sound as a method to bypass the mind and allow heavenly energy to move straight into the body. There is light and energy in the sound, and when there is surrender in the mind and adequate capacity in the nervous system to handle divine voltage, a direct transmission of heavenly energy can flow into the earth. We can feel when this is happening. The sound seems to move around us, swirl inside of us and move straight through us. Sometimes we can feel like it is dropping from the sky, right into our heads, like the young DJ yogi I described in the previous chapter. It may feel like it is somehow inside of our hearts, awakening, as if it was always there. Xi Wang Mu is the master of this art.

She is revered as the original teacher of the Tao to the mystics and the great teacher to all who tread that path of wisdom. Whether or not you relate consciously to the Tao, you will be a student of its wisdom to some degree because you are drawn to working with the Divine Feminine. Otherwise you wouldn't be reading this book! Taoist principles feature deeply in this book. The Tao is the way of life that is a feminine or yin path of allowing life and seeking to know and to become it, rather than approaching it with a view to dominating and directing it from an ego perspective. The Tao is about true power – mastery of the self rather than others, and finding fullness and accepting endless space through realising that all dwells within rather than through seeking fullness from external sources and avoiding emptiness like the plague. The Tao is about harmony, balance, the feminine wisdom of life itself and being in connection with all. For those that master it by becoming it, nothing is withheld. Yet this ultimate power will never be afforded to those with a lust for power. The divine paradox is that the great power flows through those who lay no claim to it. The Tao is not just about self-development; it is about wise surrender into all of life.

The iconography of Xi Wang Mu includes the tiger, and at times she is pictured as a woman with tiger teeth or a leopard tail. These hint at her wild qualities and the power of nature that is wielded through her. She often wears a headdress and carries the shaman's staff which can symbolise the connection between all the worlds and also be a tool through which energy is directed and flows. The crown or headdress she wears, symbolises an awakened crown chakra and that she is royalty in the truest sense which means spiritually awakened and in service to all through the exercise of her spiritual authority and power.

Her mountain home is sometimes described as the Jade Mountain, for jade contains much yin essence. Yin is life force in the feminine sense, moving in spirals rather than in the more linear, yang style of progression. The nature of the Earth Mother is yin – her coolness, her cycles, her seasons and spiralling progression of evolution, dance between day and night, always from a perspective of balance.

When we are walking this path ourselves, we will have that sense of always needing to return to balance. As we grow, we can temporarily lose our balance, as we learn to gain mastery at a new level. So the yin path is about restoring, aligning and adjusting as we grow. It is about trusting in the seasons of our soul and how they manifest as times of abundance, times of rest and withdrawal, times of activity and dynamic creativity and times of apparently doing not much at all which can result in magnetic, effortless attraction of all that is needed. On this path, we are outside of socially accepted ways of success and 'doing things' in the world. We are learning another way.

I once met a man who runs an entire spiritual community this way. We met in a Chakradance® class for the crown chakra, run by my dearest friend. We decided to meet for a cup of tea, which we did some weeks later. As I sat and listened to him talk, I was struck by several things. Firstly, how receptive he was. I am used to being the one who listens and am delightfully surprised when others can return the favour in some depth. I felt drawn into deeper connection with this man, and suspected that everyone he met was given the same attention and felt the same depth of connection. When people were making speeches at his fortieth birthday party, a woman stood up and said, "Well, I only just met you tonight because I came here with a friend of mine, but listening to all these things people are saying about you, I feel that I know you and love you too!" I found this extremely funny but I could appreciate why she was moved. This man just has an ability to be at peace within himself and to receive others. He has a lot of natural yin receptivity and draws others to him because of it.

The other thing I noticed is how unplanned and unscripted he was. He simply would choose to run an event if it felt right and came together easily. Now that is yin wisdom. His events grew and when I was in connection with him for a few years on and off, I was aware that his gatherings were attracting hundreds of people with not much more than an occasional email here and there. This indicated not only that he was living his right path but also that for him, he was approaching it in a way that was in harmony with life – he attracted what was needed for his vision of a respectful community interested in bringing positive, kind energy into his hometown of Sydney, to manifest.

Yin energy is very magnetic. People are drawn to it. It is the opposite of the hard-core sales pitch. It is the invitation to be received by someone. It is a cooling tonic in a world still so full of demands on our time and attention. Even in the metaphysical field, there are thrills and titillation a plenty in the modern world that seduce so many into believing that they have found something of worth (my personal belief – rightly or not – is that genuine worth doesn't seek to proclaim itself quite so loudly). These are the often charismatic but wounded teachers that grab our attention and apparently offer us so much. The yin way quietly unfolds underneath, with more genuine and yet more subtle beauty, until weary of the fray and the empty promises we become open to another way. We have taken a step out of what we have known and towards oneness with life.

In the Western world, understanding and appreciation of yin energy is relatively new. It requires an unlearning of pretty much everything we have been taught about how to succeed in life! We usually learn that success comes through constant effort, pushing, striving, and the yin way is instead learning how to relax, cultivate our energy through intelligent practices and discipline, and how to let go and let life do what it does – which is endlessly create. For some with strong past life training in these arts, like the man I mentioned above (whom I always see as a Buddhist monk rather than an Australian man who likes Eastern Suburbs beaches in Sydney) this yin way can feel natural.

For those of us with a shamanic healing path the story is likely to be different. We will get to yin wisdom eventually, more likely than not, but our path to that place of wisdom will more than likely involve some trouble accessing a yin state for ourselves, at least at first. A shaman is one who heals diseases of culture, body, mind and society by healing the soul or spirit within people and society. A shaman is a tool of divine evolution and is initiated to become capable of working with a disease. The initiation will involve personally experiencing whatever disease is relevant to their dedication for healing. In healing the disease – whether it be of mind, body or soul – the shaman gains mastery and power over that consciousness and can assist others in finding their way through it too.

So if you are going to heal the spiritual imbalance between masculine (yang) and feminine (yin) energies in the world, you will have to learn about the disease – how it operates, why it becomes addictive, how to unravel the patterning and how to find the way back to wellness. In this instance that means being in the yang way of society and learning how to shift into the yin path.

Part of the shamanic initiation at a soul level is that you incarnate into the relevant diseased pattern. Your soul is not diseased, your light is pure and always will be. However, you need to know what you are working with and how to work it through. So your soul will choose the right dysfunctional family dynamics or social situation, to set up your life path. Through taking a healing journey you will not only learn how to heal yourself but become prepared with the tools, understanding and capacity, to help heal the disease at a broader level and thus benefit others.

When we are drawn to the feminine or yin path, we will first learn where it is broken, denied, feared, distorted or misunderstood and even vilified and ridiculed. We go undercover, sometimes forgetting about our own purity of light and soul, and believing in the wounds and pain that we suffer through, for as long as is needed to really understand the problem as deeply as necessary in order to fulfil our spiritual life mission.

Once that first part of the path is taken, we will embark upon the second part of the path – the empowerment of the healing journey. Once we know what the wound is, we go on the journey of how to deal with it for healing purpose. We use ourselves – our bodies, our minds and our energy field – as guinea pigs in the grand healing science-lab. This is what is meant by the notion of the wounded healer, by the idea that it is through the wound that the light flows. Through the wounding, healing wisdom is attracted. It is the yin way that what is made empty shall be filled and what is broken shall attract healing.

Depending on the extent of our mission this lifetime, we might learn how to heal a disease of mind or body within ourselves, or within larger groups of family dysfunction or social dysfunction in corporations, educational or health systems, and so on.

There are entire soul groups that are working on healing various social diseases. Some are healing at the basis of the problems by rebalancing masculine and feminine energies, and some are dealing with specialised issues such as bringing healing into the corporate world or other sick systems and organisations that are based on authority rather than empowerment (we'll learn about them in the discussion on cults and cultic organisations in *Crystal Saints & Sages 777*). Still other soul groups are learning methods for genuinely healing the cause (and not just the symptoms) of cancer, part of which involves learning the difference between taking and receiving, which we have discussed in this book. Then there are those that are helping to heal the narcissistic wound, that painful psychological and emotional disease which is insidious in Western culture and an obstruction to growth of the soul. For those of you uncertain about what I mean by the narcissistic would, I would say it is a case of pretty flowers that kill. The narcissistic wound is seen in the shiny, pretty people, objects and ideas in our culture that seem gold on the surface but are actually deeply toxic and destructive underneath. We'll explore that teaching in more depth in *Crystal Saints & Sages 777* and *Crystal Stars 11.11* too.

Once we have explored the disease that is relevant to our own soul path this lifetime, come up with a set of tools that work for us, and we have the consciousness of wellness entrenched in us, we are ready for the next step. This happens when we are exposed to the illness or dysfunction again and again without being pulled back down into it, away from the purity of our light and our healing wisdom. We have developed some compassion and some immunity. It hasn't been an easy path. It will have entailed us traversing through a rather sick and distorted astral field of beliefs, opinions and energy, taking them in, living them, and learning how to heal them.

I remember walking into the lounge room when my then partner was watching a movie from the Harry Potter series. The great, wise wizard Dumbledore and his young protégée, Harry Potter, were gaining ground in their brave plan to overcome an evil dark lord . . .

However, there is an obstacle in the way of their further progress. As a safety measure, the evil lord has place a potion around a precious object which houses some of his power. The good wizard and his young student want to gain that object to help overcome the power of the dark lord. To do so however, means the potion must be removed.

The great wizard realises that it cannot be removed through magic and the only way for it to be removed is for it to be drunk. Recognising it as poisonous and knowing it will cause great pain to the being who drinks it, so much so that they will beg to be released from the suffering with all of their heart, the great wizard accepts the task and asks something of his student. He tells Harry that he will appear to be dying and may beg to be spared from drinking the entire portion of the potion. He says it must all be consumed and that when he becomes too weak to finish taking the poison himself, the young wizard must force-feed him the final amount. He must be strong. He must not give in to the suffering that the great wizard knows he will encounter.

This is exactly what happened. As I watched the scene unfold, with absolute horror, I felt something unknown stir in me at such a deep level that I was unexpectedly thrown into unfathomable depths of despair.

The scene drew to a close, and the great wizard eventually triumphed with the help of his brave young charge, but only after truly terrible suffering. I exited the lounge room and plonked myself down in my healing room where I sat in the darkness, sobbing deeply and feeling wretched for several hours without any conscious understanding why. This story had touched upon a painful truth within me and I had to let it rise out of me to be released.

It was the taking in of the poison and the need to suffer to the point of almost unbearable agony in order to overcome darkness and liberate something valuable that I could identify with. In my heart I didn't identify with the suffering of the world, or even my own. I felt it, certainly, but I always had a sense of myself as a pure being enduring something that was happening to me rather than as me. It was not in a victim sort of sense, because I had always understood that something useful could come from suffering, if we are open to realising it. Still, I couldn't get away from this notion that I was somehow taking in a sort of poison in order to be of service. It sounds very noble, but I am not the only one doing this (perhaps you are also on such a path) and it certainly wasn't my ego choosing it. It was just a function of my soul, which is shamanic in nature. I have been a shaman my whole life without actually knowing what that was until I had been on a conscious path this lifetime for decades.

Emotionally, this process can be so very frustrating and painful. I have often struggled deeply with my tendency to be profoundly and deeply affected – taken over temporarily but utterly just as Dumbledore was in that scene – by the world around me. I tend to pick up psychically and in dreams much of what is going on in the psyches of those that I am connected with physically or spiritually. I often feel like a blank page upon which the stories of whomever I am around are impressed. I cannot control that process, though I have certainly tried in various ways over the years. The resolution of this issue, that I have come to at this stage in my life, is that I can only surrender and work through any such process with wisdom and a willingness to grow. Then I can at least gain power and mastery to help others heal, and grow stronger spiritually myself, more capable of accepting all of life as serving a divine pattern, even if at the human level that is impossible to see at times. Nonetheless the process of being so impacted upon by life has been difficult for me to accept at times.

Actually, it was only last night, before I even realised I would be writing about this today, that I was reflecting upon this issue and asking the Universe to help me understand this part of my nature – the openly receptive part that sucks in poison! Eventually I was asked the question by guidance, "What happens when you do this?" My answer was that I eventually overcame it, like developing a successful immune response, and I grew more empowered and wise. That, I thought, was the answer to my concern.

Going into the disease at a psychological, emotional or physical level, that we are in service to healing as part of our divine life mission, can be a great challenge. Especially if we forget that is what is happening and judge ourselves for any issue we have going on. I have been in all sorts of situations in my life – including experiencing some truly cult-like spiritual schools and organisations (thankfully for only a relatively short, but certainly interesting period of time). I will talk about that in more depth in *Crystal Saints & Sages 777*. There are also related discussions in *Crystal Masters 333* and *Crystal Angels 444*.

As difficult as those journeys have been for me, I always had the sense underneath that I was learning about something. I didn't quite know what I was there to learn at a higher level, at the time I was in the experience, but I knew I would figure it out eventually, and so I did. I realised part of that learning was to provide an 'out' for others who needed it, but also to understand the fundamental difficulty that Western society has with taking responsibility for our own power and inner authority. It took a while for me to work this out. Eventually the wisdom came and I felt free from the pull of that issue and able to move on in my belief systems and from my involvement in those sorts of organisations. This is what we feel when we have come through to the other side of a shamanic journey. At a deeper level we have developed enough immunity to gain power over the poison and we can take the next step. We are ready to work at a greater level and we begin the third part of our life mission.

The third part is the actual healing, the demonstration of our gifts in the world. This is where we are initiated as shamans or healers, at the hand of Xi Wang Mu or one of her many forms, which might be a totem or power animal. Bats are often symbols of such an initiation taking place, and we might see them more often than not during such times of intense growth. However, we mostly sense this process internally. It doesn't automatically come with the completion of a course in shamanism or simply calling oneself a shaman in the outward world.

I have met people who are definitely shamanic but wouldn't particularly think of applying that word to themselves as well as those who use the title in a very public way but perhaps don't have the consciousness to support the use of the title in any genuine sense. The initiation of Xi Wang Mu, the grandmother of all shamans, takes place at a soul level. It is a new level of spiritual rebirth that follows a death of the old self in some way, and that rebirth brings with it a new power and wisdom that can be used to benefit the community.

When we are approaching initiation, we will always have to give something up. It might be an attachment to an identity or status quo, a situation, an attitude, an entire philosophy or belief system, a relationship or even wellness, going into a disease of mind or body for a time in order to learn how to heal it, as we have spoken of above. It might be a combination of all of these things. What happens on the other side of this, whether it be a matter of months, years or lifetimes, is that we are born anew. We pass through the initiation and we are changed. If we are not changed in a profound and far-reaching way, there has not been a passing through of initiation. Sometimes the full extent of that internal birth takes time to show itself, it might be some months or even years for it to reveal its full glory, but the signs of the change will reveal themselves to some extent immediately.

The passing of an initiation is often unexpected. We might not even have consciously known we were in one, especially if it has lasted the better part of a lifetime! We might have just thought that our life was meant to be hard and filled with struggle, and we were going to have a particular issue to deal with our whole life. When we suddenly begin to move through it, and we are perhaps gifted with a sudden flash of insight, realising that we are healing and this issue will not actually continue, it can be quite a surprise! I have a personal joke with myself that I have been taking the spiritual journey described in the Bible of wandering in the desert to the Promised Land, for forty years. At thirty-nine years of age, I looked back at some quite painful and challenging issues lasting my entire life to that point – such as my struggle to accept my fundamentally shamanic soul type – finally coming into some sort of resolution within me. I've been seeking that promised land of peace and plenty, and all that symbolises for me, for quite some time. Around forty years as it turned out.

In 2013 I was teaching a class in the gorgeous Southern Highlands town of Berry, in New South Wales, Australia. The class was going to be on rebirth. As with all my classes, I have no clue what is going to happen in them. I know the Divine will happen, of course, but that's about it. People might love it, they might be disturbed by it and deeply challenged. Normally it's the former, but occasionally it's the latter. Actually the more I consider that, it's probably most often a combination of all of the above. All I know in advance is that I will rock on up and do my job. The Divine is in the happening, and that serves the greater good, whether the grace that comes through is gentle or fierce.

On the morning of the workshop, I guided the fifty or so participants into connection with the elements of the Earth. Intuitively I felt guided to do this to ground us before working with big spiritual energies later in the day. As I guided the group through the different elements, I felt an aspect of myself open up that I had never consciously connected with before and yet as it did so, I felt like I was reconnecting with an old friend, a part of me that had been there forever and was the 'true' me in a deeper way than I had previously experienced myself. That inner door swung open and I recognised all of that in an instant, even whilst chanting and guiding the opening exercise. Sounds and movements happened in my body for each of the elements that unleashed a powerful transformative energy into the room. It was emotionally moving for all of us. There were tears, there were shifts in energy and a powerful space opened up not only inside of me, but in the entire group energy field. It was at that moment that I realised I had finally been granted formal recognition and initiation as a shaman, and permission to work with those earth energies on my healing path this lifetime. The whole realisation and initiation took less than a second. The preparation for it to be accessed at that level, during this lifetime at least, took four decades.

If we are on an intense healing path, there will be constant evolution as we master a lesson at deeper and deeper levels. It isn't as though once we are initiated, that's it, no more work for us. I once heard a man who claimed to be enlightened give a talk. His claim should have set off alarm bells anyway. However, I listened to him with an open mind and when he said he felt that his spiritual work was pretty much done, something just went 'clunk' inside of me. It just didn't feel true. He undoubtedly has his own journey and perhaps I misunderstood his words, it doesn't really matter either way. What I know is, that while there is a being in the world labouring away in suffering, the spiritual work of liberation for all of humanity is not yet done. If the work for all is not done, neither is our work done. We are always capable of evolution into greater service. Always.

Will there be deeper initiations for me on the path? Undoubtedly so. These are the steps that the soul takes on the ladder, climbing Xi Wang Mu's heavenly cosmic peach tree, until at the right concordance, the peach blossoms and the soul knows itself to be absolute divinity. Immortality is realised and the work, though not done, can happen, I suspect, from an even more expanded and radiant place, to guide others towards their moment to taste that sweet peach nectar of the goddess.

Each step we take on our path is a step towards initiation, which is a step towards the great soul transition from endless incarnations through the cycle of life and death, into the blazing love of divine immortality, such as that manifest in beloved grandmother Xi Wang Mu.

The order in which our learning unfolds has a genius to it, and we can trust in that. For me it was stars first, Earth second. The shamanic initiation, which was a result of integration of Earth consciousness and being able to serve that great being, Gaia, happened only after an integration of star consciousness as serving those great worlds in the sky felt far more natural to me for the first portion of my life. (If you feel the same, then you are one of the souls being held in my heart in the writing of *Crystal Stars 11.11* and the creation of the *Star Child* meditation CD).

For you it might be the other way around, and by that I mean that we gain spiritual nourishment from the source that is most natural to us, and then we expand how we can be spiritually nourished until it can come from any source, from all of life. That is the destiny of the shamanic soul type, and what Xi Wang Mu will lead us towards. For me, the heavens and the stars talked to me so easily, and still do, so that is where I started consciously seeking spiritual nourishment. As a child I could also draw nourishment easily from trees, the ocean and nature. It took me somewhat longer to embrace humanity and the darker parts of life as part of my spiritual food. I could only do that once I acknowledged my soul as shamanic and able to grow in love no matter what it consumes. That is part of what is healing the old wound in me that was brought to my awareness through the Harry Potter scene described above.

The prospect of there being many years of inner work (3,000 according to Xi Wang Mu's stories) or many lifetimes of dedication on the spiritual path before we attain some sense of meaningful enlightenment or resolution can trigger mixed responses in us. There is a story of two men on the spiritual path. Upon hearing from their spiritual teacher that they each had ten lifetimes until they were enlightened, the first man said, "Humph! Ten lifetimes! I cannot stand that! It is too long!" and he sunk off into dejection. The second man said, "Oh! Ten lifetimes! I am so lucky! I cannot believe I have been so blessed that I will actually reach enlightenment! I am so grateful – thank you, thank you, thank you!" – At which point he promptly became enlightened.

This funny little tale teaches us about the power of attitude. The wisdom of the path of immortality, which Xi Wang Mu leads us towards in her infinite grace, is that it places everything in context. We can feel relief and let go of the enormity of all things needing to happen right now, and find in its place, a surrendered trust that actually allows things to happen more effortlessly and often, more quickly. The immortal path is not a rushed one. It is said that when one is in flow with the Tao, all things are accomplished without rushing. Such beings are capable of tremendous power and presence in the world – often invisible unless one is somewhat conscious of spiritual energy through dreams, meditations and visions – and depending on whether or not the advanced being in question is happy to be recognised. Some prefer anonymity to better accomplish their task. Many advanced souls do work undercover, as it were, to attain their purpose their power is felt rather than seen.

When we work in a yin way, great things can happen, apparently through our own hand, and then we might expend great discipline and energy yet feel we haven't done anything at all. It can be quite odd! When I sit down to right an oracle deck or a book, for example, I certainly go through a huge – though relatively swift, I will admit – creation process. At the end of it, I have to remind myself that I have actually done something. I have to remember to honour the fact that yes, it is the divine energy that manifests itself, but it is the capacity of this channel (me!) and all the learning and application that has gone into developing this channel in this lifetime and others, and that still continues, that creates a willingness to receive the flow. I learn to honour Heaven and Earth, soul and body, as stepping stones on the divine path of immortal true self-remembrance.

When I feel the energy of Xi Wang Mu, I just melt. I can hear the music that surrounds her upon the sacred mountain, played by her Jade maidens, and there is a sense of eternity – an endless expansion of life force that is powerful beyond measure and yet somehow soft. The vision I have of her is subtle and hazy, as though it is a glimpse into her world shrouded in golden mist. I see her soft, radiant face, her all-seeing, all-knowing, kind and powerful eyes, and hear the musical instruments and voices, the rustling of the breeze through the leaves of her peach tree, the padding of tiger paws on the earth, and even her slow, even flowing breath. There is so much stillness and so much movement and life, all at once. I catch the subtle scent of a peach. There are no words, just an almost overwhelming sense of benevolence and love. I have the sense that she is both intimately aware of our darkest struggles and completely beyond them, as she gently calls our souls to her world of immortal ecstasy.

STROMATOLITE (STEADFASTNESS)

Like the ancient grandmother goddess, stromatolites are part of the original consciousness of life itself. They are some of the most ancient stones known to humanity. These stunning fossils date back over three and a half billion years. It is mind boggling (and therefore good for meditation and generally keeping things in perspective!) to consider that.

Science has suggested that these structures were actually formed by the first living bacteria on the earth. A sign of new beginnings, they resonate with new life and the tremendous creative possibilities that can unfold as the journey of life takes place. They are a sign that from the apparently insignificant, big things can grow.

They have a softness in their energy that reminds me of Xi Wang Mu. They are ancient, powerful and contain the stories of life and evolution on the Earth. Yet, to hold them brings softness and strength in a lovely combination.

I was quite mesmerised when I first saw these stones, with their swirling tones of black and various shades of chocolate and caramel. I had no idea what they were, but I fell in love with them instantly, holding them in my hands and appreciating their beauty.

They are inexpensive and available in various smoothed shapes and sizes, most often in tumbled stones or slightly larger palm stones that fit comfortably in the hand and are wonderful for calming and grounding us during stressful times of change when we really do need to remember that this too shall pass and that it's just one page of a far bigger book of our life journey.

Their connection to original life on Earth and their continued existence today, means that stromatolite can be a powerful aid for past life recollection, particularly when those lifetimes happened on Earth. (If you want to explore your past lives and bring healing, you may benefit from my *Past Life Healing* CD featuring a guided meditation and discussion of past lives and their impact in the present moment, published by Blue Angel and available on my website).

The more we connect with the soul, the more we will want to manifest our inner light in the world in meaningful ways through whatever methods speak to our heart. Xi Wang Mu guides us on the biggest path as far as our individual soul goes – which is the path of spiritual enlightenment, the soul remembering that it is divine, and claiming its divine prize of immortality. At grander levels, there is the journey of the great Earth Mother, our solar system and our galaxy, which as vast as they may seem, are still served in part by our own soul journey and certainly serve our soul journey. However, we can also look in the other direction to the smaller journeys which take place on a daily basis, the circles within the greater circle of the flower of life if you like. These are the choices we make on a daily basis and the yearly intentions that we set (and some of which we might actually carry out) that eventually accumulate into food to nourish the larger cycles.

To be able to connect these small daily actions to the larger process helps us find the joy that the man who responded, "Only ten lifetimes to enlightenment! Woohoo!" could feel. We have to be able to take delight in the small successes, for they are mirrors of the greater successes. There is nothing that cannot be celebrated if we are able to honour it as divine.

After years of therapy, I was finally able to feel my profound grief. It hurt like hell, but at another level I was grateful for it, because I could feel. I was no longer numb, and I knew that was both truthful and healing. If you have ever been sick and suddenly you start to feel better, and you are grateful for just feeling well, being able to sleep soundly without waking up to blow your nose every few minutes or to cough, then you will know what this feeling is like. It is profound gratitude for the simple successes and gifts of life. We can be grateful even for a breath, because it gives the soul the option to experience life and eventually, through a grand journey (which stromatolite embodies for us) to claim the ultimate conclusion to life, which is eternal life, the remembrance of the divinity and the awakening to it in totality.

When we need the oomph to keep going with a journey, or the calming to keep things in perspective and not try to build Rome in a day (am I the only one guilty of that tendency? I think not!), stromatolite helps bring us to balance. Just like the Tao teaching that nature never rushes and yet all things are accomplished, stromatolite helps us access the patience, steadfastness and willingness to just get on with what needs to be done, so that life can continue to flow.

For those of us that have lots of creative ideas or tend to flit from one topic to the next, which is easy enough to do when there is so much available to us in this modern world, and in such quantity at this time in human evolution, stromatolite helps us find that which will endure, that which we can let go of, and that which will nurture us into new life. The shamanic teachings of Xi Wang Mu, and the gospel of Gaia as she manifests her wisdom teachings through nature itself, show us that true life dwells as one with death, there can never be one without the other. Sometimes to say yes to something important, we have to say no to something that cannot serve our growth any further.

Recently, a beloved friend of mine was being plagued by a spirit who was stuck in this world and unable to move on to the spiritual worlds. We worked together over the telephone for a while, bringing through the energy of love and compassion to soothe the disturbed state of being of this spirit who was finding it hard to let go of her pain and go into the light. Her body had died, but her soul had not crossed over to continue on with her far grander life journey. It was a bit like those people who mourn a relationship after it has ended and find it difficult to move through the pain, let go and genuinely experience new love and new life without baggage from the past rearing up and pulling them back into old stuff. I could relate! It was a challenging journey to take.

We asked the spirit who she had loved and who loved her when she was alive on earth. A little white dog (god spelled backwards!) emerged and stood at the edge of the light. "Do you see the dog?" my friend asked the spirit. "Yes!" she responded. "Do you love the dog and does it love you unconditionally?" I asked her. "Yes!" the spirit responded. I urged the spirit on, "Well go on then, go with the dog! It's safe, it's so easy for you to do this now, off you go, enjoy!" Suddenly my friend felt a huge surge of emotion breaking through her heart, as she sobbed, and we could both feel an explosion of light as the spirit left her and crossed over, chasing her gorgeous white dog back into love.

Afterwards, my friend and I were discussing the experience. "It's one, isn't it", she mused, "life and death. It is so hard to give birth and I can see it's so hard to die too." I thought about what she said and I could absolutely see the truth in her words, wise being that she is. What is death, but another birth? Whether the ending of one phase of life so that the new can begin, or the ending of a physical life so that the next phase of the soul journey can happen, birth and death happen at once, simultaneously. It is perhaps just a different perspective of the one event. "We can't live or die by half measures," I replied. It takes complete commitment to genuinely show up to what is happening and let go.

I then shared a teaching with her that I had heard from Marion Woodman, a Jungian analyst whom I hold in high esteem. We don't need our physical eyes and ears in the womb, but they are developed there nonetheless, in readiness for our transition into the physical world where they will be of use to us. Woodman proposes that in this life, we develop the organs of the soul, our ability to hear, see, sense and feel in a way that doesn't apply to the five-sensory world around us, in preparation for the soul world we move into at the death of this physical body. We sat with the knowledge that life and death are the same, just two experiences of the one birth at yet another new level.

Stromatolite helps us commit to life. To really live with a perspective of what is happening in the here and now, and also with a view of how the now is a part of a far greater cycle of past and future, constantly being woven into one great, divine tapestry of life.

MANIFESTING THROUGH PATIENCE

Let's start by outlining what manifesting through patience is not. It is not lying about waiting for something to happen. (Well, it can be if we are genuinely connecting with rest and replenishing ourselves!) It is not becoming passive. It is not necessarily about things having to take longer.

Now let's look at what it is! It is about trusting in divine timing, through which we can actually accelerate the process of creation, when that is appropriate. It is energising because we let go of the drain on our energy that occurs when we are pushing something that isn't ready. That is rather different to pushing when pushing is required in the moment for birth. If we have rested enough beforehand, we will have plenty of energy to successfully birth the new. It is about giving ourselves permission to trust, even in the absence of immediate gratification or signs of imminent success, because we know that everyone has their own time to shine according to what is going to serve the greater good. It isn't about whether or not we deserve success, it's about the right thing, at the right time. As one of my spiritual mentors said to me, about a particular project I have been working on, "It's a good thing it's only happening now because a few years ago everyone was still so sound asleep, no one would have noticed what you were doing!" This made us both laugh uproariously.

When we are not in touch with the technique of manifesting through patience, we can make 'delays' (which are really just our expectations not aligning with the intelligence of divine timing) mean something inaccurate. We might believe we are not deserving, or our dreams are not going to manifest, that we are not worthy or that we are on the wrong path. We have to trust that with steadfastness, we will be shown one step at a time and we can take it. With a greater view of immortal progress of the soul, we will understand that our life journey is a highly complex web of meetings, happenings, manifestations and creations, all guided by a divinely loving intelligence. So we have to trust in the route by which we are taken through our life path, for it will serve, often in ways that we are not absolutely aware of at the time, or sometimes even in hindsight. With patience as our tool to manifest, we can let go and let the Divine happen so much more freely, and ultimately, enjoy the journey so much more.

HEALING PROCESS

If you groaned when you read the title for this manifestation technique, and thought, "Oh, I don't want to do that!" then you definitely need this healing process! Don't worry. You have my compassion. Patience was never my strong point.

Manifesting through patience restores our faith in the bigger scheme of divine planning and flow. We know all things happen according to a greater plan. We just have to remind ourselves of this! This healing process will help you remember.

When there is a dream in your heart, if you feel that you are waiting for it to manifest, for the way for it to come to fruition to show itself to you (in the form of the right people or opportunities) then this healing process will help you.

The Process

Start with your crystal mandala and/or crystal before you. Lie down or be seated in a comfortable manner, preferably with electronic equipment turned off or in silent mode and out of your immediate energy field.

Say aloud, "I call upon the Crystal Angel of Stromatolite and Xi Wang Mu (SHEE-WANG-MOO or SEE-WANG-MU), the ancient grandmother who loves me unconditionally. I call upon your love, patience, immortal grace and steadfast strength, so that I may manifest my divine destiny into ripe blossoming. May every step in the smaller and greater cycles of my life, be blessed and held in the protection of your grace. I am in your service, the service of unconditional love. So be it."

Imagine that you are in a place of ancient beauty and solitude upon the earth, in a place that is both present and timeless. You lie naked upon the earth, with your arms and legs gently resting, spread out on the ground. Beneath you is a vast plateau of smooth stone, in whirling patterns of black, chocolate and caramel tones.

At the edges of this plateau you sense the gentle movement of ancient wings of light, and you realise that you are resting in the healing energy field of the Crystal Angel of Stromatolite.

The whirling patterns of energy are the meridians of this angelic being, and as you breathe out, you can release anything you no longer need into the meridians of this great loving angel who will draw toxins away from you and transmute them into raw energy for life.

You may be conscious of what you are releasing or you may just have the intention to let go as much as you can mentally, emotionally and physically as you become very present, mentally empty, and simply 'be' with the great angel.

Stay here and be with this angel, gaining strength and releasing impatience, despair, doubt, worry, confusion, anger, disappointment, fear, judgment and criticism from your body, mind and energy field.

When you are ready, you see, sense or perceive a pale shimmering mountain of light.

At the top of the mountain, which you are naturally drawn towards, the face of a beautiful ancient goddess appears through golden mists. She is delighted to see you and smiles. You see that behind her is a colossal peach tree. Just looking at this beautiful tree that links Heaven and Earth is enough to bring great peace to your heart. It is the way home! To love.

Sit and be before that beautiful peach tree now. You may feel emotional without knowing why. Be with whatever happens for you, no matter how strong or how subtle, and trust. You are receiving a great blessing, whether that is obvious to you or not, so just accept it and be.

When you are ready, after at least eight breaths in and out, you can start to move your hands, fingers, feet and toes, and come back into the room. Feel the air on your skin and the warmth in your heart.

When you are ready, gently sit up and place your hands in prayer at your heart and say, 'Thank you.'

You have finished your healing process. Repeat this at any time you are struggling with impatience or concern about divine timing on your life path.

18.

PELE (DESIRE)
LAVA STONE (COOLING)

MANIFESTING THROUGH LONGING

She sees him and is on fire with love and desire. She burns for him yet he cannot be her divine partner, for he is of the human world and is not yet a god. She rages and punishes him, from her feelings of loss and anger. Then suddenly apologetic, she cools her heart and blesses him. Her desire changes lives, her apology cools the savage heat of her outrage, as once again she loves eternal, never surrendering her passionate nature.

PELE (DESIRE)

Pele, the wild, Hawaiian, volcano-dwelling goddess of fire, is ruled by passion. Her stories chronicle her wandering heavenly eye, as she searches for true love. She is considered difficult to handle, sexually overt, seductive and without moral consideration, as well as having a hot temper that is easily aroused by the mere possibility of rejection. Her volatile, fiery nature can be highly destructive to human life.

However, she doesn't hold grudges and feels remorse after she acts out in anger, once her passion has cooled (temporarily!). She then offers creative and unique blessings to mitigate the harm she caused. Even though her actions cannot be undone or reversed, she finds a way to overcome any trouble she caused by her angry reactions. Eventually she will allow the rightful course of events to take place, even if that means she doesn't get what she wants – for now!

The destructive anger of this goddess is treated with great respect in Hawaii. To this day, the story is told that if a rock is removed from Hawaii, which is actually illegal, the wrath of Pele will be invoked and the person will be cursed. Apparently hundreds of rocks are mailed back to Hawaii each year, presumably from people who scoffed at the warning, claimed a natural souvenir of their trip and experienced something that made them change their minds. Returning the rock to its rightful home is a way of trying to appease Pele.

This seems like a good time to talk about crystals and ownership. Earlier in this book we spoke about the difference between receiving and taking. We can take that a bit further and talk about the difference between enjoying a possession and claiming an object. The former holds an item more loosely, the latter grasps it with the fear of loss.

If we are lucky enough to be blessed with a crystal, whether as a gift from another or to ourselves, we will have it in our possession for as long as is helpful. It is wise to surrender to this. A friend of mine worked with a huge crystal when she ran healing groups in the United Kingdom. When it was time to move to Australia, she packed up the crystal and gave strict instructions for its careful transportation. The crystal however, had other ideas and, as my friend described it, "Decided that it would prefer to stay in the United Kingdom!" It never made it to Australia. Mother Earth decides who gets what and when. Try to take as we might, what is rightfully ours will come to us or be taken away, based on what needs to be where.

Pele's stories are filled with emotional upheaval as she is moved by huge passions, jealous rages and makes errors in judgment because of it. Her great gestures to restore and repair the situations as best as possible come once the truth is out and she is able to see past her passion. Her energy is the force of destruction that follows thwarted desire and then rebuilds in a new form because the desire is so strong she cannot and will not give it up. Her desire, which is for love, is at the core of her heart, and all the emotional drama around it will not cause her to step away from it.

On the spiritual path, we are often taught that we need detachment and dispassion. These are cooling qualities and they have a useful role in spiritual growth, but they are not the whole picture. We will meet some of the funny, quirky, inspiring rebels on the divine path in *Crystal Saints & Sages 777*, so for now it is enough to say that the great masters and teachers model an enlightened humanity that is certainly not free from passion, or even at times, destructiveness. It is, however, always in service to love. It is the fierce face of compassion.

This does not mean that working with Pele gives us some sort of divine permission to be a complete and utter brat or demand that the world and the people in it bend themselves to suit our will to avoid our temper tantrums. I have met enough people like that (even as adults) to realise it is unlikely that the world needs any more of such behaviour! The teaching stories of the goddess are given so that we can come to a deeper understanding of how the divine energy in us can interact with our human nature.

In this case, Pele is teaching us about the motivating force of desire. The great mystics have often spoken of how much love one has to have for the Divine in order to bear the great trials of having our illusions cut to shreds. This is rather excruciating to endure, to put it mildly. I know it is the absolute passion I have for the Divine and the intense desire I feel for divine union, that motivates me to do things I would not otherwise do – even things I really do not want to do at all. Sometimes my very powerful human passions have to be subjugated into the divine passion for spiritual growth and awakening. Being of a fiery nature myself, this is not easy for me. I doubt it's easy for anyone! It is only the greater desire that I have for the Divine and this path that urges me on, even in the times when I would much prefer to stay put because of the pain of letting go of what I would rather not give up. It sounds simple, and it is, but it is rarely easy.

There are various paths to the Divine. Truly advanced souls often incarnate to experience more than one of them. Sort of like going to a restaurant and having such a spectacular meal that you want to go back and go through the entire experience again, ordering something different from the menu each time.

One path to the Divine is that of devotion, known as bhakti in the Hindu tradition of India. This is the path of the heart, the path of loving the Divine with such passion that it will move you beyond your own patterns, beyond inertia or paralysis, beyond fear, to keep you progressing towards your goal of knowing the Divine as intimately as possible. It might sound soft and fluffy but the path of bhakti is intense! It is not about fluffy love and 'hugging it out' on every occasion. The genuine path of bhakti will break your heart over and over again. It is a path of passionate, loving devotion to the Divine. If you think about love at a human level and the inevitable hurts we have as we grow in relationship as well as the bliss, and amplify that a billion-fold, you will begin to sense what is possible on the path of bhakti. The Divine is a fierce lover who always calls you on your 'stuff' and will accept no obstacle to your union. To be able to endure the inevitable deaths of that which was, the constructive destruction that allows us to be alive and grow this lifetime – rather than to just age and die – requires a powerful heart.

Pele helps us learn to trust in the light that burns as holy fire in the heart. She never gives up her desire. Part of the bittersweet nature of her teachings is that she stands alone. That is why her passion for love is never doused, because it is never truly satisfied. On the divine path, the power of yearning for the Divine Beloved can motivate us to great heights, far greater than what we would be capable of contentedly sitting at home, just as our ego might wish it to be. I have been told by my guidance, at various times in my life, that my desires for certain things to happen – which would have led to a level of personal fulfilment – had to be sacrificed so that my hunger for true fulfilment wasn't sated by a smaller meal when a far bigger soul feast was awaiting me. We lose the natural joy of eating if we don't ever feel hunger. Sometimes we need to be kept in a state of yearning so that we really move along on our path.

This does not mean we must be forced into a life of discomfort in order to grow, but we must be careful that our comforts do not become suffocating to our spirit. There are times when we need pain (I suspect, it's not as often as we fear) to grow. When the dangling carrot of desire is bigger than our need for comfort, we will be urged on. Otherwise we run the risk of sitting around pretending that everything is fine when in truth our souls are going missing and we could end up losing the precious gift of immortality by swapping enlightenment for a life dedicated to watching *Game of Thrones* under the doona with a box of chocolates! Once in a while, it's not too bad, but as way of life it will douse our Pele nature, and stop us from bearing the fire of passion and getting on with what would really bring us so much aliveness and feed our spirit.

The light of the fire that burns within Pele, reminds us of what we truly desire. I have always believed that desire is not something to be repressed or thwarted, but to be engaged with and curious about, so that we may understand what we really seek. As I have said, lusting after a Porsche doesn't mean you are off your path, you just need to go a bit deeper into what that desire is really about. Maybe the person dreaming of a prestigious car wants the experience of status, admiration and power that this, bizarrely enough, tends to offer. This isn't bad – there will be learning in that for someone if they choose to follow their desire deeper into their truth. Looking beneath the desire, they might discover what it is about themselves that wants to be recognised as owning a status symbol, for example. Desire can lead us to greater self-knowledge and wisdom if we choose to work with it. The deeper we go, the more we will find that, ultimately, all desires lead to the same place. It is truly my belief that underneath all desire there is only one source to which all longing returns, the Great Divine Beloved.

When we come from that place, our actions change. When we do consume, we do so with more relish and appreciation, and with less attachment. We also tend to consume less often than when we are mindlessly acting out without real connection to what we are consuming and what it means to us. Pele isn't about indulgence or acting without regard to others. To take that interpretation of her story is to miss out on the heart of it. Pele is the light of fire in the Earth's core. She reminds us to look for the light in the core of our being, which is our heart and its capacity for love despite apparently immoveable obstacles. She teaches us not to be bound by moral constraints or societal dictates, but to move from love with fearlessness.

Pele is known as 'she who shapes the land' which helps us understand that we must use our Divine Feminine power responsibly, for we will have an effect on the world around us whether we are conscious of it or not. Pele teaches us how to make reparation when we tread too heavily upon the earth in our enthusiasm – and that is going to happen sometimes. In the teaching of this goddess, using our power with awareness and an intention to come from the heart with a pure desire for love, can move mountains and create new landscapes for the soul that will open up possibilities and change lives.

Daring to live from the heart and be open to love, can bring us the gift of cleansing, of letting go and of opening up to the energy, vitality and inspiration that fire brings. As the goddess of fire, Pele comes to us when we need passion, excitement or for something within us to be stirred up so that we can get out of a rut and more clearly see where we need to go. If you have ever felt more alive or more 'you' when you were travelling, you will have experienced that sense of being shaken up as leading to a more conscious engagement in life. This is the counterpoint to staying at home, with the powerful expectations of others pressing you to continue with your habitual ways of being and weighing you down with a lack of inspired action. Sometimes rest and repair is just what we need. Sometimes, however, we need motivation and action that is fuelled by a great, passionate love. If you are truly motivated by love in your life – for your path, your work, for another, for a cause, for the Divine – you will know what a blessing and a demand it is. It is a privilege without a doubt, but one that asks much of you. However, when it is a true desire, a true love from the core of your heart, you will be willing to give yourself up to it completely. Pele empowers us for nothing less than that.

If you are in need of cooling in your life, tempering that passionate dynamic streak that may burn you out as much as inspire you, particularly if you are doing the quite incredible work of bringing light into dark organisations and mind-sets (such as working in mental health, the corporate or political sector, working for not-for-profit causes and so on) then you will need something to calm your justifiable anger and deep ardent desire for change. You are so important and loved! You must take care of yourself not only so that your fire burns, but that it doesn't burn you out. You are too important to go to waste.

The coolness of Pele's contrition when she has caused harm in her pursuit, can help us. We might not mean to harm, but in our passion for change, we will be walking that edge between accepting the right of every being to freely choose how they wish to live and our fierce need to bring a different consciousness to the world through how we choose to be in it. We want to be careful not to try to change others according to our dictates. I have seen passionate people become so angry about the state of the oceans that they burn themselves up. They have no energy left to nourish themselves and therefore no wellspring of energy to draw upon to continue their good fight. Sometimes they unintentionally alienate people who could contribute to the cause by becoming too hard-line in their approach. I completely understand the reasons why someone would become very hard and direct in their method. They may believe with all their heart that it is absolutely justifiable, but is it the most useful and effective way to create change? Perhaps not so much. So what do we do if we want change? Pele teaches us to be on fire with our passion, but also to become all that we can be, to bring a consciousness to how we are in the world, which will then affect others in the world who are ready to receive your wisdom, rather than fruitlessly trying to force others to be what they cannot yet be.

If you have been through a difficult time in your life, have been down or negative for whatever reason or have had a moment (or two) of losing your temper, but have enough wise compassion to realise that you might have unintentionally brought someone else down, Pele can help. She brings the grace of making reparation and soothing inflammation when we have burned too brightly. In our enthusiasm for the path, we can go too far at times in telling someone something that they are not quite ready to hear, for example. Even if our intention was from a passion for that person to be free of a painful struggle, it might burn them and cause pain because they were not justly received. It can be hard to hold one's tongue but sometimes it is best.

At other times we really are moved to speak from a place of love and although we might not feel in control of it consciously, and although the other person might have had some feathers ruffled by the experience, it is a divine happening needed to come about in that way for the greatest good. It has happened to me, where I have been in a healing session and an unexpectedly strong statement that really gives someone a shove comes out of my mouth. This is not the typical way I would express myself, for I tend to be much gentler by nature. Both the recipient and I might be rather ruffled by it.

Pele is there for us in that moment, to remind us that love is behind it, and that reparation can be made by the Divine Goddess usually in the form of a shove that leads the person in question into a far better situation in their lives. I experienced this when I had to move house. I loved that house and put simply, I didn't want to go. I knew the Divine was asking me to go (because my guidance had said as much and I felt it intuitively myself anyway) but still I wasn't celebrating the move. It took about three days and I realised that although I was still going to need to grieve the loss of the old house and how much I loved living there, there were ample compensations in my new place and that I was being given a chance to live in an energy that would be much kinder and give me what I genuinely needed. Within a month or so, reluctance turned to relief and gratitude. Pele's passion had upended my world, but she had made reparation for the violence of her actions.

When our desire is cooled, we don't lose our passion, we simply gain the balance we need so as not to burn out and give up. There is a phenomenon known as compassion fatigue. Earlier on in my vocation as a healer, I experienced this from time to time. When we give our emotional energy to something, or someone, and don't take the time to cool our fevers and replenish ourselves, we will burn out. I wasn't very good at stopping my heart from simply pouring out love and emotion. I am still not good at that, but I have grown more capable of (usually) bringing myself back into balance. Back then, there were times when it was too much for me and I found that I couldn't summon the emotional energy to care about what someone was saying. I then had to step back for a day or two and just focus on myself, to restore a sense of energy and wellness. If left unchecked for too long, we might end up beyond compassion fatigue and in the terrain of 'never wanting to deal with another (supposedly) lost cause again.' This is a tragedy! We must balance our heat with coolness to survive the marathon of the path of service. In this vein, Pele's gift to us is basalt or lava stone from her very own volcanic nature.

LAVA STONE (COOLING)

Having emerged from volcanic activity, lava stone contains the energy of fire within it. Also known as basalt, it was rock so heated that it was liquefied and essentially molten lava. You could say that Pele's passionate fire had well and truly got into it! As it rapidly cools on the surface of the earth, it hardens and becomes stable.

To touch and observe, lava stone doesn't look that strong, but it has an ability to hold and radiate heat, which is why it is often chosen by massage therapists who work with hot stone therapy. It is also a very hard rock, having been forged from the hottest fires within the earth! So despite an appearance that suggests it might crumble if held too tightly, it is very tough.

In shades of black to dark grey, sometimes with a slightly brown tinge, lava stone is often shaped into jewellery although it can be used in building materials as well. The surface often features indents and bubble holes, but can also be fine grained and smooth to the touch when used in tiles and carvings.

Lava stone is born from the most challenging of situations – pure living fire. It can empower us to emerge from nearly burning to a crisp through anger, violence, burn out, exhaustion or heat-based imbalances such as arthritis or liver problems, and any form of damage to us inside or out from excessive heat, fire, passion or anger, and to be quickly cooled into a healing state of balance.

If we are stuck in apathy, boredom, overwhelm, or feel weak, victimised, taken advantage of, or for whatever reason need to get 'mad as hell and not take it anymore' to bust out of some stuck pattern or other, then lava stone can help us tap into the fire within. This is the passionate desire that will motivate and lift us more than any other force in our lives.

Sometimes we need a lot of passion to break out of the monotony of being one of the not-quite-living zombified persons that passes for a 'regular normal person' these days. Sometimes when I am with people like that, I feel as if I could be screaming like a wild woman with the walls burning down around us, and the people in question would continue to politely chat or gossip and scheme with each other, killing off their true feelings and desires under suffocating cloaks of fearful resistance to truth and life. I guess you could call my rage against where they are on their path of human development as having a 'Pele moment.'

Although I do have to make reparation, usually by coming into compassion and chiding myself for being so arrogant as to assume that I know better than the Divine what will serve the growth of that soul. However, I still passionately believe that the gift of a human soul is worth fighting for. It is a divine experiment you see, one which could succeed or not. The precariousness and preciousness of the human soul moves me like nothing else. There is nothing else that I would love enough to become a willing hand of the destructive side of the Divine for.

For a long time, I took the existence of the human soul for granted. I figured everyone would become enlightened eventually, we just needed time. It was only relatively recently that I realised nothing could be taken for granted. Souls were missing out on life experience, as bodies and minds were dissociating, distracted and disturbed by modern culture and unable to claim the powerful connection to body and earth that would keep them in the present moment and empowered enough to bear a healing journey so as to continue on their life path to the fulfilment of their spiritual destiny. Connection to the heart and its path of love – with all those challenges and triumphs – was becoming obscured by the many false lights that cluttered the way. Endlessly upgrading techno gadgets to gain some sense of superiority, believing the false promises of advertising and gorging on harsh scandal mongering by media come to mind as examples. Those things glitter with the promise of something substantial and all too easily deliver damaging discord to the mind and body. The real light, the radiance of the Divine, is getting covered up by fancier and fancier distractions, all whilst the most precious gift of all, is withering and cast aside! Yes, I can certainly relate to Pele's rage.

The tools and toys of this world are a great gift when used in service. Technology can be a weapon against connection or a means to further it. It can connect us with others or block others out. It depends on our ability to stay in tune with our genuine feelings, our hearts and our bodies to be able to monitor whether something is in or out of balance. Without that, we have nothing against which to regulate and check our behaviour.

We need to have some fierceness about this. To be philosophical about the possible extinction of the human soul is madness. It is disrespectful to all that is feminine and to all that have suffered on this path to bring the light of mastery to us so that all of life can step into divine radiance. We need Pele's passionate, her all-consuming desire to give us enough sacred fire (even if it is laced with compassion after she's had her divine rage) to cut through the lies, nonsense and tantrums of the egos of the world that want to pretend that it is okay to just continue on as things are, to not risk the comforts of life for love. I believe we are capable of so much more than that!

We have so much to be grateful for and such a promising future ahead of us, but we must be willing to tap into our desire for light, for the divine, for healing, for radiance, for wisdom, for absolutely unrestrained creative and spiritual self-expression, for freedom, happiness and inner peace, and run the risk of that passion sometimes burning too much, rather than too little.

Sometimes this is hard to bear within us, let alone share with others. Sometimes I can get so passionate about this situation that I have to be careful not to burn too brightly with it and inadvertently push people away rather than draw them closer to the light. I have to find bigger containers into which I can express that – writing and music for example – rather than trying to fit the proverbial ocean of feeling into a teacup. For example, the full force of divine rage in a psychic reading might be much more than one bargained for and not particularly helpful!

I spoke earlier of the spiritual school I began to build in Europe a few years ago. When I began that process, I worried at times that my passion burned too brightly. I certainly had a lot of spiritual ambition for what would be accomplished through that school and how to run it with integrity. Perhaps it was necessary though, as the divine message about moving on, because the karma between myself and the woman in question was finished, was easier to accept when I could see that what was happening with the school was not so well matched to what I sought to create.

However, I was worried that I had unintentionally blazed so much divine passion that I had made her shy away from what was being asked of her, rather than stepping forward. Although I understood the guidance given to me was that I was no longer to be involved with her or the school, I was concerned that I had been too forceful when I was there. I wondered if I had hindered rather than helped her and that the school had suffered and died as a result of me asking too much. I know in my heart that all things serve, but that doesn't mean I am immune to moments of self-doubt. This was one of those.

I questioned myself about it quite deeply and was given a dream in response. I dreamed of a huge, scarlet red candle, much bigger than a human being, burning in a white temple with white floors, white ceiling and white walls. The candle burned so much that it began to melt the wax and spill onto the floor. It couldn't be contained! I felt so sad in the dream. The temple could never be restored to purity! The whiteness would be stained by the scarlet wax and I would never be able to fix it. Then all of a sudden, the wax began to retract, as if in reverse slow motion and the candle was restored to perfect containment and the whiteness of the temple was as it ever was. The 'damage' was completely undone and I felt relief and wonder at it.

When I awoke from the dream, I had my answer from the Divine. It was okay. The restoration happened through an invisible hand that I knew to be the hand of divine grace. That grace would sort things out for me and make them right. Perhaps, because I would never act with recklessness and just expect the Divine to take over responsibility for the outcome, this dream foreshadowed an unexpected grace that soothed my heart. Surprised and grateful, I awoke from that dream realising that on the path of love, even if we burn too fierce at times, grace will cool us and restore the balance.

Not long after that dream I found out that *Kuan Yin Oracle* was to be translated into the language of that particular country. Even though my message didn't reach that country through the ways I had planned, the Divine still found a way. Of course! That is the reparation that comes with Pele's passion. When we act from love, grace is never far away.

Lava stone motivates and strengthens us with the power of fire and the stability of coolness. Working with lava stone and Pele brings us into the heat of our desires with the cool-headedness we need to check in with our actions and stay on the path of our truest, most ardent desires – without getting so caught up in them that we forget we are here to serve love first and foremost.

If you are feeling challenged by desperate, apparently insurmountable circumstances, or feel thwarted in love, overwhelmed by passion and sacred rage, or underwhelmed with not enough passionate fire in your belly and your life, then lava stone is helpful for you. It assists us to tap into tremendous powers of survival and adaptation, to balance extremes and in doing so, become tough in our ability to cope with life, whilst maintaining an ability to bring passion into the world. If we are encountering a lot of change, particularly those big transitions of moving house, ending a relationship or going through death or loss of some kind (including a loss of identity with a career change), then lava stone can help us find stability without deadening our feelings.

MANIFESTING THROUGH YEARNING

I read somewhere that the challenge of being a passionate individual who loved being in connection with others, was that when you were in a relationship you longed for the freedom of being single and when you were single, you longed for the comfort and passion of a relationship! I felt this was rather a depressing view, especially as I wanted to experience the joys of both situations. There is some truth to the idea that no matter where we are, or what situation we are in, yearning will be part of our life experience. It is an inbuilt emergency function, in case we get too distracted by all the shiny, pretty things on the Earth and forget to look deeper and remember why we are here. We have an inner emptiness that is expressed through yearning. It ensures that we will always have to look deeper and go further along our spiritual path to find what it is that the emptiness seeks – the completeness of divinity. Contrary to popular belief, in Western culture at least, the emptiness is not a sign that something is wrong. It is actually the means by which we can receive divine grace in various forms.

Now of course we can try to deal with our yearning in ways that seem more bearable. We might try to rid ourselves of it by stuffing the emptiness full of substitutes. As fun as they can temporarily be, they cannot do anything other than distract us for a time from our true yearning. A new car might be fun, but if you are dying of thirst it will not compare to a glass of water. Likewise, when your spirit is hungry for the Divine, it will not be satisfied with chocolate cake for long, no matter how 'heavenly' it may be. If substitutions don't work, or we lack the cash or opportunity to rely on them, we might try numbing ourselves until we can't feel the yearning within us anymore. Unfortunately our relationships then become casualties of that process, because when we stop feeling, we stop relating, communicating, and loneliness will result. Ah, the Divine is so clever! It has us in a real bind!

For me, dealing with yearning is the same as dealing with fear or anything else that we don't particularly want to deal with. Sometimes we just have to go through it, rather than trying to find a way around it. The yearning that we have for the Divine has some benefits. The bigger the desire, the more divine energy can flow in response. And it does. I have had times when the pain of separation from the divine oneness I sought was so great, I could do nothing but cry. In that sweetness of surrender, my heart cracked open enough to allow more light in and I could feel the divine response more clearly and deeply than ever. The Divine in each one of us is moved so deeply by a genuine call for love. It rallies and thrives! We must not be afraid of asking this of each other, and of the Divine.

Whenever I connect with someone in a workshop or session, or often enough in the lead up to that, I can feel the strength of their soul calling to me for love, for divine light and for radiance. It is the most beautiful experience and I am literally moved by it. I remember one time that I was to be interviewed for an internet radio show by an absolutely gorgeous woman in the United States. For some reason, I couldn't call the station in America on Skype. I had pre-purchased credit so I could call from Australia but it just wasn't working. I didn't have her number, I had emailed her, but she was already live on air. I wasn't there with her and I didn't know how to connect with her to fix the situation. I was flustered for a few moments and prayed for help. Then she made a comment. I can't even recall what it was, but I recall with absolute clarity what I felt energetically behind her words. She was calling for my soul! I felt her energetically reaching out and me not being there for her. That realisation was agony for me! To have a hand reaching for me and me not being there at a soul level to respond gave rise to an anguish in my heart. Her yearning to connect motivated a burst of passion that moved me. I literally jumped up and began Googling numbers for the station and eventually, undoubtedly through some divine intervention, a number popped up that finally worked. Shortly afterwards we were able to speak with each other on the air, and I felt, as I always do when speaking with her, the tremendous love that she has within her, and how much the Divine adores her and wants to support her on her path in all ways.

When someone is open to me and calls to me at a soul level, something in me clicks on and I am there in dreams, meditations, during classes and outside of class. They will suddenly find me online, or download music or meditations that I have created for healing. It doesn't matter how or when. It is my soul, my genuine light that responds to the genuine call for divine love from their soul. Sometimes I consciously realise it is happening. I will hear or see people on the inner planes and know that our souls are talking, but often I will not, yet I nonetheless understand that it happens.

Truly it is love that we hunger for. The yearning for that love moves us into action and pushes us to the point where there simply must be manifestation of the desired connection, without hesitation or question. Yearning always brings forth a divine response. Very early on my path in this lifetime, after having closed down emotionally, I became ready to do my inner work. For some time I prayed fervently to spirit, "Let me know you, let me be your voice, your hands, your eyes, let me serve you wholly and utterly." With passion, I claimed my divine birthright, demanding it from a place of surrender into that yearning. I knew I couldn't control the response, but only ask for it from a place of pure, heartfelt desire. The response of the Divine to that desire has been the unfolding of my life's work in my spiritual vocation in many and varied ways, some of which I would never have dreamed possible – even in my wildest dreams.

The capacity we have for yearning determines the response we call to us. It doesn't have to be a loud cry for help. It can be silent, but echo in the untouched chambers of our vast heart space. It isn't something to avoid, and we need to recognise that in the same way it is safe to be hungry and then enjoy eating our food, it is safe to be hungry for the Divine, and then really relish the growing capacity to receive holy grace. Though unlike food, the hunger for the Divine grows vaster as we journey on our path, but only to the extent that serves us. We never have to be afraid of our passion for love. It will be whatever serves our growth. As we grow, our souls can become voracious in their appetite for love, and that is as it must and should be.

Sometimes, in our yearning for divine love, we are asked to let go of what we are holding on to, so as our arms can be empty and ready to receive what is only just beginning to make its presence felt in our life. The divine response to the yearning in our heart is calling us forward. And sometimes we just can't take everything with us!

Recently this was asked of me, and I felt very, very sad about it. As I lay in the garden, gazing up at the clear blue sky, I saw a solitary Ibis circling above me. "That's me!" I suddenly thought. I watched it circle, higher and higher, wider and wider in a spiral and felt a deep sense of kinship and identification with that bird in its solitary flight. Unexpectedly, four other Ibis came into view, flying as a group even higher than the solitary bird. My heart leapt in recognition. The solitary Ibis was not going to be alone forever. It was rising up in spirals to meet with this group at a higher level.

I knew the Divine was speaking to me with gentle reassurance. I was being told I would be on my own for a time, but I was not only leaving someone behind. I was transitioning to a higher, vaster frequency where I would be able to connect with the new souls I was meant to join on this life journey, at this particular time.

I felt emotional at the kindness and unexpectedness of the message. It gave me hope, which didn't end the sadness of my loss, but helped me bear it. Eventually the birds naturally and gracefully flew into alignment with each other and soared effortlessly together, spiralling higher and wider, until I could no longer see them. The next stage of my life was going to be far beyond what I could see at that moment. I trusted in the message and returned to my rest in the garden.

HEALING PROCESS

Whether you know your passion or are yet to consciously uncover it, there are times when we need respite, fuel for our inner fire or coolness to soothe us after we have expended so much energy on our path. This healing process is for those times when we need warming up or cooling down, extra energy or help to shed something or someone that is no longer meant to be a part of our journey.

This process calls on the healing power of Pele's desire and fire. It is a strong ritual and if it is an unusually hot day, or you are already in an overheated state for whatever reason – with a fever, inflammation from injury or you've had too much sun, or are feeling irritated because you have overexerted yourself physically, emotionally or mentally, then do take care, beloved. The ritual will not harm you but you might feel it is better to rest, cool and complete the healing process on a different day or at a different time. If that is the case and you still want some simple practice to close this chapter, you can say this prayer as your substitute for the full healing process, "I call on the Crystal Angel of Lava Stone, please bless me with your cooling, healing grace now, through unconditional love, so be it!"

However, if you feel it is appropriate for you to dive into some spiritual fire, the entire healing process is outlined for you below. Remember that divine fire opened without arrogance, but with a genuine desire to receive what is needed for healing, will not harm you.

The Process

Have your lava stone and/or crystal mandala ready. You may also like to have a candle to symbolise Pele. Be careful to have the fire in a container and away from open windows. Pele is a big force to work with and you want to be sure that her fire remains on a spiritual level in this ritual.

Say aloud, "I call on Pele, who loves me unconditionally. I call upon her grace, her light and her passionate devotion to love. I call upon the Angel of Lava Stone, Basalt, and the strength to transition through my life's challenges with consciousness and grace. I call upon my own higher self and the divine guidance that loves me unconditionally. Please be with me beloveds so that I may surrender into the yearning of my heart and partake of the journey of life and the path of love, without hesitation or fear. So be it."

Imagine, sense or perceive that you are sitting at rest near an erupting volcano. You are as close or as distant from that volcano as feels good. You are either near the base or at the opening; whatever feels right for you. Perhaps you are even on a nearby island witnessing the majesty from afar. You sense the raw and wild power of this volcano and the swiftly cooling rocks as the molten lava flows and eventually hits the earth and ocean.

Say out loud, "I now surrender any part of me that is blocking my path of love, of divine fulfilment, into the transformational power of Pele."

Imagine seeing, sensing or feeling that you are releasing any energetic blockage into the active volcano. It releases huge amounts of energy from each one of your chakras, from both the front and the back of your body. It opens up the chakras in your hands and feet, and allows energy to flow freely from your feet up to your crown, down through your crown to your feet and out through your hands. Allow this energy flow to become clearer and stronger for at least eight long, slow breaths.

When you have finished, the volcano becomes silent and the flow of molten lava ceases. The energy of the cooling ocean rises up and the temperature drops.

When you are ready, imagine, sense or perceive a deposit of black lava stone near you. It is cooled by the air, the earth and the ocean. You sense the power compressed in that stone!

Say aloud, "Your power is my power, your strength is my strength."

Feel, sense or perceive that you are receiving energy from the stones that are now building a boundary around you that deflects negative energy and builds up a resource of strong, cooling, refreshing energy that you can draw upon whenever needed. Just notice it as a field around you. It may be any colour or all colours, it might be black or invisible to the eye, it might shift and change colour, substance or shape. Just be with whatever you sense and know it is happening, even if you are not conscious of it.

When you have sat with this for at least eight breaths, or however long feels good, simply open your eyes, place your hands at your heart in prayer position and bow your head in respect. When you are ready, blow out your candle to complete your healing process.

THE END IS JUST ANOTHER BEGINNING

Spiritual Guidance from the Crystal Goddesses

Do not fear our love
We reach to you through compassion
We hold within our hearts
The key to your divine passion

Now is the time for you to be born
Anew, into your wild self, loving and true
It is time to cast your shackles aside
To reclaim your natural dignity and pride

Be without shame for you are beautiful inside and out
Boldly leap with trust and surrender your doubt
We call you to the path of endless love and creative power
You are our midwives, our helpers, in this, the Earth's birthing hour

You know that you hold a sacred task to complete
We gift you with everything that you will need
You are on our path of loving liberation and divinity
Together we shall manifest all beings happy and free

Prayer – Affirmation

To invoke the healing power of all the crystal angels, at any time, you can repeat the following affirmation quietly in your mind, or aloud.

Crystal Angels help me through unconditional love
With the power of Earth below and Heaven above!

AND FROM HERE?

Every ending is another beginning, beloved. If you wish to continue our journey together you may enjoy the forthcoming books in this *Crystal Spirituality Series*.

The Blue Angel titles is this series by Alana Fairchild are *Crystal Angels 444: Healing with the Divine Power of Heaven and Earth*. Here Alana guides you into the beautiful healing worlds of angels and crystals, with her stories of life on the spiritual path. Alana shares the ancient wisdom teachings of the Ascended Masters for spiritual growth in *Crystal Masters 333: Initiation with the Divine Power of Heaven and Earth*.

Coming soon are the following Blue Angel titles in this series:

Alana will take you on a sublime spiritual journey to the loving wisdom teachers from star systems far and wide that love the Earth and wish to help human spiritual evolution and ascension in *Crystal Stars 11.11: Crystalline Activations with the Stellar Light Codes*.

In *Crystal Saints & Sages 777: Enlightenment with the Divine Power of Heaven and Earth* you will be inspired and loved by the extraordinary beings that bring the divine journey to life and help empower us to do the same with a bold fearless heart. Amazing true stories and genuine guidance supports our journey with these amazing mystics.

Alana will also be sharing the guidance of Crystal Angels, Ascended Masters and Goddesses in the forthcoming *Crystal Mandala Oracle* which features stunning crystal mandalas and divine guidance from the first three books of this series. With this oracle deck you can easily tune into guidance and do readings for yourself and others with the wisdom of the Crystal Angels and other beings of unconditional love and light.

If you want to learn more about the number sequences in the titles, you might like Alana's book *Messages in the Numbers: The Universe is Talking to You!*

ABOUT ALANA FAIRCHILD

From the earliest memories I have, I was always in conscious connection with Spirit. It has always been as natural as breathing to me. When something is natural for you, especially if it has been that way since childhood, you can assume for a long time it is natural for everyone. It took me some years to realise my sensitivity, healing ability and natural conscious connection to the spiritual was unusual and could help people. So, I chose to create beautiful offerings to support humans in discovering and manifesting the truth of their hearts. Books, oracle decks, music albums, guided meditations, training programs for healers and more. All are designed to bring out the beauty and truth of your inner divine nature, so you can live with freedom, courage, happiness and peace.

If you would like to find out more, please visit me at my online home:
www.alanafairchild.com

ABOUT THE ARTIST

Jane Marin is an accomplished artist, intuitive healer/coach, past life regressionist, author and Reiki/Seichim Master/Teacher.

She holds diplomas in Child Psychology, Hatha Yoga Teaching, Bach Flower Essences and Certificates in Past Life Regression, Journal Therapy, Angel Therapy™, Crystal Light Healing Practitioner Level III, and Motivational Kinesiology IV.

Her background in dance prompted her to explore the healing powers of music and dance leading her to the ancient art of bellydance. She has been teaching this form of dance since 2004.

Jane's spiritual art and photography can now be purchased in her online shop as can her beautiful coffee table books.

Jane is the author of *The Me Book – A Journey of Self-discovery*, published in 2011 by Balboa Press to compliment her popular "Me Book" workshops.

To find out more about Jane Marin and her work, please visit her website:
www.jaanemanart.com

THEMATIC INDEX BY CHAPTER

CHAPTER 17

CHAPTER 18

INDEX

Note to reader: The page numbers listed below refer to the page number on which the chapter dealing with each theme begins.

Crystal Angels 444
Healing with the Divine Power of Heaven & Earth

You have loving guides from the spiritual worlds of Crystals and Angels. They are ready to help you now.

In *Crystal Angels 444*, Alana Fairchild, author of the bestselling *Kuan Yin Oracle*, offers a truly unique approach to crystal healing, combining the natural healing properties of each crystal and its 'crystal angel' or 'spirit' with divine guidance channelled from heavenly angels such as Archangels Raphael, Gabriel, Metatron & Melchizedek. Together they help you bring your spirit and body together as one and live with more peace and prosperity, passion and purpose. Each chapter deals with a powerful precious stone and its heavenly angel and features a range of sacred rituals and processes to help you fully harness the healing potential of that stone, deepen your connection with yourself and the divine guidance supporting you and tap into the many gifts hidden within you.

You will delve deeply into a variety of topics including love, power and protection, eating and body image, self-esteem, addiction, feminine/masculine balance, wealth and prosperity, connecting with divinity, speaking your truth, dealing with your emotions, developing your spiritual talents and much more.

The book is enriched with many personal stories and spiritual experiences from the author which offer practical examples to bring the material to life.

You have important healing work to do on yourself and for the planet. *Crystal Angels 444* is written for you, to help you successfully complete your task, with greater happiness and fulfilment.

Featuring 18 full-colour Crystal Angel Mandalas by artist Jane Marin.

Paperback book, 368 pages.
ISBN: 978-1-922161-13-0

ALSO AVAILABLE IN THIS SERIES BY ALANA FAIRCHILD

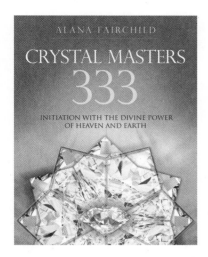

Crystal Masters 333
Initiation with the Divine Power of Heaven & Earth

You have wise spiritual guides from the spiritual worlds of Crystals and Ascended Masters. They are ready to help you on your path of spiritual growth now.

In *Crystal Masters 333*, Alana Fairchild, author of the bestselling *Kuan Yin Oracle*, continues the highly successful Crystal Spirituality Series, which began with *Crystal Angels 444*. She shares her unique approach to crystal healing, combining the natural healing properties of each crystal and its 'crystal angel' or 'spirit' with wisdom teachings from the loving Ascended Masters, such as Mother Mary, Kuan Yin, Jesus, the Buddha, Mary Magdalene and Merlin. Together they help you take the next steps on your path of spiritual growth, by preparing you with the teachings and tools you need to successfully navigate the demands of spiritual initiation.

Initiation is a path of advanced spiritual growth. When you are highly committed to your spiritual path and personal growth this lifetime, you will be on the path of initiation. This path can be very challenging but offers incredible rewards including the awakening of spiritual talents, assistance in bringing your divine light to the world and support in your own role as a healer and spiritual leader on the earth. Each chapter deals with a powerful precious stone and its heavenly angel and features spiritual teachings and stories from Alana's own life and work, as well as a healing process to help you fully harness the therapeutic potential of that stone and connect directly with the Ascended Masters, to receive their wisdom and blessings.

You will delve deeply into a variety of topics including aligning with divine will, healing the child within, planetary healing, spiritual communication, enlightenment and spiritual growth, the light body, the golden body, and much more.

You have important healing work to do on yourself and for the planet. *Crystal Masters 333* is written for you, to help you successfully complete your task, with greater happiness and fulfilment.

Featuring 18 full-colour Crystal Angel Mandalas by artist Jane Marin

Paperback book, 384 pages
ISBN: 978-1-922161-18-5

ALSO AVAILABLE IN THIS SERIES BY ALANA FAIRCHILD

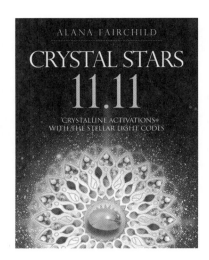

Crystal Stars 11.11
Crystalline Activations with the Stellar Light Codes

The star light within your heart will lead you to sacred fulfilment for the spiritual benefit of all.

This book is for star seeds, old souls, lightworkers, visionaries, healers and hearts who hold a curiosity for the stars. This unique and powerful approach to crystal healing connects you with loving stellar beings and the precious stones that embody and enhance their transformational energy. Alana grounds the teachings with relevant and practical examples and the healing processes help you harness the therapeutic potential of each stone and form a bond with the stars so you can receive their wisdom and blessings.

Aligned with the 11.11 frequency, your celestial guides will help you shift personal paradigms and make rapid spiritual progress. Discover the healing and belonging that only comes from experiencing unity with the stars and the earth. Connect with Sirius, Andromeda, Alcyone in the Pleiades, Vega, Arcturus and others as you delve into treasured spiritual lessons on authenticity, soul passion, dark initiations, the cosmic priestess, supreme spiritual protection and more.

Beloved, you have illuminating sacred work to accomplish for yourself and the planet. Prepare yourself for the next stage of your journey with teachings and tools to help you shine like the star being you truly are.

Featuring 18 full-colour Crystal Angel Mandalas by artist Jane Marin.

Paperback book, 328 pages.
ISBN: 978-1-925538-76-2

ALSO AVAILABLE IN THIS SERIES BY ALANA FAIRCHILD

Crystal Mandala Oracle
Channel the Power of Heaven & Earth

This unique oracle deck is encoded with crystal frequencies, and the high vibrational energy of angels, ascended masters and goddesses, to empower you to channel the divine healing power of Heaven and Earth.

In this stunning, stand-alone deck, you will work with the vibrant crystal mandalas by Jane Marin, as featured in Alana Fairchild's popular books *Crystal Angels 444*, *Crystal Masters 333* and *Crystal Goddesses 888*. Alana shares loving spiritual guidance from the angels, masters and goddesses to help you integrate the frequencies of the crystals and higher beings that are featured in each of the cards. The Crystal Angels will help you heal your body, mind and soul. The Crystal Masters will support your spiritual growth and help you successfully pass through spiritual tests and initiations. The Crystal Goddesses will empower you to embody your spirit and express your soul purpose in the world.

This powerful deck will enhance your connection to the sacred worlds of higher beings and crystal energy, opening your heart to divine beauty and empowering your soul with loving consciousness.

Artwork by Jane Marin

54 cards and 244-page guidebook, packaged in a hardcover box set.
ISBN: 978-1-922161-89-5

ALSO AVAILABLE BY ALANA FAIRCHILD

BOOKS
The 3 Cs, Crisis, Confusion, Chaos
333 Oracle of Heart Wisdom
55 Keys
Crystal Angels 444
Crystal Masters 333
Crystal Stars 11.11
Happiness
The Kuan Yin Transmission™
Love your Inner Goddess
Magic of Isis
Messages in the Numbers
Sleep
Trust
What to do when you don't know what to do
Wisdom of Kuan Yin

DVDs
Kuan Yin: A Visual Meditation

JOURNALS
Goddess Isis Journal
Kuan Yin Oracle Journal
Lightworker Journal
Rumi Journal
Sacred Rebels Journal
Wild Divine Journal
Crystal Mandala Journal
Earth Warriors Journal
Love Your Inner Goddess Journal

ORACLE DECKS
Butterfly Affirmations
Crystal Mandala Oracle
Divine Circus Oracle
Earth Warriors Oracle

Isis Oracle
Isis Oracle: Pocket Edition
Journey of Love
Kuan Yin Oracle
Kuan Yin Oracle: Pocket Edition
The Kuan Yin Transmission™
Lightworker Oracle
Love Your Inner Goddess Oracle
Mother Mary Oracle
Rumi Oracle
Sacred Rebels Oracle
White Light Oracle
Wild Kuan Yin Oracle
Wild Kuan Yin Oracle: Pocket Edition
Wings of Wisdom Affirmation Cards

AUDIO CDS
Black Madonna
Chakra Meditations
Christ Consciousness Meditations
Divine Lotus Mother
For Love & Light on Earth
Ganesha: Meditations for Spiritual Success
Holy Sisters
Inner Power
Isis Power of the Priestess
The Kuan Yin Transmission™
Meditations with God
Meditations with Sekhmet & Narasimha
Mother Mary: Meditations for Grace
Mystical Healing
Past Life Healing
Radiance
Rumi Meditations
Star Child
Voice of the Soul

1.
TARA (MOTHER OF THE WORLD)
TIBETAN QUARTZ (PURITY)
MANIFESTING THROUGH COMPASSION

2.
LAKSHMI (SELF WORTH)
DENDRITIC AGATE (PLENTY)
MANIFESTING THROUGH LIMITLESSNESS

3.
SEKHMET (SACRED RAGE)
FIRE AGATE (INNER FIRE)
MANIFESTING THROUGH PASSION

4.
SARASWATI (SOUND)
AMMONITE (SPIRAL)
MANIFESTING THROUGH WORD

5.
ISHTAR (DEFIANCE)
ASTROPHYLLITE (REBIRTH)
MANIFESTING THROUGH DIGNITY

6.
HECATE (CROSSROADS)
MICA (SYNTHESIS)
MANIFESTING THROUGH CHOICE

7.
MATANGI (DIFFERENCE)
HELIOTROPE (INNER CHRIST)
MANIFESTING THROUGH QUIRKINESS

8.
BASTET (SENSUALITY)
CAT'S EYE (UNVEILING)
MANIFESTING THROUGH PLEASURE

9.
GAIA (WILD GRACE)
OCEAN JASPER (FEELING GOOD)
MANIFESTING THROUGH TRUST

10.
KALI (REVOLUTION)
BLACK OBSIDIAN (DEFLECTION)
MANIFESTING THROUGH TRUTH

11.
RHIANNON (FREEDOM)
AMAZONITE (INTEGRITY)
MANIFESTING THROUGH RESPECT

12.
FREYA (UNTAMED)
AMBER (AGELESS)
MANIFESTING THROUGH ZEST FOR LIFE

13.
MAYA (VEILING)
RUBY AURA QUARTZ (PRESENCE)
MANIFESTING THROUGH REALITY

14.
PERSEPHONE (VIRGIN)
RUBY (POTENCY)
MANIFESTING THROUGH MATURITY

15.
ISIS (RESOURCEFULNESS)
ISIS CRYSTAL (FEMININE ENERGY)
MANIFESTING THROUGH DETERMINATION

16.
DURGA (MANY ARMS OF THE DIVINE MOTHER)
HEMATITE (GROUNDING)
MANIFESTING THROUGH GENIUS

17.
XI WANG MU (IMMORTALITY)
STROMATOLITE (STEADFASTNESS)
MANIFESTING THROUGH PATIENCE

18.
PELE (DESIRE)
LAVA STONE (COOLING)
MANIFESTING THROUGH LONGING

THE CRYSTALS:

TIBETAN QUARTZ

DENDRITIC AGATE

FIRE AGATE

AMMONITE

ASTROPHYLLITE

MICA

HELIOTROPE

CAT'S EYE

OCEAN JASPER

BLACK OBSIDIAN

AMAZONITE

AMBER

RUBY AURA QUARTZ

RUBY

ISIS CRYSTAL

HEMATITE

STROMATOLITE

LAVA STONE